'At last, a book that can be used to teach Sales Management that goes beyond 'do's and dont's'. It proves that sales management is an academic discipline and understands the importance of theoretical advances as a way of improving management of a sales force. It is an accessible, real-world and practical book that will really help readers to understand this area.' – Nektarios Tzempelikos, Anglia Ruskin University, UK

'This is an outstanding and comprehensive introduction to the fascinating world of sales management. Its coverage of key contemporary issues is excellent and the real-life cases bring the subject to life. This should be a vital part of any reading list on selling and sales management.' – Nick Lee, Loughborough University, UK

'This is an engaging book that provides an updated and comprehensive knowledge needed for successful sales management.' – Michael Marck, Strathclyde University, UK

'This is a useful textbook which offers sales practitioners a great source of ideas and hands-on applications in the field of sales & key account management.' – Nikolaos Panagopoulos, the University of Alabama, USA

'This textbook is ideal for both undergraduate students looking to deepen their knowledge of this critical area and postgraduate students encountering the management of sales for the first time.' - Laura Cuddihy, Dublin Institute of Technology, Ireland

'In the Sales Management field it is rare to find textbooks that include both a sound academic foundation and a direct contact with the real business world. This book is one of them, and it will be extremely useful both for Sales Management professionals and students alike.' – Jaime Castelló Molina, Esade Business School, Spain

'This text does an outstanding job explaining the sales function and its relation to marketing, the buying function, and the creation of value. Moreover, the detailed chapters on Key Account Management and International Sales provide valuable insights not found in other texts. I look forward to recommending this book to my sales students!' – Dawn Deeter-Schmelz, Kansas State University, USA

SALES MANAGEMENT

Strategy, Process and Practice

4th edition

JAVIER MARCOS CUEVAS

BILL DONALDSON

RÉGIS LEMMENS

BLOOMSBURY

NEW DELHI • LONDON • OXFORD • NEW YORK • SYDNEY

BLOOMSBURY INDIA
Bloomsbury Publishing India Pvt. Ltd
Second Floor, LSC Building No. 4, DDA Complex, Pocket C–6&7,
Vasant Kunj, New Delhi 110070

First published in India 2023
First published 2016 by RED GLOBE PRESS
Now published by Bloomsbury Academic

ISBN: 9789356403260
10 9 8 7 6 5 4 3 2 1
For sale in the Indian subcontinent only

Printed and bound in India by Thomson Press India Ltd

Javier – to Monica, Ismael, Adrian and Julia

Bill – to Kay

Régis – to Julie, Emily and Sophie

CONTENTS

LIST OF FIGURES

LIST OF TABLES

NOTES ON THE AUTHORS

DR JAVIER MARCOS CUEVAS is the Director of Custom Programmes, Executive Education and Senior Teaching Faculty at the University of Cambridge Judge Business School. His main areas of expertise and research are Professional Selling and Sales Management, Executive Education and Organisational Development. Javier emphasises the blend of leading-edge research with innovative training methodologies in the delivery of his programmes and in the design of consulting assignments. He has designed and delivered programmes globally and has also co-authored with Régis and Bill the book *From Selling to Co-creating* (BIS Publishers, 2014) and numerous academic and practitioner-oriented articles and reports.

PROFESSOR BILL DONALDSON is Research Professor of Marketing at Aberdeen Business School, Robert Gordon University, Aberdeen. His research interests are in selling, customer relationships and the management of sales operations.

DR RÉGIS LEMMENS is the founder of Sales Cubes, a consulting firm which helps sales organisations to innovate and co-create value with their customers. He is a member of the team of experts at Impulse Brussels (the Brussels Enterprise Agency for starting and experienced entrepreneurs) where he serves as coach for startups to help them to develop and implement their commercial strategies. He is also a professor in Sales and Sales Management and teaches at business schools in Belgium (Antwerp Management School, Solvay Business school), the Netherlands (Tias Business School) and the United Kingdom (Cranfield School of Management). He holds a Masters degree in Science from Southbank University, a Masters in Business Administration from the University of Surrey and a PhD from the Aberdeen Business School.

ACKNOWLEDGEMENTS

The act of writing or updating a book is often a lonely endeavour. The 'journey' leading to the publication of a book is always one where you meet a number of people who enrich your perspectives of the topic and your area of specialism.

Neil Rackham has always inspired us, both for his ability to make complex problems easy and for finding the right question to ask sales organisations and their leaders to bring about growth and performance. Prof Dr. Deva Rangarajan from Vlerick Business School was instrumental in helping us complete research on sales force effectiveness. We thank Gude Verhaert from Kluwer Training for her support and leadership in organising the yearly Sales Management seminar in Belgium to which we have contributed.

Our colleagues at the Centre for Strategic Marketing and Sales and the Key Account Management Best Practice Club (both at Cranfield School of Management) shared with us invaluable lessons, possibly so many that we would have needed another book (or two) to capture them. The business development team at Judge Business School Executive Education provided food for thought, helping us sharpen the presentation of some topics to enhance their applicability to the 'real' world and to the management of 'real' customers. We also want to express our gratitude to Bruno Winnen from Canon Belgium, Lieven Somers from Bekaert and Peter De Clerck from LMS/Siemens for offering us the opportunity to carry out several research projects within their organisations.

We are indebted to Michael Marck, Laura Cuddihy, Nektarios Tzempelikos and Beth Rogers for their insightful reviews of the first manuscript. In particular, Laura's comments inspired us to 'go one extra hour' on many of those days when, already late in the evening, we were updating, complementing and further strengthening the initial draft.

The interviewees featured in the book, Ian Helps, Carlos Mena, Mark Davies, Abboud Ghanem and Miguel Carrasco, generously contributed with their views and time, and we enjoyed so much talking to them.

Martin Drewe motivated us to accomplish this new edition, and Jenny Hindley and Holly Rutter made that initial commitment a reality. The production team at Palgrave turned a 'dull' manuscript into this 'vibrant' textbook.

Finally, we would like to thank our students and the delegates to our programmes. They may not be aware, but they also played a major part in motivating us to write this book. We hope you will use it and that it will help you in your practice and/or studies.

Publisher acknowledgements

The authors and publishers would like to thank Monica Franco-Santos for Figure 13.2 from Franco-Santos et al. (2010) *The Impact of Performance Targets on Behaviour: A Close Look at Sales Force Contexts*. Research Executive Summaries Series 5.5.

PREFACE

Professional Selling and Sales Management have become more complex and multi-faceted than ever before, also ever more exciting and stimulating as a function and a profession.

We initiated the 4th edition of *Sales Management* with enthusiasm and passion to bring together quality research and relevant practice in sales management. Our aim was to offer an integrated perspective of the frameworks and ideas that underpin well-informed *strategies*, robust *processes* and the best *practices* in sales management. In this sense we tweaked the subtitle of the 3rd edition to reflect the positioning of the book as closer to practice but retaining its academic grounding.

Through a combination of detailed review of the latest scholarly contributions to the field, a constant search of innovation in sales operations and extensive dialogue with colleagues and clients, we offer a fully revised and updated text. The 4th edition contains new chapters like Defining and Implementing Sales Strategies (Chapter 7) and Key Account Management (Chapter 8). Some chapters have been completely re-structured and updated like Chapter 5 (Motivation and Leadership of the Sales Force), Chapter 6 (Professional Selling), Chapter 9 (Technology and Sales), Chapter 12 (Sales Training and Development) and Chapter 15 (Sales Performance Measurement and Monitoring).

New case studies, vignettes, questions for reflection ('What do you think?') and statistics ('Did you know?') have been added throughout the text, to help readers contextualise the concepts presented in concrete markets and organisations. We invited a number of professionals to contribute with their experience and insights, and these are captured in brief interviews at the end of Chapters 1, 2, 8, 9 and 15.

Please visit the companion website: www.macmillanihe.com/companion/donaldson4 for additional resources and materials.

In the course of writing this new edition of *Sales Management* we were mindful that, nowadays, much disciplinary content is freely available online and also that, increasingly, undergraduate, postgraduate and executive education is delivered encouraging action-learning, problem-based learning and reflective practice. This text is intended to become a useful resource for lecturers and trainers in providing spaces to learn about sales management, evolving from 'transmitting content' to 'facilitating discussion and its application' to real-life sales and sales management problems.

All the existing evidence and debate in the field points to the fact that professional selling and sales management has become an established discipline in marketing education and a more strategic function in businesses of all sizes. We sincerely hope this book will contribute to further develop the standing, influence and significance of sales in education and in business.

Javier Marcos Cuevas
Bill Donaldson
Régis Lemmens

PART I
STRATEGY

1 THE ROLE OF SELLING AND ITS DEVELOPMENT IN THE KNOWLEDGE ECONOMY

OVERVIEW

The role of selling is to identify and realise opportunities to create value for customers. Value can be expressed in financial, organisational and relational terms and is often co-created with customers through a series of exchanges and interactions. Customer relations have become increasingly complex in recent years, requiring effective sales management to create maximum value for the customer and generate sustainable advantage for the supplier. Modern sales operations combine personal selling with other customer contact approaches such as telephone and Internet sales, and/or automated customer service. Despite the use of advanced technologies personal selling is still key in driving customer satisfaction in many industrial and professional sectors.

In order to remain competitive, today's firms must find the best way to connect sales operations with other functions such as manufacturing, distribution and finance. Of particular importance is the interface between sales and marketing. Leading firms constantly seek ways to improve the coordination between sales and marketing as well as to build the competence of the sales force through management development and training.

LEARNING OBJECTIVES

This chapter aims to enable the reader to:

- Understand the role of selling in the business and marketing context.
- Describe the environment in which modern selling takes place.
- Outline the key drivers of sales force transformation.
- Explain the role of salespeople in creating and delivering value.

DEFINITIONS

Personal selling is the process of creating value for the customer through personal interaction with buyers and other individuals within the customer organisation.

Sales management is the process of planning, organising, controlling and developing the sales force, and implementing sales operations to achieve the firm's objectives and business growth.

Salesmanship is the set of skills and competencies that underpin effective customer management and interactions.

Buyer refers to an individual or a team whose role is the acquisition of products and services or the management of suppliers' capabilities that are at the service of the customer.

Transactional customers are those involved in exchanges with the supplier in either short sales cycle or low value items. Limited or no direct contact is established with the field sales force.

Strategic customers are typically engaged in longer-term relationships with the supplier or in buying complex products/services or high volumes.

Servitization is the process of developing the organisational and personal capabilities to provide services in addition to product offerings, with a view of realising added customer value.

SELLING IN THE MARKETING PLANNING CONTEXT

A firm lives or dies by what it sells. Sales growth is for many senior executives the most important priority for their businesses (Baumgartner, Hatami & Vander Ark, 2011). The sales function is the engine of growth and sustainability and is increasingly recognised as a strategic function of growing importance within the firm. The role of selling is to create the maximum value for a firm at the point of contact with a customer through various channels and contact strategies. Sales revenues and profits derive from both transactional and strategic customers. Maximising value creation and efficient resource utilisation requires balancing approaches to deal in a coherent way with different customer groups. Senior management must provide guidance to salespeople regarding selling prioritisation by current and future revenue and profitability. Coherent sales strategies are not always created as part of business planning. Later chapters on sales operations will discuss how senior management can contribute to achieving the business plan objectives through a sales process that aligns selling with corporate goals as well as customer needs.

Selling is an element of the marketing mix. Indeed, the traditional marketing mix, based on McCarthy's 4Ps model (Perreault, McCarthy, Parkinson, & Stewart, 2000), shows selling as a subsidiary function within the promotional mix, an adapted form of which is shown in Figure 1.1.

Figure 1.1 – Elements in the marketing mix

This hierarchy suggests a relegation of the sales function, which does not reflect today's competitive market context. Many firms spend more resources and employ more people in selling than in any other promotional activity. In some situations, the sales budget may well exceed all other marketing activities added together. Marketing and selling, though often seen as differing functions, can indeed be very complementary. The divide may have been fuelled by a view that sees firms as having either a 'production–sales orientation' or a 'marketing orientation', which is known as 'Marketing Myopia' (Levitt, 2004). While some still operate in a production-focused fashion, successful firms have since adopted a marketing and customer-centric orientation.

Did you know?

Numbers of marketing and sales professionals.

In 2010 there were more than 8.2 million jobs directly employed in sales in the US. If we take into account top executives, who are often engaged in business development activities, this number would reach 10 million (US Bureau of Statistics, 2010). Neil Rackham estimates that there are 18 million jobs overall in sales in the US. In the UK, Benson Payne Ltd, a management consultancy appointed by the Marketing and Sales Standards Setting Board in the UK calculated there were 545,000 full-time marketing professionals in 2003, an increase of nearly 80 per cent since 1993, and 766,000 full-time sales professionals within field sales operations, an increase of 9 per cent since 1993.

Sources: Rackham, 2010.

MARKETING AND SALES STRATEGY

We argue that best practice firms translate business goals into well-defined route-to-market strategies, bringing together sales and marketing capabilities. Typically, marketing strategies include (Jobber, Fahy, & Kavanagh, 2003):

- Market and customer segmentation.
- Market research to identify the needs and wants of prospective customers.
- Decisions on products and services to be offered to each customer or prospect group.
- Design and implementation of marketing communications programmes including the sales plan.

Sales planning involves a similar strategic approach at the individual customer level, typified by methodologies such as:

- Account planning (segmentation and targeting of key customers or groups).
- Opportunity identification and value assessment.
- Distribution channel management.
- Sales targets and territory management.
- Communications with prospective and existing customers.

Effective managers will ensure that both marketing and sales strategies are consistent and coordinated by aligning people, processes and technologies. The sales strategy should be connected with marketing, drawing on marketing planning and also providing input into the marketing strategy development. This alignment is not always easily achieved.

In many organisations salespeople are not fully aware of the priorities of the marketing department/function. There is a lack of clarity from the top about market-related objectives, which results in problems of alignment of individual sales plans, targets and remuneration with marketing's overall goals. Conflict can arise between sales policies and marketing policies. For example, the firm's policy on market segmentation can affect an individual salesperson's effectiveness. The extent to which the same product/service package is offered to the market or modified to suit specific groups of customers influences sales management decisions. Selling techniques and resources must be allocated according to whether marketing is undifferentiated (no segmentation), differentiated (different offerings to different customers) or concentrated (different offerings to several groups of customers) (Kotler, Armstrong, Wong, & Saunders, 2008).

What do you think?

Salesperson: 'Marketing are OK at coming up with grandiose schemes and expensive advertising or PR stunts but it is the sales force on the ground, day-in, day-out that makes the customer contact and separates us from the competition. They all think they are customer driven but how would they know? They've never met one, far less having to deal with queries, complaints and a host of competitors in your face.'

Marketing/Brand Manager: 'The trouble with salespeople is they only see their own target customers or area as important, and if it doesn't suit they don't try to sell your product or brand no matter the overall strategy or the investment behind it.'

Q: How would you reconcile such entrenched attitudes?

Changes made to the other elements in the marketing mix will have an impact on the degree of personal selling effort. At one extreme, a firm can offer the minimum product specification and cheapest price and rely on customers ordering by phone or on the Internet. In these cases little or no personal selling is involved; overheads, such as selling costs, are minimal. At the other extreme, salespeople may be required to provide a personalised service to customers, increasing the company's overall costs to serve. Over the last few decades traditional (product) marketing has developed a greater awareness of the importance of relationships, particularly in business-to-business contexts.

Relationship marketing

Very often personal selling effort and the salesperson may determine whether a sale is made or not. This may depend on the individual salesperson's ability to build a relationship with the buyer, as well as on the intrinsic merits of the seller's product or service. 'Relationship Marketing (RM) refers to all marketing activities directed towards establishing, developing and maintaining successful relational exchanges' (Morgan & Hunt, 1994).

Thus, RM is based on an intimacy between the firm and its customers, distributors, suppliers or other parties in the marketing environment. Traditionally, owing to their boundary-spanning role, the field sales force of a company has been a vital link between the firm and its customers and they act as a platform for communicating the firm's marketing message to its customers and as the voice of the customer to the firm. RM focuses on creating the necessary conditions for a long-term relationship between firm and customers with the aim of building durable and successful sales encounters.

Truly adopting relationship marketing means reappraising conventional sales management practices, and fostering meaningful business relationships and approaches to selling that emphasise advising and counselling, listening and helping. Each contact point and selling occasion becomes an opportunity to develop mutual trust and commitment, strengthen the relationship and build customer loyalty.

The role of salespeople can be considered as 'boundary spanning' as its purpose is to link the supplier's capabilities with the requirements of the customer. The salespeople's knowledge and insight of both organisations place them in a unique position to create value for the customer and implement mechanisms to appropriate value for the supplier (Blocker, Cannon, Panagopoulos, & Sager, 2012).

Relationship selling

Just as selling is one part of the promotional mix – itself part of the marketing mix – so relationship selling is part of, but different from, relationship marketing. Relationship selling involves direct contact with the direct customer, offering a tailored service and dedicated resources, whereas relationship marketing is the more organisation-wide approach to working with customers. Customer orientation has become a key tenet of relationship selling and we argue that in practice the boundaries between the two become blurred.

In today's highly competitive marketplace, companies' marketing success is largely dependent upon sales forces, as they have the most immediate influence on customers. Sales forces adopting a relational selling approach provide the foundation for achieving a competitive advantage by adding value for clients and influencing future purchasing intention (Haas, Snehota, & Corsaro, 2012). Furthermore, the role of salespeople nowadays has expanded beyond sales generation and more towards relationship selling as a means of creating customer satisfaction and loyalty.

Paparoidamis and Guenzi (2009) define relationship selling 'as a strategic approach developed by a supplier willing to establish long-term and mutually profitable relationships with its customers'. Sales forces try to improve relationship quality by performing value adding activities, becoming a customer's partner in solving problems and challenges and ensuring the customer is able to extract maximum value from the suppliers' products and services.

The adoption of a relational selling approach to selling requires revisiting (or even abandoning) more traditional techniques that are often focused on the short term and on 'closing' deals. These techniques may not enhance customer trust of the salesperson, suggesting the adoption of more medium-to-long-term approach to maximise sales results. Relationship selling approaches often require salespeople to adapt selling behaviours in the direction of customer-oriented and adaptive selling.

Customer-oriented selling refers to the implementation of the market orientation construct at the level of the individual salesperson (Weitz & Bradford, 1999). Customer-oriented selling is fundamental in relationship development between the buyer and seller, and an important aspect of relational selling behaviour aimed at increasing long-term customer satisfaction.

Adaptive selling is conceptualised as the ability to modify sales behaviours during the interaction with the client, or across various clients' interactions, based on the perceived nature and status of the selling situation. A salesperson demonstrates a high level of adaptive selling by using different sales presentation and communication styles in different encounters with the client. Adaptive selling is particularly relevant in selling situations characterised by different needs on the part of the customer organisation, complex products or services, the need to have high levels of information and high perceived risks in the transaction.

KEY TRANSFORMATIONS IN SELLING AND SALES ENVIRONMENTS

It is widely recognised that professional selling and sales management is changing rapidly and significantly. To explain the ongoing transformation of the professional sales force, we first outline the key external drivers of change. This provides a foundation to map the evolution of selling in the remainder of the book.

In the last decade, market forces have combined with internal pressures to improve sales force effectiveness across a number of sectors. However, more recently investments in the sales function have come under scrutiny and the sustainability of some sales force models called into question with the rise of new channels and technologies. On one hand, senior sales managers recognise that the costs of transactional selling have to be optimised. The Internet and third parties such as distributors have emerged as viable alternatives to optimise sales costs. On the other hand, higher quality service expectations from important accounts suggest the appropriateness of customer-specific investments and resources (Lemmens, Marcos-Cuevas & Ryals, 2011).

Three trends have been identified as key drivers underpinning sales force transformation: the nature and expectations of professional buyers, the opportunities offered by new technologies, and enhanced levels of globalisation and competition.

New buyer behaviour and customer requirements

In the past decade business-to-business (B2B) markets have experienced significant change in the relationship between customers and their suppliers. Increasingly, sophisticated customers are more powerful and seek to achieve savings and increase value by adopting supplier segmentation and other procurement strategies. This has often resulted in reductions of 40–90 per cent in their supplier portfolio (Ulaga & Eggert, 2006).

Procurement has become a strategic function linked to the customer's business plan, with responsibility for realising higher profit margins, containing costs and contributing to superior shareholder value (Janda & Seshadri, 2001). Increasingly, professional purchasing managers use complex sourcing metrics to select the 'right' suppliers, and dictate the terms of the relationship (Boer, Labro, & Morlacchi, 2001; Talluri & Narasimhan, 2004). Overall, buyers are demanding more value, not just from the product or service but from the relationship, and want to access specialised supplier capabilities on the best possible terms and conditions.

Likewise, the process of creating value for the customer is undergoing dramatic change. Traditionally, value creation was embedded in a pre-determined product or service. This approach largely ignored the possibilities of value which is co-created with the customer and manifested 'in-use' (Vargo & Lusch, 2008). In an effort to move away from commoditisation a new definition of value creation is being developed that is due in part to a 'servicised', knowledge-driven economy. The supplier and customer now co-create value in the context of the application of products and services within the customer's business. Some sales organisations are responding to these changes by providing opportunities for joint collaboration and innovation or by adopting partnering approaches to offer superior solutions. This is now becoming the norm with strategic customers, even in arguably transactional businesses.

It has been widely argued that buyers in B2B relationships are demanding more from selling organisations. Two factors may explain the change in supplier–customer relationships; firstly, the availability of information has enabled more transparency and greater product knowledge that buyers use to their advantage. Competitive offerings in the marketplace can be easily evaluated, and feedback from current or past customers is now more widely accessible. Secondly, buying power has consolidated among fewer customers as a result of mergers and acquisitions as well as international expansion of key players in many sectors.

The result of a more powerful position is that customers can and do demand more. At the same time, senior management in customer organisations is asking the procurement function to add more value, and to achieve higher levels of cost reductions, without compromising mission delivery. A renewed focus on return on investment

(ROI) is driving companies to demand more compelling and measurable evidence of the supplier's ability to add value for their business (Enz & Lambert, 2012). Corporate procurement is becoming a strategic function, and in many industries procurement's role in driving company success is more widely acknowledged.

How sales professionals can address both challenges – meeting the expectations of more demanding customers and contributing to the sustainable growth of their business – is a key question for sales leaders and sales representatives alike.

New information and communication technologies

Over the last few decades, unprecedented advances in information and communication technologies have profoundly changed the way in which sales organisations operate. Technology is facilitating new ways of working, opening up new opportunities and challenges for sales professionals. Traditionally, field sales professionals were the primary source of product and service information for the customer. This function has, in many cases, disappeared as customers now easily access information via the Internet (Sheth & Sharma, 2008). Basic tasks such as information retrieval are handled more efficiently and often more effectively over the Internet, which calls into question the future of this traditional salesperson role.

Another traditional salesperson role was as the source of customer insight. As the primary contact with the customer, salespeople were frequently considered the best source of information about the customer. Today, information systems are providing new opportunities to store, synthesise and analyse customer information in unprecedented ways. Thus, gaining customer insight is becoming an organisational capability (Maklan & Knox, 2009) and data analytics are enabling the generation of novel and unique customer insights (Arnett & Badrinarayanan, 2005).

Technology has also accelerated a number of sales operations as a result of bringing together information from marketing, finance, operations and other functions. Advances in technology are not only facilitating customer interactions but also enabling supplier organisations to gain a better understanding of their cost structures and customer profitability. Marketing and sales investments in selected customers, segments and channels can become more transparent and accountable. Salespeople are becoming 'knowledge brokers' (Verbeke, Dietz, & Verwaal, 2011) who need to blend their tacit customer insights with information from across the organisation to better manage the customer relationship and identify untapped business opportunities.

Technologies are also transforming the 'service provision' role of sales forces. Online platforms can, in many contexts, provide opportunities to deliver quality customer service, reducing the need for expensive face-to-face sales interactions to maintain customer satisfaction and experience quality. Technology has enabled some organisations to reduce the size of their field sales force. In turn, this has challenged sales leaders to think about the strategic role of the sales force: where should sales organisations focus, and what other tools are available for adding customer value in sales? As a result, an increasing polarisation between transactional and consultative selling is emerging (Rackham & DeVincentis, 1998).

Globalisation and competition

The business landscape in many sectors and across different economies has changed dramatically as a result of greater market liberalisation in some sectors (professional services, airlines), and higher levels of regulation in others (food, pharmaceuticals). Large-scale mergers and acquisitions have resulted in increased concentration in many sectors, re-shaping the competitive arena. Thus, traditional sales territories and regions are losing relevance to regional and global customers. This suggests that more strategic customer management roles may be needed in sales organisations. Global account management programmes are proliferating as a result, and it is argued that local sales organisations play an essential role in the implementation of these programmes, considering that global customers often buy from the same supplier but at different geographic locations (Panagopoulos et al., 2011).

Over the last few years the global economy has witnessed a dramatic change of cycle in mature markets whilst the emerging economies have, by and large, maintained their growth rates. Nowadays about 10 per cent of the firms in the Global Fortune 500 index are in emerging economies (Panagopoulos et al., 2011), shifting traditional flows of trade and investments. This in turn indicates that global sales efforts in some sectors may require refocusing over the coming years to achieve/maintain growth. Within European countries for instance there is increasing concern about overseas competitors, and also a realisation of the need to adapt sales forces to new centralised and consolidated buying structures (Tanner, Fournier, Wise, Hollet & Poujol, 2008). Negotiations have become more global and suppliers need to consider an integrated approach for their offerings to global customers, while maintaining the ability to adapt to local circumstances.

THE ROLE OF THE SALESPERSON

We have introduced contemporary approaches in sales such as relationship selling and described the key trends that are affecting the transformation of professional selling. In this section we focus more specifically on the sales process, how it has evolved, and the role of the salesperson.

More than two decades ago, Wotruba (1991) argued that selling had progressed through five stages (see Figure 1.2): provider, persuader, prospector, problem-solver and procreator. The provider stage refers to a selling role focused on taking orders from the buyer for existing products and services. The persuader stage entails influencing the customers to buy the seller's offering. The prospector stage refers to the process of identifying relevant buyers who will reveal a need relevant to the seller's offering and power to make the purchasing decision. The problem-solving stage requires obtaining insights about the buyer's needs and matching those needs with the seller's capabilities. In the procreator stage, a close collaboration between the seller and the buyer may lead to the creation of unique offerings that address these identified issues.

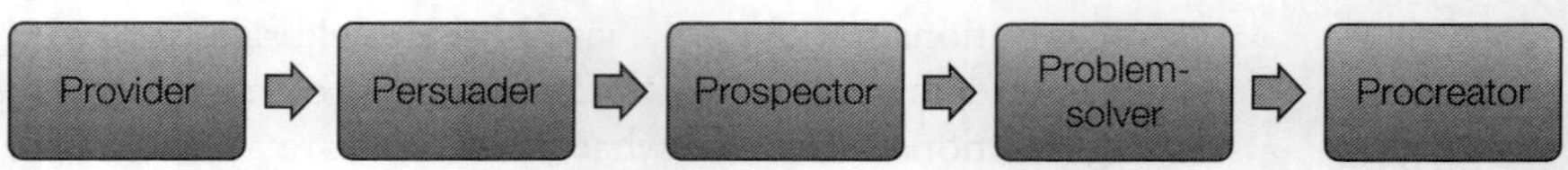

Figure 1.2 – The evolution of personal selling

Source: Based on ideas from Wotruba (1991)

Weitz and Bradford (1999) identified four major roles in the salesperson, underpinned by four conceptions of the nature of selling: (1) a production approach where the key role is to make sales and inform customers about the supplier's offerings. (2) The sales approach, in a similar way to Wotruba's (1991) persuader, is focused on influencing customers to buy the seller's product. (3) The marketing approach focuses on matching the offering to the customer's needs by influencing customers to practise adaptive selling. (4) The partnering approach emphasises the fulfilment of the customer's and the supplier's long-term needs by creating new alternatives to address the customer's problems.

Traditional views of personal selling

Historically, personal selling has been seen as having a transactional component, whereby salespeople focus on generating revenue for the company strongly motivated by incentive compensation. Traditional personal selling was dedicated to stimulate, rather than necessarily satisfy, demand for products. Furthermore, salespeople paid little attention to targeting their markets or planning their sales calls. Consumers were not very sophisticated and markets were not very competitive or transparent. Sales forces were then mostly focused on achieving short-term results for their firms using persuasive selling techniques.

What do you think?

Do buyers nowadays know more than the sellers about their products and services?

David Meerman Scott, author of the book *The New Rules of Sales and Service: How to Use Agile Selling, Real-Time Customer Engagement, Big Data, Content, and Storytelling to Grow Your Business*, contends that this is a growing trend. In the pre-Internet era customers often obtained information about products and services from the sellers. Although quality information is now easily accessible there are still companies training their sales forces in cold calling and establishing rigid scripts that attempt to persuade down a linear path to the sale.

Source: Selling Power: How to Take Control of the Sales Process, 2014.

Moncrief and Marshall (2005) provide a review of the traditional steps of selling as shown in Figure 1.3. These are: (1) Prospecting, (2) Pre-approach, (3) Approach, (4) Presentation, (5) Overcoming objections, (6) Close and (7) Follow-up. Although the traditional seven steps of selling is perhaps the oldest paradigm in the sales discipline, it has served for many years as a foundation in sales training for the process of making a sale. We briefly describe these steps below.

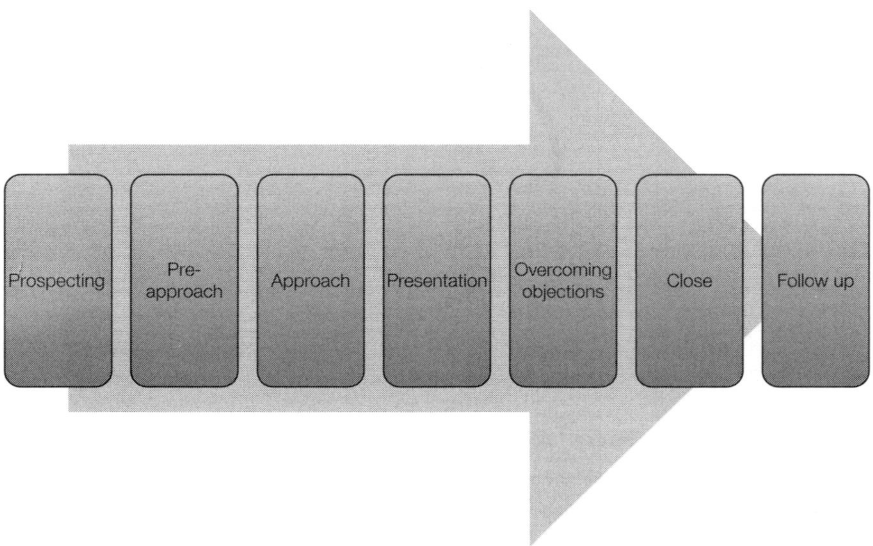

Figure 1.3 – Traditional selling steps

Source: Based on ideas from Moncrief and Marshall (2005)

Prospecting is the phase when salespeople search for new customers as most companies lose some customers every year. Traditionally, prospecting was a complex and difficult part of the selling job. In *pre-approach* salespeople conduct research on prospect clients in order to evaluate their potential and interest for the selling organisation. The *approach* usually takes place in the first minutes of the buyer–seller interaction, with the objective of creating a positive impact and rapport with the customer. This often led to the *presentation* stage where the salesperson presents information about the features and benefits of the product/service. This step should occur after the seller has explored the prospect's needs. Thorough preparation for presentation is essential as this step is very important and complex. During sales presentations and interactions, salespeople should expect clients' questions and hesitancies about products or services, leading to the so-called *handling objections*. This stage can provide an opportunity to help reveal clients' doubts, thus uncovering the buyers' true needs. This may be followed by the *closing* stage when the salesperson, using potentially endless tactics, asks for the order, thus concluding the sales process. At the *follow-up* stage, sales professionals ensure that customers are satisfied with the products or services offered.

Contemporary views of personal selling

We have depicted the sales process very much in the same way it has been seen over the last decades. However, in recent years the world of selling has changed and the transformative factors described above have triggered an evolution of selling processes. Moncrief and Marshall (2005) describe the evolved selling processes in as (1) customer retention and deletion, (2) database and knowledge management, (3) nurturing the relationship (relationship selling), (4) marketing the product, (5) problem-solving, (6) adding value and satisfying needs, and (7) customer relationship maintenance. These evolved or contemporary selling steps are briefly outlined below.

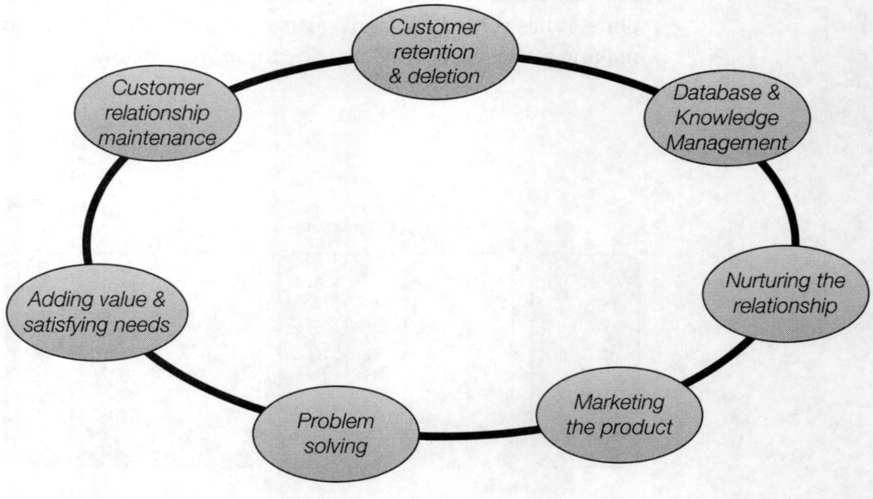

Figure 1.4 – Contemporary selling steps

Source: Based on ideas from Moncrief and Marshall (2005)

Today, prospecting customers has become an expensive and resource intensive activity. Thus, companies are placing an emphasis on *retaining customers*, which sometimes also entails 'deleting' those that may be unprofitable or non-core. Modern technologies have changed the way in which customers can be approached, and the rise of Customer Relationship Management (CRM) systems and social media mean that *data and knowledge management* is now considered a key sales function. *Nurturing and developing relationships* has also become central to most sales organisations, leaving behind short-term and transactional approaches. The traditional sales presentation has evolved to *marketing the offerings* as a result of the expansion of the salesperson role into strategic marketing activities (Leigh & Marshall, 2001) and the development of different channels. In many contexts, the modern sales force has adopted an emphasis on solution selling; thus, overcoming objections has turned into *problem solving*. Closing the sale – a key focus of traditional sales – has become a process for *adding value and satisfying needs*, uniting efforts for mutual success. The final step considers the activities after the sale to ensure that the relationship with the customer is maintained or developed even further into new territories and opportunities (Moncrief & Marshall, 2005).

SUMMARY

Professional selling and sales management has experienced a fundamental transformation over the last few decades. Rather than just a seller-initiated process, it has evolved to become a process of value creation jointly with the customer. The creation and delivery of value is becoming increasingly complex, given the heightened demands of buyers and customers, the increasing pressure of competition and globalisation, and the profound effect of new technologies – fundamentally the Internet. Thus, selling has emerged as a strategic function within the company, requiring its professionals to develop a wide range of competencies and skills. Likewise, the traditional steps of selling have opened the way to new, more nuanced and multifaceted processes that link the supplier and the customer's operations in a value creating fashion.

QUESTIONS

1. Describe the role of selling within the overall firm strategy and process.
2. Outline the key drivers influencing the transformation of sales organisations. How can companies respond to these transformations effectively?
3. What is the role of salespeople in creating and delivering value for both the customer and their own organisation?

CASE STUDY: DISCOVERATA

DISCOVERATA Ltd* is a relatively new company, which commercialises technology resulting from academic research at two leading universities. Oil exploration and production companies can use this technique to confirm the presence of hydrocarbons prior to drilling an expensive test well or to map the extent of a hydrocarbon discovery without additional appraisal wells. DISCOVERATA's technology is ready for use in deep-water exploration areas, and since incorporation the company has undertaken several commercial surveys with the largest contract around $2 million.

The founders of the company are three scientists, formerly university academics, with over 30 years of technical experience in the field between them. The company has recruited a CEO who joined DISCOVERATA with 20 years' experience in the petroleum geophysical surveying industry. This CEO is concerned that the company is working in a relatively small marketplace – with less than 100 potential clients. Therefore their operations contain many risks for the company in terms of market penetration, client relationships and long-term creation of value. The major issues thus relate to how to promote and price their service to be successful.

As world economies develop, the demand for energy is increasing and despite much interest and activity in renewable energy, this demand is met largely by hydrocarbon-powered sources. Energy consumption per individual in the Western world, and particularly in the USA, remains significantly higher than that in the developing world. However, demand from the developed countries has remained relatively stable, or in some cases declined slightly as a result of conservation efforts and high prices. The increase in demand for hydrocarbons results from the increased demand per capita in developing countries and from the growth in populations in those countries, particularly the so-called BRIC countries – Brazil, Russia, India and China. There is virtual unanimity among forecasters that hydrocarbon demand will grow – and available oil and gas reserves will diminish.

Improvements in deep-water drilling technology, enabling oil to be produced from water depths of almost 3,000 m (compared to a limit of about 300 m in the 1980s) have opened up vast tracts of ocean to new exploration. As much of the onshore and shallower water areas of the world have already been well explored, this new 'virgin' acreage represents otherwise unavailable opportunities to discover large oil and gas fields.

The oil industry has embraced remote sensing geophysical methods as the primary means of detecting and mapping structures that could contain hydrocarbon reservoirs. Advances in geophysical techniques – primarily a method known as 3D seismic – have been the major driver in improving exploration drilling success. Seismic contractors can point to direct industry benefits in reducing their customers' finding and development costs and, according to unconfirmed trade sources, the seismic business has grown steadily over the years so that today it has a value of more than $4 billion annually. Despite the widespread adoption of seismic surveying, these techniques are limited to the detection of geological structures that *might* contain oil or gas and give little direct indication of the actual presence of oil and gas inside the geological structure. As a result, although seismic surveys can detect the most promising geological structures, oil companies still resort to exploration drilling to confirm the presence of oil and gas and appraisal drilling to delineate the extent of a discovery.

In deep water, drilling exploration and appraisal wells is extremely expensive: costing from $20 million to $130 million per well. DISCOVERATA's technology currently works well in deep water but less well in shallower water.

The offshore oil industry is heavily dependent on technology to aid it in its operations. Sophisticated communications systems, complex surveying methods and leading-edge engineering solutions are essential enabling technologies, without which the exploration and production of offshore hydrocarbons would not be feasible. Accordingly the industry has an appetite for such technology, which augurs well for the future of DISCOVERATA. There is also general agreement that there will be growth in deep-water production and exploration. As drilling in these deep-water areas is significantly more expensive than shallower drilling, a technology which improves targeting even marginally is guaranteed a market. DISCOVERATA's technique does not substantially replace any of the value delivered by the seismic method, but instead largely substitutes for drilling. It is an important early realisation that the company's services compete with drilling (Table 1.1).

Table 1.1 – Analysis of clients' needs

Market need	Met by seismic	Met by drilling	With DISCOVERATA
Map structure	✓		
Detect gas or liquid in formation	?	✓	✓
Confirm presence of hydrocarbons		✓	✓
Detect oil/water contact		✓	✓

The deep-water exploration market is growing quickly as drilling technology improves and supports drilling in previously unexplored areas, many of which potentially contain large oilfields. Deep-water exploration is, however, extremely expensive and generally only the major oil companies are active players in this arena. Exploration drilling has increased steadily over the last few years and the CEO estimates the annual deep-water market for DISCOVERATA as 160 exploration well sites and 120 appraisal well sites, making 280 overall. Assuming a cost of $30 million for each offshore well, it can be projected that the industry is spending approximately $8.5 billion on the services that DISCOVERATA will substitute for.

A deep-water well can cost between $20 million and $130 million. As about one in three of these wells leads to a discovery, oil companies are conservatively thought to be drilling $60 million worth of dry holes for every discovery they make. Appraisal wells are also drilled to map the extent of each discovery, their number depending on the structural complexity of the oilfield. As DISCOVERATA's technique can accurately map the edge of the reservoir, this appraisal drilling (1–6 wells per field at similar costs to an exploration well) can be drastically reduced or completely eliminated. Both these steps potentially deliver immense value to DISCOVERATA's clients (Table 1.2).

Table 1.2 – Value delivered by DISCOVERATA

	Without DISCOVERATA		With DISCOVERATA	
Seismic survey	$5m		$5m	
Exploration well	$90m	3 wells = 1 find @$30m per well	$45m	Conservative est. 2 wells = 1 find
Appraisal well	$60m	1–4 wells @$20–40m per well	$30m	1–2 wells only required
Total spend	$155m		$80m	

**Name is fictitious*

DISCUSSION QUESTIONS

1 Examine the marketing communication options, including personal selling, that DISCOVERATA might employ as a route to market. Recommend a specific programme that would be compatible for a company this size, making clear your assumptions.
2 Taking into account market penetration, client relationships and long-term creation of value, recommend to DISCOVERATA how to set prices for their new technology – which has little competition but potentially high value for their clients.

INTERVIEW: IAN HELPS, CONSALIA

Ian is currently General Manager EMEA and Director at Consalia (consalia.com), an international sales consultancy dedicated to improving sales performance. Ian has extensive expertise in growing businesses by transforming their sales and account management functions in global organisations such as BP, Shell and E.ON and Invensys.

Q: How do you think selling is changing?

Ian: What a lovely broad question! Clients' buying habits are changing dramatically, driven by I guess lots of freedom, access to information, on doing a lot more research before they even engage with sellers. A lot of reliance on networks, even more so I think than there used to be. I think clients' expectations have gone up, in terms of what they're looking for from suppliers – looking for a better, richer set of solutions brought more proactively to them.

Q: To what extent do you think sales organisations are sufficiently good at adapting to these new changes in customer/sellers relationships?

Ian: I think most organisations are a bit lost, when you get inside them, when you really see what they do they are miles behind what the customer's looking for and even the smartest, most well invested companies are really, really struggling to keep up with the trend.

Q: What are some of the trends that will actually shape the way selling organisations go about managing their customers in the future?

Ian: I think at the highest level companies are going to have to be much more ruthless at segmenting their customers. I see a great inefficiency in not really understanding which are the high value, high potential customers and which are the ones that you just can only sell transactionally to. I think they've [sales organisations] got to be much more process orientated, much faster acting, cutting corners or however you want to describe it – you can't afford the same cost to serve for that channel.

Q: What else do you think is likely to have a big impact on the way sales organisations operate in the near future?

Ian: Well I think that there is going to be some form of 'HR revolution' in terms of what people are looking for from successful salespeople. When we do the client interviews about the proportion of salespeople who they think are successful, they estimate that around 5–10 per cent deliver the value they've been talking about. I just think that that ultimately must lead to a transformation of the quality of people in sales. That's something that not many people want to talk about but it is a revolution that's going to have to happen.

REFERENCES

Arnett, D. B. & Badrinarayanan, V. (2005). Enhancing customer needs-driven CRM strategies: Core selling teams, knowledge management competence, and relationship marketing competence. *Journal of Personal Selling & Sales Management*, 25(4), 329–343.

Baumgartner, T., Hatami, H. & Vander Ark, J. (2011). *Sales Growth: Insights from Leading Sales Executives*. McKinsey & Company.

Blocker, C. P., Cannon, J. P., Panagopoulos, N. G. & Sager, J. K. (2012). The role of the sales force in value creation and appropriation: New directions for research. *Journal of Personal Selling & Sales Management*, 32(1), 15–28.

Boer, L. de, Labro, E. & Morlacchi, P. (2001). A review of methods supporting supplier selection. *European Journal of Purchasing & Supply Management*, 7(2), 75–89.

Enz, M. G. & Lambert, D. M. (2012). Using cross-functional, cross-firm teams to co-create value: The role of financial measures. *Industrial Marketing Management*, 41(3), 495–507.

Haas, A., Snehota, I. & Corsaro, D. (2012). Creating value in business relationships: The role of sales. *Industrial Marketing Management*, 41(1), 94–105.

Janda, S. & Seshadri, S. (2001). The influence of purchasing strategies on performance. *Journal of Business & Industrial Marketing*, 16(4), 294.

Jobber, D., Fahy, J. & Kavanagh, M. (2003). *Foundations of Marketing*. London: McGraw-Hill.

Kotler, D., Armstrong, G., Wong, V. & Saunders, J. A. (2008). *Principles of Marketing* (5th edn). Harlow, Essex: Prentice Hall.

Leigh, T. W. & Marshall, G. W. (2001). Research priorities in sales strategy and performance. *Journal of Personal Selling & Sales Management*, 21(2), 83–93.

Lemmens, R., Marcos-Cuevas, J. & Ryals, L. J. (2011). Selling in the 21st century: mapping the transformations of selling and sales management. *The 9th Sales Management Research Conference*. Paris, 5 May.

Levitt, T. (2004). Marketing myopia. *Harvard Business Review*, 82(7/8), 138–149.

Maklan, S. & Knox, S. (2009). Dynamic capabilities: The missing link in CRM investments. *European Journal of Marketing*, 43(11/12), 1392–1410.

Moncrief, W. C. & Marshall, G. W. (2005). The evolution of the seven steps of selling. *Industrial Marketing Management*, 34(1), 13–22.

Morgan, R. M. & Hunt, S. D. (1994). The commitment-trust theory of relationship marketing. *Journal of Marketing*, 58(3), 20–38.

Panagopoulos, N. G., Lee, N., Pullins, E. B., Avlonitis, G. J., Brassier, P., Guenzi, P. & Weilbaker, D. C. (2011). Internationalizing sales research: Current status, opportunities, and challenges. *Journal of Personal Selling & Sales Management*, 31(3), 219–242.

Paparoidamis, N. G. & Guenzi, P. (2009). An empirical investigation into the impact of relationship selling and LMX on salespeople's behaviours and sales effectiveness. *European Journal of Marketing*, 43(7/8), 1053–1075.

Perreault, W. D., McCarthy, E. J., Parkinson, S. & Stewart, K. (2000). *Basic Marketing*. Maidenhead: McGraw-Hill.

Rackham, N. (2010). The role of professional salespeople. Retrieved 28 September 2013, from http://www.youtube.com/watch?v=ktMMblAlass.

Rackham, N. & DeVincentis, J. (1998). *Rethinking the Sales Force: Redefining Selling to Create and Capture Customer Value*. New York: McGraw-Hill.

Selling Power http://www.sellingpower.com/content/article/?a=10428/how-to-take-control-of-the-sales-process (accessed 8 Sep 2015)

Sheth, J. N. & Sharma, A. (2008). The impact of the product to service shift in industrial markets and the evolution of the sales organization. *Industrial Marketing Management*, 37(3), 260–269.

Talluri, S. & Narasimhan, R. (2004). A methodology for strategic sourcing. *European Journal of Operational Research*, 154(1), 236.

Tanner, J. F., Fournier, C., Wise, J. A., Hollet, S. & Poujol, J. (2008). Executives' perspectives of the changing role of the sales profession: Views from France, the United States, and Mexico. *Journal of Business & Industrial Marketing*, 23(3), 193–202.

Ulaga, W. & Eggert, A. (2006). Value-based differentiation in business relationships: Gaining & sustaining key supplier status. *Journal of Marketing*, 70(1), 119–136.

US Bureau of Statistics. (2010). Occupational outlook handbook. Retrieved 8 October 2013, from http://www.bls.gov/ooh/sales/home.htm.

Vargo, S. L. & Lusch, R. F. (2008). Service-dominant logic: Continuing the evolution. *Journal of the Academy of Marketing Science*, 36(1), 1–10.

Verbeke, W., Dietz, B. & Verwaal, E. (2011). Drivers of sales performance: A contemporary meta-analysis. Have salespeople become knowledge brokers? *Journal of the Academy of Marketing Science*, 39(3), 407–428.

Weitz, B. A. & Bradford, K. D. (1999). Personal selling and sales management: A relationship marketing perspective. *Journal of the Academy of Marketing Science*, 27(2), 241–254.

Wotruba, T. R. (1991). The evolution of personal selling. *Journal of Personal Selling & Sales Management*, 11(3), 1–12.

2 THEORIES AND APPROACHES OF PROFESSIONAL BUYING AND SELLING

OVERVIEW

The best conceived and implemented sales management strategies take into account purchasing and procurement practices at the customer and sector level. This chapter presents established conceptual frameworks of professional selling and buying processes distilled from decades of research in buyer–seller relationships. The chapter aims to integrate process-based perspectives with economic and behavioural views in understanding buying and selling in business-to-business contexts. The models presented in this chapter emerge from these theories and aim to help interpret a buyer's behaviour in different circumstances, and therefore help predict likely future buying behaviour. This understanding improves the effectiveness of the sales process on one hand, and the customer's ability to engage with sales organisation for enhanced value creation on the other.

LEARNING OBJECTIVES

This chapter aims to enable the reader to:

- Understand established theories and frameworks of selling and buying in business-to-business contexts.
- Gain insights to understand professional buyer behaviour.
- Structure the sales interaction with professional buyers.

DEFINITIONS

Industrial marketing is the traditional term now superseded by business-to-business (B2B) marketing. It still applies where marketing and selling takes place between those buying goods and services for use in the production and supply of their own products and services.

B2B marketing involves the supplying of goods and services to businesses, intermediaries and public bodies for consumption, use or resale. B2B marketing therefore embraces industrial marketing and also trade marketing, which involves the sale of goods and services to retailers for selling on to the end consumer. It also embraces public sector procurement.

Direct selling to consumers is still an important route to market for some companies. Avon cosmetics, for instance, uses this approach in reaching its consumers. Direct selling is also widely used for products and services such as home improvements and financial services.

Fast-moving consumer goods (FMCG) sales are made through trade marketing teams, category managers and others as part of customer and account management process.

Decision-making unit (DMU) refers to the structure and organisation of buying centres including key individuals and the role they play in the process of deciding and appointing suppliers and sourcing products and services.

ECONOMIC AND BEHAVIOURAL THEORIES

The core concepts underpinning the theories of buying and selling are best studied and understood in chronological order. Thus, some of the references in this chapter go back into the history of buying behaviour to help us understand how selling approaches have changed from a relatively simple process to a highly complex and participative one. Also, many authors have separated theories of buying behaviour and their derived models between consumer and industrial/organisational buying contexts. Throughout this chapter this distinction is made with special emphasis on industrial/organisational purchasing.

Traditionally, economic theory was used to analyse buying and selling activities. Purchasing was thought of as problem-solving behaviour undertaken by rational individuals whose goal was to maximise satisfaction (called 'utility' in economics) by choosing the ideal combination of goods from a 'range of affordable commodities' (Arrow, 1951). The environment and process was one of atomistic transactions; that is, multiple, discrete and anonymous trades (Turnbull, Ford & Cunningham, 1996). Buyer would 'meet' seller in the market to engage in a rational 'exchange transaction' (Alderson, 1995). The final transaction was a price match between supply and demand, after taking account of all the influencing factors on each party's decision to buy or sell.

Alderson (1995) and others recognised the limitations of applying strict economic theory to buyer–seller processes. Katona (1995, p. 134) combined behavioural sciences, namely psychology, with economic theory, aiming to study 'forms of rational behaviour, rather than the characteristics of the rational man'. Marketers and salespeople were urged to 'take a closer look at the nature of the participants' and understand the overall behaviour of the 'system' (Alderson, 1995, p. 26). This system could range from well-organised groups such as firms and households to loosely structured networks such as trading centres. Social sciences (sociology, psychology and cultural anthropology) were also used to explain the behaviours of such systems and also influenced theories of selling, in the quest to understand the nature of the interaction between buyer and seller.

The sales process in an industrial B2B and services situation commonly involves personal interaction between participants. The human aspect of the interaction between buyers and sellers is one that requires attention given its implications for sales performance and relationship effectiveness. Researchers have long tried to identify the buyer–seller characteristics that affect the outcome of a sales interaction, in particular focusing on buyer–seller similarity. Empirical studies confirm that buyer–seller similarity has been more influential in achieving sales success than seller expertise across a number of sectors (Lichtenthal & Tellefsen, 2001). They reviewed all the research literature on buyer–seller similarity in B2B situations and proposed two categories of similarity: internal and observable, comprising several characteristics. Lichtenthal and Tellefsen (2001, p. 1) suggest that 'internal similarity can increase a business buyer's willingness to trust a salesperson' and that, in the main, 'observable similarity exerts a negligible influence'. Gaur, Herjanto and Bathula (2012) studied the effect of similarity on a buyer's sense of satisfaction with a firm represented by a salesperson in the banking context. Their research showed that appearance similarity and status similarity have a significant effect on the salesperson–buyer relationship, whereas lifestyle similarity has no effect. Furthermore, they concluded that the buyer's satisfaction with a salesperson is found to mediate the relationship between similarity in appearance and the buyer's satisfaction with the supplier firm.

Buyer–seller similarity has implications for sales recruitment and training. Sales organisations should consider appointing sales executives and relationship managers for customers whose buyers are compatible. A challenge to overcome is the tendency of some sales managers to hire people with similar characteristics to their own. Research on persuasion (Cialdini, 2001) has shown that the perceived degree of similarity between two individuals affects likeability, a key dimension of persuasion in interpersonal relationships. It has been argued that in buyer–seller relationships, similarity in work attitudes, sex, life stage and personality have differential effects in facilitating open communication, relationship investment, and relationalism (Smith, 1998).

ORGANISATIONAL BUYER BEHAVIOUR

Organisational buyer behaviour is the decision-making process that customers go through to source needed resources from the marketplace. For suppliers, understanding the dynamics of customers' procurement processes is essential to define priority customers and segments, and for devising the strategies and tactics that will most likely result in effectively reaching organisational buyers and in providing offerings that address their needs (Hutt & Speh, 2012). Typically, organisational buying comprises the following stages, as depicted in Figure 2.1 (Biemans, 2010; Hutt & Speh, 2012):

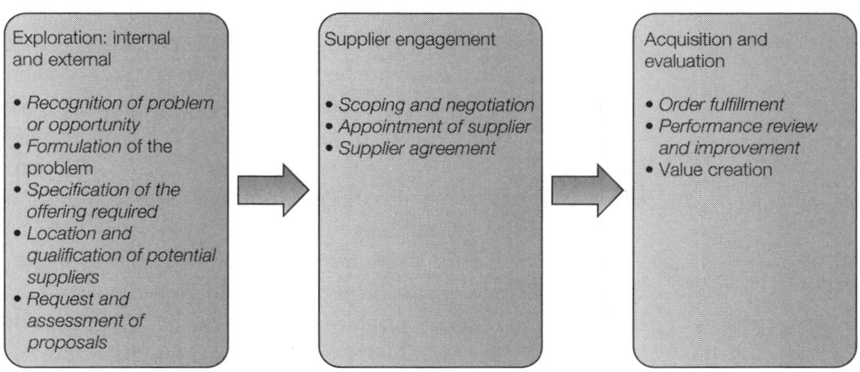

Figure 2.1 – Organisational buying process

Source: Based on ideas from Biemans (2010) and Hutt and Speh (2012)

Stage 1. Exploration: Internal and external

- *Recognition of problem or opportunity*: the customer identifies an area that poses a challenge to the organisation and therefore needs to be addressed, or the possibility to enhance the effectiveness of the organisation or market growth.
- *Formulation* of the problem or opportunity determining broadly the outcomes to be achieved by addressing them.
- *Specification of the offering required*, whether a product or service or a combination of the two, organisations stipulate the characteristics, features and requirements of the solution sought.
- *Location and qualification of potential suppliers*, whether through previous preferred supplier list or through referrals, market research and other sources, suppliers are identified and evaluated in terms of capability and fitness for purpose and potential value for money.
- *Request and assessment of proposals*. Prospective suppliers are invited to respond to a (formal or informal) briefing outlining the details of their proposed solution terms and conditions. These proposals are then evaluated against a set of predefined criteria.

Stage 2. Supplier engagement

- *Scoping and negotiation*. Often a short list of vendors is invited to present and discuss their proposed solutions, their terms and the extent to which their proposals address the customer interests and needs. Some re-definition of requirements may occur at this stage. Bargaining and exchange of concessions often also take place.
- *Appointment of supplier*. A supplier, or sometimes a group of suppliers, is selected.
- *Supplier agreement*. A contract or formal agreement is signed establishing or further extending the relationship with a supplier.

Stage 3. Acquisition and evaluation

- *Order fulfilment*. The provision of the service or the delivery of the product is initiated.
- *Performance review and improvement*. A regular review of the offer being delivered is undertaken. Communications and discussions are held with the supplier in order to improve relationship effectiveness and
- *Value creation*.

Process and task models of buying behaviour

During the 1960s to early 1970s, new theories and frameworks of buying and selling emerged. These concentrated on understanding the purchasing decision act by examining purchasing processes and tasks. Typical of the process approach was the complex, inputs–outputs model of buying behaviour first proposed by Howard and Sheth (1969) as a means of understanding consumer behaviour. This model has been simplified to the buying-decision process (Wilson, Gilligan, & Pearson, 1992), better known as the decision-making process or DMP – a hierarchical decision model. The DMP is a time-based sequential flow of activities, which represents the process a buyer follows from problem recognition, through identification of options, selection and purchase, then post-purchase evaluation. At each stage, there are internal and external influencing variables affecting the final purchase decision, including the type of purchase; for example, whether it is a product or a service (explored in more detail in the next chapter).

The length and complexity of a DMP will also depend on the characteristics and importance of the product to the buyer (see Table 2.1).

Table 2.1 – Buying importance matrix

	High involvement	Low involvement
Significant differences between products/services	Complex buying behaviour	Variety-seeking buying behaviour
Few differences between products and services	Dissonance-reducing buyer behaviour	Habitual buying behaviour

Complex buying occurs when a product is not purchased recurrently, a mistake in supplier selection can be costly, the customer's knowledge about the product is low and there are significant differences between brands. The customer will tend to spend a long time at the search and evaluation stages, for example buying aircraft systems in the aerospace industry.

Habitual buying occurs when there are few brand differences and the product is of low importance. The customer is likely to make a quick decision and race through the DMP.

Variety-seeking customers tend to indulge in brand or supplier switching. The DMP will not be long or complex.

Dissonance-reducing behaviour occurs because some purchase decisions trigger feelings of dissatisfaction or dissonance afterwards. In these situations, the purchase tends to be important, but there may be little to choose between brands; for example, kitchen equipment.

In another study, Robinson, Faris and Wind (1967) looked at the nature of the purchase task, from which they developed the Marketing Sciences Institute (MSI) industrial buying model. This defined three separate tasks or 'buyclasses' in a buying situation: new task, modified rebuy and straight rebuy. Each task requires a different sales process and selling approach.

New task is where the buying centre members view the purchase as different or new. Significant information has to be collected, assimilated and evaluated. This is referred to as extensive problem-solving (Howard & Sheth, 1969). There is usually a lack of well-defined criteria for comparison and also no strong predisposition to one particular solution. The implication is that marketing effort should be directed not to selling product but to customer problem-solving. Clear information, detailed proposals of benefits, cost/revenue evaluation plus evidence of previous and current successes have most effect. Sellers are required to monitor needs and respond accordingly.

Modified rebuy – in this situation, some or all of the members of the DMU/buying centre feel that reappraisal and re-evaluation of alternatives are necessary. This manifests itself in a need for further information and consideration of alternatives. Triggers for this may be the need for cost reduction, quality improvement, delivery performance, other sources of dissatisfaction or external forces. This is described as limited problem-solving with defined criteria needing reappraisal. Actions here depend on whether you are an 'in' or 'out' supplier. If 'in', attempt to move towards a straight rebuy, identify problem, correct it, and reinforce benefits. If an 'out' supplier, examine the source of advantage most appropriate to the buyer's needs. Usually, individual responses are required through salespeople to match these customers' needs.

Straight rebuy – for many organisations, there is a continuing or recurring requirement for the product or service. Buyers and buying organisations are experienced and require little or no new information. Decision processes in this case are routine: one or a few suppliers are used repeatedly. Marketing effort is geared to reinforcing the buyer–seller relationship and building, or at least maintaining, inertia. For a new entrant or 'out' supplier, life is very difficult. To change supplier or product requires a break in this routine, which involves uncertainty and risk for the buyer. An 'out' supplier must painstakingly research the market, assess buyers' needs and preferences and wait for or create opportunities.

The buying centre or DMU

The role of buying centres, also termed decision-making units or DMUs, and their impact on the sales process have been studied extensively. The number of people involved in a buying decision will vary depending on the cost and the complexity of a purchase. Therefore, it was judged important for suppliers to identify the most influential participants in a buying centre and understand the role that each played.

The participants in a DMU were classified by Webster and Wind (1972) as follows:

- Users.
- Influencers.
- Decider and/or approver.
- Buyer.
- Gatekeeper.

This simple model has since undergone several updates. It can be applied to both consumer and industrial situations. Table 2.2 represents one version suitable for industrial purposes, with a description of the role each participant normally plays.

Table 2.2 – Classic DMU used in industrial/B2B marketing

User	• An individual or team who will be employing the service. • Influenced by personal relationships and previous experience. • May have little influence but high 'grumble factor'. • Will understand the benefit of the product.
Influencer	• Persuades as to what company is selected. • May be outside the organisation, e.g. a consultant. • Is driven by a variety of factors (brand, personal relationships). • May be a subject matter expert and assist in the specification of products/services.
Decider/Approver	• Person who makes the final choice. • The reputation of the supplier and its brands. • They may detail standards and establish the purchasing criteria. • Likely to be influenced by performance guarantees.
Buyer	• Places the contract/order. • Likely to be motivated by price and conditions. • Negotiates the terms and conditions.
Gatekeeper	• Controls access to others, e.g. secretaries, assistants or other team members. • Has 'negative power', i.e. power to prevent things happening. • Can be anyone in the organisation, from a receptionist to an external specialist.

What do you think?

Procurement professionals have traditionally been measured by their ability to achieve cost reductions. Some believe that an excessive focus on this indicator may jeopardise their ability to engage with strategic suppliers in value creation activities in the long run. It has also been suggested that a number of high-profile cases of irregularities in reporting corporate accounts may be due to the fact that both the procurement and commercial departments in companies are incentivised and bonused on savings delivered to the business.

Source: Ball, 2014

Several researchers attempted to combine all these theories into a single framework for describing buying behaviour – the most famous being Sheth's (1973) integrative model of industrial buying behaviour that combined economic theory with behavioural sciences (sociology, psychology and culture) and demonstrated the complexity and dynamics of purchasing within organisations. However, it concentrated only on process, task and role, with little attention paid to the nature or dynamics of the interactions or relationships between the component parts and the participants (Turnbull, 1987). As a result, models that included the interactive behaviour of buying centres emerged in the early 1970s.

Webster and Wind (1972) argued that organisational buying involved the aggregation of the decision-making purchasing process with both the behaviour and interactions of multiple persons in a buying centre. Their model for understanding organisational buying behaviour was considered 'truly comprehensive' by Turnbull (1987, p. 158) as it encompassed economic theory, behavioural sciences, organisational and management theories, and corporate politics. Their model described the psychological and sociological behaviour of the individuals in the buying centre. It omitted, however, any reference to what Turnbull (1987, p. 161) regarded as the 'fundamental' variables; that is, the personal relationships between buyer and seller and the interactive context within which such relationships develop.

The IMP interaction model

The next phase in buying theory evolution came with the Interaction approach, proposed by the Industrial Marketing and Purchasing (IMP) Group in the early 1980s. The IMP Group was formed in 1976 to 'conduct co-operative research' into the nature of supplier–buyer business relationships, which were by then recognised as complex, multi-person phenomena (Turnbull, 1987).

IMP researchers emphasised buyer–seller interpersonal influences and relationships in the purchase decision over size, structure and DMP of the buying centre. The ensuing IMP Interaction Model (Hakannson, 1982) described organisational buying as a function of four variables:

1. The Environment is the cultural/political/socio-economic conditions surrounding a trading relationship.
2. The Interaction Process is a series of active and episodic exchanges between the participants.
3. The Participants are the individuals or 'actors' involved in the exchanges.
4. The Atmosphere is formed from the expectations, balance of power, collaboration and cooperation in the relationship – a product of the exchanges between the actors.

The four areas of the model are interrelated. The origins of the interaction approach appear to have evolved from a dissatisfaction with the 4Ps paradigm (described in Chapter 1) as an adequate managerial framework when applied in an industrial marketing context and as a result of a series of empirical studies in a variety of industrial international situations. The main arguments against the traditional view centre on the idea that buying is not a single discrete purchase, that marketing management consists of more than the manipulation of the marketing mix to a generalised passive market operating in an autonomic way and that marketing and purchasing do not operate in separate and discrete ways. In industrial exchange, the relationship is more likely to be characterised by small numbers of buyers and sellers who are both active participants in the process and whose actions are identifiable by others and have long-term effects (interaction rather than transaction). There are likely to be specific investments in technical and organisational routines which result in a relationship characterised by stability, source loyalty and inertia. To explain marketing activity requires an understanding of the differences between buyer–seller relationships as they apply in concentrated and diverse markets. The IMP group refer to this as the interaction approach. Their focus is the relationship rather than the buyer or the supplier. This work is helpful in describing, understanding and classifying relationships but depends on the nature of the product, the number and degree of alternative sources of supply, the relative importance of the seller's product to the buyer and the distribution network (availability of product).

The interaction model shown in Figure 2.2 can be described as follows. In B2B market transactions, the parties involved, buyer and seller A and B, interact within their environment, the outcome of which depends on the characteristics of the parties, the interaction processes and the atmosphere surrounding their exchange. The interaction process consists of episodes and relationships. The episodes include the core product or service exchange, the information exchange (content, width, depth and formality), financial exchange and social exchange (reducing uncertainty, trust). The relationship embraces the degree of formality (institutionalised), the contact patterns and the adaptations of buyer and seller. The characteristics of the parties refer to both individuals and organisations and will reflect the technology, organisation, experience and individual personalities, experience and motivation. Impinging on this relationship are the effects of the external environment and the atmosphere surrounding the parties. The interaction environment encompasses the market structure, dynamism, internationalisation, channel structure and social systems. The atmosphere is 'the power-dependence relationship which exists between the companies, the state of conflict or co-operation and overall closeness or distance of the relationship as well as the companies' mutual expectations' (Hakannson, 1982). Such an atmosphere has both economic and behavioural dimensions.

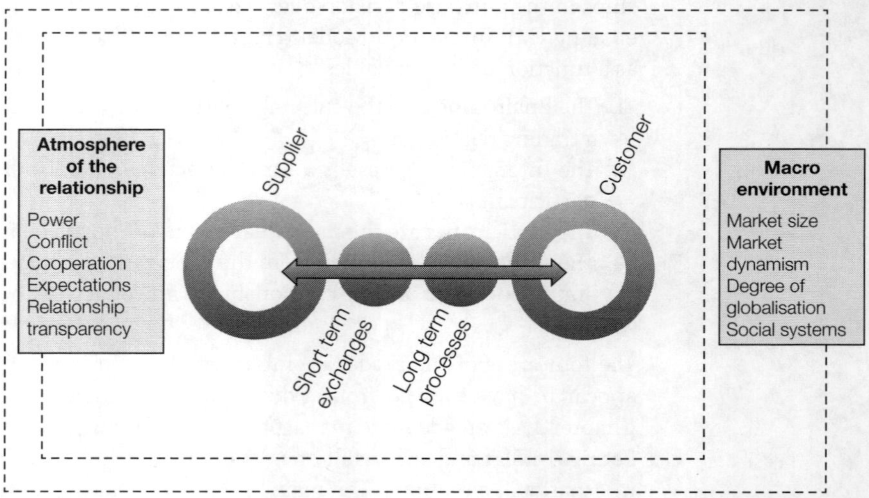

Figure 2.2 – The IMP interaction model

Based on ideas from Hakannson (1982)

In support of the model, a number of case studies and surveys have been conducted by the IMP group which add empirical support for the variety of relationships which can and do exist, revealing variations in the relationship and the closeness between the parties (Ford, 1990). This empirical research suggests that the Interaction approach is a better approximation of the realities of organisational buying than the earlier DMP and buying centre models.

PROFESSIONAL SELLING: PROCESSES AND APPROACHES

Neil Rackham, in his foreword to *The Challenger Sale* (Dixon & Adamson, 2011) outlines the history of selling, arguing that the evolution of the profession witnessed at least three breakthroughs. The first, about a century ago, was the split of customer-related tasks such as selling and collecting payments, which meant the creation of professional selling in its own right. Early in the development of selling as a function, formulae were used throughout to either describe or predict buyer or seller behaviour. A famous selling formula is AIDAS (attention, interest, desire, action, satisfaction). This mnemonic and its variations are used to explain the sales process in terms of mental-states theory, which was first attributed to Sheldon (1902) with his mnemonic AIDR (attention, interest, desire, resolve).

The second breakthrough came about with the publication of *The Psychology of Selling and Advertising* (Strong, 1925), which describes sales techniques as a set of skills that can be learned. Strong modified AIDR into AIDA (attention, interest, desire, action). Later the S, for 'satisfaction', was added. The AIDAS formula is known as the hierarchy of effects and is often used in communication theory – although its relevance is widely debated on both theoretical and empirical grounds. The model can be matched to a series of distinct steps in the sales process (Table 2.3).

Table 2.3 – AIDAS selling formula

Hierarchy of effects	Steps in the sales process
A Attention	Making contact
I Interest	Arousing interest
D Desire	Creating preference / specific proposals
A Action	Closing the sale
S Satisfaction	Retaining business

Many critics, in both advertising and personal selling, have questioned the appropriateness of this model. For example, Palda (1966), in advertising research, criticises the hierarchy for implying closer probability of an intended action as a potential buyer proceeds on this sequential process of mental states. In other situations, the sequential order may be distorted, out of predicted sequence, telescoped or even omitted. Rackham (1987) accumulated data on numerous sales situations. He suggested that, particularly in larger sales, the hierarchy may be inappropriate.

The third breakthrough in professional selling came about in the 1970s. Research led by Neil Rackham himself resulted in seminal work such as SPIN Selling (Rackham, 1995) providing evidence of the difference between small and complex sales. Recently the publication of *The Challenger Sale* (Dixon & Adamson, 2011) has provided counter-intuitive findings that help explain salesperson performance, arguing that high performers have something in common: they understand their customers in depth and push them to think differently about their business, thus creating opportunities to sell. We now describe these two approaches in more detail.

The SPIN model

As firms began to realise the importance of considering the buyer's actions before the seller's, models were re-oriented towards customer needs first, then benefits and features. Rackham (1987, 1995) devised an approach termed SPIN – an acronym for the order of questions raised by the salesperson during the sales process: situation, problem, implication and need/payoff.

In Rackham's model, the emphasis is on salespeople being more effective – working smarter and not just harder. Asking questions and getting the buyer to do most of the talking in a sales interaction is more powerful and more effective than a slick presentation. By studying successful salespeople, Rackham found that these people ask questions which get the buyer talking, revealing both explicit and implicit needs and enabling the salesperson to match their offer more closely to the customer's requirements. Furthermore, successful salespeople ask certain types of questions, as outlined in the model. For example, they ask situation questions to establish background facts, but not too many, which may bore or irritate the buyer. They quickly move on to problem questions, which reveal difficulties or dissatisfaction. The possibility of solutions may emerge at this stage but implication questions increase the scale of the problem and confirm the relevance of a solution. Need-payoff questions suggest benefits for the customer. While this may sound stylised, it has proved to be a powerful approach to fulfilling the salesperson's primary task – solving the customer's problem and revealing what has to be done to win the customer's business. Sometimes it may be necessary to provoke the customer to think through the issues to more fully understand what their problems really are.

The Challenger Sale

In 2009 the global economy was in a period of severe difficulty, in particular the selling environment. Despite this, senior officers at the Sales Executive Council, part of the Corporate Executive Board, realised that there were a group of sales professionals that were selling and achieving outstanding results even in a difficult economic environment. This led them to initiate a study into sales representative productivity that resulted in the publication of *The Challenger Sale* by Dixon and Adamson (2011).

A key finding of the study was five distinct profiles of sales representatives. First, the *hard worker*, someone who is always willing to go the extra mile, who doesn't give up easily and is self-motivated. Second, *the challenger*, the individual who has a different view of the world, understands the customer's business and pushes the customer to also think differently about their business. The third type was the so-called *relationship builder*, an individual who builds strong advocates in the customer organisation and gets along with most people in the customer organisation. The fourth type, the *lone wolf*, is someone who follows their own instincts, is self-assured and difficult to control. Finally, the fifth type, the *reactive problem solver*, is described as a reliable person who responds to internal and external stakeholders and ensures that all problems are solved.

Furthermore, Dixon and Adamson's work revealed that the highest percentage of high performers (up to 39 per cent) in sales belonged to the *challenger* type. On the contrary 25 per cent fitted the *lone wolf* profile and only 17 per cent, 12 per cent and 7 per cent of all star performers fell into the *hard worker*, *reactive problem solver* and *relationship builder* profiles respectively. The work carried out by the Sales Executive

Council further shows that sales professionals best fit the challenger type (p. 23) in that they:

- Offer the customer unique perspectives.
- Have strong two-way communication skills.
- Know the individual customer's value drivers.
- Can identify economic drivers of the customer's business.
- Are comfortable discussing money.
- Can pressure the customer.

Insight and solution selling

Insight Selling is the title of Schultz and Doerr's (2014) book, in which they propose that high-performing professionals in sales sell radically differently from average performers. In their study of more than 700 business-to-business purchases made by buyers (representing a total of $3.1 billion in annual purchasing power) they reveal a three-level model that explains buyers' preference to award their purchases to (high-performing) sellers:

- Level 1 'Connect': High-performing professionals better connect the customer needs and the suppliers' capabilities and solutions, while also being able to connect with buyers as people; as individuals.
- Level 2 'Convince': The best sellers convince buyers to purchase their offer by demonstrating how they can achieve maximum return, the acceptability of risks, and the reasons why the seller is the best choice amongst all options.
- Level 3 'Collaborate': Winning sales professionals collaborate with buyers by suggesting new ideas, and revealing new insights. They adopt a team approach when working with buyers.

'Solution selling' is a term popularised in the mid-1990s (Bosworth, 1994) that also found interest and further development in the academic literature (Sharma, Iyer & Evanschitzky, 2008). According to Storbacka, Polsa and Sääkjärvi (2011) solution selling often entails a protracted sales process that starts before the formal procurement process, and shows a certain degree of customisation and the involvement of functions other than sales. Overall, as the B2B relationships become more complex, the adoption of solution selling is seen as a promising approach to address the ever-growing requirements of demanding buyers.

SUMMARY

For theories to be useful, they need to help marketers and salespeople understand what happens and why in the sales interaction process. Next, they need to help the seller anticipate how the buyer is likely to behave and act in the sales process, and what the outcome is likely to be. Importantly, a theory can also help explain failure as well as success in a selling situation. Theories that have been developed from historical observations should be overlaid by other changes in the environment that also drive buyer behaviour: increased global competition, easily accessible information from the Internet and increased technology enabling e-auctions all have a profound effect, albeit on some businesses more than others – for example automotive. This knowledge can improve the planning and management of future sales processes and sales force training. All the above theories and models were built from observation and research into how firms sell and customers buy. The ability to put them into practice will depend on the firm's marketing structure and processes, plus the actual selling situation.

QUESTIONS

1. Why is it important for B2B salespeople to understand the concepts of organisational buying behaviour?
2. Which factors in buyer behaviour are likely to be the most important to a consumer purchasing a home improvement product?
3. In what ways might the sales behaviour of a business development manager pursuing a large contract differ from that of a salesperson's repeat calling on retailers?
4. If you were invited to prepare a training programme for salespeople, how much emphasis would you put on helping salespeople understand buyer behaviour? Why?
5. Using the SPIN model, prepare a list of questions you would use if selling office furniture to professional firms (accountants, lawyers, estate agents and so on).

INTERVIEW: CARLOS MENA, MICHIGAN STATE UNIVERSITY

Dr. Carlos Mena is an Assistant Professor in the Department of Supply Chain Management at Michigan State University. Formerly he was a Reader in Procurement at Cranfield School of Management. He led the Strategic Procurement and Supply (SPSF), a joint initiative with the Chartered Institute of Purchasing and Supply (CIPS) in the UK to develop a vibrant network of procurement professionals engaged in creating and disseminating thought leadership in the field of procurement.

Q: Carlos, thank you for contributing to the chapter 'Theories and Approaches of Professional Buying and Selling' by offering your insights in this short interview. In the sales literature, it is argued that procurement has changed significantly over the last two/three decades. In your view, how has this changed happened?

Carlos: In the last two decades there has been a shift in focus from solely driving down costs, to a much more holistic focus. Procurement professionals have started to realise that they can deliver much more than just cost savings to businesses. They are the gateway to quality, to innovation, to sustainability and as they understood this new role, they have been developing these functions. Obviously there are differences depending on the industry.

Q: What are the key factors you think are driving these changes in procurement?

Carlos: An important recent driver has been the emphasis on sustainability, because the impacts that an organisation can have are not within their own 'four walls', but across the supply chain: the organisation's suppliers, the supplier's suppliers, or even further upstream. If you want to contain the impacts on society you need to reach out to these suppliers to help them change their behaviour to become more sustainable.

Innovation is also driving different approaches to managing suppliers. In advanced technological sectors, suppliers become an integral element in businesses' innovative capabilities. So with certain suppliers, those that can help provide a competitive edge, organisations will want to establish a collaborative approach.

Q: Professional buying is thought of as problem-solving behaviour undertaken by rational individuals. However, to what extent are personal factors such as perceived trust, likeability and similarity important in professional procurement?

Carlos: Most procurement professionals I know would like to think they are very rational, very structured in their decision-making, by and large trying to avoid 'soft issues' in dealing with suppliers. Having said that, we are all humans, and I think it is impossible to avoid biases towards those individuals we like or whom we have enjoyed working with before. So I think it plays a role, but it is not intentional – it is something that happens out of human nature and relationships, rather than a conscious decision of the procurement professional.

Q: In this book we argue that sellers should adapt to the way in which the customer likes to buy. In general, to what extent do you think suppliers are flexible in accommodating customers' buying methods and processes?

Carlos: I think this varies enormously from industry to industry and from company to company. Some of them are very good at adapting to the needs and the style of the customer, whilst others are not.

We recognise the move towards increased customisation in sales. However, in procurement people can be sceptical and ask themselves, is this vendor really customising their offer for us, or is it just an off-the-shelf package dressed to meet our purpose?

Q: What is your view of the future of procurement? How is procurement likely to evolve over the next, say, ten years?

Carlos: There is a belief that collaboration is important for doing business, so this is likely to continue, particularly in certain sectors. Procurement is unlikely to adopt a collaborative approach for every input they buy. They are looking to collaborate with those suppliers that will give them some competitive edge. For the rest, we should expect to continue seeing transactional relationships. However as quality, innovation, sustainability, etc., become more important, collaboration is likely to increase.

Q: What advice would you give to a young professional sales executive in order to be effective in her/his relationships with corporate buyers?

Carlos: I think if they want to understand how procurement professionals behave and make decisions, to spend some time within their own companies, on the buying side of their business. Real experience of living 'in the other side' gives you a lot of insights into how decisions are made.

The other advice is pretty obvious: to try understand the buyers, try to develop a relationship, and be flexible and adaptable over time to the changing needs of the customer.

REFERENCES

Alderson, W. (1995). The analytical framework for marketing, in *Marketing Classics*. Englewood Cliffs, NJ: Prentice-Hall, pp. 22–32. From conference of marketing teachers from Far Western States, 1958.

Arrow, K. (1951). *Social Choice and Individual Values*. Wiley: New York.

Ball, Daniel (2014). Supply chain transparency: The key challenge in 2015? Daniel Ball (December 18). Procurement leaders website: http://www.procurementleaders.com/blog/my-blog--guest-blog/2014/12/18/supply-chain-transparency-the-key-challenge-in-2015

Biemans, W. G. (2010). *Business to Business Marketing: A Value-Driven Approach*. London: McGraw-Hill Higher Education.

Bosworth, M. (1994). *Solution Selling: Creating Buyers in Difficult Selling Markets*. New York: McGraw-Hill.

Cialdini, R. B. (2001). Harnessing the science of persuasion. *Harvard Business Review*, 79(9), 72–81.

Dixon, M. & Adamson, B. (2011). *The Challenger Sale*. Penguin.

Ford, D. (ed.) (1990) *Understanding Business Markets*. London: Academic Press.

Gaur, S., Herjanto, H. & Bathula, H. (2012). Does buyer–seller similarity affect buyer satisfaction with the seller firm? *International Review of Retail; Distribution & Consumer Research*, 22(3), 315–335.

Hakannson, H. (1982). *International Marketing and Purchasing of Industrial Goods*. London: John Wiley.

Howard, J. A. & Sheth, J. N. (1969). *The Theory of Buyer Behavior.* New York: John Wiley.

Hutt, M. D. & Speh, T. W. (2012). *Business Marketing Management B2B* (11th edn). Mason, OH: South Western Cengage Learning.

Jackson, B. B. (1985). *Winning and Keeping Industrial Customers.* Lexington, MA: D. C. Heath.

Katona, G. (1995). Rational behaviour and economic behaviour, in B. M. Enis, K. K. Cox and M. P. Mokwa (eds.) *Marketing Classics*. Englewood Cliffs, NJ: Prentice-Hall, pp. 125–136.

Lichtenthal, J. D. & Tellefsen, T. (2001). Toward a theory of business buyer-seller similarity. *Journal of Personal Selling & Sales Management*, 21, 1–14.

Palda, K. S. (1966). The hypothesis of a hierarchy of effects: a partial evaluation. *Journal of Marketing Research*, 111 (February), 13–24.

Rackham, N. (1987). *Making Major Sales*. Aldershot: Gower.

Rackham, N. (1995). *Spin Selling*. Aldershot: Gower.

Robinson, P., Faris, C. & Wind, Y. (1967). *Industrial Buying and Creative Marketing*. New York: Allyn and Bacon.

Schultz, M. & Doerr, J. E. (2014). *Insight Selling: Surprising Research on What Sales Winners do Differently*. New Jersey: John Wiley & Sons.

Sharma, A., Iyer, G. R. & Evanschitzky, H. (2008). Personal selling of high-technology products: The solution-selling imperative. *Journal of Relationship Marketing*, 7(3), 287–308.

Sheldon, A. F. (1902). *The Art of Selling*. Chicago: Sheldon School.

Smith, J. B. (1998). Buyer–Seller relationships: Similarity, relationship management, and quality. *Psychology and Marketing*, 15(1), 3–21.

Storbacka, K., Polsa, P., & Sääkjärvi, M. (2011). Management practices in solution sales – A multilevel and cross-functional framework. *Journal of Personal Selling & Sales Management*, 31(1), 35–54.

Strong, E. K. (1925). *The Psychology of Selling*. New York: McGraw-Hill.

Turnbull, P. W. (1987). Organizational buying behaviour, in M. Barker (ed.) *The Marketing Book*. London: William Heinemann, pp. 147–164.

Turnbull, P. W., Ford, D. & Cunningham, M. (1996). Interaction, relationships and networks in business markets: An evolving perspective. *Journal of Business & Industrial Marketing*, 11(3/4), 44–62.

Webster, F. E. & Wind, Y. (1972). *Organisational Buying Behavior*. Englewood Cliffs, NJ: Prentice-Hall.

Wilson, M., Gilligan, C. & Pearson, D. J. (1992). *Strategic Marketing Management* (1st edn). Oxford: Butterworth-Heinemann.

3 ETHICAL ISSUES IN SALES

OVERVIEW

The impact of ethical issues on the sales profession has grown significantly over the last decade, and is increasingly influencing decision-making, the definition of sales processes and the implementation of customer engagement strategies. There is recognition following high-profile corporate scandals over the last few years that we live in an ethically challenged business environment. For sales activities, predefined corporate ethical codes need to inform the resolution of day-to-day dilemmas faced by sales representatives and customer managers. Also, these codes need to be implemented and made compatible with the business context, trading conditions and the circumstances and moral positions of individuals involved in sales. Managing the ethical dimension of sales is intricate: what may be seen as unethical by one person could be considered normal practice by another. Individual and business ethics are complex themes and, in this chapter, the focus is on ethical issues affecting sales operations. This concerns the moral problems and potential rights and wrongs of sales practices.

LEARNING OBJECTIVES

This chapter aims to enable the reader to:

- Understand the scope of ethical issues in sales.
- Consider how ethics might affect sales operations.
- Evaluate ethical relationships between salespeople and the company, co-workers, customers and competitors.
- Draw up guidelines for managing ethical behaviour in sales.

DEFINITIONS

Ethics are the set of values held by a group, profession or community that result in a code of behaviour considered to be moral and socially accepted.

Ethical climate, closely related to organisational culture, refers to the perceptions, codes and norms that define issues of right and wrong, determining whether certain dilemmas need to be addressed and resolved.

SCOPE OF ETHICAL ISSUES

Ethics in the workplace have gained prevalence and relevance in business and organisational life. Ethics can be viewed as the values which an individual uses to interpret whether an action or behaviour is considered acceptable and appropriate (Stanwick &

Stanwick, 2013). In professional selling and sales management, a number of ethical dilemmas exist which may create role stress and potentially dysfunctional outcomes. Sales leaders and sales professionals have to decide how to approach these ethical issues. Being ethical includes being fair, truthful and impartial and not profiting unjustly at someone else's expense. Sometimes, managers regard ethics as 'soft' issues of secondary importance when compared to the profit maximisation ethos which drives many firms. This view is limiting; firms must acknowledge that their prosperity depends upon the interdependence and principled exchanges with a variety of stakeholders, who may have different interests (see Figure 3.1). Furthermore, firms that focus solely on achieving and maximising profits may not be the most profitable ones. On the contrary, emphasising the fundamentals of research and innovation, and excellence in customer care may lead firms to obtain the profits and financial results they seek. Profitability is often the result of an overriding effort to deliver a meaningful mission (Kay, 2012).

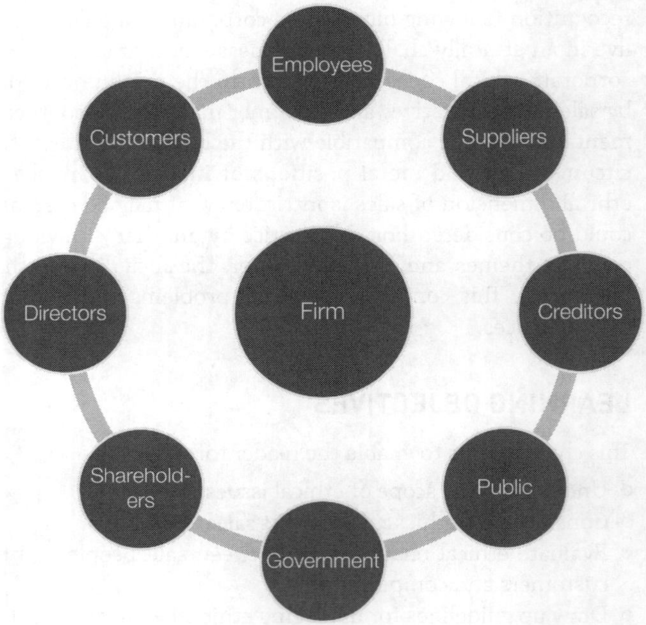

Figure 3.1 – Stakeholders in the firm

The culture implicitly or explicitly promoted within a firm may influence the behaviours sales personnel display in their day-to-day operations. For instance an organisation that is excessively focused on financial results may induce behaviours in salespeople that make them prone to bend the rules in order to make a sale or to achieve targets. Schwepker and Good (2012) argue that the application of sales quotas has far-reaching organisational implications affecting the perceived levels of organisational trust, customer-oriented selling, and sales performance. Setting targets in businesses and organisations are well-established practices that are grounded in goal-setting theories (Locke & Latham, 1990) and have been found effective in driving behaviour and increased performance. However, in certain contexts, the use of targets can lead to dysfunctional effects such as unethical behaviour (Ordóñez, Schweitzer, Galinsky & Bazerman, 2009).

From a personal and company perspective, ethical standards can be seen at different levels (see Figure 3.2). At one level, there are the basic right and wrong issues, which, as a minimum, means keeping within the law and abiding by rules and regulations – this is the legal minimum level of ethical behaviour. A second level is setting ethical standards, with company rules and procedures written as part of a job description or contract of employment. This implies that the ethical standards expected of an employee are set out and are reciprocated by the company. A higher ethical level is to establish a code of conduct that raises ethical standards in the way you do business. This code of conduct may involve looking after employees and customers in responsible ways. A further level is that of social awareness, where every effort is made to increase benefits to a wider public than just your customers, perhaps including the local and wider communities and other groups that could be affected by the organisation's operations. Finally, firms can proactively pioneer ethical agendas and standards for others, promoting high ethical standards in corporate social responsibility and sustainability.

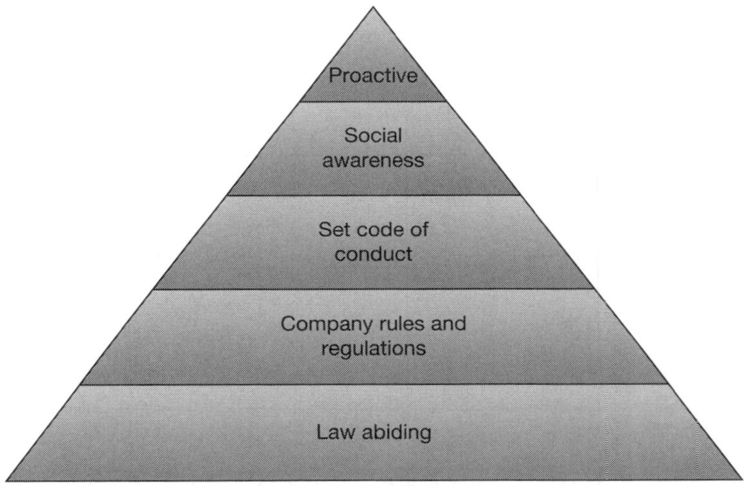

Figure 3.2 – Hierarchy of ethical standards

The Global Business Standard Codex (Paine, Deshpandé, Margolis & Bettcher, 2005) captures eight major underlying principles to assess and evaluate ethical behaviour within businesses and organisations. (1) The fiduciary principle refers to the legal duty to act in the best interests of stakeholders and other employees within the firm. (2) The property principle is the principle by which employees and other stakeholders are expected to respect property and the rights of the owners of property. (3) The reliability principle is translated as the belief that employees will honour the commitments made to the firm. (4) The transparency principle means that employees will conduct business in a truthful and open manner. (5) The dignity principle is the principle by which employees are expected to respect others' dignity, avoiding humiliation, coercion, or other types of human offences. (6) The fairness principle refers to the need to treat others fairly. (7) The citizenship principle assumes that employees will act in a responsible manner in the communities where they work and operate. (8) The responsiveness principle refers to the responsibility to respond to requests for information from various stakeholders about the operations.

Increased transparency and visibility in the operations of businesses and organisations as well as their implications has resulted in increased consumer concern for responsible products and services. Kuhlmann (1994) derived a list of six basic duties for sellers and manufacturers, drawing on various consumer rights statements. These were as follows:

1. Manufactured and offered products must provide a minimum level of security.
2. Supplier communication must not contain any deceiving or misleading information but rather educate the consumer with regard to important product qualities.
3. Contracts must not be drawn up to the consumer's disadvantage but must enable both parties equally to attain their interests. Furthermore, they should provide the consumer with the right to demand redress for damages.
4. Suppliers should be open to customers' complaints and attend to their problems as well as to the reasons for satisfaction and dissatisfaction concerning products and services.
5. The environmental pollution caused by the production, distribution, use and waste disposal of goods should be minimised.
6. Suppliers of goods can help to educate the consumer. Companies offering high-quality products and services at reasonable prices have nothing to fear from a well-informed customer.

Did you know?

In a 2012 study conducted by Ernst & Young among 1,700 executives from 43 countries:

15% stated they would take cash payments in the form of a bribe

39% responded that bribery and corruption are common in their countries

24% stated that bribery and corruption have increased

Source: Ernst & Young Global Fraud Survey (2012)

ETHICS IN PROFESSIONAL SELLING

The importance of ethics in personal selling and sales management has increased substantially in recent years, resulting in a growing body of knowledge about complex dimensions of ethical decision-making (McClaren, 2013). In order to fulfil their mission, sales professionals need to make decisions and devise sales tactics that may have ethical implications not only at a personal level but also for their companies, competitors and customers. In a survey of ethical issues in marketing, Chonko and Hunt (1985) listed important concerns for marketing practitioners:

1. *Bribery* – gifts from outside vendors, money under the table, questionable commissions and rebates.
2. *Fairness* – manipulation of others, conflict between company and family, inducing customers to use services not needed.
3. *Honesty* – misrepresenting services and capabilities, lying to customers to obtain orders.
4. *Price* – differential pricing, meeting competitors' prices, charging higher prices than firms with similar products while claiming superiority.

5 *Product* – products that do not benefit consumers, copyright infringements, product safety, exaggerated performance claims.
6 *Personnel* – hiring, firing, employee evaluation.
7 *Confidentiality* – temptation to use or obtain classified, secret or competitive information.
8 *Advertising* – misleading customers, crossing the line between puffery and the misleading.
9 *Manipulation of data* – distortion, falsifying figures or misusing statistics or information.
10 *Purchasing* – reciprocity in supplier selection.

At the personal level, salespeople are faced with several ethical dilemmas. The most obvious, and probably the most frequently encountered, ethical conflict is the salesperson offering gifts and incentives to buyers in order to obtain favourable treatment for their offerings in the customer's procurement process.

What do you think?

In the US and Europe the marketing practices of pharmaceutical companies have been subject to heated debates over the past few years. A key controversy has been generated by the incentives, gifts and inducements that large pharmaceutical companies provide to physicians to influence their prescriptions towards branded drugs.

The industry is facing increasing regulation of its business practices to limit the effects of inappropriate financial incentives. Companies such as Abbot (2012), Allergan (2010), AstraZeneca (2010), Eli Lilly (2009), Glaxo Smith Kline (2012), Merck (2011), Novartis (2010) and Pfizer (2009) have since 2009 been issued fines in excess of US$11 billion after investigations revealing inappropriate business practices, mostly misleading or illegal use of information designed to persuade clinicians to prescribe their drugs.

Q: Is it acceptable to offer incentives to physicians so they promote a particular branded drug? Some companies are abandoning practices that remunerate their sales forces based on number of prescriptions. What other practices can you suggest?

The nature of gifts that sellers can use to influence the customer's buying decisions may range from large economic sums in the form of grants and subsidies to small gifts such as entertainment, meals and expenses related to engagement with customers at social events. Sales people must understand what is reasonable and ethically acceptable with regard to incentives to customers. This is often not straightforward. Suppose that a distributor requires help to attend a trade show but your company also supplies a close competitor. This help may require financial aid, merchandising and salesperson's time. How do you reconcile this with regard to your other supplier? Offer no help to anyone, offer help in proportion to the business they do, or help anyone who asks for it? Could incentives to one of your customers induce unfair competition against other customers?

Building close relationships with some customers may affect relationships built up over many years with other customers or distributors and can have ethical implications. The trend towards more relationship-based selling creates difficulty in differentiating between principled and ethical decision-making and the opposite. Fundamental aspects in individual relationships such as friendship, care, support, loyalty, honesty, trust, openness and self-sacrifice (Duck, 1991) need to be made compatible with high ethical standards. In business-to-business, cooperation, trust and commitment (Morgan & Hunt, 1994) have to be aligned with principled strategies and customer management tactics. In order to ensure objectivity and to remove bias in procurement, some companies rotate their buyer teams to avoid the establishment and development of close personal relationships with salespeople.

Difficulties can and do arise for salespeople when performing the activities of their role, particularly when gathering insights to design a customer solution. For example, in the process of understanding customer operations, a salesperson can have access to practices and processes that, whilst not disclosed, may still influence the salesperson's understanding and dealings with a competitor business. Ensuring that confidential and sensitive information is not revealed and used inappropriately is a key challenge in the so-called 'knowledge economy'. Other areas that can potentially challenge ethics are the use of discounts and rebates. Published discounts are unambiguous, but less transparent loyalty rebates based on retrospective sales may be earned by the customer have to be paid later. Do all customers know of these rebates? Are they the same for all customers or biased towards one customer over another?

Salespeople may also find that ethical issues arise with co-workers. A common problem here concerns who makes the sale. Many customer accounts may have several branches that operate across different sales territories. The initial contact may be made at one branch, a subsequent order placed at another, while the ultimate level of business may be determined by company performance on a range of product, service and information issues. Another dilemma between co-workers might involve whether a manager should tell a prospective recruit that they are planning to leave the company to join another organisation. These are just a sample of the ethical issues affecting co-workers.

Finally, dealing with competitors is another area that particularly affects the sales force. Do you meet with competitors' salespeople and make unlawful agreements or pacts, for instance regarding price of a product in the marketplace? Is it ethical to agree not to poach from each other's customers?

THE ROLE OF THE SALES MANAGER IN PROMOTING ETHICAL STANDARDS

The foundation for an ethical supervisor–employee relationship in business is honesty and fairness. Sales managers are faced with ethical dilemmas when, for instance, tackling underperformance. If a salesperson is not performing as expected, one approach is to put pressure on the person or to threaten the individual with dismissal. An episode often pictured in movies and cartoons is that of an individual being called to the manager's office for their annual review, and told at that meeting that they have been made redundant (and asked to leave the company car keys, with the mobile phone and laptop). A more responsible approach is to intervene earlier to avoid such situations of underperformance and to help employees with coaching and training to perform to their best.

Other decisions with ethical implications may emerge from the opposite cases: in the case of a highly successful salesperson, would you, if in the role of sales manager, split his/her territory in two in order to offer improved service for customers but affecting the salesperson's bonus or commission? Whilst 'doing a good job' is a key motivator for industrial salespeople (Donaldson, 1997), performance-related pay is also considered a key driver of behaviour (Steenburgh & Ahearne, 2012) thus a balance between the organisation and the individual's interests must be achieved to enhance fairness and transparency – key features of ethical decision-making.

Sales managers often need to deal with ethically questionable occurrences such as anti-citizenship behaviour in the sales force (Jelinek & Ahearne, 2006). For instance, a study (Strout, 2001) revealed that 60 per cent of sales managers have caught their salespeople cheating on expenses. Falsifying sales reports and concocting expenses are also commonly reported unethical practices (Smith, 1995). Other possible grey areas from an ethics perspective include the misuse of company equipment, the improper use of company cars, cheating on time and doing two jobs. The freedom salespeople enjoy can give them the possibility to be involved, for instance, in running a family business, which may or may not be permitted in the employment contract.

For the sales manager, an integral dimension of the role is to discipline salespeople and instil high ethical standards fairly and consistently. The manager's ethical standpoint is an important consideration given that staff observe and take as a reference the manager's ethical standards as well as what the senior managers say or do (Schwepker, Ferrell, and Ingram, 1997).

What do you think?

Sam is an average performing salesperson with 20 years' service for the firm, who becomes quite seriously ill and is away from work for several months. On his return, there is a noticeable decline in performance and most people agree that Sam, although only 52, can no longer perform as expected. The long hours, the travelling and the increasingly difficult job in a changing environment all take their toll. The sales manager has to decide how to handle this situation.

Q: Does the sales manager offer Sam another job, propose offering a redundancy or early retirement package? What is appropriate, ethical and also in the best interests of both Sam and the company?

For sales managers another potential issue with ethical implications is the selection and recruitment of sales personnel. In most developed countries there is legislation protecting employees against discrimination on age, religious, racial or sexual grounds. However, some of these may be difficult to implement; for instance, totally removing the bias towards younger (or otherwise) candidates to fulfil sales positions. Sales managers can subconsciously be tempted to practise positive discrimination when they recruit people with similar ethnic or social backgrounds and values. While subtle ways of discriminating still exist, in most sectors these are being gradually eradicated and minimised. Overall, managers need to recognise the importance of being ethical in dealing with all staff, customer and other stakeholders, set the standards and abide by a code of conduct to reinforce ethical practices.

MANAGING ETHICS IN SALES ORGANISATIONS

Most contexts where businesses and organisations operate have established legal frameworks that prescribe constraints on how business is conducted in order to avoid or minimise unethical practices. However, many organisations operate standards well above those required by law. In sales, given the boundary-spanning nature of the profession, approaches to manage ethics that go beyond legal requirements may need to be developed and may have advantages. Customers are increasingly demanding higher levels of ethical behaviour (Gilbert, 2003).

What do you think?

It is difficult to give rules to promote ethical leadership. Some people base their moral position on religious or humanitarian grounds while others base their ethical position on the own personal value system. Smith (1995) suggests a number of maxims to decide whether or not actions are ethical. First, the golden rule is to do onto others as you would have them do unto you. Second is the media test – would I be embarrassed in front of colleagues/family/friends, if my decision was publicised in the media? The third item is the invoice test – are payments being requested that could not be fully disclosed in the company accounts? Fourth, good ethics is good business, the belief that the best interests of the firm are served by good ethics. Fifth comes the professional ethic – would the action be viewed as proper by an objective panel of professional colleagues? Finally, when in doubt, don't proceed.

In order to outline the dimensions of ethics that sales organisations may need to manage, we draw on McClaren's (2013) comprehensive review of ethics research in personal selling and sales management covering the period 1998–2010. This review showed increasing interest and growing empirical contributions to the field. The framework devised by Ferrell, Johnston, and Ferrell (2007) was used as an organising structure synthesising topics relevant to understanding ethical decision-making in sales into five categories. These are briefly described below specifying how managers can implement and enhance this aspect of ethics in sales derived from McClaren's (2013) review.

1 *Organisational culture* comprises the ethical climate, leadership style, norms and values, codes of conduct and policies, and socialisation (Ferrell et al., 2007). Taken for granted assumptions and artefacts also constitute organisational culture (Schein, 1992). To develop strong ethical cultures, organisations need to devise training interventions that focus on specific work-related norms; and they also need to devise corporate ethics codes that will generate higher levels of compliance the more consistent they are across different sales roles, companies and industries. In addition organisations will need to devote efforts to communicate breaches of professional and corporate codes of ethics. Overall, ethical climates are reinforced by directive leadership that delimits clear boundaries of ethical behaviour for salespeople.
2 *Sales activities* refers to the tasks associated with professional selling and challenge ethical standards when salespeople engage in aggressive selling, deceptive sales tactics, and distort stakeholders' values and norms (Ferrell et al., 2007). Overall, ethics in sales activities are associated with the structure and content of selling activities, the perception that customers have about the selling activities and the salesperson's supervisor, the applicable supplier/buyer ethics policies, and the supervisor's perceptions of selling activities and the customer.
3 *Ethical issue intensity* denotes the characteristics of a moral issue (Jones, 1991) and is an important influencer in decision-making. DeConinck (2005) examined the influence of ethical control systems and moral intensity on sales managers' ethical perceptions, showing that perceived moral intensity is a predictor of sales managers' perceptions of ethical problems. Thus, organisations need to consider implementing both compliance and values-oriented ethics programmes in order to increase the perceived moral intensity of managers and to help reduce unethical behaviour. The nature and frequency of unethical behaviour in salespeople is related to the extent to which their moral intensity is similar to that of the customer; therefore, where possible suppliers could consider influencing ethical standards in their customers.
4 *Sales ethical climate*, arguably a sub-element of organisational culture, refers to the perceptions, values, codes and norms that define issues of right and wrong,

determining whether certain dilemmas need to be addressed and resolved. Ethical climate is associated with job performance, job stress, turnover intention, role ambiguity and organisational commitment. The sales ethical climate can be fostered by organisational control mechanisms, such as codes of ethics and evaluation processes, and explicit corporate social responsibility statements.

5 *Individual factors*, such as education level and personal values, together with personal demographics have been studied in sales ethics. It is argued that the level and type of formal education as well as regularity of corporate ethics training are related to the ethical behaviour of sales executives. Leaders in sales organisations need to recognise that individual standpoints have a bearing on ethical conduct, given that the ethical judgements of sales managers differ according to their personal conceptions of virtue, morality and integrity.

Table 3.1 – Interventions to promote ethics in sales organisations

Element	Interventions
Organisational culture	• Training interventions that focus on specific work-related norms. • Devise corporate ethics codes. • Communicate breaches of professional and corporate codes of ethics. • Directive leadership that delimits clear boundaries of ethical behaviour.
Sales activity	• Establish frameworks to monitor the structure and content of selling activities, and capture the perception that customers have about the selling activities. • Promote supplier/buyer ethics policies.
Ethical intensity	• Implementing both compliance and values-oriented ethics programmes.
Sales ethical climate	• Establishing organisational control mechanisms, such as codes of ethics and evaluation processes. • Devising explicit corporate social responsibility statements.
Individual factors	• Promote active formal educational programmes to balance differences in individuals' ethical conceptions.

Source: Based on ideas from McClaren (2013)

To implement ethical practices does not necessarily imply the need for a democratic process but certainly one of consultation and participation. Organisations need to have formal groups or committees with ethical responsibilities, part of the organisation's strategic purpose. A necessary part of creating an adequate ethical position is fostering an ethical climate and communicating it to other stakeholders, particularly customers.

Did you know?

Kwik-Fit, the car service workshop chain, used to reward their branch managers on sales performance. The result was higher sales of tyres, shock absorbers and related products, Unfortunately, unsuspecting customers did not realise that these replacements were not always required and the company began to get a reputation as a 'rip-off merchant'. To be fair, the company quickly rectified this and rewards are today related to overall performance and customer satisfaction. Tom Farmer, founder and former chief executive and chairman of the company, set his own standards and exhibited what was expected by his qualities of leadership and example. As a result the company set as its mantra 100 per cent customer satisfaction every time a customer visited a Kwik-Fit outlet.

SUMMARY

Society's expectations of business are today much higher than in the past, which puts pressure on managers to behave in a more responsible and ethical way. Customers and consumers have both more information and greater choice and freedom to purchase what they want from where they want. This makes ethics a critical issue in leading and managing marketing and sales organisations. Despite the importance of ethical issues, customers are still conned, cheated and misled. Sustainable and responsible management involves not only the generation of profits and return on investments but also addressing human and moral issues that concern employees, customers and the public at large.

QUESTIONS

1 Are some stakeholders more important than others? If so, which ones and why?
2 Can a staff committee deal with ethical issues more effectively than individual leadership from senior management?
3 Outline some of the ways in which a firm operating at the top of the ethical standard hierarchy can set the agenda for others to follow.
4 List some of the key ethical issues faced by sales management and suggest how they can be resolved.

CASE STUDIES

Grampian Leasing

Grampian Leasing (name disguised) is part of a large international group with substantial interests in financing and real estate. Grampian's main business is in the market for supplying finance to companies that sell office equipment. Basically, they facilitate businesses to purchase the benefits of office machinery without having the risks of ownership associated with purchasing the machinery outright. Grampian's customers are primarily the equipment supplier, although deals are done with the individual consumer or business firm. A typical transaction is for the supplier to contact Grampian with a proposed new client who typically wants to lease some type of office equipment. Grampian underwrites this proposal before accepting the contract. Effectively, Grampian buys the equipment from the supplier and leases it to the end user.

Grampian typically uses a telephone prospecting system, contacts the account and grades them by size. The salesperson will then call to evaluate the supplier, who is likely to be in reprographics, telephone communications, computers and information technology or vending. Many customers are loyal and known, and use Grampian because of previous experience and service. These customers will be offered a more competitive rate than a new customer since less work is required because of the previous trading history. Grampian is very aware of competitors' prices and each salesperson is expected to work around a different rate sheet for the end user. The sales approach is to deal not only with the company but also with the employee. Grampian prefers to allocate the same salesperson to the same dealer, thus building up the relationship. Part of their relationship-building is an extensive programme of corporate entertainment; sports events in particular are popular. The sales force are appraised every six months and training and refresher courses are periodically held. The regional sales team meets on a Friday, once a fortnight, for an open exchange of ideas and information and to encourage team building. Schemes that are run include longer holidays for longer service and bonus schemes, for both individuals and groups, if targets are met. A normal bonus is of the order of 10 per cent of salary, paid quarterly.

Ian has worked for the company for several years and has three particular contracts in the pipeline as he begins his week on Monday. First is a potentially lucrative deal with a computer company, but he knows that his major competitors will also be bidding. Ian has built up a good relationship with the marketing director of the computer firm, who use a supplier evaluation form to grade the bids. This director has informed Ian that Grampian is behind on their performance evaluation against one of their competitors. On a number of performance dimensions Ian knows Grampian to be the better offer, and he is sure that this competitor has falsified the return.

A second potential contract is with a smaller company with limited potential. As part of relationship-building, Ian had entertained this client to dinner. He is being specifically asked by the customer to repeat the event but Ian knows that the expense cannot really be justified. Furthermore, the buyer is fond of 'a little libation', and Ian knows that there will be a long evening of drinking without much work being discussed and that he personally will be seriously out of pocket on expenses.

Finally, Ian has good prospects of interesting a major company in a deal but he knows that, if the deal goes through, it will be from their head office and the credit for the contract will go not only to another salesperson but to the region where the head office is located. He is undecided whether it is worth the effort (Figure 3.3).

1. Discuss the ethical issues involved in all three situations that Ian faces.
2. Suggest a course of action to Ian for each of the customer relationships mentioned.

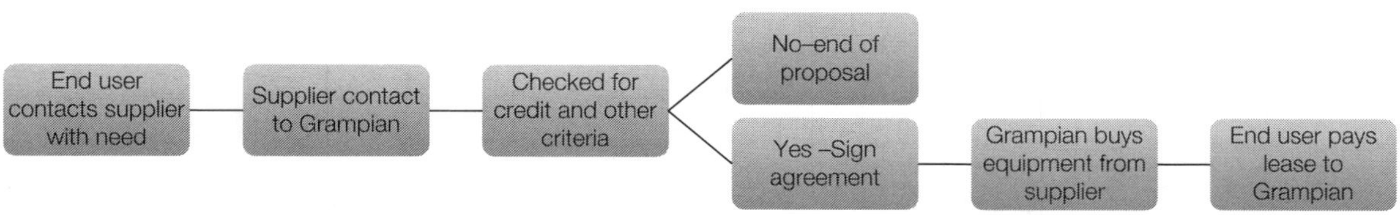

Figure 3.3 – Grampian Leasing proposal process

Barings Bank

A widely recognised global economic decline and financial crisis that began in December 2007 with a financial liquidity crisis, and as further complicated by the bursting of the US housing bubble, caused the values of securities tied to US real estate pricing to plummet, with a severe negative impact on financial institutions globally. This led to the collapse of a number of institutions. The fall of some of these institutions and the findings of inadequate risk control mechanisms, was compared to the case of Barings, a financial services organisation which collapsed, arguably by the ethically questionable practice of a key member of staff.

Barings plc was the oldest investment bank in the United Kingdom, with total assets of $9.37 billion and 4,000 employees worldwide. Following the deregulation of London's financial markets in 1986, Barings established a subsidiary Barings Securities to commence trading in securities and derivatives. In April 1992, Barings Securities sent Nicholas Leeson, an employee at their London office, to Singapore to set up the settlement operations for securities trading. In February 1995 Barings incurred huge losses and went into bankruptcy.

The following factors contributed to the development of the conditions that caused the collapse of the bank:

- The work was distributed in terms of both physical and temporal settings, with long physical distances separating the two offices and time differences (London–Singapore). This precluded timely flow of information.
- Interdependent activities with little third party involvement that could facilitate error detection. An internal audit team that reviewed BFS's operations in July–August 1994 pointed out that the current arrangement whereby Leeson was solely responsible for trading and settlement, deviated from standard industry practice as well as from Barings' own operational risk management.
- Increasingly risky positions that led Lesson to accumulate about 28,000 contracts valued close to $29 billion. Leeson's huge positions were based on the assumption that stock prices and interest rates would go up.
- The organisational setting suffered from certain instability.
- Primacy of the profitability goal – incentive systems that rewarded revenue generation but not safety/control. Resource allocation strategies de-emphasised safety-related activities such as monitoring and correcting error.
- Inadequate resources devoted to monitoring and corrective mechanisms.

Leeson booked deviant trades in a newly created account, which was reported periodically to Barings, which failed to initiate follow-up inquiries and corrective actions. Increasingly risky positions that led Lesson to accumulate about 28,000 contracts valued close to $29 billion. Leeson's huge positions were based on the assumption that stock prices and interest rates would go up.

By giving the trader complete control over the transactions, this latent error in infrastructure facilitated subsequent latent errors in execution. Similarly, errors in monitoring further facilitated latent errors in execution. Positive feedback systems such as trading losses led to increased volume of trading, which in turn led to further losses. Trading losses and volumes were directly linked.

The regrettable ending of the bank initiated on January 17, 1995. An earthquake in Kobe, Japan, led to a steep drop in Japanese stock prices and interest rates. Within a period of a month, Barings was exposed to losses of $1.3 billion and was forced into administration, a legal proceeding similar to Chapter 11 bankruptcy-court proceedings in the United States.

1. Discuss: how could this major event have been avoided? Think about firm-, team- and individual-level initiatives.
2. What might have been the role of financial incentives in promoting the excessive risk taken by Nicholas Leeson?

REFERENCES

Chonko, L. B. & Hunt, S. D. (1985). Ethics and marketing management: An empirical investigation. *Journal of Business Research, 13,* 339–359.

DeConinck, J. B. (2005). The influence of ethical control systems and moral intensity on sales managers' ethical perceptions and behavioral intentions. *Marketing Management Journal*, 15(2), 123–131.

Donaldson, B. (1997). The importance of financial incentives in motivating industrial salespeople. *The Journal of Selling and Major Account Management*, 1(1): 4–16.

Duck, S. (1991). *Understanding Relationships*. New York: Guilford Press.

Ernst & Young (2012). 12th global fraud survey. Retrieved 20 December 2013, from http://www.ey.com/GL/en/Services/Assurance/Fraud-Investigation---Dispute-Services/Global-Fraud-Survey---a-place-for-integrity.

Ferrell, O. C., Johnston, M. W. & Ferrell, L. (2007). A framework for personal selling and sales management ethical decision making. *Journal of Personal Selling & Sales Management*, 27(4), 291–299.

Gilbert, J. (2003). A matter of trust. *Sales and Marketing Management*, 155(3), 30.

Jelinek, R. & Ahearne, M. (2006). The ABC's of ACB: Unveiling a clear and present danger in the sales force. *Industrial Marketing Management*, 35, 457–467.

Jones, T. M. (1991). Ethical decision making by individuals in organizations: An issue-contingent model. *Academy of Management Review*, 16(2), 366–395.

Kay, J. (2012). *Obliquity: Why Our Goals Are Best Achieved Indirectly.* London: Penguin Books, p. 240.

Kuhlmann, E. (1994). Customers, in Harvey, B. (ed.) *Business Ethics: A European approach*. Trowbridge: Prentice-Hall, Chapter 5.

Locke, E. A. & Latham, G. P. (1990). *A Theory of Goal Setting & Task Performance*. Englewood Cliffs, NJ: Prentice Hall.

McClaren, N. (2013). The personal selling and sales management ethics research: Managerial implications and research directions from a comprehensive review of the empirical literature. *Journal of Business Ethics*, 112(1), 101–125. doi: 10.1007/s10551-012-1235-4.

Morgan, R. M. & Hunt, S. D. (1994). The commitment–trust theory of relationship marketing. *Journal of Marketing*, 58 (July), 20–38.

Ordóñez, L. D., Schweitzer, M. E., Galinsky, A. D. & Bazerman, M. H. (2009). Goals gone wild: The systematic side effects of overprescribing goal setting. *Academy of Management Perspectives*, 44(1), 6–16.

Paine, L., Deshpandé, R., Margolis, J. D. & Bettcher, K. E. (2005). Up to code. *Harvard Business Review*, 83(12), 122–133.

Schein, E. H. (1992). *Organizational Culture and Leadership* (2nd edn). San Francisco, CA: Jossey-Bass.

Schwepker, C. H., Ferrell, O. C. & Ingram, T. N. (1997). The influence of ethical climate and ethical conflict on role stress in the sales force. *Journal of the Academy of Marketing Science*, 25(2), 99–108.

Schwepker, C. H. & Good, D. J. (2012). Sales quotas: Unintended consequences on trust in organization, customer-oriented selling, and sales performance. *The Journal of Marketing Theory and Practice*, 20(4), 437–452. doi: 10.2753/MTP1069-6679200406.

Smith, N. C. (1995). Marketing ethics, in Baker, M. J. (ed.) *The Companion Encyclopedia of Marketing*. London: Routledge, pp. 905–929.

Stanwick, P. & Stanwick, S. (2013). *Understanding Business Ethics* (2nd edn). Thousand Oaks, CA: Sage, p. 584.

Steenburgh, T. & Ahearne, M. (2012). Motivating salespeople: What really works. *Harvard Business Review*, 90(7/8), 70–75.

Strout, E. (2001). Are your salespeople ripping you off? *Sales and Marketing Management*, 153(2), 56–62.

REFERENCES

4 SALES FORCE ORGANISATION AND DEPLOYMENT

OVERVIEW

One of the key principles in sales management is determining the optimal structure and size for the sales force as a fundamental mechanism to deliver the corporate and marketing strategy. In this chapter, we first focus on the principles of organisational theory and practice as they relate to the sales force, in order to contextualise the problem and the factors which influence management choice in organisational structure. Second, acknowledging the need for a re-examination of the role of salespeople in achieving sales, marketing and corporate objectives (see Chapter 1), in this chapter we set out the principles for organising the sales function. In so doing we explore possible approaches taking into account the product, market and characteristics of the company's offering, as well as the size of the sales force and how to deploy it.

LEARNING OBJECTIVES

This chapter aims to enable the reader to:

- Understand the principles of good organisational design and the difficulty with implementation of these principles in a sales context.
- Consider different types of sales force structures.
- Evaluate methods for calculating the optimal size of the sales force.
- To establish sound principles for managing the territory covered by the sales force.

DEFINITIONS

Agents are firms or individuals acting on behalf of another.

Sales force structure refers to the 'blueprint' of functions and roles as well as formal relationships of the sales function.

Sales territory is an area of responsibility for an individual or team of salespeople in which to develop sales.

Telesales is the use of inbound and outbound telephone communication for the purposes of making a sale and/or providing service to a customer.

PRINCIPLES OF ORGANISATION

Drucker (1968) claimed that 'Good organisation structure does not by itself produce good performance. But a poor organisation structure makes good performance impossible no matter how good the individual managers may be.' Consider how an organisation, in particular the sales organisation, may evolve from its inception as a small business to its maturity as a large organisation. The example below, for an industrial product, should help to show the nature of the problems that sales managers face in organising selling effort and add realism by referring to a dynamic situation which demonstrates a means of applying the theory and principles discussed in this chapter.

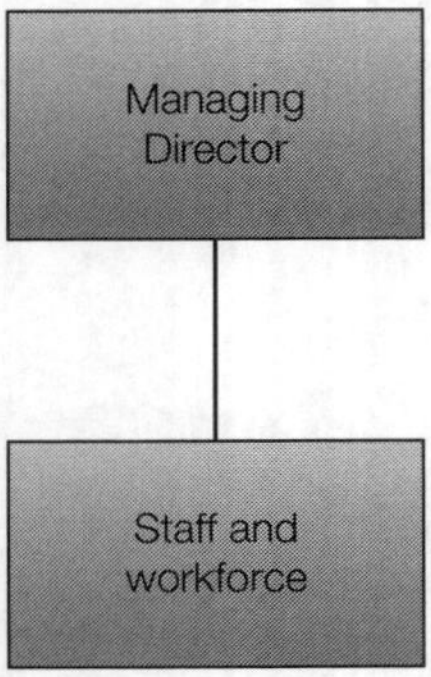

Figure 4.1 – Structure of a newly created business

In stage one (Figure 4.1), a business emerges, the owner acting as managing director employing a small workforce. Lines of communication are short and direct, with low organisational complexity and thus few management problems. As a result of product acceptability in the market, a period of rapid growth is experienced. Salespeople are employed to inform and persuade customers and distributors of the product's benefits, resulting in an expansion of the business.

The growth of the company is associated with some initial challenges with the control of operations, sales and finance. This suggests the creation of specialised roles for leading these functions. The sales force focuses on selling to distributors (intermediaries) and subsequently on to users (Figure 4.2).

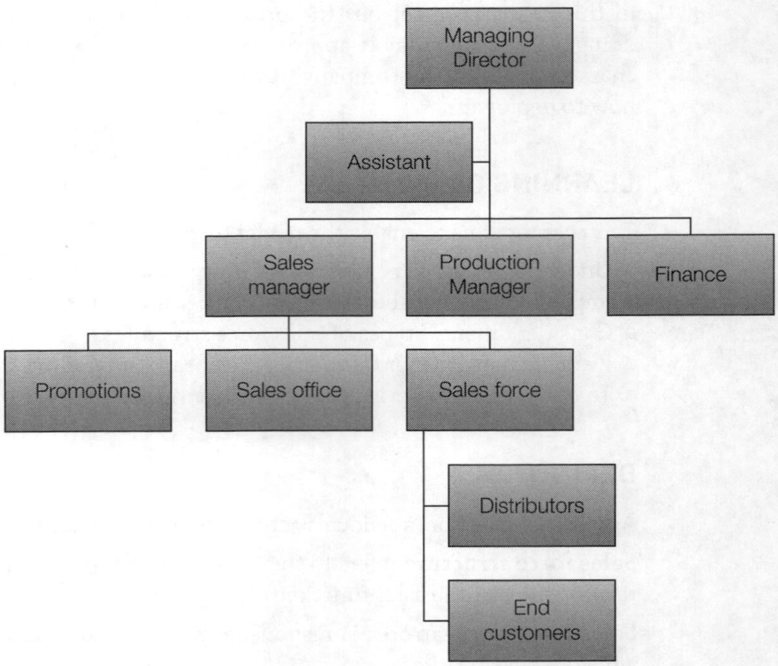

Figure 4.2 – Evolved structure for the new business growth phase

Further development of the business occurs both from organic growth and by integration with other companies. A more formal structure is defined to cope with the size of this business, which grows progressively though at a more moderate level. Salespeople sell to intermediaries but are increasingly expected to secure orders with specifiers and users of the product to protect the market share against competitors (Figure 4.3).

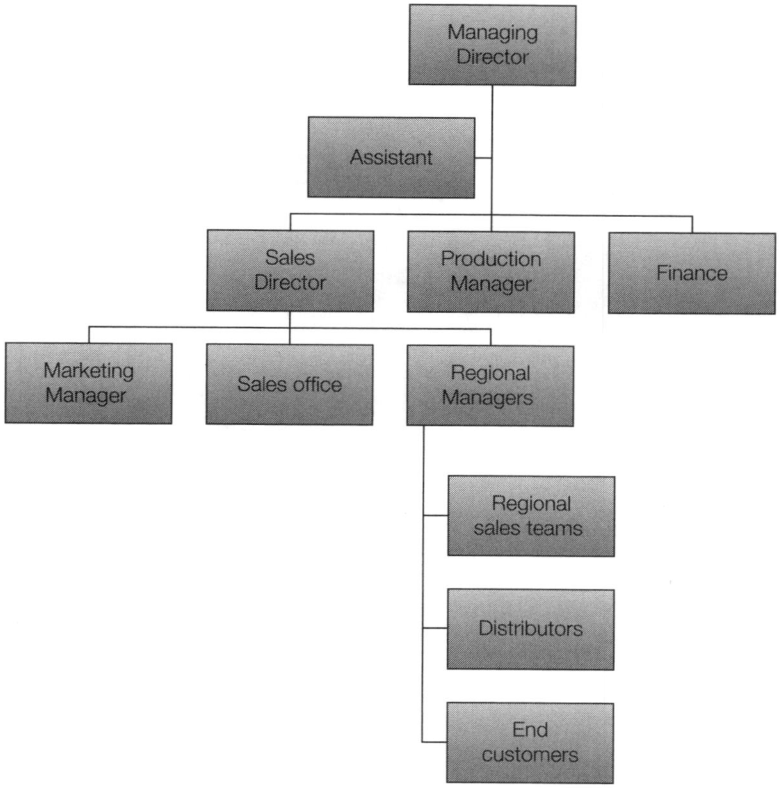

Figure 4.3 – Structure to support business maturity

Finally, the organisation, now with a sales force of about 50 professionals, is established in the market. Growth, however, is comparatively low while sales costs have increased. Problems arise in maintaining control in a diverse multi-product organisation. The resulting organisational structure is shown in Figure 4.4. At this stage, sales force organisation problems often depend on particular circumstances such as market conditions, product acceptability or competitive pressures. Consideration of organisational theory and the specific role of selling provides some help with this problem.

The definition and deployment of the optimal organisational structure is a complex process. There are, however, a set of principles that inform the adequacy and desirability of an organisation:

1 *Organisational structure* should be market- and customer-oriented. The previous example showed that, in a small company, the need to serve and service customers is fundamental, although a shortage of resources may limit what can be done. Senior management in larger organisations become distanced from their customers, sometimes losing the close contact necessary for true market-orientated firms. There is a danger, as size increases, of organising to suit the company's internal requirements or convenience rather than that of the customer. Such moves should be resisted at all levels and functions, and it is particularly crucial that this does not happen in the sales force.
2 Organisations should be designed according to *processes and activities* rather than people. The raison d'être of organising is to perform tasks, not to accommodate people, and management's task is to specify what is to be done by whom rather

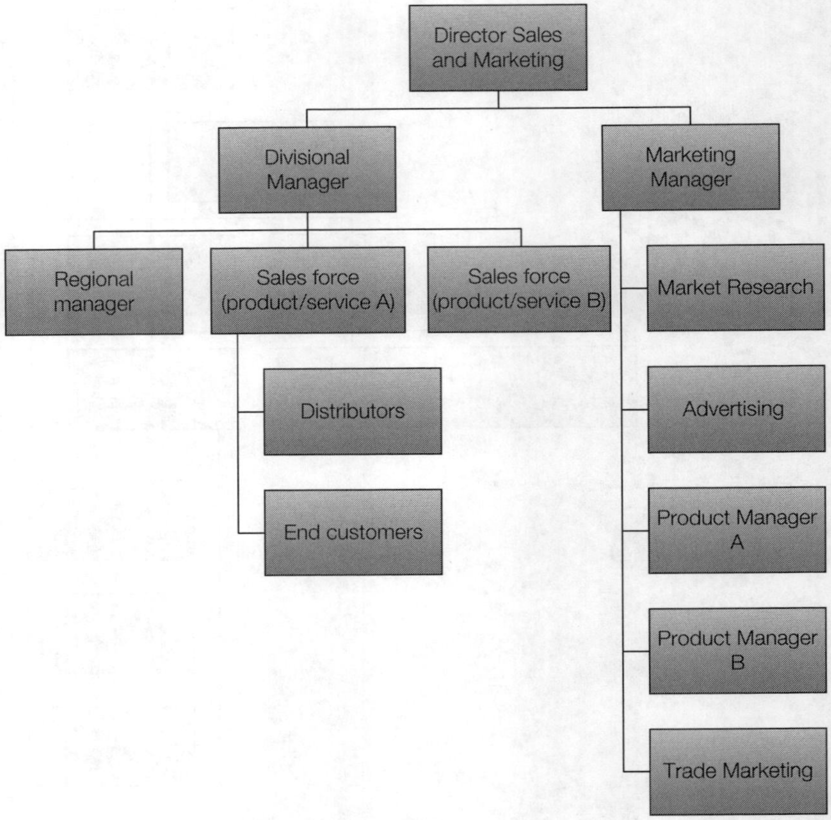

Figure 4.4 – Large organisation structure

than who is available to do what. This is a more common problem in sales organisations where frequent changes in structure occur, the result being that jobs are created for certain people rather than people for the identified jobs.

3 *Delegation of authority* and defined *responsibility*. The rule here would be that the more authority and responsibility that can be delegated to subordinates, the more involved and committed individuals will be to the organisation. The size and complexity of the sales force will affect the ease and practicality with which this can be accomplished. It is, for example, easier to delegate pricing responsibilities to a stable sales force of five than to a larger sales force of 50. While such problems can never be resolved without some compromise, the job description should clearly communicate the expectations held on the sales representative.
4 Reasonable *span of control*. Much debate is given to define numbers which equate with 'reasonable'; somewhere between four and ten appears to be the consensus. The actual number will vary depending on the ability of the supervisor, the ability of the subordinate and the nature of the work. Certainly, a span of control such as 1:1 or in excess of 10:1 creates problems for both superior and subordinate. A shorter span of control has been found to reduce role ambiguity and may have a bearing on sales performance (Bagozzi, 1980).
5 Organisations should be *stable* and *flexible*. As a result of internal pressures attempts are made to routinise and systemise activities in the interests of cost efficiency, but this can be myopic if the result is customer alienation or if the delivery of customer solutions is compromised.

6 Organisations should be *balanced* and *coordinated* in the activities to be performed. As with the aims of stability and flexibility, so too the aims of balance and coordination of activities will tend to conflict rather than naturally complement each other. One of the skills in management is to resolve differences, unifying the operations and personnel within complex organisations. This is more likely to be achieved where there is a unified purpose or corporate culture, where these principles of good organisation are considered and implemented and care and effort are given to the recruitment, training and motivation of employees.

Having described key underpinning principles of sales organisation design, we now turn to the key decision points for executives on the type and size of the sales force organisation and the role of salespeople.

TYPES OF SALES ORGANISATION STRUCTURES

Sales managers have the task of determining how sales force effort should be allocated to specific sales tasks, to groups of customers, to geographical regions or to specific products or product groups. Overall, decisions around sales structures and processes are fundamental in embedding strategic customer management (Piercy & Lane, 2009), and necessary to design sales organisations that are responsive and in sync with the demands of contemporary markets and customers (Panagopoulos et al., 2011). The key design parameters for sales forces relate to ownership, space and focus; these are described below.

Inside versus outside sales

The activities related to the deployment of sales personnel, organisational structures, and the definition of job responsibilities of salespeople are key in sales practice and also the subject of much interest in extant sales research. However, it is argued that more research is needed investigating the 'next generation' of salesforce deployment options (Williams & Plouffe, 2007). Questions that sales leaders face when designing sales forces include:

- Should my organisation employ its own sales personnel or independent agents?
- Will my defined sales strategy require field sales forces, or could telesales and online processes undertake the necessary sales activities to support business growth?

A useful way to consider these decisions is to analyse both efficiency and effectiveness of sales operations (Zoltners, Sinha & Lorimer, 2004). Generally speaking, where products are easy to understand, customers are small or not sophisticated, and sales activities are of moderate complexity and value, then the need for personal contact will be less, and more efficient customer contact methods can be considered. In cases of higher customer sophistication and risk, personal selling in the form of field sales forces or account management will be required.

Agents versus own sales force

Sales agents are independent professionals or organisations rather than employees of the supplier company. In the case of organisations often referred to as re-sellers (or distributors or dealers), they are given sales concessions, sometimes with exclusivity, to sell products and services in a given domain in terms of geography or product portfolio.

Independent professionals are sales representatives that act on behalf of the supplier but are not on the payroll of the company. Companies that use independent sales agents may lack the resources to maintain their own sales force, or may wish to achieve a quick roll-out in the market, thus benefiting from the scale and flexibility of outsourced sales teams. Agents are recruited for their territory and specialist market knowledge or their technical or sales competence. Changes and developments in a number of sectors with the expansion of franchise systems and independent sales agencies demand a rethink on the organisational choice of sales structure. There are several factors to consider, such as:

- Company resources.
- Market potential.
- Industries where agents may be the normal practice.
- Where one product complements other products from different manufacturers.
- Where local market knowledge is important.

It is usually recommended to use an internal sales force where close control over the selling situation is required, careful customer management is needed or technical knowledge is essential to maintain sales growth. In economic downturns, when cutting costs and overheads become necessary, having a flexible sales force in the form of independent agents can be a more realistic alternative to balance revenues and costs. The decision on whether to use outside agents or employ the company's own sales force has been researched by Anderson (1985). He tested several hypotheses and found that companies were more likely to use their own direct sales force:

- The greater the investment of company-specific resources (plant, equipment, promotional expense and so on) in a market.
- The more difficult it was to evaluate sales performance.
- The higher the combination of environmental uncertainty and transaction specific assets.
- The more favourable the price–quality combination; that is, the more attractive the product line.
- The greater the importance of non-selling activities (advice, service and so on).

Some characteristics, such as travel time, company size and nature of the goods, were less important in the decision than predicted. The conclusion is that, while almost any marketing function can be contracted out to agents, there are circumstances in which it is imprudent to do so. Furthermore, it is wrong to think that sales managers can abdicate their responsibilities merely by using independents. Whether independent agents or company-owned salespeople, there is still a need for a coherent sales strategy and detailed sales plans, and a need to train and motivate. In some respects, the motivation problem is not only different but also greater with independents.

Telesales

Another way to optimise costs is by employing telesales people, also known as 'inside sales'. Today telesales people tend to use multiple methods to communicate with customers and prospects including direct mail, email and the Internet. It is generally acknowledged that telesales can make up to five times the number of contacts that a field salesperson can achieve, and the cost is about half. According to a joint study conducted by InsideSales.com and InfoUSA, the inside sales model is growing 15 times faster than the traditional sales model. Telesales overcome the problems of geographical distance and time since they can be used, if required, 24 hours per day, seven days per week.

According to a recent report (SAP, 2013) roles found in telesales organisations can be classified as:

- *Inbound.* Refers to a team of people that respond to leads from the web and inbound marketing response (phone and online).

- *Social listening.* Is in charge of tracking social media for potential buyers and customers.
- *Chat.* Interacts online in real time with customers and or prospective customers.
- *Outbound.* These professionals use phone, email, and/or social media channels to engage, educate and prospect customers.

The decision of how to best use telesales needs to be considered in terms of the sales process the company has defined. For presales, telesales agents can generate and qualify new leads to assign a subsequent visit by a field sales representative. Telesales can also handle information requests and further appointments. During the sales stage, the telephone channel can be used to take orders and to offer advice and service support in a very effective way. Telesales teams often have on-screen customer information, and they can advise about order and delivery status, credit and other details to customers in real time. In the post-sales stage, telephone follow-ups can provide information and services to enhance customer satisfaction.

What do you think?

IBM (www.ibm.com) is a fine example of opportunity management. As an IT director of a medical company put it to us in our research, the IBM salesperson was able to add value by providing a solution to his problem. The product supplied by the medical company was of relatively low unit value but crucial to operating theatres in hospitals. The IBM representative was able to bring in a company specialist, with experience in bar coding grocery products, to provide a similar solution for the pharmaceutical company. Linking the product to computerised stock control ensured it was always available when and where required. For the medical company the result is increased sales and few out-of-stock situations. For IBM they were able to offer other pharmaceutical companies a similar solution. The readiness of the salesperson to solve the customer's problem and the ability of the organisation to mobilise company resources behind customer solutions provides a clear win-win situation.

Q:To what extent can the skills and proficiency of the sales force be a source of competitive advantage?

Field sales forces

In most sectors, it is necessary to consider adopting multi-channel and a variety of routes to market and in order to maintain sales growth and remain competitive. Our research in this area (Tzokas & Donaldson, 2000) suggests that as a result of new technology, more demanding and expert customers and increasing competition, salespeople with direct, face-to-face contact with customers have a role to play in creating and delivering customer value. As a result, the sales job has become more strategic (Shapiro, Slywotsky & Doyle, 1998) and requires a greater range of skills and abilities than hitherto (Lassk, Ingram, Kraus & Di Mascio, 2012; Moncrief, Marshall & Lassk, 2006). How this enhanced value is produced and delivered, how it is perceived by customers and how it affects the long-term performance of the organisation is a key challenge that sales leaders face in modern sales organisations.

Did you know?

Nicky Robinson, the Director of Field Sales at Coca-Cola Enterprises UK, is responsible for managing and inspiring 320 people who manage retail customers. The combined value of this channel is £1.4 billion. She believes that flexible working arrangements could have a positive effect on retention, particularly female talent in sales, with positive impact on overall business performance.

Source: Journal of Sales Transformation, Issue 1. January 2015

Customer value will be enhanced if organisations consider three core issues. Firstly, the process of creating and delivering value. Customers perceive value in relationships and in the role of salespeople across multiple dimensions. There are approaches and activities that often result in the creation of customer value. These include focusing on the priorities of the customer, providing a value proposition that addresses those priorities, and only making promises that the supplying firm can fulfil and that seem 'sensible' in the eyes of the buyer. Being aware of the financial constraints and cost drivers of their customers also enhances the esteem and credibility of the salesperson in the eyes of the buyer.

Secondly, establishing and developing customer relationships. Salespeople need to acquire new skills and competencies to perform in their role as 'boundary spanners' across suppliers and partners (Flaherty & Pappas, 2009). These skills suggest that salespeople need to develop conceptual, managerial abilities, which in the past were associated with the middle and top-level management of the firm. In addition, they need to change their mentality from selling products and services to supporting competitive advantage and career paths of their customers, and from simply capitalising upon product and service characteristics to promoting differentiators emanating from the existing and planned competencies and capabilities of their firm (Lemmens, Donaldson & Marcos, 2014). As such, they need to understand their customers' business and that of their own firm to a much greater extent than before. Furthermore, they need to develop the ability to 'orchestrate' their firm's capabilities to 'match' customer needs with the supplier's capabilities.

Finally, organisational support for salespeople. Management must provide support for their salespeople as shown in Figure 4.5

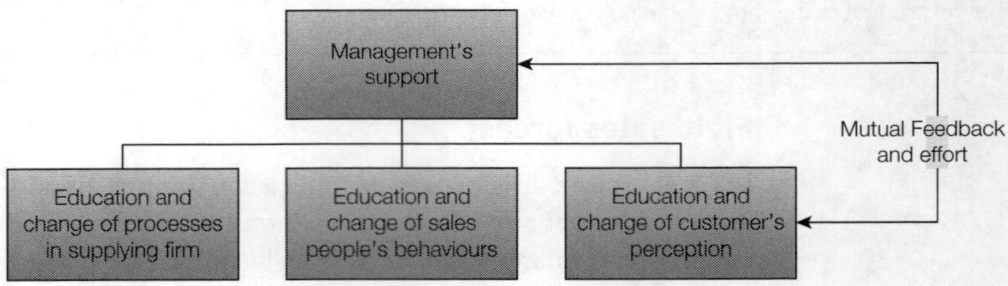

Figure 4.5 – Management's support for relationships

There are three interrelated directions of this support, namely: educating internal personnel and changing processes in their own firms, educating and changing salespeople's behaviour, and educating and changing customers' perceptions. Overall, we found evidence that both customers and suppliers recognise the need to mutually support the new role of salespeople. This joint recognition stems from the appreciation that contemporary salespeople operate in an extremely complex selling environment. To perform effectively in this environment they should have access to internal resources, as well as access to the customer's organisation. Internal resources include training and skills development, and the customer organisation includes close collaboration, trust, honesty, commitment and mechanisms to jointly evaluate value creation. Suppliers employing field sales force need to:

- Evaluate the relationship orientation skills and capabilities of their existing salespeople and those to be recruited in the future.
- Qualify the relationship propensity of their customers.

This enhanced role for the salesperson has been evidenced in a number of studies emphasising aspects of the role of modern field sales representatives in areas such as adaptive selling (Chakrabarty, Brown & Widing, 2013), effective presentations (Cicala, Smith & Bush, 2012), value creation and appropriation (Blocker, Cannon, Panagopoulos & Sager, 2012; Haas, Snehota & Corsaro, 2012) and relationship management (Davies, Ryals & Holt, 2010).

Organisation by geography and territory management

Geographical specialisation is the traditional and most widely used type of sales organisation in business-to-business selling. In this type of sales force, each salesperson is responsible for all tasks, all products and all existing and prospective customers within a geographical area. It is most appropriate in larger rather than smaller organisations, where there is a widely spread customer base, where regional variations are more important than national standards and where personal contact between buyer and seller is frequent rather than occasional. The advantages of a geographical split are likely to be that travel time and expenses are less. Each salesperson can build good customer and area knowledge, which is itself a motivating factor in that salespeople manage their territory. There is less confusion since multiple calling on a single customer is avoided and customers know who their point of contact is. Finally, management control and evaluation are more easily administered. A disadvantage of the geographic organisation refers to the complexity of today's selling job and the dynamics of the business environment. Sales forces organised under geographical criteria may not have the specialised product or customer knowledge that some products and services require (Johnston & Marshall, 2013).

Territory management is one aspect of sales management and a key determinant of organisation, performance and control. It would be wrong to isolate organisation, especially sales force size, from territory management or to suggest that suitable territories can be determined and evaluated without studying other determinants of performance, such as salesperson ability, distribution, economic conditions or marketing effectiveness. A related problem is to establish which comes first – the sales territory or the sales. Interaction effects between sales force size and design plague measurement of the disparate elements which contribute to sales performance.

Sales territories are established to facilitate effective sales force operations. This is achieved by allocating a number of present and potential customers to a particular salesperson within a given area – usually, but not always, a geographical area. The reasons for establishing territories and the basis for their allocation can vary greatly. A reason for not having territories may be where the market is small, the customers few or the sales force size itself does not justify such divisions. If information is not readily available about prospects, or where the acceptability of a new product is not yet known, management may want to withhold the establishment of territories until the position is clarified.

Most companies do establish territories for one or more of the following reasons:

- To gain thorough coverage of the market. Territories permit identification of existing and prospective customers in a given area, thus reducing the possibility of missing business or duplicating calls, which can create excessive travelling time.
- To define the salesperson's responsibilities more accurately and specifically, if possible, by account name, number and call frequency.
- As a means of performance evaluation. Sales against the previous period, against the plan or against some measure of potential is both easier and more specific within a defined territory. The sales manager can in turn make comparisons between territories, which may in itself suggest improvements for all sales force personnel.

- To improve customer relations. Salespeople with a specified territory can learn more about their customers and build up rapport with them through regular contact, itself a possible source of time-saving. However, the possibility of overcalling or time wasting on too many courtesy calls should also be avoided.
- To reduce selling expense. Travel and expenses are much less in a defined sales territory. For this reason, most companies would insist that salespeople live in their territory.
- To match selling effort to fit customer's needs. This may be for parochial reasons such as a knowledge of local conditions or customs. Again, similarity between the salesperson and prospect may be important.
- To help the salesperson. This facilitates coordination with other functions of the business, specific marketing and publicity effort while contributing in a positive way to the morale and motivation of salespeople whose job is enhanced by being managers of a territory.

The most compelling of all reasons is that territories facilitate implementing the marketing strategy by contributing to better identification of customer needs and permitting more suitable actions to satisfy those needs. However, consideration of the new types of selling referred to earlier in this chapter suggest that new, innovative approaches are required for 'the territory management problem'. Again, we will compare the traditional approach to sales territory design with some new, innovative ideas.

Did you know?

Sales operations managers is an increasingly common position in sales organisations.

'People in sales often say: "When things calm down, I'm going to take a look at all that"', says Price Burlington, director of field operations for SAP America. 'But they're so busy managing the day to day of selling and managing customers that they let the big-picture stuff drop.'

This has led to the increasing adoption of the sales operation manager position in large organisations. This is an often cross-functional position for overseeing functions such as sales management, including technology adoption, revenue growth, and process efficiency. The sales operations manager often supports the VP of sales or sales director in designing optimal sales organisations and processes.

Source: Adapted from Kim Wright Wiley, The Evolution of Sales Operations, Selling Power Magazine.

Traditional sales territory design

The generally agreed procedure for establishing sales territories follows a five-stage process:

Stage 1: Selecting the basic unit The starting point for defining suitable territories would be on the basis of economic planning regions or possibly television areas. The inequalities of population, income and industry spread do not necessarily make this equal in terms of potential. Where possible, the smaller the start unit the better, since sales areas can then be built up from a compilation of more equal districts. Market characteristics, the distribution systems and the particular standing of the company are likely to have more influence than simple geographical lines.

Stage 2: Evaluating accounts and sales potential The market information system should provide the necessary input to assist in this decision. Where there is accurate market and customer information, the compilation of territories should be relatively easier. This means listing all potential accounts into categories such as unqualified lead, existing, past or potential customer. The advantage of a computerised system is the ability to select potential accounts by a relevant characteristic very rapidly. Information can also be stored on account status, value and prospects. Most firms use some form of A B C classification of accounts: A = most important, B = average importance, C = least important.

Stage 3: Analysing salesperson workload Salesperson workload is an estimate of the time and effort required to cover a geographical territory. This means the number of accounts of different types, the frequency of calls required, the time at each call, the travel time between each call plus other time spent on non-selling activities. To suggest that workload is a matter of arithmetic disguises the complexity of the problem, however. Consider some of the difficulties which can arise in calculating the workload figure:

- The type of selling. Salespeople may be involved in developing and establishing an account, which requires on average much more time than servicing existing accounts. Calls may have to be made on several people in each account; in others, only the buyer needs to be seen. Some types of selling require more missionary or development work while in others extensive merchandising activity may be required.
- The type of product. Fast-moving consumer goods require less explanation or demonstration than more technical products. Business is repeated on a regular, mostly routine pattern. Certain industrial products or speciality goods require more explanation of benefits, requiring more time per call.
- The newness of product or market. With market or product development, more time per call and lower sales per account are expected than with existing products or accounts. Each account has to be built up over time. More accounts mean a higher workload in a developing territory than for the equivalent sales in an established territory.
- The market share, standing and competitiveness of the firm in the territory. If the competition is well established, the salesperson's task per account is more difficult, usually more time consuming. Most firms enjoy a stronger market share in their own locality and the salesperson's task is considerably harder in other more distant regions. Other salespeople may be more successful, but this may be due to the effectiveness of distributors in that territory rather than to individual selling skills.

Stage 4: Designing basic territories The objective in this stage is to establish the sales potential for one salesperson in a given area. This must in turn relate to sales force objectives. As with sales forecasts, two different approaches can be used: the build-up method and the breakdown method. The build-up method is similar to the workload method for establishing sales force size described in the previous chapter. The procedures are:

1. Establish the number, size and location of customers, including current, past and prospective accounts. If desired, these accounts can be graded and grouped on a suitable basis such as size or whatever segmentation criteria may be used by the company.
2. Determine the number of calls per account, the time required at each and the call frequency.
3. Calculate how many accounts can be handled by each salesperson. The use of some A B C classification may be helpful. In particular, there will be an average number of calls per day, an average frequency and, if possible, an average allocation of selling time which can be calculated.
4. Draw boundary lines around a realistic load per person commensurate with the geographical base unit. For example, one salesperson covering all of Scotland might be more realistic despite not having exactly the same average as other sales areas.

The build-up method can be calculated using a computerised information system. Customer knowledge from data acquired through sales calls can be used to maintain a customer information file. It does, however, require up-to-date accurate information on accounts and the assumption that sales performance can be standardised to get the right outcome. These assumptions are often difficult to justify. Alternatively, management can adopt the breakdown method for territory planning. Given a countrywide assessment of market potential and target share, the sales potential can be estimated. This estimate then has to be allocated to the number of salespeople available (or to be recruited). Each salesperson is then allocated accounts which equalise workload and potential. Realistic geographical boundaries can then be drawn. The difficulty with this approach is that, when sales potential is equalised, workload will vary and geographical boundaries may be unrealistic. The problems of different market conditions and the varying effectiveness of distributors combine to complicate this rather simplistic approach.

Good territory design is achieved where:

- Territories are easy to administer.
- Sales potential is relatively easy to estimate.
- Travel time and expenses are minimised.
- Equal sales opportunity is provided across customers and prospects.
- Workload is equalised.

Stage 5: Assigning salespeople to territories When territories have been established, the task of assigning individuals to a territory must be completed. Salespeople vary in knowledge, ability and skills, making some people more effective than others. The evidence suggests that matching salespeople to customers is important but many factors contribute to the effectiveness of salespeople. Management's task is to prioritise these variables in search of an improvement, if not an optimum solution. Variations in ability as well as the desire or inclination for individuals to move to other territories may create less than optimum but at least workable compromises.

What do you think?

Advantages and disadvantages of geographic sales territories.

According to a report by the consultancy company Sales Benchmark Index, there are some advantages to the geographical organisation of sales forces:

- Decreased travel and increase selling time.
- Reduced conflict amongst the sales team.
- Strong local knowledge and decreased language barriers.

This approach to structuring the sales force also has some disadvantages, however:

- Limiting growth from ambitious sales professionals.
- Lack of specialisation.

Source: Sales Benchmark Index. February 2012. http://www.salesbenchmarkindex.com/bid/78171/The-Pros-and-Cons-of-Geographic-Sales-Territories

Improving time and territory management

Geographical improvement The high proportion of time that salespeople spend travelling is an obvious area in which to look for time-saving. Whether this saving can be achieved by management-imposed routes is more doubtful, except in the most routine forms of selling, such as the delivery salesperson or merchandiser. The widespread adoption of satellite navigation systems is an obvious help in avoiding wasting time on incorrect routes. The advantages of a properly designed system will be lower costs, improved territory coverage and better communication between management and salespeople and between salespeople and customers.

The first way in which time can be saved is by utilising the most appropriate shape pattern for the territory. Three possibilities are:

1 *The circle system*, which is useful when customers are of similar size and type, being evenly distributed: the salesperson's base should be as near the centre as possible (Figure 4.6); variations within this enable a mix of size and type of call to be planned, together with a reduction of journey time.

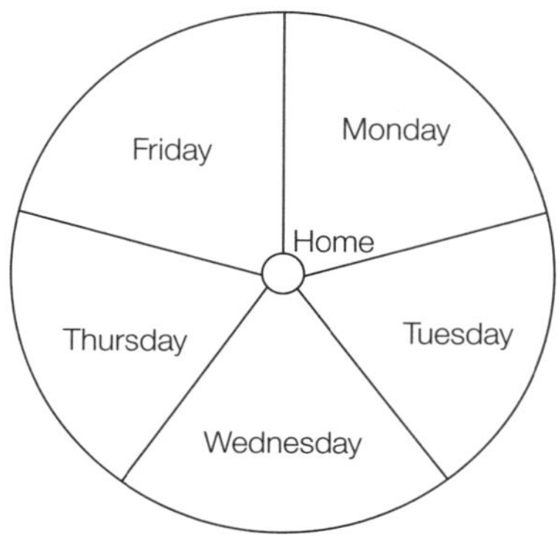

Figure 4.6 – The circle system to manage sales territories

2 *The hopscotch system*, which might help to reduce overall journey times if the distance from home is great; that is, travel to the furthest point and work back (Figure 4.7).
3 *The petal system*, which establishes a minimum working time, for example, a day's or week's work, the journey time being minimised (Figure 4.8).

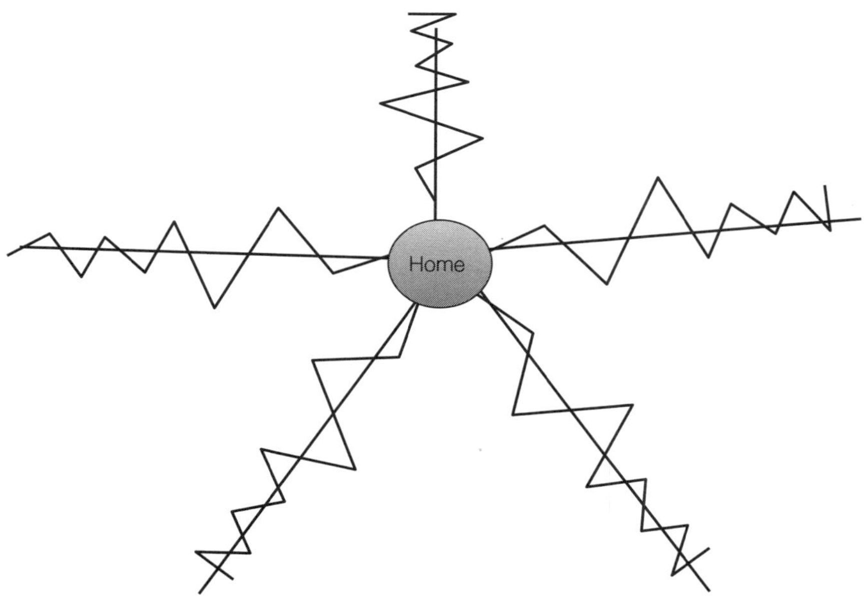

Figure 4.7 – The hopscotch system to manage sales territories

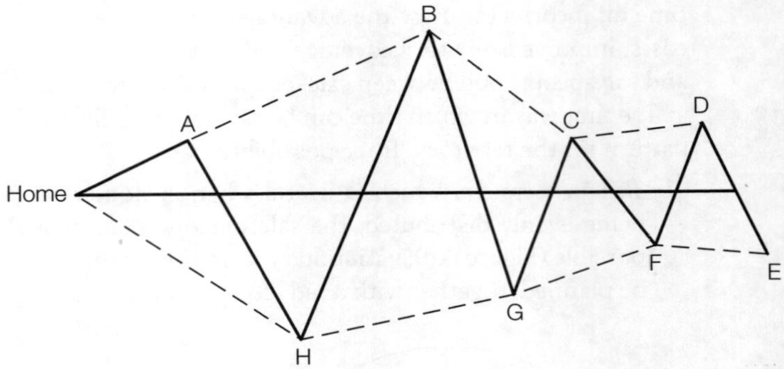

Figure 4.8 – The petal system to manage sales territories

Within these overall shapes, more efficient routes are sometimes possible as the features of motorways and call schedules are adjusted. In Figure 4.8, the route shown by the straight line is shorter than the route shown by the zig-zag line. It is almost certain that a more efficient route could be found for an existing sales call pattern on a given territory. However, the difficulty of not calling on one customer in the same area as another is that it may be considered rude rather than efficient. Extra travelling to some calls may yield higher sales than more calls.

Pipeline quality improvement The idea of measuring the sales process is one that is also spoken of in the commercial literature, and it is often referred to as a sales funnel, a version of which is shown in Figure 4.9.

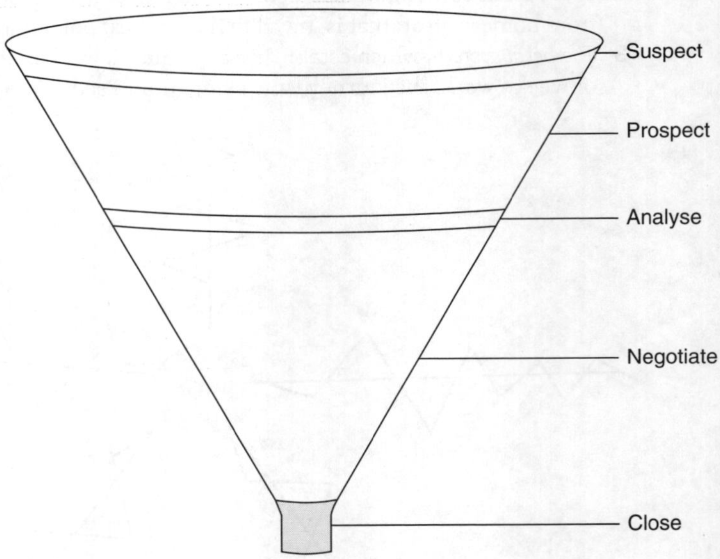

Figure 4.9 – Sales funnel

According to Heiman, Sanchez and Tuleja (1998), the sales funnel enables the manager to evaluate the current sales situation and the sales strategy. They claim that the use of sales funnel or process to report sales opportunities provides:

- More clarity in terms of where each opportunity really stands.
- Better communication as it provides a common way to view opportunities.

- A clearer perspective as it makes it possible to see how different opportunities are linked together.
- Better forecasting as it provides a detailed view of how far each opportunity really is from being closed.

They also argue that this overall process would enable a sales manager to detect problems related to sales skills and to time and territory management. Low conversion ratios would reflect sales skills problems, and unbalanced numbers of opportunities at each stage would reflect time and territory management problems.

Bosworth (1995) shares this view and extends it by arguing that statistical analysis should be used to measure and manage the sales process. In Bosworth's view historical process measures, combined with average sales cycle duration and average order value, enable the development of process objectives needed to accomplish the sales targets.

Activity-based improvement Several authors have provided classifications of selling types based on the actual activities performed by the salesperson (McMurry, 1961; Moncrief, 1986; Moncrief, Marshall & Lassk 1999; Newton, 1969). The latest and perhaps most complete list of sales activities is that of Moncrief et al. (1999) which lists the following main activities: selling, working with orders, servicing the customer, working with distributors, travelling, entertaining clients, information management, servicing the product, attending conferences and meetings, training and recruiting new salespeople, managing customer relationships, using new technologies and team management. Chonko, Low, Roberts and Tanner (2000) argue that the sales manager must identify the relevant sales activities and for each of these activities define its goals, objectives, performance standards, what behaviours are needed to complete the activity and the relative importance of each behaviour.

The problem of time allocation, not to mention the opportunity for profit, has attracted the attention of IT vendors and others in devising models which optimise on such factors as sales calling effort, number of salespeople, location and journey planning. The aim is to find the position of the optimum line between the extremes of maximum coverage and minimum cost.

The recommended solution to the analysis of sales territories is a six-stage approach:

Stage 1: Select one or more appropriate measures of performance such as sales or profit per salesperson.

Stage 2: Develop operational measures of the factors considered to be determinants of sales territory performance. These were considered to be:

- Market potential (forecast industry sales).
- Territory workload (measured by annual purchases and concentration of accounts).
- The salesperson's experience (length of time employed).
- The salesperson's motivation and effort (management rating scale).
- Company experience (historical market share and change in market share).
- Company effort (advertising expenditure).

Stage 3: Analyse criteria and predictor variables using empirical data in a multiple regression model.

Stage 4: Determine the relationship: evaluate the above multiple regression model.

Stage 5: Determine performance benchmarks for each territory to spot poor areas requiring attention.

Stage 6: Evaluate individual territory performance. This can be achieved by comparing actual sales with target sales and the response predictors using the multiple regression model between two different territories (Table 4.1).

Table 4.1 – Comparison of two territories

	Sales (units)	
	Territory A	**Territory B**
Constant		
Number of accounts		
Industry sales		
Market share change		
Workload per account		
Performance of salesperson		
Market share		
Length of employment		
Advertising expenditure		
Total	Units	units
Actual	Units	units
Actual to benchmark	%	%

Before claiming success with these models in predicting territory sales response, the problems and difficulties of measurement should be reiterated. Remember that the impact of other variables is likely to be large and significant. This occurs where markets undergo rapid change. Also, assessing market share on a territory basis can be particularly difficult in many markets for different products. What is likely is that companies with much of this information as part of a sales or marketing information system can find alternative and improved ways of setting targets and improving sales performance evaluation. Indeed, there is no general agreement on the factors to be included. Consider some of the possible variables which are omitted rather than measured or relegated to the 'other' category, for example environmental factors (economic, technological, social or political), competitive activity, the company's own marketing strategy and tactics, the salesperson's motivation and rewards, sales manager characteristics and particular customer factors.

These limitations to models of territory response should not disguise the fact that they provide a better explanation and measure of performance than traditional 'sales versus target', 'last year plus 10 per cent', or other rule-of-thumb methods. They also provide a better framework for the student to understand what contributes to territory sales and a ground for further empirical studies. It is the author's contention that any company can improve its territory allocation, management and evaluation by adapting these conceptual models to the specific company conditions in which they operate to yield improvements in sales force productivity. The limited evidence available so far confirms this to be the case. Ryans and Weinberg (1979), in reviewing the evidence, found territory potential and geographical concentration to be much more important in sales performance than measures of workload. This confirms part of the folklore which good salespeople know or learn quickly yet sales managers often forget. That is, put the effort where potential is greatest and take the necessary actions to achieve it by, for example, working longer hours or travelling further. Sales follow potential rather than historical sales or workload. Top sales performers work harder to overcome workload problems.

Predominant in the discussion of territory allocation and management is the most effective use of the salesperson's time. Most of the improvements can be achieved by salespeople themselves being more disciplined and more professional.

Disciplined time-management improvements include:

- Starting earlier.
- Finishing later.
- Cutting down on social chit-chat.
- Fewer breaks.
- Less entertaining, fewer lunches and less drinking.

More professional time management would include:

- Better planning of work.
- Less calling on unqualified or unimportant prospects.
- A systematic travel plan.
- Better use of travel and waiting time.
- More use of the telephone, including for appointments.
- Systematic paperwork.

Factors that salespeople have to assess in their time allocation include the following:

- When to deal with paperwork.
- How long to spend at each call.
- Travelling time.
- Number of calls.
- Order of calls.
- New business development.
- Non-selling activities.
- Social conversation.

Desirable though it may be to leave time-management problems to individual salespeople, managers have a responsibility not only to monitor but also to control time inefficiency and promote more effective sales practices.

Organising around products

Product specialisation would appeal where a company has product lines which differ in technical complexity, end user and profitability. Each salesperson can then gain the necessary expertise in product knowledge to handle different customer requirements more effectively. Companies that take over or merge with others sometimes continue to operate separate sales forces. Also, the case for expertise with a new product may require specialist development salespeople. With this type of organisation, problems may arise with duplication of effort and multiple calling on one customer. This requires management to promote cooperation between salespeople and to minimise conflict and confusion over who does what job.

Organisation by customers and markets

The implementation of relationship marketing would suggest that the most appropriate form of specialisation is that based on the customer. Where market segmentation policies can be applied, it is sensible to operate the sales force specialising in the respective segments. Grouping of customers into suitable classifications means that salespeople can develop customer expertise and implement marketing policy and programmes. This process can also work in reverse where knowledge of customers' customers can be used as a basis for differentiation (Smith & Owens, 1995). In dynamic, innovative markets, the information exchange process may require this form of specialism. In other cases, too much specialisation will result in excessively high selling costs.

Did you know?

Many of the large management consulting and technology firms are organised across verticals; that is, specific industries and sectors for which a suite of solutions are developed such as

- Financial Services.
- Communication, Media & Entertainment.
- Manufacturing.
- Utilities.
- Information & Technology.
- Oil and Gas.
- Retail, etc.

These suppliers offer solutions to help customers manage integrated communications and processes with partners, end customers and even other suppliers.

Combined organisational structures

The advantages and disadvantages of the three previous methods encourage many firms to seek combination systems of organisation which merge the benefits of specialisation with reduced selling costs. The increasing complexity of the selling job in dynamic, changing markets gives impetus to this organisational dilemma. Whichever approach is adopted it should incorporate the key principles of sales organisation outlined earlier in the chapter and reflect the many specific factors affecting the firm operating in its environment.

No single organisational solution can fit all, nor can it remain unchanged over time. For example, a product–market combination may be operated by separate divisions, groups or product managers as well as separate sales forces. A market organisation may split customers into key accounts, by different channel members or by industry type and is best served by multiple sales teams. In several markets, particularly food, do-it-yourself (DIY) and household goods, the disproportionate effect of major customers' control on the market necessitates specialist sales treatment. For instance, in addition to field sales forces, a separate merchandising sales force may be used to call on branches rather than to sell to buyers. In some markets, such as office equipment, a junior sales force establishes contact and evaluates prospects. Similarly, an inside sales force or telemarketing operation may be used to complement the outside sales force for specific tasks. It should be borne in mind that, despite the theories, concepts and principles of organisation which can assist sales management to establish the 'one-best' system, marketing and sales management decisions apply in a dynamic and uncertain environment. As such, numerous diverse influences have to be considered in any organisational proposal and changing the way in which the sales force is deployed can provide an opportunity to increase sales force productivity.

SALES FORCE SIZING

Sales management problems are complex and their solutions seldom permanent. In determining sales force size, the temptation to look for a simple, universal formula should be avoided. The type of sales organisation will affect the size of the sales force, particularly the degree of specialisation considered appropriate. The nature of the selling task between development and service selling will be fundamental. Other aspects of the selling task will be affected by the time that needs to be spent on activities such as:

- Demonstration presentation.
- Negotiating on price.
- Explaining company policy.
- Providing information on competitors and customers.
- Dealer support programmes.
- Stock-checking.
- Display work.
- Complaint handling.
- Credit problems.
- Prospecting for new business.
- Report-writing.

These activities should be included as part of the salesperson's job description to reflect their importance to the firm. This importance will in turn affect whether six or 16 calls per day are possible. Questions about sales force size will also depend on company objectives, company resources and competitive or other environmental factors. Issues of sales force size cannot be divorced from the form of organisation, the method of specialising or territory allocation. A number of methods for sizing sales forces have been described in core texts (Ingram, Laforge, Avila, Schwepker & Williams, 2012; Johnston & Marshall, 2013; Zoltners et al., 2004) and below we summarise three of them.

Workload method

The workload method is a composite figure made up from the total work time available, the allocation of this time to sales tasks and the time spent with each customer or prospect. It is usually based on the sales revenue per account. It is the most commonly used technique in UK sales management and calculated as follows:

(i) Determine the total work time available for each salesperson. This is likely to be a maximum of 35 hours per week × 46 weeks (excluding holiday) = 1,610 hours.

(ii) Determine the work time allocated to selling activities. A salesperson's time may consist of:

travel	25%
food and breaks	12%
waiting	15%
selling tasks	30%
administration	18%

Selling time available is 1610 × 30% = 483 hours.

(iii) Classify customers on the basis of sales volume potential or profitability. This might be, for example:

A – large accounts, say	500
B – medium accounts, say	2,000
C – small accounts, say	4,000

(iv) Decide on the appropriate length of call and call frequency per account type. On average this might be:

Type A – 60 minutes per call every two weeks
Type B – 30 minutes per call every four weeks
Type C – 15 minutes per call every eight weeks

(v) Calculate the company workload to meet the required calls:

A = 500 × 60 mins × 24 calls per year = 12,000 hours
B = 2,000 × 30 mins × 12 calls per year = 12,000 hours
C = 4,000 × 15 mins × 6 calls per year = 6,000 hours
TOTAL = 30,000 hours

(vi) Calculate the number of salespeople required:

30,000/483 = approximately 62 salespeople

With this approach, each salesperson should have a similar workload in terms of size of accounts, number of calls and travel time. It is rarely the case that accounts can be distributed evenly, so that travel time in some areas will inevitably be much greater than in others. Other weaknesses in this approach may be that larger accounts may not be those with the highest potential in the future. If potential is used, these may not be the most profitable if costs of servicing the account are higher or a less profitable product mix is taken. The most serious problem is the simplistic assumption that quantity equals quality. Each account and each salesperson will be different in quality, a factor not incorporated in this method. Put simply, different call frequencies (and time per call) may yield higher sales and profits.

Sales potential method

In this method, an estimate is made of sales potential for the company's products (sales forecast) based on management objectives and a desirable market share. If each salesperson performs to their job description, an average productivity level per person can be calculated. Some allowance should be made for the loss of someone leaving, for example, 10 per cent per annum, and the sales force size can be calculated using the formula:

$$N = \frac{S}{P} + T\left(\frac{S}{P}\right)$$

or

$$N = \frac{S}{P} + \left(\frac{S \times T}{P}\right)$$

This is the same as:

$$N = \frac{S}{P} \times (1 + T)$$

where N = number of salespeople
S = sales forecast
P = productivity level per person
T = turnover rate in sales force

Assuming that S = £20 million, T is 10 per cent and P is £500,000, the sales force size can be calculated as:

$$20/0.5 \times (1 + 0.10) = 40 \times 1.1 = 44 \text{ people}$$

Part of the problem with this method is the accuracy in estimating each variable, particularly P (productivity) and the accuracy of T (turnover) where the lead time in recruitment, the effect of lost sales and the desired level of productivity per person will vary. Also, it assumes a rather static market position when most companies will experience growing or declining sales productivity and perhaps regional variations within an overall sales forecast.

Incremental method

In order to overcome weaknesses in both the previous methods, the incremental method is suggested. Intuitively, this makes good business sense since the sales force should be expanded if additional sales revenue exceeds additional costs. The difficulty of estimating incremental revenues and costs can be quite daunting. This formula oversimplifies the economics of selling by assuming that the product mix is uniform and extraneous factors can be correctly assessed in advance for each area. The costs of selecting, recruiting or dismissing salespeople can seldom be accurately predicted. Other forms of promotion, such as advertising, may have unequal effects on different prospects. The simplicity of sales responding to personal selling effort where all other factors are constant is not tenable. The dynamic nature of markets, coupled with economic growth or decline patterns, distorts the calculations of the effectiveness of salespeople in terms of a sales response function. Seasonal, cyclical and competitive fluctuations create market uncertainty with a possible danger of overstaffing leading to cost inefficiencies. Companies may compound these problems by adding salespeople as long as profits are positive, that is,

$$S(P) - C > 0$$

where S = sales volume; P = profit margin on sales; and C = cost of maintaining salesperson.

The important weakness here is that salespeople become the result of sales rather than the creators of sales. Furthermore, it fails to take account of the effects of differing abilities, knowledge, skills and aptitudes of salespeople.

Consideration of these three methods should confirm that no one method will be perfect in establishing sales force size. The dynamics of the marketing environment increase the complexity of this problem. The best solution will be one which incorporates individual time and territory considerations as well as organisational expediency. Shapiro (1979) suggested that a rational process for structuring a sales organisation should follow a six-step process:

1. Analyse the needs which the organisation must meet. Remember that organisations should be based on tasks to be accomplished. A clear statement of sales strategy should be specified. The customers to be approached, call frequency and selling tasks help to focus the organisational purpose.
2. Structure the sales force at the bottom level. This way, the organisation will be designed to manage the sales force rather than the sales force being designed to fit a management structure.
3. Once the salesperson-level structure is established, keep changes to the management level. This is because the basic level is task-oriented – the prime purpose of the organisation.
4. Integrate units and staff support into the structure. If possible, this can be done concurrently but not prior to previous levels.
5. Develop control systems (measurement, evaluation and rewards) to support the organisation structure.
6. Allocate people to fit the job to be done.

Shapiro points out two problems that arise in operationalising this process. First, implementation has to follow marketing decisions on the role of personal selling in the marketing mix, as these decisions determine objectives. The second problem is that organisations are seldom formed from scratch on a blank sheet. Most decisions concern restructuring, which is often costly, unpalatable or both.

Another key consideration in determining the size of the sales force is the growth cycle of the company. Zoltners, Sinha and Lorimer (2006) propose four considerations to determine the optimal size of the sales force:

- Start-up phase: The main tasks in this phase are to create awareness of the product or service and generate quick uptake of the company's offering. Salespeople must also chase as many opportunities as possible in order to drive business, thus the size of the sales team needs to be moderate to large.
- Growth phase: Customer teams need to penetrate deeper into existing segments and develop new ones; therefore, the size of the sales force must be optional and understaffing must be avoided.
- Maturity phase: Businesses focus on serving and retaining existing customers efficiently, which suggests a decrease in the size of sales forces and the appointment of account managers.
- Decline: Efficiencies are further emphasised, and critical customer relationships protected. Companies may decide to leave unprofitable segments or customers, thus reducing the size of the sales force.

SUMMARY

Organising the sales force involves applying the principles of good organisational design to the dynamic needs of customers and markets. Personal selling, and in particular the activities of field sales forces, must operate in coordination with other functions within the company. Sales force structures need to be informed by the objectives of the organisation and the marketing function. Methods of calculating salesforce size must be used with caution since these methods may fail to acknowledge the differences between quantity and quality in personal selling. Designing sales territories and allocating people to these areas is a key task of sales management. While established procedures can be helpful, the conventional approach is often much less than the optimum. Models of territory response and call-planning schedules offer some improvement over traditional approaches but have not yet been widely accepted. The key factors to consider in designing territories are market potential, account concentration and dispersion.

QUESTIONS

1. In what ways might changing market structures and market conditions necessitate a review of the organisational structure of the sales force?
2. Sales forces are often organised along geographical areas. Give examples of where alternative means of specialisation could be used.
3. Critically assess the workload method for determining sales force size.
4. Strathclyde Cutting Tools manufactures industrial products. Until recently, they employed 12 salespeople to call on accounts and prospects. Dissatisfied with the results, the sales manager discharged all 12 in favour of nine independent agents who were self-employed and sold a number of other products to the same customers. Sales immediately began to increase, and new accounts were obtained. Analyse the possible reasons for this improvement, and point out the possible drawbacks in the scheme.

5 A sales management consultant arrives at your organisation with what she claims is a user-friendly software package to assist in the design of sales territories and the improvement of calling schedules. What questions need to be asked and answered before deciding on the adoption of such a package?
6 If potential is the major factor in sales performance, what restricts the sales manager in allocating more accounts to the best salespeople?

CASE STUDY

Scotia Ltd

Scotia Ltd (name disguised) have been suppliers of packaging materials, that is, cardboard boxes, paper board and carding, for 50 years. Their works occupy a site owned by the company adjacent to vacant land also owned by the company and cleared for industrial development. At present, this land makes no contribution to the income of the company.

Analysis of the company's present sales show a dominance by traditional customers in a 50-mile radius of their works. Market penetration tends to decrease noticeably as distance from the base increases. There are no exports.

Although the company has a large turnover in its own regional area, this is relatively small compared with other UK suppliers. Scotia does very little advertising beyond the Yellow Pages and a small stand at the Printing and Packaging trade exhibition once every two years. There is no publicity manager, and any promotional activity is handled by the managing director or sales director. The company has no branding, all material being supplied printed for the particular user or unmarked.

Sales representation is well below that of competitors of equivalent size, but the company considers that this is offset by the regional location of the representatives. Of the ten-strong sales force, about half are within ten years of retirement, and all are male. The company has no systematic programme for training salespeople, sales manuals as such do not exist and new inquiries are dealt with by the sales manager and inside service personnel using the salesperson as liaison. Any contact after the initial enquiry is usually made informally between the representative and inside production personnel.

The firm has never been a product leader, and there are no unique product advantages. There are relative weaknesses in that the company is unable to produce the newer packaging materials sought by many of its customers, although an investment in shrink-wrapping machinery lies underutilised. Competitors have always led on innovations in materials and printing techniques.

The company's products are competitive on price and sales have been increasing steadily in absolute terms. At present, the competition seems to be increasingly active, and in the last financial year sales volume for Scotia fell. The current managing director, son of the founder of the business, has called you in for advice on their sales operations:

1 In your evaluation of the sales function of Scotia, what would you wish to know in addition to what is stated?
2 Consider the strengths and weaknesses of this company, and discuss how Scotia can hold its own and even increase sales. Consider how the company can meet the challenge it now faces.
3 In particular, what are your proposals for improving the effectiveness of the salesforce?

REFERENCES

Anderson, E. (1985). The salesperson as outside agent or employee: A transaction cost analysis. *Marketing Science*, 4(3), 234–254.

Bagozzi, R. P. (1980). Performance and satisfaction in an industrial sales force: An examination of their antecedents and simultaneity. *Journal of Marketing*, 44(Spring), 65–77.

Blocker, C. P., Cannon, J. P., Panagopoulos, N. G. & Sager, J. K. (2012). The role of the sales force in value creation and appropriation: New directions for research. *Journal of Personal Selling & Sales Management*, 32(1), 15–28.

Bosworth, M. (1995). *Solution Selling.* New York: McGraw-Hill.

Chakrabarty, S., Brown, G. & Widing, R. E. (2013). Distinguishing between the roles of customer-oriented selling and adaptive selling in managing dysfunctional conflict in buyer-seller relationships. *Journal of Personal Selling and Sales Management*, 33(3), 245–260.

Chonko, L. B., Low, T. W., Roberts, J. A. & Tanner, J. F. (2000). Sales performance: Timing and type of measurement make a difference. *Journal of Personal Selling and Sales Management*, 20(1), 23–36.

Cicala, J. E., Smith, R. K. & Bush, A. J. (2012). What makes sales presentations effective – a buyer-seller perspective. *Journal of Business & Industrial Marketing*, 27(2), 78–88.

Davies, I. A., Ryals, L. J. & Holt, S. (2010). Relationship management: A sales role, or a state of mind? An investigation of functions and attitudes across a business-to-business sales force. *Industrial Marketing Management*, 39(7), 1049–1062.

Drucker, P. F. (1968). *The Practice of Management.* London: Pan Books

Flaherty, K. E. & Pappas, J. M. (2009). Expanding the sales professional's role: A strategic re-orientation? *Industrial Marketing Management*, 38(7), 806–813.

Haas, A., Snehota, I. & Corsaro, D. (2012). Creating value in business relationships: The role of sales. *Industrial Marketing Management*, 41(1), 94–105.

Heiman, S., Sanchez, D. & Tuleja, T. (1998). *The New Strategic Selling. London*: Kogan Page.

Ingram, Thomas N., Laforge, R. W., Avila, Ramon A., Schwepker, Charles H. & Williams, M. R. (2012). *Sales Management: Analysis and Decision Making* (8th edn). London: M. E. Sharpe Inc.

Johnston, M. W. & Marshall, G. W. (2013). *Sales Force Management*. New York: Routledge.

Lassk, F. G., Ingram, T. N., Kraus, F. & Di Mascio, R. (2012). The future of sales training: Challenges and related research questions. *Journal of Personal Selling & Sales Management*, 32(1), 141–154.

Lemmens, R., Donaldson, B. & Marcos, J. (2014). *From Selling to Cocreating*. Amsterdam: BIS Publishers.

McMurry, R. N. (1961). The mystique of super-salesmanship. *Harvard Business Review, 39*, 113–122.

Moncrief, W. C. (1986). Selling activity and sales position taxonomies for industrial salesforces. *Journal of Marketing Research*, 23(3), 261–270.

Moncrief, W. C., Marshall, G. & Lassk, F. (1999). The current state of sales force activities. *Industrial Marketing Management*, 28(1), 87–98

Moncrief, W. C., Marshall, G. W. & Lassk, F. G. (2006). A contemporary taxonomy of sales positions. *Journal of Personal Selling & Sales Management*, 26(1), 55–65.

Newton, D. A. (1969). Get the most out of your sales force. *Harvard Business Review*, September–October, 16–29.

Panagopoulos, N. G., Lee, N., Pullins, E. B., Avlonitis, G. J., Brassier, P., Guenzi, P., Humenberger, A., Kwiatek, P., Loe, T. W., Oksanen-Ylikoski, E., Peterson, R. M., Rogers, B. & Weilbaker, D. C. (2011). Internationalizing sales research: Current status, opportunities, and challenges. *Journal of Personal Selling & Sales Management*, 31(3), 219–242.

Piercy, N. & Lane, N. (2009). *Strategic Customer Management: Strategizing the Sales Organization*. Oxford: Oxford University Press.

Robinson, Nicola (2015) "Simply the best" The International Journal of Sales Transformation Issue 1:1 April, p.6 Bill

Ryans, A. B. & Weinberg, C. B. (1979). Territory sales response. *Journal of Marketing Research*, 16(4), 453–465.

SAP (2013). *Inside Sales Success: A Guide for Global Leaders*. Retrieved 8 January 2014, from http://cloudforminfo.sap.com/rs/successfactors/images/SAP_RWG_InsideSalesSuccess_eBook_June2013.pdf.

Selling Power http://www.sellingpower.com/content/article/?a=9540/the-evolution-of-sales-operations (accessed 8 Sep 2015)

Shapiro, B. P. (1979). *Account Management and Sales Organisation New Developments in Practice*, in Sales Management: new developments from behavioural and decision model research American Marketing Association and MSI Proceedings, August: Atlanta.

Shapiro, B. P., Slywotsky, A. J. & Doyle, S. X. (1998). Strategic sales management: A boardroom issue. Note 9-595-018. *Harvard Business School*, Cambridge, MA.

Smith, D. C. & Owens, J. P. (1995). Knowledge of customers' customers as a basis of sales force differentiation. *Journal of Personal Selling and Sales Management*, 25(3), 1–15.

Tzokas, N. & Donaldson, B. (2000). A research agenda for personal selling and sales management in the context of relationship marketing. *Journal of Selling and Major Account Management*, 2(2), 13–30.

Williams, B. C. & Plouffe, C. R. (2007). Assessing the evolution of sales knowledge: A 20-year content analysis. *Industrial Marketing Management*, 36(4), 408–419.

Zoltners, A. A., Sinha, P. & Lorimer, S. E. (2006). Match your sales force structure to your business life cycle. *Harvard Business Review* (August 2006), 81–90.

Zoltners, A. A., Sinha, P. & Lorimer, S. E. (2004). *Sales Force Design for Strategic Advantage*. New York: Palgrave Macmillan.

[illegible] (2018). [illegible]

[illegible]

Sethu Power [illegible] [illegible] operation [illegible]

Sandra [illegible] [illegible] (2017) [illegible]

[illegible] *Nature* [illegible]

[illegible] International [illegible]

[illegible] (2017) [illegible]

Williams, B. [illegible] (2017). [illegible]

[illegible] (2020) [illegible]

[illegible]

5 MOTIVATION AND LEADERSHIP OF THE SALES FORCE

OVERVIEW

Motivating the sales force is a critical component of sales force management, given its profound effect on sales performance. Drawing on literatures from disciplines such as management, behavioural theory and psychology, we provide an overview of motivation theories that are relevant to sales force management. The chapter then focuses on sales force leadership – also a crucial issue for organisational sales success. We argue that the complex work environment described in Chapter 1, where sales professionals are dealing with greater levels of complexity, requires leadership styles that are more sophisticated and mindful of the context in which sales forces operate.

LEARNING OBJECTIVES

This chapter aims to:

- Provide a summary of key theories of motivation and their relevance to selling jobs.
- Identify the link between motivation and job performance.
- Describe different approaches to leading the sales force.
- Outline the how sales leaders may influence salespeople's performance.

DEFINITIONS

Motivation is the willingness to exert additional effort in pursuing the achievement of activities and tasks associated with the job.

Job satisfaction is the extent to which the individual salesperson finds the job fulfilling and rewarding.

Sales leadership refers to the range of behavioural approaches that sales leaders adopt to direct and influence salespeople with a view to enhance their performance and sustain their motivation.

MOTIVATING THE SALES FORCE

Motivation theories aim to explain people's attitudes towards work and the behaviours they display when putting effort into accomplishing tasks. Key questions are: How do people get motivated? Why do people work? Why do they put in the effort they do? Why do some work harder than others? Why do individuals respond differently to attempts to increase their motivation?

As a starting point, the sales manager has to understand the 'why?' of salespeople's behaviour. Figure 5.1 illustrates a basic process for motivation. It draws on classical theorists such as Schein (1965) who argue that the fulfilment of people's needs is paramount in achieving organisational effectiveness. A 'motive' is seen as a need or driving force within a person. The process of motivation involves choosing between alternative forms of action in order to achieve some desired end or goal.

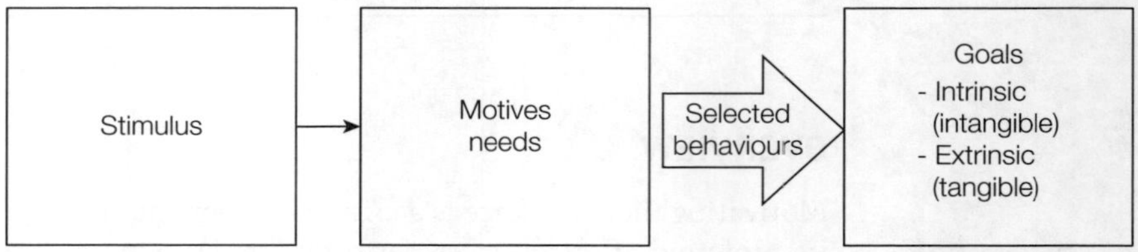

Figure 5.1 – The process of motivation

Stimuli influence and activate individuals depending on their perceived motives and needs. Then individuals choose to display specific behaviours that are directed towards the attainment of specific objectives or goals. The fulfilment of these goals may derive from intrinsic motivation, extrinsic motivation, or both.

Motivation theories

If a sales manager is to motivate salespeople, it is necessary to have some underlying theory that can identify the factors that influence motivation taking into account the uniqueness of the individual and the situation. Influential theories are Maslow's (1954) hierarchy of needs, Herzberg, Mausner and Snyderman's (1959; see also Herzberg, 1987) motivation–hygiene theory and Vroom's (1964) expectancy theory.

Maslow's needs theory

Maslow suggests that an individual has an hierarchy of needs which vary in order of importance from the basic physiological level (hunger and thirst) through various other levels – safety and security, a desire for love and belonging, a need for status and enhanced self-esteem – and culminating in the highest-order needs of self-actualisation. These needs are structured from the bottom upwards, hence the pyramid (see Figure 5.2). The lowest level must be satisfied before the next level needs become a motivating factor. When each level of needs is satisfied, it is no longer effective as a motivator. For example, work may initially be undertaken to acquire money to feed oneself and one's family. Later, money may provide some of the symbols of status. At the highest level, work is a means of achieving maximum personal satisfaction or self-actualisation. In this way, the model is robust enough to apply to every individual in work and to salespeople in their particular context. The implication for sales managers is that, for some, money soon loses its power as a motivator and other incentives or goals, such as opportunity for promotion and status-enhancing benefits, better meet an individual's needs. These higher-order factors have a more profound effect on motivation.

Figure 5.2 – Maslow's hierarchy of needs

Source: Based on ideas from Maslow (1943)

Herzberg's motivation–hygiene theory

Herzberg's theory distinguishes between factors which cause dissatisfaction (hygiene factors), such as working conditions, salary, company policies and supervision, and those factors creating job satisfaction (motivators); for example, achievement, recognition, responsibility and opportunity for growth and advancement. The underlying premise is that the hygiene factors do not motivate and do not improve performance but can cause a decrease in performance if they are absent. Sales managers must maintain hygiene factors while providing motivators to improve performance.

This theory has certain managerial implications. The nature of the job, in terms of delegating responsibility and enhancing status, may work more effectively as a motivator than factors such as job security and salary. Sales managers must provide adequate levels of hygiene factors but attention to job enhancement works better as a motivator. This includes providing new challenges, giving respect for expertise, communicating clearly and offering objective feedback on performance. These practices will be significant motivators and thus more likely to enhance effort.

The proviso to this argument is that individual needs and reactions are different. Greater rewards and non-financial incentives work on individuals' behaviour and motives in different ways. Solutions which are individualised rather than generalised offer better results. If individual solutions become too complex and unmanageable, some compromise solutions may be both workable and effective. One approach is to segment the sales force into types of salespeople who are similar in some key respects yet different from other identifiable groups.

Ingram and Bellenger (1982) identified three styles of salesperson who may respond differently to motivators. First are the 'comfort-seekers', who are likely to be older, less educated and with higher incomes, a proportion of which is concentrated on commission. This person seeks greater value in job security and in liking and respect from colleagues and managers. Second, also an older group, are the 'spotlight-seekers', who favour highly visible pay and rewards. This group has lower incomes than the first group but is more concerned with extrinsic rewards. They are more likely to respond to promotion opportunities and incentives such as contests. Third are 'the developers', salespeople who are more highly educated, younger, with good incomes and small families. These people seek opportunities for personal growth although not necessarily status through promotion. As a group, they are most likely to benefit from training and career development.

Vroom's expectancy theory

The theories by Maslow and Herzberg were further developed by Vroom (1964), who made more explicit the link between effort and performance – particularly useful in understanding salespeople's behaviour. Vroom's expectancy model forms the basis of much work in sales-related motivation (Walker, Churchill & Ford, 1977). People are motivated to work by choosing between different behaviours if they believe that their efforts will be rewarded and they attach value to these rewards. Three factors underlie their behaviour – choice, expectancy and preference. Motivation is a key factor in sales performance, perhaps the key factor, but it is not the only factor. Aptitude, rewards and organisational and managerial factors will also be important.

Walker et al. (1977) contend that motivation responds to a variety of personal and organisational variables (experience, training, closeness of supervision, emphasis on meeting standards), is related to the nature of the job itself and is influenced by the individual's role perceptions. Motivation is also goal-directed behaviour and has two dimensions: the direct goal of improved performance and the indirect goal, which stems from achievement of the direct goal. For example, increased sales achieve the direct goal but may also result in promotion – an indirect goal. An individual may choose between different goals. Salesperson A may be given a target to meet, which is higher than any previous sales objectives. That person may decide that the target is way above their capability and may not aim for it. Salesperson B, given a similar target, may decide to put in extra effort, intending that this will be enough to reach the target expected and the resultant gain will be worth the effort. This is expectancy theory.

What do you think?

When David Snow, VP of Commercial Operations Astra-Zeneca, was asked in an interview about the key to encouraging people to strive for their best, he said 'You have to provide information about where they stand quickly and effectively, and second, sales leaders need to know what success looks like, so that they can do a good job of setting the goals for their own teams.'

Source: Selling Power. How To Motivate and Reward Top Performers. (Accessed February 17, 2015)

Motivation and behaviour are affected by the perceived value or worth of attaining the goal. This perception is itself based on the expectancy of the individual that performance is the result of particular actions (e.g. more calls) and is profitable and desirable. The link between effort and performance can be expressed in terms of expectancy, particularly the magnitude of expectancies and their accuracy. For example, magnitude will be influenced positively by a belief in one's own ability, by higher levels of self-esteem and by experience. Environmental factors such as competition and trading conditions may have a negative effect. Accuracy of expectancy will relate to role perception. Another major factor in role perception is experience, which then becomes a common antecedent. It can be hypothesised that salespeople will have greater accuracy of expectancies the longer they are in the job, the greater their role accuracy, the lower their role ambiguity and role conflict, and the more closely they are supervised. Motivation, in terms of expectancy, will also be affected by rewards and the desirability of higher rewards. These rewards can be externally mediated (pay incentives) or internally mediated (self-fulfilment and career growth), which provide different levels of satisfaction for the individual.

The link between expectancies and performance requires understanding of two further concepts: ***instrumentality*** and the salesperson's ***valence for rewards***. Instrumentality is the salesperson's perception that their individual actions will result in the required performance and that this performance will lead to other desired goals. Valence for rewards is the expected value placed on the goals/desired results. This has either a positive or a negative effect depending on the value placed on achievement. Expectancy theory suggests that the effort expended on the job depends on the valence (anticipated satisfaction) in accomplishing it and the expectancy of a result (probability of achievement).

Satisfaction, motivation and performance

The relationship between salesperson satisfaction and the evaluation of performance has been a key issue in sales management research. However, the link between job satisfaction and job performance is not a straightforward one; as Bagozzi has suggested (1980), four possibilities exist:

- Satisfaction causes performance.
- Performance causes satisfaction.
- The two variables are reciprocally related.
- The variables are not causally related at all, and any empirical association must be a spurious one owing to common antecedents.

Job satisfaction is related to performance, but differences in performance can also be attributed to individual differences in, for example, skills, aptitude and self-esteem. Furthermore, longitudinal studies are required to assess the true nature of the satisfaction–performance–satisfaction sequence. Bagozzi tentatively suggests that enhancement of self-esteem through personal recognition, monetary rewards or visible acknowledgement of good performance would be a better means of management style than job enhancement per se. Salespeople can perhaps be motivated more by challenging targets, by achieving these targets, by receiving accurate and complete feedback and by appropriate visible rewards than by job enhancement or job enrichment. These increase job satisfaction, leading to lower recruitment costs and lower staff turnover but may or may not be the prime movers in higher job performance (Figure 5.3).

The motivation of salespeople is neither easy nor straightforward. Part of the complexity is due to the multiplicative nature of the variables which impact on performance, such as aptitude, role perception and the components of motivation itself. The problem is compounded by the individuality of the selling job since the nature of the task and the individual's perception of each element, and their reaction to them, will vary. The problem of industry-specific contexts, the type of selling and

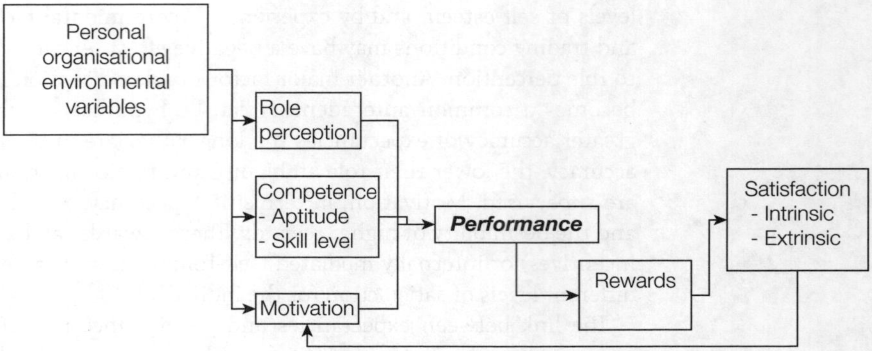

Figure 5.3 – Motivation and performance

Source: Based on ideas from Ingram, Laforge, Locander, Mackenzie and Podsakoff (2005)

the characteristics of individuals all hamper the search for definitive solutions and create unique problems.

> **Did you know?**
>
> According to the Office of National Statistics 63% of people working in sales and customer service are women but less than 30% of salespeople are women. Yet the changing role of sales, the use of technology and the need for teamwork suggest higher social skills which are often attributed to women.

Overall, managers can enhance a salesperson's satisfaction and motivation by considering and addressing the following dimensions:

- ***Personal, organisational and environmental*** variables refer to a wide range of circumstances in the salesperson's context. Accuracy and regularity of feedback has a positive effect on job performance (Bagozzi, 1980). Participation, particularly in target-setting (see Chapter 13), has a positive effect on sales force motivation. Sense of belonging increases commitment and also staff morale. A fair code of behaviour and an ethical climate (Schwepker, 2013) also have positive effects on sales performance.
- *The job itself (role perception).* If a salesperson does not find the job challenging or interesting, there will be a motivation problem. Sales managers should be careful that excessive routines, job simplification or overly strict discipline do not demotivate. Job attractiveness is related to the degree of autonomy combined with the variety of tasks and their perceived importance. These characteristics can be quantified and a motivating potential score (MPS) calculated (Hackman & Oldham, 1975) whereby MPS = (Skill variety + task identity + task significance)/3 × autonomy × feedback.
- *Competence level*, in terms of product knowledge and competitive intelligence, is a key requirement to achieve high levels of performance (Mariados, Milewicz, Lee and Sahaym, 2014).
- *Motivated people*. Salespeople who have drive and a need for achievement will tend to perform better than their peers. Demirdjian (1984) suggests that this motivation can be expressed as a function of a salesperson's economic, social and self-actualising needs: M = f [(+ En) + (Sn)+ (+ SAn)] where M = Motivation; En = economic needs of the salesperson; Sn = social needs of the salesperson; SAn = self- actualising needs of the salesperson.

- *Rewards*. Remuneration is a fundamental reward used to motivate salespeople. A wide variety of payment plans can be implemented, with an equally wide variety of subtle effects on the sales force. For this reason managers need to fully understand the effect of payment on their employees' motivation. Monetary rewards will foster extrinsic satisfaction and motivation whilst non-monetary rewards enhance intrinsic motivation and satisfaction.

The importance and complexity of motivation and its effect on performance has led to the idea of the motivational mix. These factors, individually and collectively, influence an individual's motivation to work and ultimately their job performance. The individual may respond positively or negatively to the different factors which management can deploy to motivate the sales force. Solving the problems of individual salespeople and providing definite solutions will resolve some of the motivational problems in the sales force.

LEADERSHIP OF THE SALES FORCE

The role of the sales manager

There is agreement that the sales manager is one of the most important individuals affecting salespeople's job-related outcomes, besides the salespeople and their customers (Evans, Schlacter, Schultz, Gremler, et al., 2002). Firstly, sales managers are responsible for motivating the salesperson towards effort and performance, for supervising & controlling and for the development of the salesperson, particularly providing on-the-job training (Johnston & Marshall, 2013).

Recent developments in sales management research have pointed out the importance of leaders in developing customer-oriented sales forces (Chakrabarty, Brown & Widing, 2012) and how certain leadership styles have impact on sales performance (Jaramillo, Gristaffe, Chonko & Roberts, 2009). Very often sales management and sales leadership are used interchangeably. Indeed, sales managers engage in both management and leadership activities. Management behaviours are primarily focused on changes, while leadership behaviors focus on changing the way people think about what is 'desirable and necessary'.

The strategic role of the sales manager has also been described in terms of functionality including tasks, responsibility, personality and required skills (Deeterschmelz, Goebel & Kennedy, 2008). Dubinsky et al. (1999) classified the tasks of the sales manager into 'Planning and Organising Tasks', 'Management and Development Tasks' and 'Evaluation and Control Tasks'. Their study of the perceptions of sales managers revealed that 'Management and Development Tasks' are perceived to be the most important tasks of all. The second most important group was 'Planning and Organising Tasks'.

Leading the modern sales force

Providing leadership to sales professionals has been recognised as one of the most crucial issues for future sales force organisational success (Ingram et al., 2005). In a complex work environment where sales professionals are dealing with greater competition, a rapid rate of change and response time driven by advances in technology and globalisation, sales leadership is becoming even more important. Key changes in the sales environment identified in Chapter 1 are placing a different set of demands on today's sales forces (Evans, McFarland, Dietz & Jaramillo, 2012) and as a result on sales leaders. Therefore, a more sophisticated level of understanding regarding leadership styles and sales performance in the sales context is required.

Research has demonstrated over a few decades that sales managers have a strong influence on how salespeople develop customer relationships and ultimately increase sales (e.g. Dubinsky, 1999; Evans et al., 2002). The literature demonstrates that sales managers influence a range of sales outcomes including financial, job performance (DelVecchio, 1998, Rich, 1998), organisational citizenship behaviours (Mackenzie, Podsakioff & Rich, 2001), trust (Brashear, Boles, Bellenger & Brooks, 2003), and ethical decision-making. Boyatzis, Good and Massa (2012, p. 191) claim that 'although the characteristics of what leads to successful salespeople have long been an area of interest for both researchers and practitioners, the characteristics of leaders in sales organisations that affect performance has been largely neglected'. In spite of the recognised importance of leadership in sales management, the sales literature does not provide clear and consistent definitions of the activities and behaviours implied by sales management and leadership.

What do you think?

Jim Dickie, Partner CSO Insights, claims that one of the keys to higher sales performance is to help salespeople work smarter. This means (1) investing in sales talent by hiring higher quality sales professionals, not only with the right skill profile but also industry/sector knowledge, (2) improving the ramp-up period, for that person to perform at his/her best within a shorter period of time, and (3) higher investment in sales process and in sales training.

Source: Selling Power. Trends in Sales Leadership. (Accessed February 17, 2015)

Leadership styles

Leadership is a widely studied topic across a variety of disciplines (for recent reviews of the topic see Northouse, 2010; Schedlitzki & Edwards, 2014). In this section we focus on reviewing leadership in sales literature to provide insights applicable to sales force management. In Table 5.1 the most salient leadership styles are highlighted and include transformational and transactional, servant leadership and authentic leadership amongst others (Boehnke Peesker & Marcos-Cuevas, 2014).

Table 5.1 – Description of leadership styles and behaviours

Key leadership styles	Associated behaviours
Transformational leadership	• Visioning • Inspiring • Stimulating • Coaching • Teambuilding
Transactional leadership	• Rewarding • Correcting
Authentic Leadership	• Self-awareness • Internalised moral perspective • Balanced processing • Relational transparency
Servant Leadership	• Serving the needs of the follower • Enabling growth of the follower • Power distribution versus power consolidation

Transformational vs. transactional leadership

For the past 30 years transformational/transactional leadership has been one of the most researched areas within the field of leadership studies. There is a significant and growing body of evidence demonstrating that transformational leadership is an effective form of leadership in a variety of settings in many countries (Bass & Riggio, 2006). The continued interest in transformational leadership may be because there is evidence that this model works well during times of change (Bass & Riggio, 2006), and the current sales environment fits that model. It provides a more inspiring and people-focused form of leadership to motivate individuals, and yet still fits the sales business model by focusing on delivering results. There is a 'neatness about such an approach which is highly attractive' (Ladkin, 2010, p. 4), and while there are limitations to this method, this leadership style accounts for some of the features present in a sales environment.

The concept of transformational and transactional leadership was first introduced by Burns (1978) with his classification of political leaders. Burns argued that transformational leaders inspire others to achieve performance beyond expectation, while transactional leaders lead by exchange such as offering rewards and recognition. Transformational leaders:

> [H]ave goals that transcend their own self-interest, and work towards the common good of their followers ... and look for potential motives in followers, seek to satisfy higher needs, and engage the full person of the follower. The result ... is a relationship of mutual stimulation and elevation that converts followers into leaders and may convert leaders into moral agents. (Burns, 1978, p. 4)

Burns focused on the concept and morale basis for transformational leadership; however, he did not explain what types of action or behaviours were used by transformational leaders (Sashkin, 2004). Bennis and Nanus (1985) built on this work to include behaviours and characteristics, and they also considered the organisational context.

Bass (1985) described transformational leadership as a style that creates the positive development of followers. Bass believed that transformational leadership was not a substitute for transactional leadership but a complement. Transformational leadership involves encouraging individuals to commit to a shared vision, inspiring individuals and challenging them to solve problems, as well as developing followers' skills through coaching (Bass & Riggio, 2006). Transformational leaders behave in ways to achieve exceptional results by applying certain behaviours that these authors outlined in their model.

Transactional leadership is focused on an exchange between the leader and the follower. Leaders explain what is required of the team and outline what compensation they will receive if they fulfil these requirements. This transactional leadership process provides a reward for good performance, and correcting actions for poor performance.

There is evidence that transformational leadership creates performance beyond expectation and transactional leadership creates performance at expectation (Bass & Riggio, 2006; Boehnke, Bontis, DiStefano & DiStefano, 2003; Howell and Avolio, 1993). Transformational leadership is now part of what Avolio and Luthans (2006) have defined as 'new genre leadership theory'. This leadership style can be seen as an expansion of transactional behaviour and is defined in terms of the leader's effects on followers (Felfe, Tartler & Liepmann, 2004).

Research has shown that transformational and transactional styles are used by high performing sales leaders (Dubinsky, Yammarino, Jolson & Spangler, 1995; Howell &

Avolio, 1993; MacKenzie et al., 2001). They have argued that transformational leadership positively impacts performance because by inspiring salespeople to perform (Dubinsky et al., 1995; MacKenzie et al., 2001). Jolson et al. (1993) suggested that recruiting, training and developing sales recruits with transformational leadership skills and adding to a transactional leadership setting that already exists can foster sales performance.

Critics have stated that they find that transformational leadership does not take into consideration the organisational context of leadership (Sashkin, 2004). A key criticism of transformational leadership is that the focus has been on leaders rather than considering leadership as a collective process encompassing both leaders and followers (Ladkin, 2010). Beyer (1999) suggested that the approach of transformational leadership was too narrow and there was a tendency to recycle the same methodological approaches (Diaz-Saenz, 2010).

Authentic leadership

Authentic leadership is a style in which leaders are greatly aware of their thoughts and their behaviour, in the context in which they operate. The theory was proposed by Luthans and Avolio (2003), and further developed by Gardner, Avolio, Luthans, May and Walumbwa (2005). It has been described as:

> [A] pattern of leader behavior that draws upon and promotes both positive psychological capacities and a positive ethical climate, to foster greater self-awareness, an internalized moral perspective, balanced processing of information, and relational transparency on the part of leaders working with followers, fostering positive self-development. (Walumbwa, Avolio, Gardner, Wernsing & Peterson, 2008, p. 94)

The four components that form the foundation of authentic leadership include: (1) self-awareness, (2) internalised moral perspective, (3) balanced processing, and (4) relational transparency (Northouse, 2010).

The life story of the leader and the meaning the leader attaches to this experience is an important element enabling authentic leadership. In addition, an important consideration of this leadership style is that the role of the follower is equally important to understanding the leadership process as is the role of the leader (Gardner et al., 2005). This leadership style has an integrated approach that recognises that leadership can be shared, enabling leaders to act as followers, and followers to act as leaders. This is especially relevant in the sales environment when salespeople are acting as leaders with their customers and other team members, as well for when salespeople are as acting as followers.

Servant leadership

The servant leadership style focuses on putting the followers' needs first. In this school of thought, serving the needs of the follower is a greater priority for the leader than achieving organisational objectives. This leadership style proposes that a sales leader is responsible for the success of the organisation and the success of his or her subordinates (Greenleaf, 2002). Servant leaders place the needs of their subordinates before their own needs and focus their efforts on helping subordinates grow to reach their potential and achieve optimal success (Greenleaf, 1970). This leadership style develops high levels of trust in the relationship as a result of the leader's actions being considered moral and honest by their team (Liden, Wayne, Hao & Henderson, 2008).

Servant leadership has been discussed as a subset of transformational leadership (Bass & Riggio, 2006). The servant leadership style is similar to the transformational leader who brings about the moral uplifting of their followers as discussed by Bass and Riggio (2006). However, this leadership style differs by its emphasis on the follower versus organisational outcomes. Servant leadership focuses on serving followers first, while transformational leadership is primarily focused on delivering performance outcomes.

Servant leadership has been researched in the sales environment (Jaramillo et al., 2009), suggesting that servant leadership values held by sales managers have a significant effect on salesperson values about customer interactions, ultimately affecting salesperson performance.

Other leadership styles in sales

Other leadership styles discussed in the sales literature included leader member exchange, contingency leadership theories (e.g., situational leadership) and path goal theory. The leader member exchange style focuses on the relationship between the leaders and the followers via a social exchange process. The sales leadership research examined the concept of trust between sales managers and sales professionals. This research has generated important findings concerning the sales manager–salesperson relationship and the critical role that trust plays in the relationship (Ingram et al., 2005).

The contingency leadership school of thought prescribes leadership behaviour given different situations that a leader might face. In the early years, sales researchers focused on this leadership style with mixed results. Butler and Reese (1991) found that the situational leadership model did not lead to superior performance in a sales management setting, and was associated with inferior performance.

The path goal theory proposed that leaders engage in behaviours that facilitate goal attainment and motivate their team to reach goals. Path goal theory has helped define behaviours of effective sales leaders (Jaramillo & Mulki, 2008). There is some evidence that salespeople are responsive to this leader style when sales leaders help the salesperson to grow by performing activities (Jaramillo et al., 2009).

Leadership and sales performance

Sales leaders have a significant influence on salespeople, the sales process and sales performance. It was found that high-performing sales managers create a culture where sales teams work harder and smarter (Jaramillo et al., 2009), which can result in greater sales performance. Sales managers impact the sales process by helping develop customer relationships, providing evidence that sales leadership can impact sales performance indirectly. Weitz (1981) incorporates many elements such as salesperson resources which are influenced or controlled by the sales leader into the performance model. Interactions between the sales representative and sales manager have an impact on performance (Good, 1993).

Transformational leadership and sales performance

The practice of transformational leadership behaviours can lead to positive sales performance outcomes. Empirical evidence across a number of studies (Howell and Avolio, 1993; MacKenzie et al., 2001) supports the positive effects of transformational leadership on performance outcomes, and even more so for the indirect selling efforts (Ingram et al., 2005). Howell and Avolio (1993) demonstrated that transformational leadership positively predicted unit-level performance across a variety of divisions in a large Canadian bank. MacKenzie et al. (2001) also found evidence that transformational leadership behaviours influences salespeople to perform beyond expectations in a group of insurance sales agents. This study also showed that transactional behaviours such as avoiding and correcting behaviours may have negative effects on performance (MacKenzie et al., 2001). A limitation of this study is the unit of measurement – inexperienced sales representatives in the insurance industry selling to consumers. There is scope for additional research in business-to-business sales environments.

Jaramillo and Mulki (2008) demonstrated that supportive leadership results in higher salesperson effort, impacting sales performance through a process that involves intrinsic motivation and self-efficacy. While the study did use self-reporting measures, which does not always produce the most accurate results, it provided evidence that under a supportive leader, salespeople are more motivated, and provide a higher degree of effort to ensure their customer needs were met (Jaramillo & Mulki, 2008).

Transactional leadership and sales performance

In contrast with the finding that supportive leadership styles will lead to greater sales performance, Dubinsky et al. (1995) provided evidence that transactional leadership may be more suited to a sales environment. They aimed to 'determine if the use of sales managers' transformational leadership induces improved levels of salesperson work outcomes beyond transactional leadership' (Dubinsky et al., 1995, p. 25). Of 11 work outcomes measured (job satisfaction, commitment, role conflict, role ambiguity, job stress, burnout, salesperson extra effort, job congruence, multidimensional performance, percent of quota, percent of prior year sales), transformational leadership was only significantly related to two work outcomes, commitment and role ambiguity, while transactional leadership was significantly related to three work outcomes – job satisfaction, commitment, and multidimensional performance (Dubinsky et al., 1995).

These results were unexpected; and the authors postulated a variety of reasons why they occurred, including the nature of the sales role and the context of the sales environment of the study (a low change environment). They suggested that the selling position did not foster the development of a strong linkage between the sales manager and sales employee. Based on the research the authors suggested that 'given that a traditional planning and evaluation "window" for salespeople is twelve months (or less), perhaps transactional leadership is better suited for a selling context than transformational leadership' (Dubinsky et al., 1995, p. 27). This demonstrates the importance of understanding context in sales when determining a leadership style.

Did you know?

According to Accenture 62% of top-performing companies say that the most important factor to improve their organisations's agility is to have the right leadership team.

Source: Acccenture.com

SUMMARY

One of the most important factors in sales performance is the motivation of salespeople. Motivation is the amount of effort that a salesperson expends on each of the activities or tasks associated with their job. Theories of motivation such as Maslow's hierarchy of needs, Herzberg's motivation–hygiene theory and Vroom's expectancy theory help our understanding of why people work and behave the way they do. An integrated managerial approach to motivate the sales force needs to be considered.

Leadership styles will influence salesperson performance but in a number of different ways, related both to the context and the individual. Approaches to improve sales force effectiveness should consider both the leader and the follower.

QUESTIONS

1. Explain how and in what ways salespeople may differ in their motivations from workers in other occupations.
2. A company is about to launch a new product range on the UK market. What are the probable effects of low sales force morale on this venture? Outline steps which could be taken to increase sales force commitment to the new range.
3. Discuss the link between a salesperson's motivation and job performance.
4. In which ways can sales managers' leadership styles influence salesperson performance?

REFERENCES

Avolio, B. J. & Luthans, F. (2006). *The High Impact Leader: Moments Matter in Accelerating Authentic Leadership Development.* New York: McGraw-Hill.

Bagozzi, R. P. (1980). Performance and satisfaction in an industrial sales force: An examination of their antecedents and simultaneity. *Journal of Marketing*, 44(Spring), 65–77.

Bass, B. (1985). *Leadership and Performance Beyond Expectations.* New York: Free Press.

Bass, B. & Riggio, E. G. (2006). *Transformational Leadership* (2nd edn). Mahwah, NJ: Lawrence Erlbaum.

Bennis, W. & Nanus, B. (1985). *Leaders: The Strategies for Taking Charge.* New York: HarperCollins.

Beyer, J. M. (1999). Taming and promoting charisma to change organizations. *Leadership Quarterly,* 10, 307–330.

Boehnke, K., Bontis, N., DiStefano, J. & DiStefano, A. (2003). Transformational leadership: An examination of cross-cultural differences and similarities. *Leadership & Organization Development Journal*, 24(1), 5–15.

Boehnke Peesker, K. & Marcos-Cuevas, J. (2014). Exploring leadership styles and salesperson performance: A review and framework, in *Global Sales Science Institute 8th Annual Conference*. London 11–13 June 2014.

Boyatzis, R. E., Good, D. & Massa, R. (2012). Emotional, social, and cognitive intelligence and personality as predictors of sales leadership performance. *Journal of Leadership & Organizational Studies,* 19(2), 191–201.

Brashear, T., Boles, J. S., Bellenger, D. & Brooks, C. M. (2003). An empirical test of trust-building processes and outcomes in sales manager–salesperson relationships. *Journal of the Academy of Marketing Science,* 31(2), 189–200.

Burns, J. M. (1978). *Leadership*. New York: Harper & Row.

Butler, J. K. & Reese, R. M. (1991). Leadership style and sales performance: A test of the situational leadership model. *Journal of Personal Selling and Sales Management,* 11(3), 37–47.

Chakrabarty, S., Brown, G. & Widing, R. E. (2012). The role of top management in developing a customer-oriented sales force. *Journal of Personal Selling & Sales Management*, 32(4), 437–450.

Deeter-schmelz, D. R., Goebel, D. J. & Kennedy, K. N. (2008). What are the characteristics of an effective sales manager? An exploratory study comparing salesperson and sales manager perspectives. *Journal of Personal Selling & Sales Management*, 28(1), 7–20.

DelVecchio, S. (1998). The quality of salesperson-manager relationship: The effect of latitude, loyalty and competence. *Journal of Personal Selling & Sales Management*, 18(1), 31–47.

Demirdjian, Z. S. (1984). A multidimensional approach to motivating salespeople. *Industrial Marketing Management*, 13(1), 25–32.

Diaz-Saenz, H. R. (2010). Transformational leadership, in Bryman, A., Uhl-Bien, M., Collinson, D., Grint, K. & Jackson, B. (eds.) *The Sage Handbook of Leadership*. London: Sage Publications Inc., pp. 299–310.

Dubinsky, A. (1999). Salesperson failure: Sales management is the key. *Industrial Marketing Management*, 28, 7–17.

Dubinsky, A., Yammarino, F., Jolson, M. & Spangler, D. (1995). Transformational leadership: An initial investigation in sales management. *Journal of Personal Selling and Sales Management*, 15(2), 17–29.

Evans, K., McFarland, R., Dietz, B. & Jaramillo, F. (2012). Advancing sales performance research: A focus on five underresearched topic areas. *Journal of Personal Selling and Sales Management*, 32(1), 89–105.

Evans, K. R., Schlacter, J. L., Schultz, R. J., Gremler, D. D., Pass, M., & Wolfe, W. G. (2002). Salesperson and sales manager perceptions of salesperson job characteristics and job outcomes: A perceptual congruence approach. *Journal of Marketing Theory and Practice*, 30–44.

Felfe, J., Tartler, K., Liepmann, D. (2004). Advanced research in the field of transformational leadership. *Zeitschrift für Personalforschung – German Journal of Research in Human Resource Management*, 18(3), 262–288.

Gardner, W. L., Avolio, B. J., Luthans, F., May, D. R. & Walumbwa, F. (2005). Can you see the real me? A self-based model of authentic leader and follower development. *Leadership Quarterly*, 16, 343–372.

Good, D. J. (1993). Coaching practices in the business-to-business environment. *Journal of Business and Industrial Marketing*, 8(2), 53–60.

Greenleaf, R. K. (1970). *The Servant as Leader*. Cambridge: Center for Applied Studies.

Greenleaf, R. K. (2002). *Servant Leadership: A Journey into the Nature of Legitimate Power and Greatness* (25th anniversary edn). Mahwah, NJ: Paulist Press.

Hackman, J. R. & Oldham, G. R. (1975). Development of job diagnostic survey. *Journal of Applied Psychology*, 60, 159–170.

Herzberg, F. (1987). One more time: How do you motivate employees? *Harvard Business Review*, September–October, 109–120.

Herzberg, F., Mausner, B. & Snyderman, B. B. (1959). *The Motivation to Work*. New York: John Wiley.

Howell, J. & Avolio, B. (1993). Transformational leadership, transactional leadership, locus of control, and support for innovation. *Journal of Applied Psychology*, 78(6), 891–902.

http://www.sellingpower.com/content?video/?mid=78/how-to-motivate-and-reward-top-peprformers (accessed 17 February, 2015)

http://www.sellingpower.com/content?video/?mid=394/trends-in-sales-leadership (accessed 17 February, 2015)

Ingram, T. N. & Bellenger, D. N. (1982). Motivational segments in the sales force. *California Management Review*, 24(3), 81–88.

Ingram, T. N., Laforge, R. W., Locander, W. B., Mackenzie, S. B. & Podsakoff, P. M. (2005). New directions in sales leadership research. *Journal of Personal Selling & Sales Management*, 25(2), 137–154.

Jaramillo, F., Gristaffe, D. B., Chonko, D. B. & Roberts, J. A. (2009). Examining the impact of servant leadership on sales force performance. *Journal of Personal Selling and Sales Management*, 29(3), 257–276.

Jaramillo, F. & Mulki, J. P. (2008). Sales effort: The intertwined roles of the leader, customers, and the salesperson. *Journal of Personal Selling and Sales Management*, 28(1), 37–51.

Jolson, M. A., Dubinsky, A. J., Yammarion, F. J. & Comer, L. B. (1993). Transforming the salesforce with leadership. *Sloan Management Review*, 34 (Spring), 95–106.

Johnston, M. W. & Marshall, G. W. (2013). *Sales force management* (11th edn). Routledge.

Ladkin, D. (2010). *Rethinking Leadership: A New Look at Old Leadership Questions*. Cheltenham: Edward Elgar.

Liden, R. C., Wayne, S. J., Hao, Z. & Henderson, D. (2008). Servant leadership: Development of a multidimensional measure and multi-level assessment. *Leadership Quarterly*, 19(2), 161–177.

Luthans, F., & Avolio, B. J. (2003). Authentic leadership development, in Quinn, R. E. (ed.) *Positive Organization Scholarship*. San Francisco: Barrett-Koehler, pp. 241–261.

MacKenzie, S., Podsakioff, P. & Rich, A. (2001). Transformational and transactional leadership and salesperson performance. *Journal of the Academy of Marketing Science*, 29(2), 115–134.

Mariadoss, B. J., Milewicz, C., Lee, S. & Sahaym, A. (2014). Salesperson competitive intelligence and performance: The role of product knowledge and sales force automation usage. *Industrial Marketing Management*, 43(1), 136–145.

Maslow, A .H. (1943). A theory of human motivation. *Psychological Review*, 50, 370–396.

Maslow, A. H. (1954). *Motivation and Personality*. New York: Harper.

Northouse, P. G. (2010). *Leadership Theory and Practice* (5th edn). Thousand Oaks, CA: Sage.

Rich, G. A. (1998). Selling and sales management in action: The constructs of sales coaching: Supervisory feedback, role modelling and trust. *Journal of Personal Selling and Sales Management*, 18(1), 53–63.

Sashkin, M. (2004). Transformational leadership approaches, in Antonakis, J., Cianciolo, A. T. & Sternberg, R. J. (eds.) *The Nature of Leadership*. California: Sage Publications Inc., pp. 171–196.

Schedlitzki, D. & Edwards, G. (2014). *Studying Leadership Traditional and Critical Approaches*. London: Sage.

Schein, E. H. (1965). *Organizational Psychology*. Englewood Cliffs, NJ: Prentice Hall.

Schwepker, C. H. (2013). Improving sales performance through commitment to superior customer value: The role of psychological ethical climate. *Journal of Personal Selling & Sales Management*, 33(4), 389–402.

Vroom, V. H. (1964). *Work and Motivation*. New York: John Wiley.

Walker, O. C., Churchill, G. A. & Ford, N. M. (1977). Motivation and performance in industrial selling: Present knowledge and needed research. *Journal of Marketing Research*, 14, 156–168.

Walumbwa, F. O., Avolio, B. J., Gardner, W. L., Wernsing, T. S. & Peterson, S. J. (2008). Authentic leadership: Development and analysis of a multidimensional theory-based measure. *Journal of Management*, 34, 89–126.

Weitz, B. A. (1981). Effectiveness in sales interactions: A contingency framework. *Journal of Marketing*, 45(1), 85–103.

PART II
PROCESS

6 PROFESSIONAL SELLING

OVERVIEW

Becoming a market-oriented and customer-focused organisation demands close relationships with customers in order to discover what the genuine customers' needs are. Changes in the marketplace are driving sales forces to move beyond communicating benefits towards co-creating value beyond the exchange process. A renewed focus on customers often renders geographical areas irrelevant, bringing to the forefront customer segments and different customer types. As introduction to part II, Process, this chapter attempts to synthesise current thinking in selling, outlining how conceptual developments in sales management theory translate into everyday practice for the salesperson in their job.

LEARNING OBJECTIVES

This chapter aims to:

- Review well-established perspectives of selling, the traditional processes and roles.
- Present contemporary approaches to professional selling.
- Outline the competencies and skills required for the 'future' sales professional.

DEFINITIONS

Professional selling is the process of creating value for the customer through personal interaction with buyers and other individuals within the customer organisation.

Traditional classification of selling roles refers to pre-internet sales approaches.

Contemporary selling refers to the additional knowledge, skills and attributes that are required to deliver real customer value in the inter-connected marketplace.

INTRODUCTION

Throughout this book we emphasise the fact that professional selling and sales management have changed fundamentally over the last few decades, giving rise to a polarisation between traditional and contemporary sales roles and processes. We have argued that the differences between traditional and contemporary selling derive from fundamental changes in technology, competition and customer demands, among other factors. Nevertheless, it is necessary to examine the evolution of selling to the present day in terms of *value*, *relationships* and *customers* as we try to understand the fundamental tenets of professional selling.

Value added

A key difference between the old and new sales approach is based on the value the salesperson brings to the sales process. Rackham and DeVincentis (1998) argue that there are three types of selling: transaction, consultative and enterprise selling. In a transactional selling approach the added value a salesperson can bring is limited to communicating the existence of the product and demonstrating its features. These functions are disappearing as customers become more aware of the existence of products and their features through other means of communication. Transactional selling is a sales process that matches the needs of intrinsic value buyers, who treat suppliers as a commodity, and are exclusively interested in price and convenience. Consultative selling is a sales process that matches the needs of extrinsic value buyers who are willing to pay for a selling effort that adds value by providing additional benefits to their product or service. Enterprise selling is a sales process that works most effectively with strategically important customers who demand an extraordinary level of value creation from a single supplier (Rackham & DeVincentis, 1998).

Rackham and DeVincentis (1998) argue that it is the added value you can bring to the sales transaction that will determine the appropriate sales approach and the relationship potential. Determining the level of added value a salesperson can bring is done by looking at the different stages of the customer buying cycle and determining at which stage you can help the customer.

Relationships

The evolution in marketing from product towards relationship marketing (Sheth & Parvatiyar, 1995) was echoed in sales with a fundamental shift that gave rise to relationship selling (Ingram, 2002; Johnston & Marshall, 2008; Weitz & Bradford, 1999). The study of relationship development is particularly pertinent in the context of managing strategic customers. The transactions with strategic customers evolved from selling to management of key accounts (Millman & Wilson, 1995). Relationships in key account management (KAM), according to Millman and Wilson (1996), can evolve through several stages: pre-KAM, early KAM, mid KAM, strategic KAM and synergetic KAM. Relationship selling requires the existence of contacts between the customer and the vendor across levels (from lower to more senior management) and across functions. Relationships developed in KAM represent the transition from transaction to collaboration (see Figure 6.1).

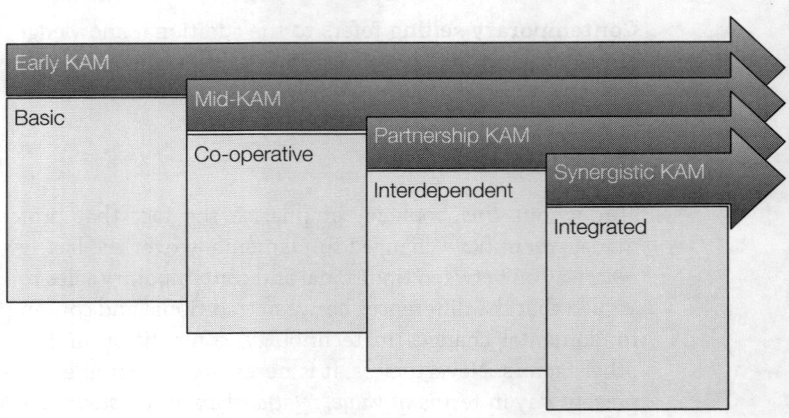

Figure 6.1 – Relationship development in KAM

Source: Based on ideas from Millman and Wilson (1995)

Customers

The key transformation in modern selling is the evolution from treating the customer as target to treating the customer as an active participant in the process of creating value (Lemmens, Donaldson & Marcos, 2014). Customer needs identification became central in professional selling (Rackham, 1995) and the sales approach adopted based on the needs of the customers (Ingram, Laforge, Avila, Schwepker & Williams, 2012). The terms 'customer-oriented selling' (Schwepker Jr., 2003) and 'adaptive selling' (Spiro & Weitz, 1990) are now well established and converge in stressing the fact that the salesperson must focus on the customer situation and adapt his or her sales approach to this situation. According to Ingram et al. (2012) the sales method used in relationship selling varies according to the stage the customer is at in his or her purchasing process. If a customer is looking for help on how to achieve their strategy the consultative selling method is appropriate. If a customer knows how to achieve their strategy and is looking to solve some of their problems then the problem-solving method is best, showing how different solutions may be appropriate. If a customer knows what solution he or she needs then the need satisfaction method is appropriate, showing how the vendor's product or services meet those needs. Overall, customer-centricity (Gummesson, 2008) has become a fundamental underpinning of modern sales strategies.

Next, we take a detailed look how professional selling has evolved. The chapter finishes with an outline of future skills for the sales professional.

TRADITIONAL CLASSIFICATIONS OF TYPES OF SELLING

For more than five decades, classifications of types of selling have attracted the interest of academics. For instance back in the late 1960s Derek Newton at Harvard developed a four-way classification of selling types (Newton, 1969). These types were trade, missionary, technical and new business selling. Newton related these categories to measures of performance by salespeople and to turnover rates in personnel.

In *trade selling*, Newton found that the high performers were older, used extensive reporting and were paid at least in part on commission. Less emphasis was placed on order-taking and selling could be termed low key, where objectives centred on the need to build and maintain longstanding customer relationships. This may explain why older (more experienced) salespeople performed better. The extensive reporting emphasises the need for accurate and informed feedback, possibly as a surrogate for closer supervision. The commission element of pay seems to reflect a need by salespeople to relate effort and reward to retain the necessary motivation, which may otherwise decline. This is very much service selling where the sales force's main objectives are retaining and increasing volume with existing customers. Effort is concentrated on sales support activities such as promotional deals, service aspects and so on.

Missionary selling is typified by the pharmaceutical salesperson calling on doctors who specify the product but may neither stock nor use the product. Similar salespeople may be found in the building industry selling to specifiers such as architects. Here the emphasis is on good coverage and presentation to make sure that these influencers know of the product, its benefits and competitive advantages. These types of salespeople create different problems for management, particularly in trying to relate selling effort and skill to performance. Newton found that this type of selling suited younger salespeople and performance related to the number of calls and coverage of a territory. Unfortunately, this also correlates with a high turnover of personnel. Sales managers must offer support through supervision and training.

In *technical selling*, more emphasis is placed on the professional level of salespeople who are technically competent with high levels of product knowledge – most common in industrial goods and services. In certain industries, technical qualification or a degree may be a prerequisite upon which selling skills can be built. As a result, such people are paid higher rates, they are usually paid more on fixed salary and turnover rates are lower. More emphasis is placed on training younger people but supervision, at least initially, must be closer.

With *new business selling* and development work, salespeople need the security of stable earnings but tend to be older and less trained than average. The implication is that young people find it difficult to cope with rejection and the lack of regular call patterns and customer relationships. The enigma in this position is that it suits people who may enjoy cold calling and the challenge but do not necessarily seek the mature customer relationship sought by many salespeople. Sales management practices seem to confirm that such people are hard to find and retain.

With Newton's type of analysis, classification problems may arise in creating too many or too few categories. Newton suggested that sales managers are better at avoiding failure (low turnover of salespeople) than they are at producing success (increased sales performance).

Various other classifications of selling have been suggested based on both theoretical and empirical grounds. One of the most widely quoted is that suggested by McMurry (1961), and McMurry and Arnold (1968). They built on the development/service spectrum to classify sales positions in terms of both the difficulty of making a sale and what they refer to as the creativity required by salespeople. Their nine categories in order of increasing difficulty were:

1. *Inside order-taker*, such as a retail salesperson, whose function is to serve the already committed customer. Critics might suggest that many customers for many products are not committed, and therefore salespeople have the scope to either close a sale or inadvertently put off customers. Some firms, aware of the importance of this moment of truth, ensure they have their own salespeople within the store; for example, a bed manufacturer in a department store.
2. *Delivery salesperson*, where the prime function is the end result of the physical movement of goods. The importance of such a person will vary depending on the nature of the relationship between buyer and buying organisation and seller and selling organisation. In McMurry's (1961) first classification, this person was rated 'below' the inside order-taker. However, there are variations in the role of delivery salesperson – from delivery with little or no other service, through delivery plus order processing or invoicing functions, to delivery salespeople who have a direct influence on the size of an order or even whether or not an order is placed at all.
3. *Outside order-taker*. In the previous category, the prime function was physical delivery of the goods. In this category, the salesperson takes orders but does not deliver and may also fulfil other services such as checking stock, merchandising and maintaining goodwill with retailers. In this case, their sales ability may determine the shelf space their product is given in a retail outlet – a major factor in sales success.
4. *Missionary salesperson*. In this case, orders are not normally taken but the salesperson is expected to educate prospects, generate goodwill and encourage the product to be used or specified. As referred to earlier, it can be exceptionally difficult to evaluate a salesperson's performance in these important but indirect selling activities.
5. The *technical salesperson* acts not only as a salesperson to the company but also as an adviser/consultant to the client. Again, it is difficult to assess how well the selling job is being performed, and this leads to a potential area of conflict between

giving the customer professional help and achieving company sales. The two, it is hoped, are not mutually exclusive but there may be a conflict of interests.

6 *Creative salesperson – tangibles*. Included in this category is the direct selling of such products as double glazing, encyclopaedias and vacuum cleaners.
7 *Creative salesperson – intangibles*. Similar to point six for services such as insurance, advertising or sales training programmes.
8 *Political or indirect salesperson*, normally associated with large-scale contracts for raw materials such as coal to power stations, cement for road contracts or other 'big-ticket' items.
9 *Multiple salesperson* deals with an organisation usually over a period of years, for example selling aircraft or turbine engines or services such as management consultancy, auditing and other financial services.

Different products, markets and customers create situations requiring different levels of creativity and presenting different levels of difficulty. The salesperson's job can be quite varied while the scope for creativity and innovativeness in, for example, merchandising may be much greater than this classification would suggest. Certainly, the degree of difficulty in achieving additional shelf-space for the number three product line in a supermarket sales portfolio of soups, soaps or yoghurts should not be underestimated.

A good way to compare traditional and new sales processes is to consider the activities that the salesperson or sales team need to undertake. In his seminal article Moncrief (1986) developed a taxonomy of selling activities (121 activities in total) organised across ten factors that enabled at least five sales jobs to be defined: missionary, trade servicer, trade seller, order-taker and institutional. Twenty years later Moncrief, Marshall and Lassk (2006) updated their taxonomy to develop a contemporary one as illustrated in Table 6.1. This contemporary taxonomy resulted in six sales positions: Consultative Seller, New Business/Channel Development Seller, Missionary Seller, Delivery Seller, Sales Support, Key Account Seller.

Table 6.1 – Clusters of sales activities

Traditional taxonomy	Contemporary taxonomy
Selling functions, e.g. make sales presentations	Relationship selling, e.g. building trust
Working with orders, e.g. write up orders	Promotional activities and sales service, e.g. at the point of purchase
Servicing the product, e.g. performing maintenance	Product support, e.g. expedite orders
Servicing the account: e.g. performing the inventory	Prospecting, e.g. responding to referrals
Information management, e.g. providing feedback	Computer-related tasks, e.g. checking email, entering data
Attending conferences/meetings	Training/recruiting, e.g. coaching new sales representatives
Training and recruiting, e.g. new sales staff	Educational activities, e.g. attending sales training
Entertaining clients, e.g. at social events	Entertaining, e.g. dining with clients
Travel	Travel
Distribution	Channel support, e.g. establishing relationships with distributors
	Office, e.g. completing expense reports
	Delivery, e.g. product samples

Source: Moncrief (1986), Moncrief et al. (2006)

TYPES OF SELLING IN TODAY'S BUSINESS ENVIRONMENT

Direct selling to consumers

It has already been suggested that salespeople who deal directly with the public are the most visible and most familiar type of salesperson, but they do not represent the majority of people employed in selling jobs. Nevertheless, this is an important type of selling, employing many people, and it also presents particular difficulties in their management and control. Direct salespeople are often order-getters who rely on selling skills and use predefined presentations and conditioned response techniques to close sales. They normally earn directly related to their sales effort/ability, and payment by commission or depending on sales results is very common. While word-of-mouth may be important in identifying and locating prospects, management support in generating sales leads and maintaining a positive image is also crucial to effective selling. Sales territories may be much less clearly defined.

There is much discussion on what contributes to success in this type of selling. It is often by watching or experiencing direct salespeople in action that the myth of 'born salespeople' is generated. Clearly, those who enjoy meeting people and the challenge of making a sale and have a high level of persuasive skills seem best suited to this type of job. Also, since these types of sales are mostly one-off events, salesmanship techniques can be particularly effective. The rewards can be high and, hitherto, relatively little in the way of formal qualification is demanded.

Did you know?

The direct selling industry has flourished and engaged over 60 million people, despite the impact the Internet is having on this type of selling. The International Direct Selling Educational Institute (IDSEI) was formed to provide academic credentials to direct selling and network marketing professionals. They have accredited programmes that teach learners the basic fundamentals of the industry's practice and how to adapt and benefit from changing times and trends.

Source: International Direct Selling Educational Institute. www.idsei.com/

Selling in retail establishments

Retailers' business model rests on their ability to maximise their sales per square metre. Thus, the product mix is a vital ingredient in optimising revenue and profits. The combination of leading brands, specialised brands and own-label products has a dramatic effect on their profitability. As a result, the role of food broker, category manager and merchandiser has emerged as a key part of sales teams in companies supplying to retailers.

The food broker: The idea of an agent representing many principals or manufacturers is not new and has been used in small tools, publishing and other product markets. In the food industry, the growth of multiple chains to a dominant position and the importance of larger non-retail users have led to a problem in representation for the smaller company and the large buyer. One type of selling to overcome the problem of size is the use of the food broker, who acts on an agency basis for several manufacturers selling a variety of products to retailers. The tasks mostly relate to merchandising and promotional offers in which the cost of individual salespeople for each company is too high and for each store manager too time-consuming. The specialist in, say, delicatessen items, dairy products or confectionery is preferred to individual representation on individual lines. The retailer gets a 'mix' of product from one broker.

The manufacturers get representation that they could otherwise neither obtain nor afford. The skill of such brokers is in balancing the items carried and matching these to customers' requirements. In retailing a new area, category management has emerged to handle the complexities involved in these situations.

The category manager: The efficacy of food brokers to add value in distribution has led to greater adoption of the concept of category management in the modern supermarket supply chain. An example of this approach is the Glasgow-based McCurrach's, which is one of the largest food brokers in the UK. Although founded over 100 years ago, this company has seen its sales grow rapidly in recent years. Representing over 30 clients such as Guinness, Campbell's and A G Barr, their role is to maximise customers' sales by getting products into stores and ensuring appropriate shelf-space and in-store promotions. McCurrach's at present employs over 100 people and has invested in new technology to provide the best possible service for client and customer. Such an operation involves specialist salespeople competent in selling, merchandising, logistics and account management. This requires a product information and service mix which meets the demanding needs of retail customers. For more information see www.mccurrach.co.uk/grocery.aspx.

The merchandising representatives: An important aspect of many companies' marketing success is to have available product, superbly presented and displayed at the point-of-sale to maximise distributors' margins and to make it easy and a pleasure for the end customer to buy. For this reason, an important aspect of many salespeople's job specification is to merchandise their company's product or service in the most competitive way. For some companies, this is most effectively achieved by separating merchandising from other sales activities. Mars confectionery, for instance, have for some time maintained a separate merchandise force from their conventional sales force, calling on large and small outlets to maximise the effectiveness of their point-of-sale displays. Others, such as Procter & Gamble or Unilever, have their own employees in major supermarkets to more effectively coordinate their operations on behalf of their distributors. Such personnel not only sell but also carry out merchandising planning and operations and a range of logistic-related activities.

Telesales

Ever cognisant of the high costs of selling and the low face-to-face selling time, an important consideration is to balance sales with other elements in the marketing mix and to consider the most effective selling mix. Is a personal call necessary? Would a telephone call suffice or be of more benefit to the customer? Can groups of small customers or non-customers be approached by telephone? The use of the telephone in selling can be both a replacement for personal contact and a complement to personal selling. So pervasive has the telephone become, and so vital a part of sales operations, that much of Chapter 4 addressed the problems and opportunities of communicating with customers via the telephone and other modern communication systems.

Did you know?

The cost of customer contact

Industrial sales call	$300
Telemarketing	$35
Direct mail	$2.50
Internet	$1.25

Source: www.e-marketinggroup.com/the_costs_content.htm

Telephone selling, like personal selling, requires good communication skills, empathy and professionalism. Certain techniques will be different. On the telephone, it is essential to record details of the caller's name and number and the approach to asking questions is different since the call is very often in response to a request. The resources at the salesperson's disposal are also different in that a visual display unit (VDU) is likely to be used, making information more readily available. Closing the call and follow-up are vital so that customers are satisfied with their treatment and their problem is resolved. Good telephone salespeople need to speak clearly and be polite and courteous so that rapport is established. They need to ensure that they are clearly understood by the customer and that they in turn understand the customer's request accurately. Telephone selling is most effective in a conditioned response mode, preferably with a script and a standardised response format. Also, if the request cannot be met in full, there needs to be a clear line of communication to a more senior manager who can deal with the problem. Telephone salespeople usually have the advantage of working in teams which can be supportive for the individuals involved. For this reason, the growth in teleworkers operating from home has proved less effective than the modern call centre operation as a sales and service operation.

Selling to consumers is also done through the Internet; see Chapter 9, Technology and Sales for reference to this type of selling. (Figure 6.2)

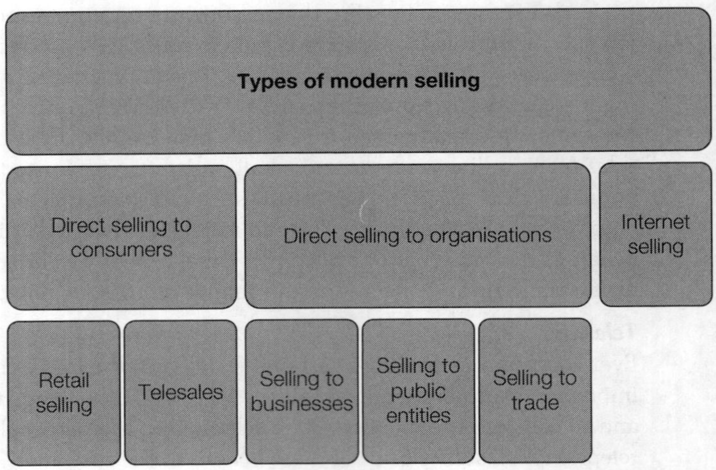

Figure 6.2 – Types of modern selling

Direct selling to organisations

In this category one finds most *field sales forces*; that is, professional groups that deal directly, face to face with customer organisations. In this category, salespeople often take orders from customers and maintain customer portfolios, the so-called 'farmers'. In most organisations field sales forces are also expected to gain new customers, thus adopting the 'hunter' role. In direct selling to organisations, there are three core types of selling: to businesses (for profit organisations), to public entities and to retailers.

Selling to businesses

The scale and the value of the purchase, the length of negotiation, the organisational nature of the buying decision, etc., are broad and diverse in B2B selling. Items sold range from industrial products such as machine tools, raw materials and component parts to products for foodservice operators, office furniture or business insurance. Other examples may be telecom systems, network computer solutions and marketing and advertising services. All these sectors employ professional sales forces to engage the customer and to find ways to deliver value. High-level technical and negotiating skills are necessary, as are business acumen. Overall, a core skill is the ability to develop solutions appropriate to the unique circumstances of the customer and aligned with the company's product/service and customer management strategy. Whereas in direct consumer selling salespeople must learn 'how to sell', in direct B2B they must also learn 'how to add and then claim value'.

Selling to resellers or distributors

In this the type of selling the salesperson will have a dual role: first, to influence the reseller to adopt a product or service as the preferred option for the end customer; and second, to ensure that the service that the reseller, distributor or installer provides is adequate and in line with the manufacturer's expected standards. The joint cooperation between intermediaries and manufacturers is essential in ensuring end customer satisfaction. Therefore, the salesperson employed by a building materials company works with and through a builder's merchant on specific contracts for a house builder or contractor. The skills required are product knowledge and application and also detailed understanding of logistics and other associated costs that impact on the overall distributor's profitability. Overall, business objectives are to defend existing business, retain inertia between buying and selling organisations and promote service aspects to the selling job in addition to the other elements of the traditional marketing mix (product, price and distribution).

Selling to the public sector

This category has some similarity to B2B but differs in the organisational buying processes and usually in the way in which business is conducted. Here, the system of tender that most public sector organisations establish, requires salespeople to have insight into the organisational complexities as well as the personal characteristics of buyers' needs. Included here are the purchases of central and local government, hospitals and health boards, schools, colleges and universities, which vary in their purchasing organisations and procurement procedures, each requiring different and sometimes unique sales approaches. In some of these organisations, such as military establishments, there are guidelines and publications on how to sell to their organisations. In some cases, the rules for the business and even the profits that suppliers are expected to make can be specified. For salespeople, the selling job here involves managing very long sales cycles, and ensuring customer rules and procedures are adhered to.

Selling to retail businesses

Traditionally this has been one of the most common types of selling, in which salespeople are primarily employed for retailer service selling. However, the concentration of the retail trade into a small number of very large organisations that dominate their retail sector has changed the nature of this type of selling. Usually, selling will now be conducted on a team basis with a combination of roles often led by a customer account manager. In their team, there will be logistics experts, merchandisers, consumer marketers, new product and special promotions representatives. In Chapter 8, Key account management, some of the approaches to dealing with the complexity of these types of customers are presented.

Some manufacturers that still maintain this type of sales force require salespeople to understand buyers' needs and to ensure adequate stocks of products, assist with point-of-sale displays, promote the company's advertising programmes to retailers and assist in coordinating merchandising tasks. Some fast-moving consumer goods companies (FMCG) employ future sales and marketing managers in this type of sales job to provide them with an immersion into the business, the competitive position of their company and its products and the way in which buyers operate. All these first-hand experiences are believed to be invaluable and ideal for training future managers who will have to make marketing decisions in more senior roles.

Detailing

This category, referred to as missionary sales by Newton (1969), seems to warrant special mention. This is a difficult form of selling in which the sale is to have the product or service specified by a major influencer in the purchase decision, rather than by the user of the product. Architects and doctors are two examples of such influencers. Most prevalent in the pharmaceutical industry, missionary selling attempts to educate and train customers (i.e. prescribers) in the use of the product and therefore aims not at the one-off sale but at building relationships for future orders. Detail selling of this type is most effective where:

- The product has clear benefits over the competition.
- The selling cycle is long term yet the information needs of the potential customers are many and urgent.
- Other forms of communication, such as advertising, cannot convey the whole message the supplier wishes to communicate, and the buyer needs to know to specify the product with confidence.
- The buying process is complex and involves a number of influencers in the purchase decision.

Key account selling

Another category which warrants special mention but which would normally be part of either consumer or industrial indirect selling comprises the so-called key account salespeople. The changing structure of major retailers, distributors and others means, for many companies, that certain customers are of strategic importance. The Pareto rule, which states that 80 per cent of the business comes from 20 per cent of customers, necessitates that these important accounts are given the attention and service they deserve. Furthermore, since these are normally large organisations with buying groups, a more customised approach similar to the government direct category may apply. We conceptualise key account management as distinct from direct selling, thus we have dedicated a specific chapter to this topic. It is mentioned here for reasons of completeness.

CLASSIC SELLING STEPS

For many years, the seven steps of selling (Moncrief & Marshall, 2005) have underpinned the thinking behind professional selling. These phases are well accepted in the field, and often referred to in sales training programmes and selling skills workshops. Although selling steps have changed significantly they are still applicable to a wide range of selling situations. Below we describe these steps and offer some tips to effectively address each step.

Prospecting

Is the process of finding new customers. This is done through *external sources* that may include: the use of a referral by asking a prospect or a current customer for the name of another prospect; using community contacts such as relatives and friends to get the names of potential prospects; obtaining an introduction from one customer or prospect to another via letter, email or phone; contacting organisations, service clubs or chambers of commerce to seek sales leads. Prospecting strategies seek to cultivate visible and influential accounts that will help persuade other buyers.

Prospecting can also be done by leveraging *internal sources* such as company records, directories, membership lists and other documents to obtain names of prospects; responses to customer inquiries from company advertising and promotional campaigns; and responses to phone, mail or email inquiries from potential prospects.

If you use marketing leads ensure that proper follow-up of those leads is arranged. Not following up is a mistake and many businesses seem to overlook the amount of follow-up required (Cardell, 2004):

- 48 per cent of businesses never follow up with a prospect.
- 25 per cent of businesses make a second contact and stop.
- 12 per cent of businesses only make three contacts and stop.

These figures are problematic, since according to Cardell's report only 10 per cent of businesses make more than three contacts, implying that you lose business because:

- 2 per cent of sales are made on the first contact.
- 3 per cent of sales are made on the second contact.
- 5 per cent of sales are made on the third contact.
- 10 per cent of sales are made on the fourth contact.
- 80 per cent of sales are made on the fifth to 12th contact.

Good prospecting requires the use of personal observation to look and listen for evidence of genuine interest in buying from the prospects; it often requires making cold calls and attending trade shows where potential prospects can be identified.

Pre-approach (planning and preparation)

This step is focused on contacting the prospect customer. The seller sends the prospect a personal letter/email to present him/herself and request an interview; alternatively, have a present customer send a letter to a prospect introducing the salesperson and requesting an interview; phone for an appointment; call the prospect in order to set up an appointment for a sales interview.

Information sources: Gather intelligence about the prospect's business before the appointment; ask current customers specific information about a particular prospect; use other company salespeople for information about a particular prospect; read local newspapers or search the Internet to obtain information about the prospect.

Planning activities: Determine the sales objective and intended outcome of the meeting; plan the subject areas that need to be addressed during the meeting; establish a valid business reason why the prospect should meet with you; plan the questions that will be asked. Table 6.2 illustrates the differences between poor preparation and good practice in professional selling.

Table 6.2 – Differences between poor and good practice in sales planning and preparation

Poor preparation	Good practice
1. Focused on the sales representative's objectives	1. Focused on the customer's strategic goals
2. The aim is to get the order	2. The aim is to establish a long-term relationship
3. Focused on the sales organisation	3. Focused on contributing to the customer's business success
4. Based on intuition	4. Based on reliable, verified evidence
5. Focused on selling a product	5. Focused on selling solutions
6. Conducted by the sales representative alone	6. Conducted in discussions with the area manager and the client

Approaching the customer and exploring needs

The approach occurs in the first minutes of the interaction. Established conventions include handshake, small talk and personal connection, all intended to create a positive good initial impression. Figure 6.3, 'Structured opening approach', illustrates a well-established approach to commence sales interactions. The purpose communicates to the customer what the intended/expected outcome for the sales meeting is. The benefit outlines the value the customer can derive from the time invested in the meeting. The 'check' phase confirms the customer's agreement and understanding of the specified purpose before moving to the next stage.

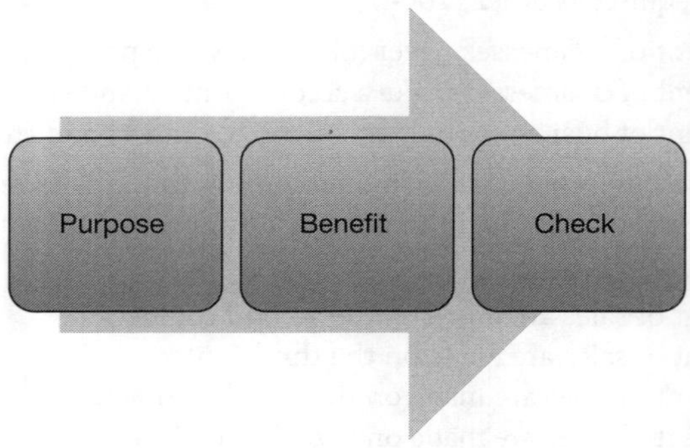

Figure 6.3 – Structured opening approach

Problem/Need Information: Do a situation analysis; request information about the prospect's business situation; identify potential problem areas the prospect might have, assess their needs and how to satisfy/solve them; enquire about the costs of the problem and the benefits it will bring if solved.

Purchase information: Assess the decision-making unit (DMU); enquire about the people and their role involvement in the purchasing decision; enquire about the budget and the decision date; assess competitors and inquire about which other vendors the prospect is seeing; identify the steps in the prospect's buying process and which step they are at now; identify the criteria that will be used to make the purchase; assess how the individual influencers will personally benefit from this purchase.

In his seminal work Rackham (1995) revealed how customer needs can typically be divided between explicit and implicit or latent. Competent sellers are those able to 'surface' the implicit needs and help the customer frame them as explicit, action-oriented desires (Figure 6.4).

Give information to obtain credibility: Establish credibility by presenting an overview of the company, experience, products and references; use company brochures to provide the prospect with documentation about the company and the product.

Planning the next activity: Understand the DMU and ask the contact person at the prospect firm to facilitate a meeting with other members of the DMU; schedule meetings with other members of the DMU; obtain commitment by requesting some form of action from the prospect in order to move the sales process forward.

Presentation

For many, sales presentation is the fundamental step in traditional selling where the seller has an opportunity to present the company and its product/services. The most effective way to persuade the customer, particularly in complex sales, is

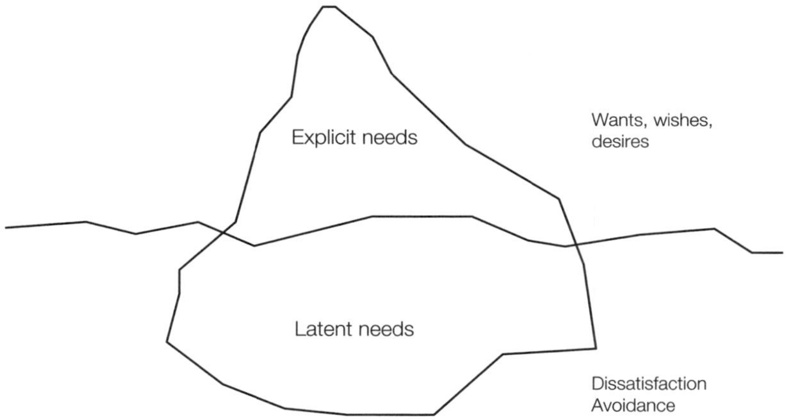

Figure 6.4 – Explicit and latent needs

Source: Based on ideas from Rackham (1995)

to offer benefits rather than simply advantages or features. According to Rackham (1995) (Figure 6.5):

- Features: are characteristics and qualities of a product or service. Typically facts, data and information that help describe a product or service. Features are unpersuasive, and in small sales there is a slight positive relationship between the use of features and sales outcomes. In large sales calls, using features early in the sales process is counterproductive.
- Advantages: are statements that describe how a product or a solution can be used by the buyer. Advantages explain how certain features of the product can help the client and may trigger objections when not linked to explicit needs. In small sales, the use of advantages is positive but in larger sales the effect is less positive.
- Benefits: show how a product or service meets an explicit need expressed by the client. Benefits are powerful statements that are highly correlated to sales success in both large and small sales.

When presenting to customers: Tailor the sales presentation specifically for the prospect; but, where possible, ensure coherence with other presentations to similar customers in order to reflect the organisation's key messages to its market; develop an initial business proposal for the customer; cover the DMU, if necessary, making the presentation to other members of the DMU.

Visual display techniques: Make a product demonstration for the prospect; provide proof and guarantees about the product/service performance; provide detailed

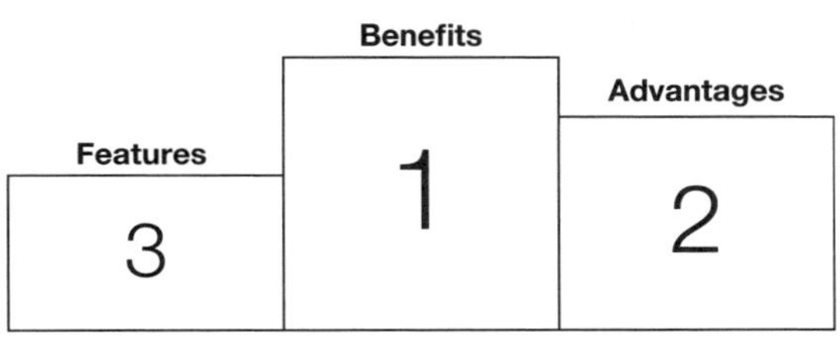

Figure 6.5 – Features, advantages and benefits

Source: Based on ideas from Rackham (1995)

product documentation; provide a copy of the presentation material. Provide proof and guarantees about the product/service performance.

Overcoming objections

Objections are concerns and reservations the customer has about the product/service. Very often they are seen as 'negative' hesitancies about the product or service. They will almost always appear during the sales process. They are often seen as negative episodes by professional sellers; however, there is an alternative perspective: to consider them as 'unique' opportunities to understand the customer's genuine needs.

When dealing with objections it is useful to distinguish between *misconception*, *scepticism* and *drawbacks* of the product or service. If the customer presents an objection which is a misconception, for instance 'I believe implementing the control system you propose may require reconfiguring existing machinery', an effective response may be to clarify to the customer the extent of reconfiguration really needed. Alternatively, if the objection reveals scepticism, such as 'I don't see how your software will improve the productivity in our dealerships', then the seller can address this objection by demonstrating and providing evidence of how the solution works in practice. An objection about a drawback in the product/service, for instance 'Your fees are too expensive', may be tackled by balancing the advantages and disadvantages of the solution.

Closing

Closing is the stage (almost) every salesperson focuses on, and there is plenty of literature on how to become more effective at closing. Closing techniques in small sales differ significantly from those in larger sales (Rackham, 1995), suggesting that frequent, compulsive closing techniques may only work in low-value products. These techniques reduce the chances of making a sale with expensive and complex products. Figure 6.6, 'A non-manipulative closing approach', outlines some principles to manage the closing process in a customer-centred fashion.

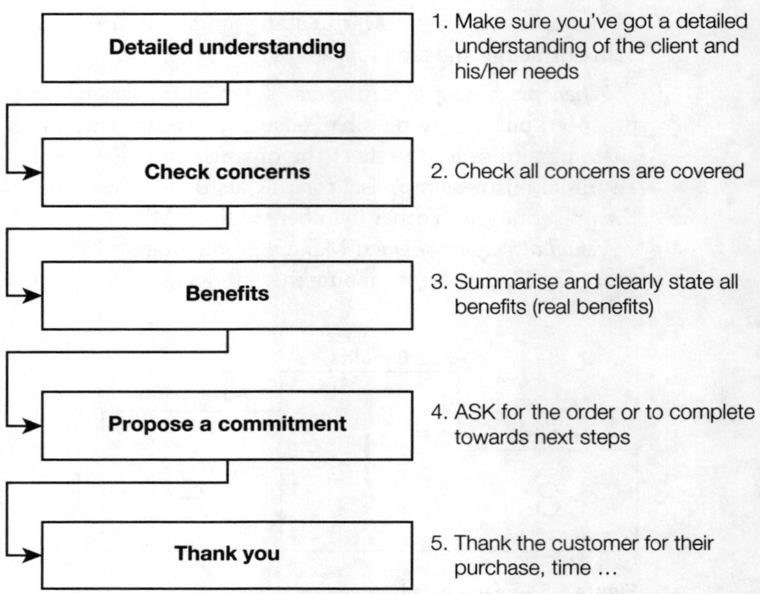

Figure 6.6 – A non-manipulative closing approach

Tailored proposal: Develop a tailored formal proposal; organise a reference visit or contact; demonstrate the product to counter objections; make an implementation plan for the product or service; consider a price discount to counter objections; reduce prospect risk by offering a smaller solution to start with.

Follow-up

Customer service activities: Serve as a consultant by giving special advice to the customer; ensure proper billing procedures and policies; interpret the firm's policies and procedures to the client; provide customer training and also training to their employees in the use of the product; if appropriate, install the product for the customer and service it when necessary.

Customer satisfaction activities: Handling complaints: address any customer complaints expeditiously after the order has been signed; follow up by ensuring that preparation for the acceptance of the product is in order and that initial use is satisfactory; periodically check with the customer to ensure that the customer continues to be satisfied; reassure the customer by seeking to rebuild or maintain the customer's confidence in his or her purchase; send thank you notes to the customer; send a letter of appreciation to the customer.

Customer referral activities: Continue to seek customer referrals by asking the customer for new sales leads; develop account penetration through contact with other employees within the company to sell the products.

Concomitant with individual activities, the sales manager needs to manage *the account*, particularly in terms of information and customer contact flows.

CONTEMPORARY SELLING STEPS

A fundamental shift in professional selling has been the evolution from transactional to relationship selling approaches (Boles, Brashear, Bellenger & Barksdale, 2000; Mark, Johnston & Marshall, 2013). Moreover, a differentiation between transactional, consultative and relationship selling (TCR) is recognised and established in the sales management field (Marshall & Michaels, 2001). Modern selling has evolved across a number of dimensions including sales activities, value added, the nature of the relationship and customer types.

Recognising the recent transformations in sales professionals, Moncrief and Marshall (2005) derived a set of evolved selling processes. These processes recognise the prevalence of the seven steps mentioned above, and can be summarised as follows (Figure 6.7):

- *Customer management*: Rather than blindly *hunting* for new customers, and given the substantial costs involved in pursuing new customers, sales professionals need to consider whether all the opportunities with current customers have been exhausted.
- *Learning*: The definition of mechanistic sales meetings' objectives needs to be revised and extended to incorporate insights from past experiences with comparable customers. What did we learn? What were the approaches we adopted in the past that resulted in value creation recognised by the customer?
- *Developing relationships*: In certain industries such as life sciences, defence, etc., engaging certain customers in a sales process is difficult if a relationship does not exist with the customer beforehand. Increasingly, many other industrial markets are becoming more reluctant to be openly involved with suppliers. Thus, the option

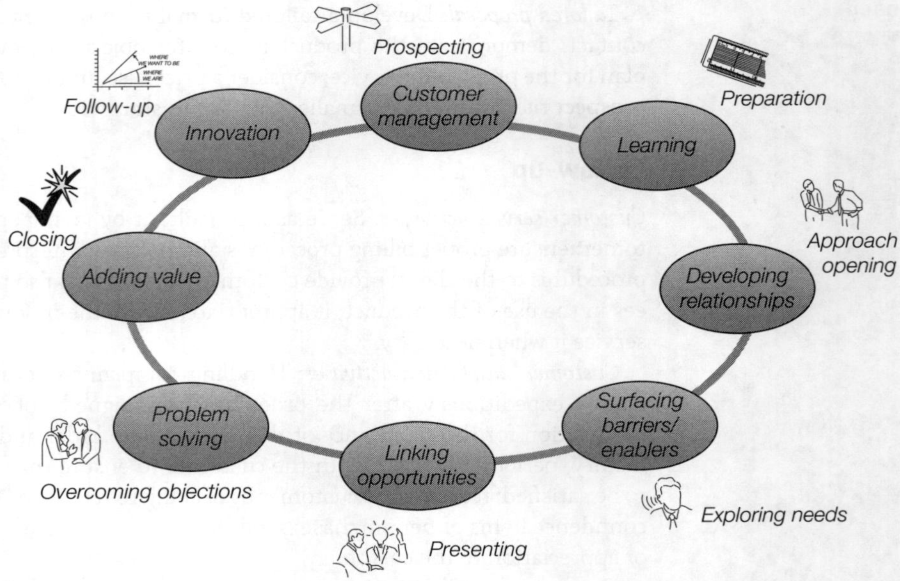

Figure 6.7 – Evolution of the selling steps

Source: Based on ideas from Moncrief and Marshall (2005)

of developing relationships first and then establishing sales process may need to be considered.

- *Surfacing enablers and barriers to change*: In the sales literature, the notion of discovering and addressing customer needs is well established. Another way of looking at the traditional concept of 'needs' is to surface the facilitators and the impediments to change for the customer. For instance, in a presentation at one of our client's events at Cranfield University, a senior representative from Oracle declared that the company has the ethos of engaging with customers that have a 'transformational aim at heart': Oracle does not just provide IT but technology-driven business transformation.
- *Linking opportunities*: Sometimes customers do not have a well formulated and well articulated set of needs, which makes the presentation of 'benefits' difficult. Also, in some sectors such as civil engineering or transport systems, there is not a scoped solution that fits a predetermined specification. In these contexts the customer and supplier come together, linking their respective capabilities to co-create new solutions (Lemmens et al., 2014).
- *Problem solving*: Moncrief and Marshall (2005) argue that there is a shift from meeting the predetermined needs of customers that demands an evolved process of selling which focuses on problem solving – adopting a consultative selling approach with a view of becoming a trusted advisor.
- *Adding value*: In relationship selling and in strategic customer relationships, the 'close' of one sales process is the beginning of the next. Therefore, the emphasis is not on 'concluding' but quite the contrary, on continuing a relationship where the creation and delivery of value is demonstrated.
- *Innovation*: Similarly, in order to maintain and further develop the relationship with the customer, both product and service/process innovation must be demonstrated.

What do you think?

In 1998, Neil Rackham and John DeVincentis in their book *Rethinking the Sales Force* argued that sales as a profession had changed very slowly and was almost the same function it had been half a century earlier. However, back then in 1998, they predicted that professional selling was about to undergo a fundamental change. In 2015 the processes to create customer value, the nature of the interactions between sales organisations and customers, and professional selling skills have all changed substantially when compared to what they were 18 years ago.

SKILLS FOR THE CONTEMPORARY SALES PROFESSIONAL

The role of the future sales professional appears to be one that will require constant development in the relevant area of expertise/business and in customer management tools and techniques. In addition to sector-specific knowledge, future salespeople will have to cultivate customer relationships and attain greater know-how to become consultative sellers.

One of our studies (Lemmens, Marcos-Cuevas & Ryals, 2011) revealed that there are four skill areas that are important for the future salesperson: Functional, Relational, Managerial and Cognitive. Functional skills primarily refer to those that would traditionally be called 'selling skills'; in the context of future sales professionals, skills that underpin the creation of customer value. Relational skills refer to the ability to interact and connect with individuals across boundaries and across functions. Managerial skills are general know-how related to the achievement of goals in organisations. Finally, cognitive skills refer to analytical abilities and the extent to which individuals can process and act upon information. Table 6.3 outlines key skills in each category.

Table 6.3 – Skill requirements of the new sales role

Functional	Relational	Managerial	Cognitive
Financial insight	Multi-level and multi-functional relationships	People management skills	Innovative problem solving
Business acumen	Understanding of human dynamics	High ethical and integrity standards	Time management and task prioritisation
Marketing knowledge	Ability to contribute and to work in teams	Influencing skills (internal organisation)	Lateral thinking
Business opportunity discovery and qualification	Ability to integrate marketing – sales efforts	Openness to change and adaptability	Mental toughness and resilience
Strategic negotiation (beyond price)	Ability to inspire trust	Clarity of communication	
Market and research	Listening skills	Time management skills	
Customer insight		Business process understanding	

Organisations that participated in the study recognised that the speed by which transformation in sales have occurred have superseded their ability to develop new talent that can cope with the new context of sales.

The war for consultative selling talent across sectors is recognised as a real one, as illustrated by one of the senior business development executives of an IT service company quoted in the study: 'we want to be in the value added business where we're helping achieve differentiation, helping make our customers be more competitive – so the biggest challenge is finding the people's skills in the market place'.

The topic of recruitment and selection of sales professionals is presented in Chapter 11. The next chapter focuses on defining and implementing sales strategies.

SUMMARY

This chapter has presented some fundamental aspects of selling that need to be understood before exploring core processes and practices. First, it has reviewed traditional classifications of types of selling providing a 'map' of the different ways in which customers can be reached. This traditional view has then been complemented with a description of the ways in which selling organisations today organise their structures and sales personnel. The chapter has devoted special effort to describing classic selling steps and sales roles and how these have evolved over the years to provide an up-to-date contemporary description of professional selling.

QUESTIONS

- What are the fundamental differences between traditional and modern sales roles?
- How would you describe professional selling in a structured way?
- What are the competencies and skills required for the 'future' sales professional?

REFERENCES

Boles, J., Brashear, T., Bellenger, D. & Barksdale, H. (2000). Relationship selling behaviors: Antecedents and relationship with performance. *Journal of Business & Industrial Marketing*, 15(2–3), 141–153.

Cardell, C. (2004). 10 Essential strategies to ensure that your marketing is a success. Retrieved 28 July 2014, from http://www.cardellmedia.co.uk/Reports/marketing.html.

Gummesson, E. (2008). Customer centricity: Reality or a wild goose chase? *European Business Review*, 20(4), 315–330.

Ingram, T. (2002). Selling in the new millennium A joint agenda. *Industrial Marketing Management*, 31(7), 559–567. doi:10.1016/S0019-8501(02)00175-X.

Ingram, T. N., Laforge, R. W., Avila, R. A., Schwepker, C. H. & Williams, M. R. (2012). *Sales Management: Analysis and Decision Making* (8th edn). London: M. E. Sharpe Inc.

Johnston, M. W. & Marshall, G. W. (2008). *Relationship Selling*. New York: McGraw-Hill.

Johnston, M. W. & Marshall, G. W. (2013). *Sales Force Management – Leadership, Innovation, Technology* (11th edn). New York: Routledge.

Lemmens, R., Donaldson, B. & Marcos, J. (2014). *From Selling to Co-creating*. Amsterdam: BIS Publishers.

Lemmens, R., Marcos-Cuevas, J. & Ryals, L. J. (2011). Selling in the 21st century: Mapping the transformations of selling and sales management. *The 9th Sales Management Research Conference*. Paris, 5th May.

Marshall, G. W. & Michaels, R. E. (2001). Research in selling and sales management in the next millennium: An agenda from the AMA faculty consortium. *Journal of Personal Selling & Sales Management*, 21(1), 15–17.

McMurry, R. N. (1961). The mystique of super-salesmanship. *Harvard Business Review*, 39(2), 113–122.

McMurry, R. N. & Arnold, J. (1968). *How to Build a Dynamic Sales Organisation*. New York: McGraw-Hill.

Millman, T. & Wilson, K. (1995). From key account selling to key account management. *Journal of Marketing Practice: Applied Marketing Science*, 1(1), 9–21.

Millman, T. & Wilson, K. (1996). Developing key account management competences. *Journal of Marketing Practice*, 2(2), 7–22.

Moncrief, W. C. (1986). Selling activity and sales position taxonomies for industrial salesforces. *Journal of Marketing Research*, 23(3), 261–270.

Moncrief, W. C. & Marshall, G. W. (2005). The evolution of the seven steps of selling. *Industrial Marketing Management*, 34(1), 13–22.

Moncrief, W. C., Marshall, G. W. & Lassk, F. G. (2006). A contemporary taxonomy of sales positions. *Journal of Personal Selling & Sales Management*, 26(1), 55–65.

Newton, D. A. (1969). Get the most out of your sales force. *Harvard Business Review*, 47(5), 130–143.

Rackham, N. (1995). *Spin-Selling*. New York: Gower Publishing Company Limited, p. 260.

Rackham, N. & DeVincentis, J. (1998). *Rethinking the Sales Force: Redefining Selling to Create and Capture Customer Value*. New York: McGraw-Hill.

Schwepker Jr., C. H. (2003). Customer-oriented selling: A review, extension, and directions for future research. *Journal of Personal Selling & Sales Management*, 23(2), 151–171.

Sheth, J. N. & Parvatiyar, A. (1995). The evolution of relationship marketing. *International Business Review*, 4(4), 397–418.

Spiro, R. L. & Weitz, B. A. (1990). Adaptive selling: Conceptualization, measurement, and nomological validity. *Journal of Marketing Research*, 27(1), 61.

Weitz, B. A. & Bradford, K. D. (1999). Personal selling and sales management: A relationship marketing perspective. *Journal of the Academy of Marketing Science*, 27(2), 241–254.

7 DEFINING AND IMPLEMENTING SALES STRATEGIES

OVERVIEW

This chapter brings together key concepts of B2B marketing to develop a sound sales strategy and a route to market plan. It starts by framing sales growth as a crucial endeavour for businesses and, indeed, the sales and marketing functions. Then it outlines established approaches to segmenting customers in business markets and describes the underpinnings for developing compelling customer value propositions. The chapter then focuses on outlining contemporary approaches to co-create value with customers and on presenting established principles to deploy a sound channel strategy.

LEARNING OBJECTIVES

This chapter aims to enable the reader to:

- Undertake a segmentation of business customers.
- Define an account relationship strategy.
- Develop value propositions.
- Establish approaches to co-create value with key customers.
- Articulate channel strategy.

DEFINITIONS

Segmentation: the process of grouping customers into meaningful categories based on relevant similarities.
Value proposition: the set of expected benefits a company provides to its customers; the promise of the value to be delivered that is believed to have a positive impact on the customer's organisation.
Customer value co-creation is the approach to achieve competitive advantage by developing capabilities to identify and deliver value to customers in unique ways.
Multichannel routes to market refers to the combination of channels that a firm uses to achieve its sales objectives. These channels include, among others, a direct sales organisation, telesales, agents, licensing, joint distribution agreements, the Internet and other means of connecting to customers.

INTRODUCTION: SALES GROWTH IN MODERN SALES ORGANISATIONS

Sales growth is a key item on the agenda of most businesses, and perhaps one of the most pressing issues for both sales executives and general managers. As the recession (2007–2014) is giving way to higher levels of dynamism in Western markets, organisations are starting to focus on capturing higher levels of growth. Generally speaking, shareholders' expectations of returns are growing, and while these can be fulfilled in the short term with a focus on efficiency, returns in the medium and in the long term require investments that enable profitable growth.

Achieving profitable growth is a complex endeavour. In Chapter 1 we outlined some of the challenges sales organisations are currently facing, such as the nature and expectations of professional buyers, the opportunities offered by new technologies, and the enhanced levels of globalisation and competition. Growth in markets where the organisation is already operating will require a renewed look at customers' preferences both in terms of expected benefits of the product or service and in terms of preferred purchase channel. Sales growth in most sectors requires leaders to think critically about the dilemma, not mutually exclusive, of growing domestic vs. growing internationally.

Overall, a key challenge for sales executives is that sales growth will require significant internal transformation in structures, systems and processes. Sales leaders are now required to become increasingly influential internally, to persuade the organisation to become more customer-centric and to re-focus activities and allocation of resources to enable sales growth.

What do you think?

A study by McKinsey found that key questions for senior sales leaders on how they can drive and sustain growth include:

- How can an organisation capture growth before competitors, both in existing and in new markets?
- How can a business use multiple channels to serve customers with different profiles and needs, optimising direct and indirect channels?

Source: Baumgartner, Hatami and Vander Ark (2011)

In this chapter we will address issues of sales strategy definition and implementation. The chapter should be seen as a pivotal one, providing a link between the strategies and principles outlined in Part I and the processes and practices presented in Parts II and III.

DEFINING SALES STRATEGIES

Sales strategy is the process of defining who the customer is, what the offer the company brings to them is, and how selling is done (Zoltners, Sinha & Lorimer, 2004, p. 54). In this section we will cover the first two aspects: the definition of the target customer groups (segments) and the development of the value proposition. We look at the 'how' aspects of sales strategies in the section below titled 'Implementing sales strategies: account and channel strategy'.

In defining sales strategies, three key elements need to be articulated:

1. Segmentation of the customer base.
2. Account and relationship strategy.
3. Development of the value proposition.

Segmentation in business markets

Segmentation is a crucial activity in Marketing and a pillar of any well-conceived sales and marketing strategy. Kotler (1991) defines segmentation as 'the act of dividing a market into distinct groups of buyers who might require separate products and/or marketing mixes' (p. 263). Therefore a segment constitutes a group of customers with the same or similar needs. Segmentation is the bedrock of successful marketing (Mcdonald, 2012).

Realistic segmentation should have the following characteristics:

- Segments should be of an adequate size to provide the company with the desired return for its efforts.
- Members of each segment should have a high degree of similarity, yet be distinct from the rest of the market.
- Criteria for describing segments must be relevant to the purchase situation.
- Segments must be reachable.

There are a number of segmentation techniques in business-to-business:

Demographic. This typically uses the size of customer, industry sector, number of employees of organisations or geographic location. These techniques are easy to use, but rarely result in competitive advantage: most sales and marketing organisations implement them.

Attitudinal. This segmentation strategy is based on the customer's attitude towards the supplier, or towards issues related to the product or service; motivation and values. This technique gives insight, but as people don't always do what they say, it is of limited value in delivering superior offerings.

Behavioural. This is based on how customers behave; their needs; patterns of usage; susceptibility to the supplier's offer. This segmentation technique is powerful but may not give insights into the reasons for a particular behaviour.

Service-based segmentation. This is developed based on differentiated service levels, and linked to customer profitability. This approach is very useful in business markets and can be applied to existing segments, making them even more meaningful for the supplier. With this type of segmentation, the supplier offers different service levels for each segment, e.g. gold, silver and bronze. Typically, service levels are based on the value of that segment to the company and to get service levels above their segment customers may have to pay extra, or service packages may have to be negotiated with customers based on the business they may bring.

Example: Segmentation in DHL

DHL, the global logistics company, recognises that an increasing level of partnership is often required by companies connected in a supply chain. In order to provide an enhanced service, they have developed industry-specific solutions for sectors such as aerospace, automotive and others. DHL has implemented some very strong customer marketing programmes, whereby the company, in addition to segmenting channels, also takes into consideration customer behaviour with the ultimate aim of achieving higher levels of customer-centricity.

As a result of efficient customer relationship management, product and service levels are tailored to individual customer segments and developed and offered through so-called product service agreements (PSAs). For DHL an important aspect of customer relationship management is to identify key customers and customer groups that represent a high strategic value to the company.

Sources: www.dhl.co.uk; http://www.dmnews.com/

Service-based segmentation draws on *needs*-based approaches, grouping the customers according to the drivers of their purchase decisions such as cost, technologies and relationships. For instance, suppliers may organise customer groups according to the following (Zoltners et al., 2004, p. 65):

- Need for service offerings. For instance in addition to buying air-conditioning systems, whether the customer also purchases maintenance services.
- Preferred buying approach: For instance for an office supplies company whether ordering online, on the phone or directly to a sales representative.
- Need for customisation. Refers to the extent to which a company requires the product or service to be tailored to their specific circumstances, such as the formula for cleaning chemicals in a food factory.
- Importance of product to the buyer. Markets can be segmented depending on whether the customer considers the supplier to be in tier 1, 2 or other level in the supply chain. For example, metal bearings may be a commodity for manufacturers of furniture but critical for automotive systems integrators.
- Procurement function. Whether centralised or decentralised, requiring a customer-centric approach.

What do you think?

The most effective approach to segmenting customers in business markets is by focusing on the benefits the customer will derive from the supplier's offer. In industrial markets some products and services are difficult to differentiate, thus making it difficult for suppliers to command price premiums. How the customer will use the product and service and the impact of these on the customer's operation is a good way to devise an informative segmentation criteria. For example Dupont, the chemical company, segmented its market for Kevlar (a fibre used to make a variety of clothing, accessories and equipment safer and more durable) according to three distinct benefits:

- Fishing boat owners: based on Kevlar's lightness deriving in fuel savings and increased boat speed.
- Aircraft manufacturers: based on Kevlar's strength: weight ratio
- Manufacturing plans: providing an opportunity to replace asbestos used in some machinery.

Q: What other criteria could Dupont use to segment its customers?

Source: Rangan (1994)

Perceptual mapping

Perceptual mapping is a technique to visually display the 'perceptions' of customers in relation to competing products in the market place. Perceptual maps use determinant attributes on a graph. The main advantage of this presentation format is that it is very simple to construct and interpret. Two product or service attributes or customer traits can being considered. By combining the scores across these two criteria, the different customer groups can be placed onto the map.

Figure 7.1 shows an example of a perceptual map of customers of a financial services firm. The vertical axis describes the degree of sophistication of the service provided. The higher the sophistication of the customers, the wider the scope of the services that can be offered. The level of income is represented on the horizontal axis. In financial services higher levels of income make these customers more attractive. The combination of sophistication and income results in a series of groups (bubbles) plotted across the four quadrants. The bigger the bubble the higher the value of that customer segment. In the example, segment 'I' is the largest customer segment and 'H' the most attractive one.

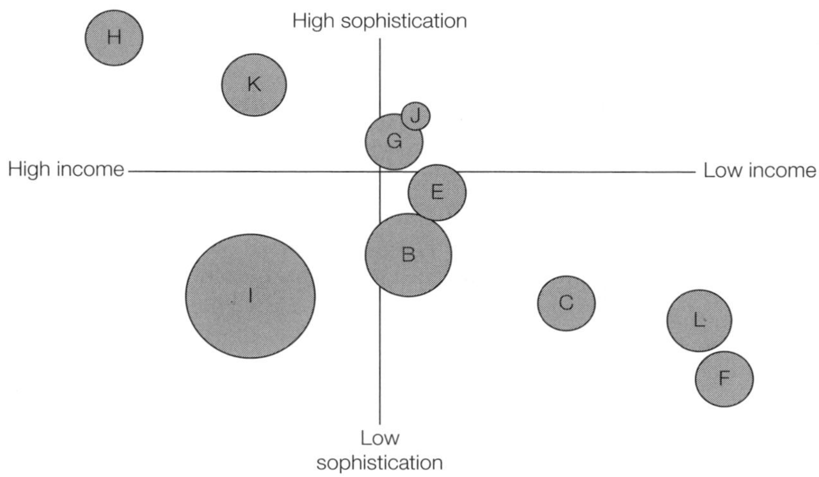

Figure 7.1 – Perceptual map of customers, financial services organisation

A process to segment your customers

Segmenting customers in business markets typically comprises a staged process that can be summarised as follows (Dowling, Lilien & Soni, 1993):

*Stage 1: **Define objectives for segmentation**.* The first step is to ensure tight alignment between the segmentation process and the strategy of the company. For instance if the strategy of the company is to develop and market logistics services, the segmentation needs to group customers according to their existing transport capabilities, networks and reach.

Stage 2: Macrosegmentation.

a) Obtain a sample that is representative or illustrative of the overall customer base.
b) Gather data on relevant characteristics such as potential needs, current configuration, asset base, etc.
c) Develop a macrosegmentation delineating first the customers that have broadly similar needs, thus reducing the total market to generally manageable segments.
d) Validate macrosegments showing that the resulting macrosegments differ from each other on the basis of the criteria specified in stage 1.

Stage 3: Microsegmentation.

a) Implement microsegmentation by further segmenting each macrosegment based on benefits and/or needs, resulting in microsegments of companies employing similar solutions to satisfy similar types of needs.
b) Validate microsegments as in Step 2 (d) above. Microsegment should be both analysed for both face validity and the statistical significance of differences.

Stage 4: Link microsegements to strategy.

a) Characterise microsegments for managerially relevant demographic, purchase decision-making, and organisational variables (segment descriptors). If done rigorously, analysis of variance-based methods or multiple discriminant analysis can be used to test for segment-specific differences.

b) Use the segmentation results to inform and re-develop the company's strategy.

As argued above, segmentation is a core foundation of a successful marketing and sales plan. Most action plans and sales approaches derive from a thorough understanding of customer segments. Therefore, sales organisations need to devote resources and time to ensure the identification of meaningful segments underpinned by solid analysis.

Account and relationship strategy

After the segmentation has been performed, the contact and relationship strategy with certain accounts needs to be defined. This process comprises the identification, analysis and specific action plans for selected accounts as follows:

Identification of potential account: Assess account attractiveness by identifying account size, purchasing volume, current suppliers, purchase criteria; identify the requirements and chances to win over the account based on price/promotion/place/product/service/information mix; estimate the amount of effort that will be needed to sell to this account.

Account analysis: Assess industry position and identify how the account is doing in its industry; identify the account's strategy and how they are planning to implement it; analyse the account's current financial situation; identify all the key activities within the client's business and which areas are likely to have problems; understand how these problems can be solved to benefit the customer; identify the employees and their role as part of the DMU; identify the main competitors and the products they are selling; identify what the main selection criteria are for a supplier; identify the typical buying steps and the buying process in the company; conduct a SWOT (strength, weaknesses, opportunities and threats) analysis for the account; analyse the value of the product service for the account.

Account strategy development: Set targets by estimating yearly volumes; define account objectives; determine the relationship wanted with the account; quantify investments needed to implement the plan.

Account action plan: Identify which account objectives are the most important ones; plan the objectives that can be accomplished during the coming year; identify all the activities needed to accomplish the objectives; review the selling proposition; identify how the objective/activities will help the customer achieve better results.

Sales and support programme: Identify how customer service problems can be solved; identify how the customer product problems can be solved; identify how you could be perceived as a higher added value provider by the account; identify how you can help the account to increase their sales revenue; identify how you can help the account to decrease their costs; communicate by making the account objectives and plan formally known to other colleagues within the organisation.

Account review: Review the account situation and see if the objectives and plan are still valid; review and communicate what has been accomplished so far on the account; review sales opportunities that have been lost and identify the reasons why.

Relationship strategy: A determinant of the type of relationship that will be developed with different accounts and account groups (Ingram, Laforge, Avila,

Schwepker & Williams, 2012). The nature of the relationship is determined not only by how an organisation will develop a relationship but also on account potential. Thus, for each of the target segments in the marketing strategy an account plan by customer or customer group is needed to estimate account relationship potential and objective. The attractiveness of an account in terms of sales volume will be the main factor in an organisation wanting to develop close and strong customer relationships. This must be a two-way process taking into account the relationship needs of the customer as well as the sales objectives of the supply firm. Customer needs are determined by the amount of risk involved in the purchase and the availability of substitutes. Some organisations may purchase large volumes of products or services but may see no added value in developing a relationship with the vendor because they regard the product as a commodity. All relationship development attempts of the vendor will therefore be wasted on that account (Donaldson & O'Toole, 2002).

Developing the value proposition

In business markets, the segmentation of customers should lead seamlessly to the development of customer value propositions (VP). The notion of VP was developed by Lanning and Michaels (1988) and has been pervasive in the marketing literature since then (De Bonis, Balinski & Allen, 2002).

We have defined value proposition as the set of expected benefits a company provides to its customers – the promise of the value to be delivered that is believed to have a positive impact on the customer's organisation.

What do you think?

Examples of value propositions:

Xerox Business Services: 'A business enterprise works on knowledge. Knowledge lives in documents. Our basic customer value proposition is that we will manage the customer's documents more effectively and more efficiently. We can do more with the document than any other company in the world!'[1]

William R. McDermott, senior vice president

3M: 'We at 3M make our living by developing products for specific customer applications. We view and present ourselves as a solution provider rather than product sellers. We go in, for example, and say to the customer, "We are specialists in protection, bonding, masking, etc. How can we improve the way you protect, bond, or mask materials in your own production of goods that you make?" It is from such dialog that potential applications are identified. And what can be better performance value than products developed to precisely match a specific user's specific application need?'[1]

Kevin Ries, Director of Marketing,
Industrial Tapes Division, 3M.

CoBank: '... is a financially strong, dependable, cooperative bank that provides credit and financial solutions to rural America. We are knowledgeable, responsive and committed to enhancing our capacity to deliver a superior customer experience and competitively priced products, while maintaining the safety and soundness of the bank for future generations. We consistently demonstrate our focus on rural America, repeatedly strive to be a trusted advisor for our customers and provide a consistent return on their investment and ownership in CoBank.'[2]

ESI: (world-leading provider in virtual product engineering). Users of OpenFOAM will experience the benefits of full control over their CFD software. Users can: modify the software freely, assess code quality, know what the software is doing, deploy OpenFOAM however they wish, e.g. own hardware, cloud, etc., influence development priorities, manage costs, i.e. choose when and how to get something for their money.[3]

Q: What would you add/change/delete in these value propositions?

Sources: 1 Mittal and Sheth (2001), 2 www.cobank.com, 3 www.esi-group.com

While the majority of enterprises use the term 'VP', less than 10 per cent of companies have successfully developed and communicated an actual value proposition (Frow & Payne, 2011). Structuring a value proposition typically entails three phases: quantifying value, comparing value and assessing the impact of the value created to the customer organisation (Figure 7.2).

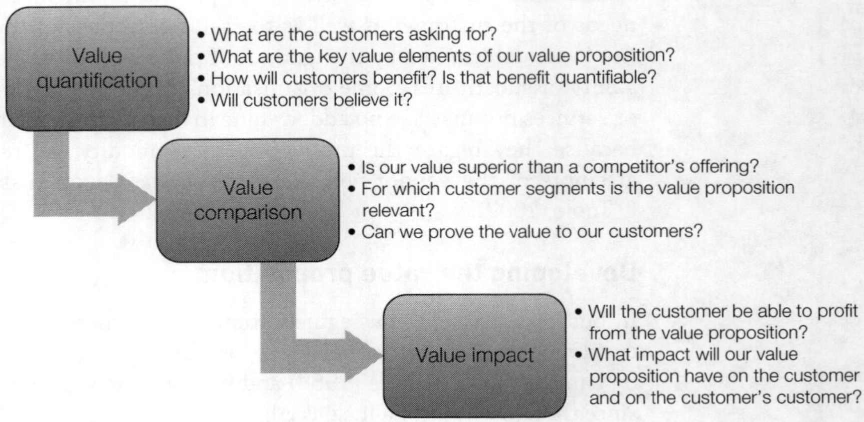

Figure 7.2 – Structuring a value proposition

There are, according to Anderson, Narus and Rossum (2006), three types of value propositions. Firstly, 'all benefits', which describes all benefits customers receive from an offering by addressing the question 'why should our company buy your offer?' Secondly, 'favourable points of difference', which determines all favourable points relative to the next best alternative by answering the question 'why should we buy your product/service instead of X?' Thirdly, 'resonating focus', a proposition that emphasises few points of difference with greatest impact by responding to the question 'what is most worthwhile for our company about your offering?' (Anderson et al., 2006).

When suppliers choose to emphasise the features of their offering that are more tightly linked to the customer's recognised value drivers, then it 'resonates' and the customer is more likely to choose the supplier's proposition over alternative offers. According to Anderson et al., (2006), the development of compelling value propositions requires the supplier to:

- Clarify points of difference/parity: points of parity are features that can also be found in the next best alternative. Points of difference make the supplier's offer better (or worse) than a competitor's offering in some way. When points of difference are positive, this allows the supplier to differentiate from other incumbents.
- Conduct customer value research or 'critical success factors' (CSFs) to determine the key requirements for the customer and the aspects of the supplier's offer and capabilities they value most.
- Document and demonstrate value: claiming that a customer can benefit from the suppliers' offer is not enough. Buyers need evidence and proof of the superiority of an offer rather than a promise of superior performance.
- Embed in organisational practice: in order to develop organisational capabilities that can be offered to a wider range of selected customers.

A well-established framework to analyse value propositions from business and organisations is provided by Treacy and Wiersema's (1995) value model. They argue that highly successful enterprises focus on operational excellence, product leadership or customer intimacy, although only outstanding organisations can pursue more than one of these simultaneously.

What do you think?

Analyse the following companies and discuss which 'value discipline' best describes each of them.

- Siemens
- Ikea
- Singapore Airlines
- Ryanair
- Dyson
- BMW
- HSBC

IMPLEMENTING SALES STRATEGIES: ACCOUNT AND CHANNEL STRATEGY

Above we outlined key aspects of defining sales strategies, namely *who* the customers are and *what* the offering is. Once the sales strategy has been defined, a granular and detailed approach needs to be defined to explain how this strategy will be implemented. Typically, the implementation of a sales strategy is materialised in the definition of *how* value will be added and the channels through which the customer will be served. We introduce the notion of value co-creation with customers, and outline key considerations for the selection and optimisation of channels.

Co-creating customer value

We argue that an organisation's competitive advantage today is largely dependent on its ability to understand subtle mechanisms to create value and to develop the systems to make value creation work (Lemmens, Donaldson & Marcos, 2014). Knowledge and know-how are increasingly the source of competitive advantage. We also claim that there is a shift in focus from just selling products and services to delivering value propositions and co-creating value with the customer. The principles that underpin the sales strategies for value co-creation are different from those that characterise traditional sales. These principles are outlined below.

Principle 1: Focus on ends instead of means

In the traditional sales approach, the salesperson provides value to their customers by selling them a product or a service. This is also referred to as value-in-exchange. In the co-creation approach, the customer ultimately defines the value of a supplier's goods and services. The customer perceives and assesses the value based on their total experience dealing with the supplier and using their goods and services based on their needs and requirements. The co-creation approach implies a protracted sales cycle, which requires:

- Salespeople to focus on customer experience rather than on mere customer satisfaction.
- Salespeople to acquire knowledge about the customer business processes rather than product knowledge.
- The whole organisation to become customer-centric rather than product-centric (Figure 7.3).

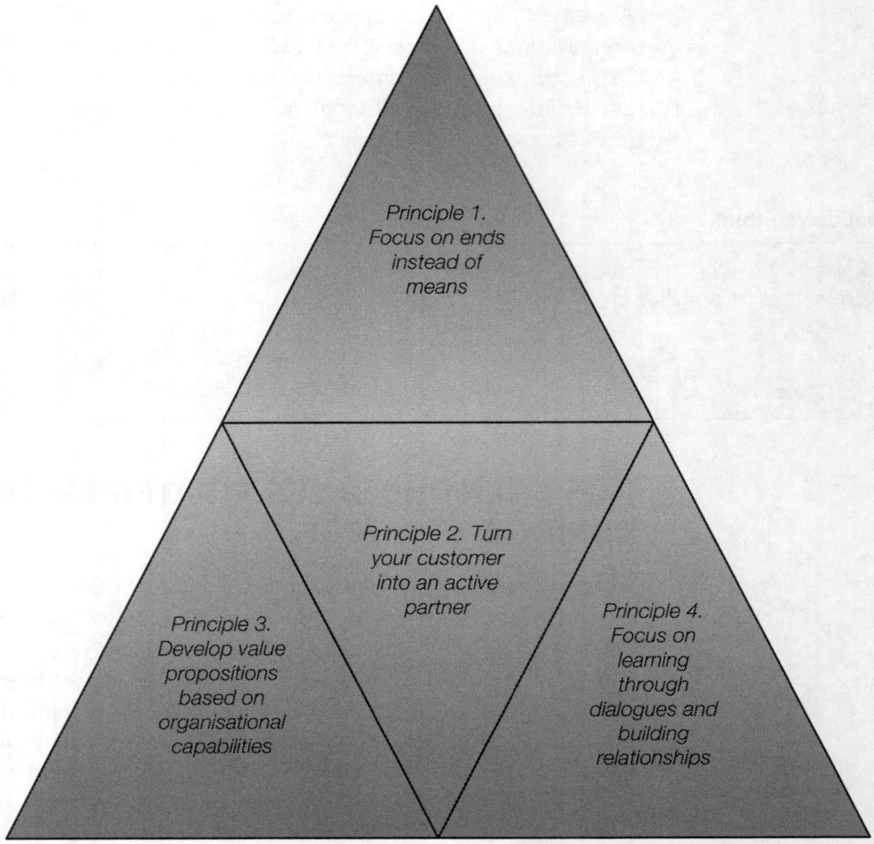

Figure 7.3 – Key principles of customer value co-creation

Principle 2: Turn your customer into an active partner

In the sales approach, suppliers tend to view customers as 'adversaries', who they must persuade to buy their offer. Consultative selling and solution selling methods helped introduce the notion that, in order to persuade customers, you have to learn about their problems and needs by means of a two-way dialogue. In order to define the solution for the customer, the customer must engage in a collaborative and dialogic process with the salesperson. Often, customers are encouraged to participate early at the product or service development stage. The co-creation approach requires a very different conception of roles and sales processes, as shown in Figure 7.4:

- Customer: changes from being an informant to being a partner.
- Information gathering: evolves from classic interviews to ongoing dialogue between the partners. In the sales approach, the salesperson follows well-crafted interview methods that enable them to uncover the problems and needs of their customers. In the co-creation approach, the salesperson and the customer have an open dialogue on how they can help each other co-create value to solve not only pressing current problems but also future challenges.
- The design of the solution changes, from the salesperson matching the customer's needs to their products and service, to the salesperson and the customer analysing the best available information together and co-defining

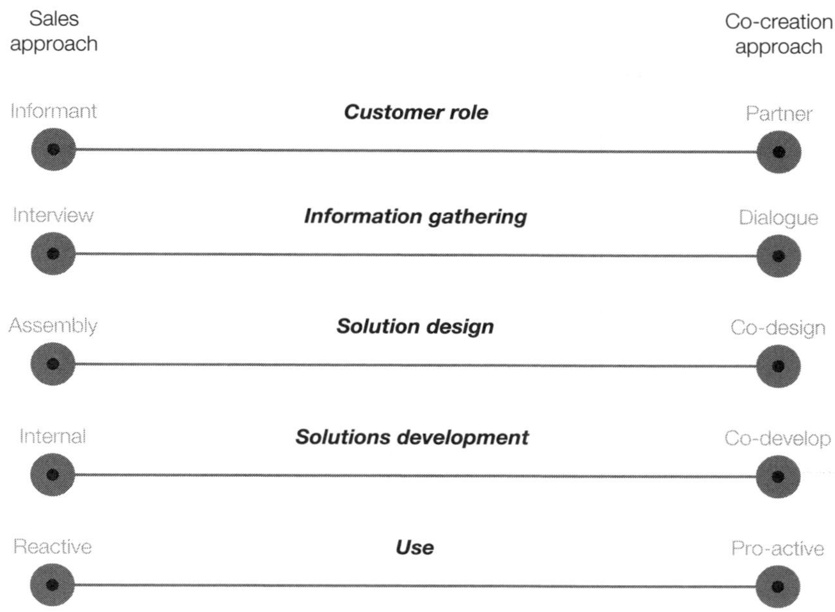

Figure 7.4 – The roles of the seller and the customer in the co-creation approach

the appropriate solution – sometimes to well defined problems, often to ill-structured challenges.

- The development of the solution, moves from internal development and subsequent contract negotiation, towards a method where the supplier and the customer develop and implement the solution together, sharing risks and benefits.
- Installation and use of the solution is typically reactive in traditional sales approaches. In a co-creation approach, the development of the solution is not considered completed after the product or service is configured and installed: it does not end until the customer is able to achieve their desired outcomes. Helping the customer use the value proposition to its maximum benefit is the most important part of the value proposition development. The supplier remains proactive during the whole process.

Principle 3: Develop value propositions based on organisational capabilities

In the sales approach, the salesperson's objective is to sell their products and services. They employ sales methods to identify the customer needs and link these with the features of their offering. In this context, solutions consist of different combinations of largely standardised products and services. In the co-creation approach, the salesperson does not present the organisation's value propositions but instead presents its capabilities. From there, both the seller and the customer investigate how these capabilities could help the customer to improve its performance or to deliver its mission better. The focus is on how to share resources and capabilities to jointly develop solutions that will help the customer do their 'job'. The salesperson's products and services are the means to help the customer create value and not the end themselves.

In this context, the supplier's know-how, partners and skills are equally important elements of the total value proposition. Approaching customers based on organisational capabilities rather than on individual products or services requires identifying what the supplier and the customer can do together. It is not about 'what do you need?' but 'what can we do together?' Typically, the dialogue that characterises this approach is very open-ended, a structured and focused conversation with a meaningful purpose. The aim is to uncover areas where the customer and the salesperson can collaborate.

Principle 4: Focus on learning through dialogues and building relationships.
In the traditional sales approach, the more a salesperson visits his/her customers the more chances they have to sell. The rationale is that frequent sales calls ensure that the supplier does not miss any opportunity to sell their products and services when the need arises within the customer. Through these interactions, the customer learns about the salesperson's products and services and the salesperson learns about the customer's problems and needs. Both use that information to select the most appropriate strategy to interact with each other. The learning is limited to improving the efficiency of existing processes. In the co-creation approach, interactions are part of dialogues between the salespeople and their customers. The dialogues are centred on various issues, including the customer's customers; trends and evolutions in the market that affects the supplier's customer and their customers. Organisations willing to become engaged in co-creation will have to be prepared to question their own organisational practices and beliefs. Salespeople need to identify with whom and when to co-create, develop relationships based on trust and transparency and organise and manage multi-level dialogues.

Channel strategy

A channel is the customer contact point through which the company and the customers can interact with one another (Neslin & Shankar, 2009). In today's market place, most organisations operate in a multichannel environment. Thus, multichannel customer management is defined as 'the design, deployment, coordination, and evaluation of channels ... with the goal of enhancing customer value through effective customer acquisition, retention, and development' (Neslin et al., 2006, p. 95). Channel strategies ensure that accounts receive selling effort coverage in an efficient and effective manner (Ingram et al., 2012). Channels in business-to-business relationships include Internet, telesales, distributors/business partners, retailers, field sales forces, technical and specialised sales forces and key account teams/managers.

Types of channels
According to Zoltners et al. (2004), based on the nature of the activities that are required, the selling organisation has to decide who is going to perform which type of selling activity though which channel. Costs are usually key drivers when choosing the channel strategy; the other driver is often quality of the customer experience. Some activities when performed by a direct sales force can generate response where other methods would generate no response at all. Efficiency and effectiveness provide a natural framework for examining the costs and benefits of alternative go-to-market strategies. Efficiency is measured by the amount of customer response based on the sales investment. Effectiveness is measured by the results of the customer contacts (see Figure 7.5). In many industries hybrid go-to-market strategies are being developed whereby the role of the traditional sales force is complemented with new online channels. Table 7.1 outlines some of the advantages and disadvantages of various channels (Linda, 2012):

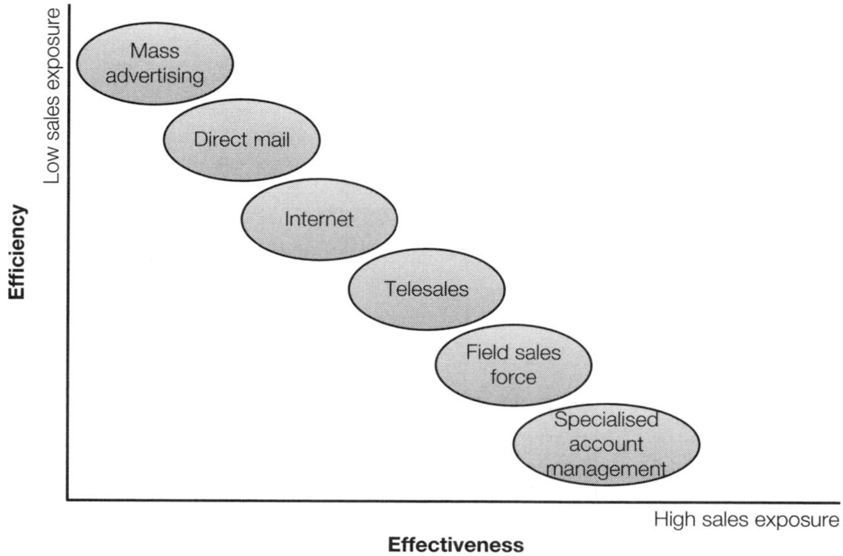

Figure 7.5 – Channel strategy

Table 7.1 – Advantages and disadvantages of various channels

Type of channel	Advantages	Disadvantages
Personal selling, own sales force	• Established relationship with the customer and development of deep customer understanding. • Better/expert/technical product knowledge. • Enhances loyalty. • Higher levels of control over the activities. • Focused in selling your own products and services. • Can offer value added services. • Higher levels of control over brand image, positioning, etc. • Faster communications to the market.	• Very expensive channel, not suitable for all goods/services, or for all customers. • Coverage and network may be limited. • When solid relationships are established, the sales representative can take business with him/her when leaving. • If variable remuneration packages are established, these might affect focus on bonus and not customer satisfaction. • Cannot call on large customer base. • Requires big commitment to recruiting and training.
Internet	• Low cost, overhead. • High profit potential. • Instantly global access if desired, wide exposure. • Easy to upgrade and to update. • Often easy to use. • Can be linked to other sites. • Can provide a good source of customer feedback/research. • Increasingly higher levels of customer confidence given increased security.	• Lack of one-to-one interaction, can be perceived as impersonal. • Instances of security problems, trust. • Requires large back office and logistics investment (inventory, warehousing, packing, shipping, record keeping, billing, etc). • Decisions often driven by price concerns.
Telesales	• Direct contact. • Inexpensive, and often very efficient. • Can reach remote areas. • Can be easily integrated within a CRM system. • Provides personal contact. • Can be used to generate leads.	• May become unpopular with customers when cold, outbound calls. • If outsourced off-shore, language barriers and cross-cultural understanding issues. • Need to structure and clarify the role of inbound vs. outbound calls. • Need to define processes for effective follow-up.

(Continued)

Table 7.1 – *(Continued)*

Type of channel	Advantages	Disadvantages
Distributors	• Focused customer base. • The distributor assumes financial and inventory risk. • Often provide an additional sales force. • Have potential to cover larger geographies. • Carry the final shipping expense. • Often technically trained. • Can offer bundled pricing.	• May carry products from the competition and thus have low levels of loyalty. • Can control final pricing to end customers. • Can be difficult to manage and have their own agenda. • The manufacturer can lose control of product presentation. • Often requires training/education costs. • Complex relationships that need to be managed strategically.

Channel selection

When articulating the channel strategy, organisations need to decide how to prioritise channels. A starting point is to identify how customers choose a certain channel or channels. Table 7.2 summarises factors that affect customers' choice of channel (see Black, Lockett, Ennew, Winklhofer & McKechnie, 2002; Jindal, Reinartz, Krafft & Hoyer, 2007).

Table 7.2 – Influencing factors in choice of channel

	Influencing factors
Channel attributes	Ease of use Convenience Cost Information quality Aesthetic appeal Service quality Risk/Security Personal contact Assortment Integration Privacy
Customer attributes	Involvement Demographics Lifestyle Previous experience Channel expertise
Product attributes	Complexity Risk Price Availability
Organisation attributes	Incentives/promotion Channel provision Image/brand
Situational attributes	Physical setting Social setting

An in-depth understanding of the customer and the advantages and disadvantages of each channel will provide the foundation to select the most appropriate combination of channels.

Did you know?

Proliferation of routes to market and the need for management of multiple channels have been cited as reasons for sales becoming a strategic issue. We have suggested that the need for more sophisticated segmentation, account and relationship planning and developing a credible and long-term value proposition drive sales as a strategic issue, yet only a small percentage of companies have a board-level member with a sales background.

Channel management

Once the channel selection is made, companies need to manage and continuously refine operations across channels. Wilson and Daniel (2007) argue that increasingly new capabilities in e-commerce, and customer demands on price and service are leading to shifting combinations of channels being offered to the customer in the search for advantage and differentiation. Marketing and sales managers in this context need to develop 'dynamic capabilities'; in other words, the processes to 'integrate, reconfigure, gain and release resources to match and even create market change' (Eisenhardt & Martin, 2000 p. 1107). Organisations that possess dynamic capabilities for addressing the challenges of multichannel contexts are characterised as having (Wilson and Daniel, 2007 p. 14):

- Active review of the route to market in a cycle of strategy development and implementation.
- The alignment of route to market with different segment and product characteristics.
- The creation of innovative channel combinations.
- Iterative development of customer value proposition melding planned and experiential approaches.
- Integration of processes and IT to support multichannel customer relationships.
- An organisational structure which balances the need for innovation and integration.
- Metrics and rewards which reflect multichannel customer behaviour.

SUMMARY

In this chapter we have presented key tools and frameworks to develop a sales strategy. First, approaches to segment customers in business markets were presented. Then, ways to develop compelling customer value propositions were outlined. The chapter also outlined contemporary approaches to co-create value with customers and key considerations to effectively formulate the channel strategy.

QUESTIONS

- Imagine a company that sells construction products such as cement and aggregates. Develop a framework for segmenting its business customers.
- Discuss the view that selling has always been customer-based and new approaches are merely a case of 'the emperor's new clothes'.
- Unilever traditionally organised their marketing and sales around brands. Now their sales organisation is based on customer account management teams. What environmental factors may have precipitated this type of organisational change?
- Take the example of IBM Global Services. What are the different ways in which this company can co-create value with its customers?

- Sales managers are under pressure to make the sales effort more effective and more efficient. Explain how integration of multichannel routes to market with the sales operation might achieve this objective.

REFERENCES

Anderson, J. C., Narus, J. A. & Rossum, W. van. (2006). Customer value propositions in business markets. *Harvard Business Review*, 84(3), 91–99.

Baumgartner, T., Hatami, H. & Vander Ark, J. (2012). *Sales Growth: Five Proven Strategies from the World's Sales Leaders.* Hoboken, NJ: Wiley.

Black, N. J., Lockett, A., Ennew, C., Winklhofer, H. & McKechnie, S. (2002). Modelling consumer choice of distribution channels: An illustration from financial services. *International Journal of Bank Marketing*, 20(4), 161–173.

De Bonis, N. J., Balinski, E. & Allen, P. (2002). *Value-based Marketing for Bottom-line Success.* New York: McGraw-Hill.

Donaldson, B. & O'Toole, T. (2002). *Strategic Market Relationships: From Strategy to Implementation*. Chichester: Wiley.

Dowling, G. R., Lilien, G. L. & Soni, P. K. (1993). Business market segmentation procedure for product planning. *Journal of Business-to-Business Marketing*, 1(4), 31–62.

Eisenhardt, K. M. & Martin, J. A. (2000). Dynamic capabilities: What are they? *Strategic Management Journal*, 21(10–11), 1105–1121.

Frow, P. & Payne, A. (2011). A stakeholder perspective of the value proposition concept. *European Journal of Marketing*, 45(1/2), 223–240.

Ingram, T. N., Laforge, R. W., Avila, R. A., Schwepker, C. H. & Williams, M. R. (2012). *Sales Management: Analysis and Decision Making* (8th edn). London: M. E. Sharpe Inc.

Jindal, R. P., Reinartz, W., Krafft, M. & Hoyer, W. D. (2007). Determinants of the variety of routes to market. *International Journal of Research in Marketing*, 24(1), 17–29.

Kotler, P. (1991). *Marketing Management: Analysis, Planning and Control* (7th edn). New Jersey: Prentice Hall.

Lanning, M. & Michaels, E. (1988). *A Business is a Value Delivery System*. McKinsey Staff Paper No. 41 July.

Lemmens, R., Donaldson, B. & Marcos, J. (2014). *From Selling to Co-creating*. Amsterdam: BIS Publishers.

Linda, G. (2012). *Advantages and Disadvantages of Alternative Channels of Distribution.* Retrieved 2 April 2014, from http://www.gla-mktg.com/id22.html.

Mcdonald, M. (2012). *Market Segmentation: How to Do It and How to Profit from It*. Chichester: Wiley.

Mittal, B. & Sheth, J. N. (2001). *Value Space: Winning the Battle for Market Leadership*. New York: McGraw-Hill.

Neslin, S. A., Grewal, D., Leghorn, R., Shankar, V., Teerling, M. L., Thomas, J. S. & Verhoef, P. C. (2006). Challenges and opportunities in multichannel customer management. *Journal of Service Research*, 9(2), 95–112.

Neslin, S. A. & Shankar, V. (2009). Key issues in multichannel customer management: Current knowledge and future directions. *Journal of Interactive Marketing*, 23(1), 70–81.

Rangan, V. K. (1994). Segmenting customers in mature industrial markets: An application, Harvard Business School Case, 9-594-089.

Treacy, M. & Wiersema, M. (1995). *The Discipline of the Market Leaders*. London: HarperCollins.

Wilson, H. & Daniel, E. (2007). The multi-channel challenge: A dynamic capability approach. *Industrial Marketing Management*, 36, 10–20.

Zoltners, A. A., Sinha, P. & Lorimer, S. E. (2004). *Sales Force Design for Strategic Advantage*. New York: Palgrave Macmillan.

8 KEY ACCOUNT MANAGEMENT

OVERVIEW

Unprecedented levels of change in business markets and customer demands have made managing key customers a crucial process for companies that aspire to remain competitive and profitable. In this chapter, we present key challenges senior business development leaders face in the design and implementation of key account management (KAM) programmes. Defining a high-performing key account management approach requires a clear selection of strategic customers. These customers will require differentiated levels of investment, thus relationship strategies across the customer portfolio need to be articulated. Appropriate relationship types will have to be agreed and the relevant structures and roles created. The implementation of strategic account management initiatives will often follow several phases that span various years and involve a number of intra- and inter-organisational practices. This chapter describes the importance and relevance of key account plans, holistic account measurement systems and an approach to continuously review strategic account management programmes.

LEARNING OBJECTIVES

This chapter aims to enable the reader to:

- Systematically identify the portfolio of key customers.
- Plan the mechanisms and approaches to best engage and develop relationships with these customers.
- Understand the appropriate structures for the organisation and roles for the key account managers.

DEFINITIONS

Key account: a customer of strategic importance to the supplier.
Key account management: an integrated process to manage customers of strategic importance for the firm in a profitable way.

INTRODUCTION

Managing accounts strategically has become a key requirement for companies that wish to achieve competitive advantage and succeed in business markets. This is due to unprecedented levels of change in the sales environment (Jones, Brown, Zoltners & Weitz, 2005), as discussed in Chapter 1, that are prompting sales organisations to redefine their customer management strategies and associated structures. Changes in the market have gradually triggered the evolution of sales professions from predictable and structured sets of activities (see Moncrief, 1986) to complex and dynamic relationship management roles (Moncrief & Marshall, 2005; Davies, Ryals & Holt, 2010). This means that classic activities of selling to customers primarily focused on the product or the service, have evolved towards consultative selling and account management roles, focused on the customer business and on adding value beyond the product or service.

Defining strategic account management

A key account is a customer of strategic importance to the supplier (McDonald & Woodburn, 2007). KAM has become one of the most significant relationship marketing development over the last few decades (Abratt & Kelly, 2002). Shapiro and Wyman (1981, p. 104) described KAM as 'an extension, improvement, and outgrowth of personal selling'. Later, in the mid-1990s, KAM emerged as a discipline with challenges and processes distinct from those of traditional selling (McDonald, Millman & Rogers, 1997). Therefore, rather than a tool or technique, key account management is conceptualised as an integrated process for the profitable management of customer relationships (McDonald & Woodburn, 2007; Ryals, 2008).

In KAM, emphasis is placed in the 'integrated' and 'profitable' dimensions of supplier–customer relationships. When a company is dealing with its most important customers, the key account manager is often the person responsible for integrating the response and the delivery of products and services. Processes need to be aligned, across marketing, operations, finance and logistics. This is important since manufacturing companies, for instance, may schedule production and delivery in the most efficient manner possible. This means that similar orders are manufactured and grouped together. When a strategic customer has a requirement that does not fulfil pre-defined parameters, this needs to be acknowledged and often given priority.

The other important dimension of managing accounts strategically is profitability. Suppliers benefit from introducing KAM by increasing their share of customer spend and revenues. It can be more efficient to manage a few larger customers than a lot of smaller ones. Introducing these approaches may help achieve cost reductions, for instance, optimising inventory costs. In addition, managing important customers strategically may improve account team communication, the gathering and disseminating of customer information and enable an increased focus on resource utilisation. However, customers will often try to bargain away these benefits in the form of lower prices, higher services, or both (Kalwani & Narayandas, 1995). Thus, the relationship with the customer needs careful management or it can become unprofitable (Piercy & Lane, 2006).

The primary aim of key account management is to build relationships that will enable the creation of value that otherwise would not be created. Value is therefore a central concept in key business-to-business relationships. Pardo, Henneberg, Mouzas & Naude (2006) argue that there are three types of key account management value: exchange value, proprietary value, and relational value. *Exchange customer value* is deemed critical and needs to be demonstrated to ensure sustainability of the KAM programme. It often includes enhanced supplier–customer coordination, better operational integration, broader customisation of offerings, better responsiveness, and inter-connected information and communication technologies. *Proprietary supplier value* is the type that most often justifies KAM programmes and refers to the achievement of efficiencies for the supplier. These may be realised through better customer processes and focused resources. *Relational value* is created as a result of the existence of the relationship and requires the cooperation of both parties. It can manifest in joint innovation and discovery.

FOUNDATIONS OF KEY ACCOUNT MANAGEMENT

Managing accounts strategically can be seen as an organisational capability that comprises a set of complex *structural designs* and *processes* that need to be taken into account in the definition of a strategic account programme. The following subsections describe some of these factors, positioning them as the foundations or design parameters of key account management. Executives can take these as guidelines to configure and define the key parameters of the architecture of KAM programmes. Important dynamic processes for managing strategic customers are also outlined.

Types of business to business relationships

The essence of managing accounts strategically is defining relationships models that fit both the purposes of both the supplier and the customer. There are at least five different types of key account relationships in a KAM relational development model (Ryals & McDonald, 2008). It is important to understand that none of the relationship types is intrinsically better,or worse – they are just different. Nor is it necessarily the case that a company would try to move from one type to another – this in fact would not be appropriate if the customer had expressed a preference for a particular type of relationship. The relational development model comprises five different structures. The relationships range from arms-length to highly integrated. The type of relationship is determined by the strategic intent and commitment of the supplier and of the customer (McDonald & Woodburn, 2007; Ryals & McDonald, 2008).

Exploratory relationships

Exploratory KAM is about potential key accounts. These are relationships where the two companies are initiating communications and contacts, but no commitment has been made to working together. Exploratory KAM is, by definition, an arms-length relationship. Signalling is important, and it is critical to ensure that the customer receives the message the supplier seeks to send. How the supplier introduces the organisation and the account managers and attention to details of business relationships (sales meeting organisation, style of communication, etc.) may be very important here, as the customer will make judgements about the supplier based on these. In addition, the supplier's corporate brand and public statements will influence the customer's decision to pursue the relationship further. Exploratory KAM relationships may be expensive, time-consuming and unpredictable (McDonald & Woodburn, 2007; Ryals & McDonald, 2008) (Figure 8.1).

Basic KAM relationship

The basic KAM relationship is where the two companies are doing business, but still at arms-length. The expression 'basic' should not be taken to imply that these are not valuable relationships. They can be very valuable indeed, and large volumes of business are often undertaken on a transactional basis in a wide range of industries. The most frequent shape of this relationship is one where a key account manager is

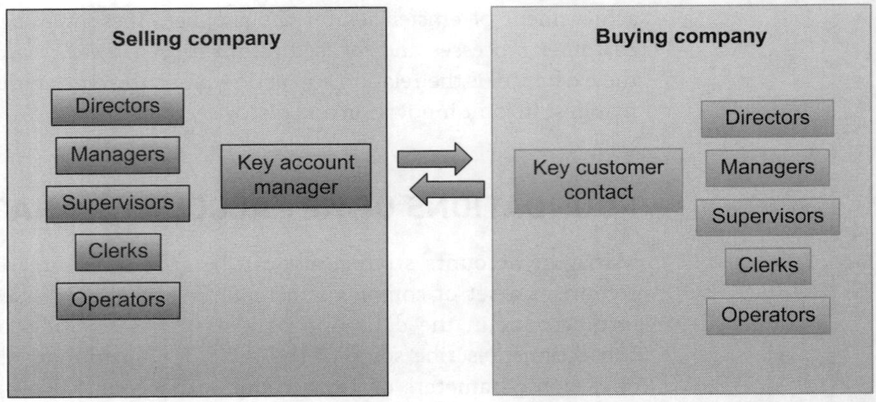

Figure 8.1 – Exploratory KAM relationship

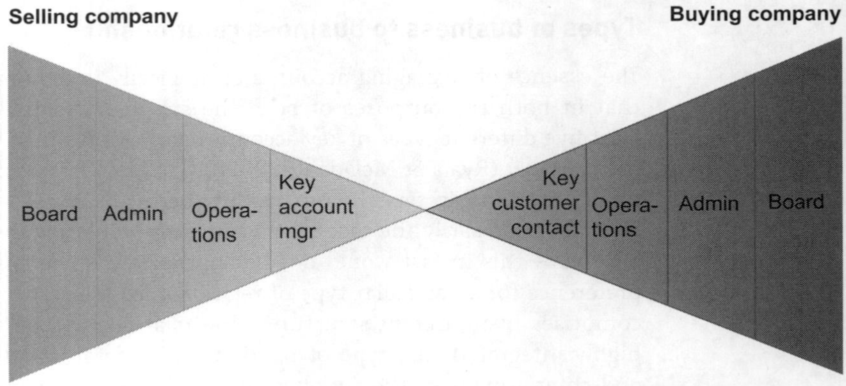

Figure 8.2 – Basic KAM relationship

talking to one customer contact; thus, this relationship type is known as the 'bow tie' or as the 'butterfly' (McDonald & Woodburn, 2007; Ryals & McDonald, 2008) (Figure 8.2).

Cooperative KAM relationship
Cooperative relationships are characterised by multiple links between two companies. Many key account relationships can be classified as cooperative. These relationships require coordination efforts and clear communication patterns, as otherwise problems and conflict may emerge. Sometimes, cooperative KAM relationships are in transition to interdependent status. At this point, both parties are investing in the relationship but it can still prove an expensive failure (McDonald & Woodburn, 2007; Ryals & McDonald, 2008) (Figure 8.3).

Interdependent KAM relationship
Interdependent KAM relationships are close, collaborative relationships between suppliers and customers. They are characterised by a high degree of trust and openness. These relationships are underpinned by a desire to achieve common goals. They are often solid relationships and are represented by 'diamond' shaped diagrams (McDonald & Woodburn, 2007; Ryals & McDonald, 2008) (Figure 8.4).

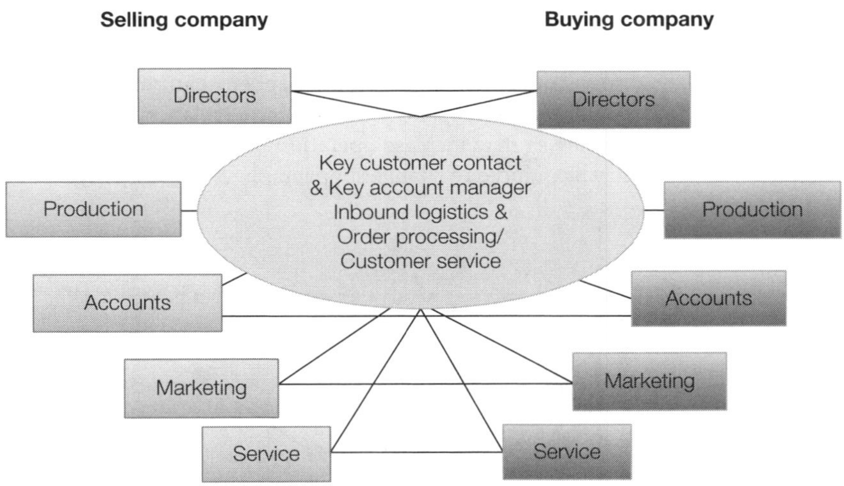

Figure 8.3 – Cooperative KAM relationship

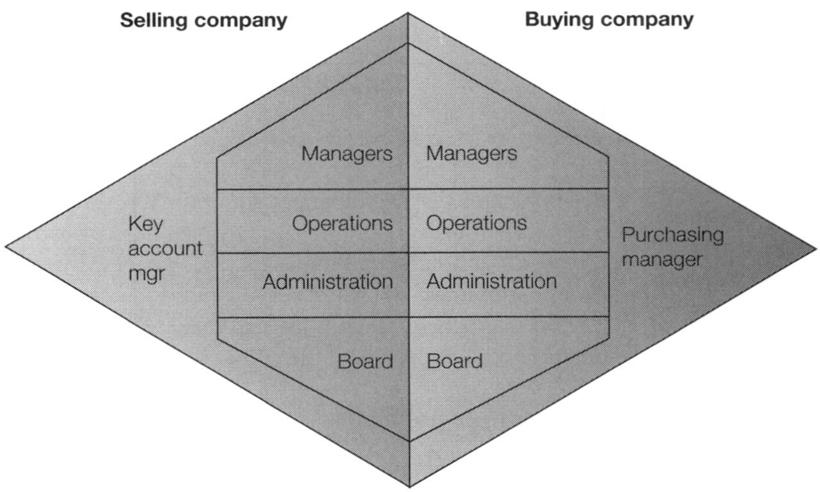

Figure 8.4 – Interdependent KAM relationship

Integrated KAM relationship

Integrated KAM relationships are characterised by blurred boundaries between the two companies. These types of relationships are sometimes seen in professional services or the manufacturing of advanced technology where the supplier literally moves into their customers' premises and they operate as though the two businesses are one. This characteristic makes integrated KAM relationships very difficult to break apart, and the costs of switching are generally high (McDonald & Woodburn, 2007; Ryals & McDonald, 2008).

To best define the optimal relationship type, two aspects need to be taken into consideration. The first is the driver of relationship intent. Generally speaking, it is the customer who dictates the degree of commitment that governs the relationship and thus the ideal relationship type. When the intent of the supplier is not matched by similar degree of commitment by the customer, a phenomenon termed the 'supplier delusion' may occur. This zone is where the supplier thinks it is more important to the customer than it really is, so it over-commits time and money to the relationship. The second aspect is that disintegration can happen at any stage of a KAM relationship, although it is rarer for interdependent or integrated relationships to cease. The closeness of the two businesses may increase operational costs. However, there are cases where customers may be induced to change suppliers, such as after mergers and acquisitions (Figure 8.5).

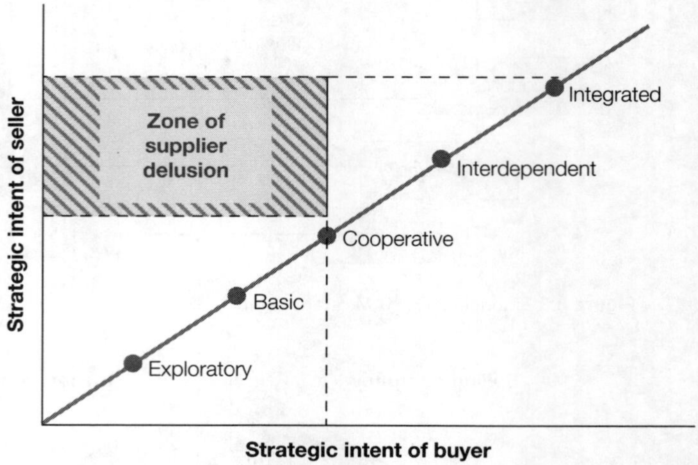

Figure 8.5 – Strategic intent of seller and buyer

Relationship types are important for optimal KAM performance. In addition to relationship form, the degree of inter-firm fitness has an important bearing on relationship effectiveness and ultimately financial performance. Inter-firm fit acts as a multiplier of coordination mechanisms, synergies and resources devoted to the customer. A high degree of congruence between the customer and the supplier intent improve the effects of organisational support and the efforts of account managers (Richards, 2006).

Key customer portfolio

Best practice key account management materialises in processes for managing customers of strategic importance *in the context* of a wider group of customers. Thus, a foundation of KAM is the idea that the company's customers form a portfolio. The portfolio concept dates back as far as Fiocca (1982) and has since been widely adopted by companies implementing KAM.

The portfolio is constructed based on the attractiveness of each key account to the business (vertical axis), bearing in mind that all of these are important customers because they are all key accounts, but that some are more attractive than others based on their revenues, profit, potential for growth, corporate brand, or other factors. The other dimension of the portfolio is the supplier's relative business strength with each customer (horizontal axis), measured relative to the best competitor. Thus, on the horizontal axis, the supplier will either be better than its best competitor and have high business strength (left side) or weaker than the best competitor and therefore have low strength (right side) (Figure 8.6).

The key customer portfolio

Once the portfolio is constructed, each of the key accounts can be plotted on it. Each circle represents a key account (or a customer segment) and the larger the circle the

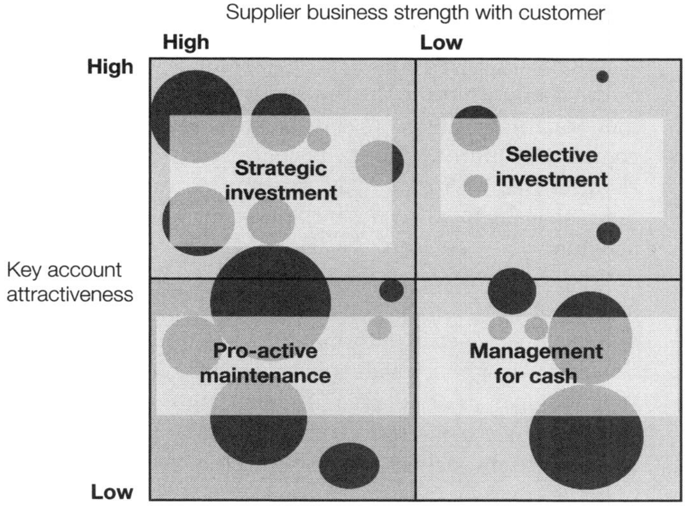

Figure 8.6 – The key customer portfolio

bigger the current or potential business. The customer portfolio can be used to define appropriate relationship strategies that often can be distinguished as:

- Strategic investment.
- Selective investment.
- Manage for cash.
- Pro-active maintenance.

Key accounts plotted in the top half of the portfolio are strategically important and need investment, although the supplier may not be able to afford to invest in all of them and some will therefore be selective investments. Key accounts plotted in the lower half of the portfolio need to be managed. These relationships are not priorities for additional investment.

Key account managers are sometimes puzzled about the 'low / low' box in the portfolio matrix, which is labelled 'Manage for Cash'. How can this be a key account, they ask, when it is not very attractive to the supplier and it performs less well than its competitors? The answer is that this matrix is constructed relative to all the supplier's key accounts, not relative to the rest of the customers. All the key accounts are important customers. However, there can be some big, important customers who fall into the 'low / low' box. For example, some of the major retailers (e.g. Wal-Mart) put a lot of pressure on their suppliers to reduce prices, whilst demanding high service levels. These customers may not be interested in partnerships with these suppliers but since they are well-established players, they are important customers to have.

What do you think?

In an interview we conducted with one senior procurement executive as part of a research project, he suggested that if a supplier told him that they were a key account he saw it as an opportunity to squeeze them further on price. This suggests that the spirit of KAM is important but often absent, and raises the question of how to manage an effective KAM programme. Davies and Ryals (2014) found nine measures of effectiveness in KAM practices, with customer-focused outcomes such as customer satisfaction, relational improvement and joint investments the most achievable rather than short-term growth or profit targets. In a separate study in the hotel sector, Wang and Brennan (2014) demonstrated the need for, and benefits of, linking revenue management and KAM.

Account business planning

A fundamental tenet of effective account management is the long-term orientation of the relationship and the investment in the strategic account. Key account management orientation refers to the extent to which a supplier adopts KAM as part of the company's culture and the behaviours they promote (Tzempelikos, 2006). Companies characterised by strong KAM orientation feature attitudes and behaviours such as top management commitment, inter-functional coordination and customer-oriented activities.

One such customer-oriented activity is the systematic gathering, synthesis and sharing of customer insights. By customer insights we mean both market intelligence and customer-specific information about their strategies, structures and processes. Customer insights provide a platform for joint learning and thus help the effective functioning of cross-functional teams within and across organisations. Furthermore, KAM business planning is focused on identifying opportunities whose exploitation may lead to mutual benefits for both the customer and the supplier. A key premise of value creation and benefit realisation is the utilisation of customer insights and market opportunities. The formalisation of a KAM programme (for instance through the design and completion of key account plans) enhances the utilisation of customer knowledge (Salojärvi, Sainio & Tarkiainen, 2010).

Joint business planning, particularly in inter-dependent and integrated relationships, enables the identification of resources needed to realise the opportunities identified in the insight generation phase. Thus, structured approaches to agree on joint future exploitation strategies are more likely to attract top management support and investment. Top management involvement with key accounts in terms of social interaction with customers can help further strategic relationships. Moreover, senior managers can support KAM by aligning the goals of different functional areas in the company to the interests of strategic customers (Guesalaga, 2014).

Overall, we argue that best practice companies are able to translate insights and investments into detailed action planning. In so doing, shared customer–supplier developments can be more effective in creating value and new solutions and less risky than endeavours led only by the supplier.

Definition and delivery of the value proposition

A key difference between customer management and strategic customer management is the degree to which value propositions are specific to the account (McDonald et al. 1997; Homburg, Workman & Jensen, 2002). Whilst consumer markets and companies supplying to large portfolios of customers tend to standardise their products and services, suppliers of key accounts are often expected to tailor aspects and sometimes the entire value proposition. In particular powerful customers may require tailored solutions or demand exclusivity of supply if it is believed that this will enhance their competitive position.

Thus, key account and senior managers need to decide about the balance between standardisation/customisation of the offering. Higher levels of customisation will likely increase the costs of delivery, potentially jeopardising customer profitability. In terms of quality of the offering for the customer, a firm may not be able to guarantee superior performance in all dimensions of a new, customised value proposition simultaneously. For instance, some companies (such as Dyson and Apple) are known to be product leaders, i.e. the design and performance features of their products are often recognised. Other organisations have developed operational excellence (e.g. McDonald's) whilst other are known for delivering superior customer experience and intimacy (e.g. Singapore Airlines). Only a few organisations can excel in all of these dimensions of their value proposition (Treacy & Wiersema, 1995), as we argued in the previous chapter.

Value is increasingly co-created with the customer (Vargo & Lusch, 2008; Lemmens, Donaldson & Marcos, 2014) in the context of the relationship with the key account. Therefore, rather than merely 'adding' or 'delivering' value, the work of the strategic account manager is to design and to engage in approaches so the supplier's capabilities can be matched with the key account's requirements, enabling the *co-creation* of value.

The role of strategic account managers

As argued above, strategic account managers (SAMs) or key account managers (KAMs) are boundary-spanning individuals whose function is to coordinate the deployment of the company's resources and who are responsible for enhancing and further developing strategic accounts relationships. KAMs operate across two key domains, the customer organisation and their own business (Holt, 2003). In the customer organisation, KAMs focus on identifying new business opportunities, developing new ideas and building strategic relationships. Internally, besides account and goal achievement planning, KAMs spend a significant amount of time managing the internal team, promoting internal alignment and facilitating the interpretation and implementation of service contracts. The importance of the internal dimension of the KAMs has gained relevance and recognition over the last few years (Guesalaga & Johnston, 2010; Speakman & Ryals, 2012) (Figure 8.7).

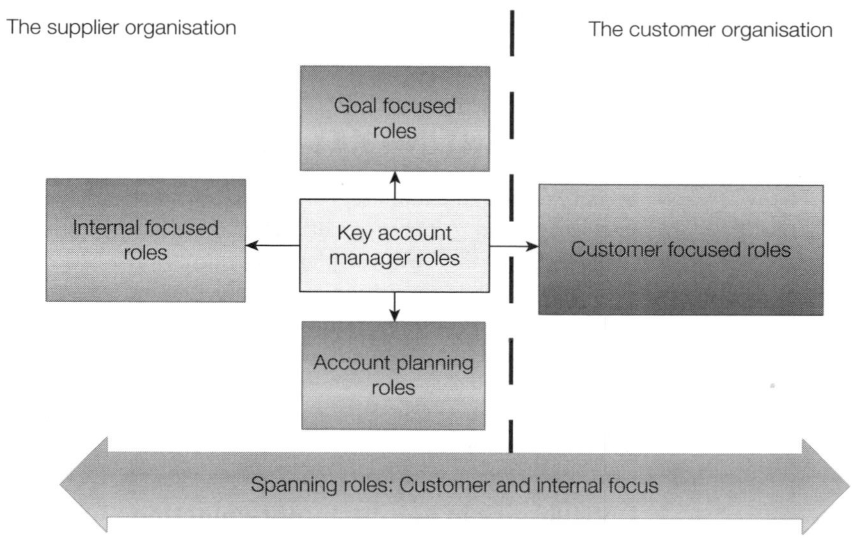

Figure 8.7 – The key account manager roles

Another dimension of the strategic account manager that has traditionally been recognised as critical is that of the relationship manager. Davies et al. (2010) conducted a study of the key activities of relationship managers, arguing that they have evolved from those found in traditional selling roles; these activities are summarised in Table 8.1.

Table 8.1 – Activity clusters of relationship managers

Activities of relationship managers	
Managing information	Selling and negotiating externally and internally
Undertaking strategic marketing and planning	Ability to work with different types of accounts
Generating customer knowledge	Operational delivery and supply chain management
Being aware of organisational/corporate cultures	Managing external and internal relationships
Managing complexity, risk and uncertainty	Managing the account teams
Strategy development	Prioritising customer relationships
Strategy implementation	

Source: Based on ideas from Davies et al. (2010)

The role of the key account manager requires a set of competences and skills that are more complex than those needed for the traditional salesperson (Gosselin & Heene, 2003). KAMs need to develop cross-functional understanding of the organisation, to facilitate seamless delivery of the value proposition. KAMs are increasingly required to have legitimacy and influence, which may come from seniority or from enlisting the support of a senior manager. Evidence has shown that effectiveness in managing key accounts requires strategic ability in analysing customers' organisational and business problems and in focusing on their long-term interests (Sengupta, Krapfel & Pusateri, 2000).

IMPLEMENTING KEY ACCOUNT MANAGEMENT

So far, key design parameters or foundations for managing accounts strategically have been presented. After the relationship type has been defined, the strategic accounts identified and the business planning frameworks established, organisations have to articulate a value proposition and create account teams and roles.

What follows is a set of processes that underpin the effective implementation of key account management. These processes are by nature dynamic; that is, they need to be reviewed on a regular basis and are contingent upon an industry and an organisation. Therefore, these processes need to be designed with specific contextual circumstances in mind.

Consistency in key customer selection

One of the critical processes of key account management is the designation of the strategic accounts. Since these customers will require significant investments from the supplier, only a finite number of accounts will be viable. The number may vary from sector to sector but typically, key customers of a given organisation vary from 5 to 20 in number (McDonald & Woodburn, 2007). The required investments mean that opportunity costs are high – another reason to suggest the careful selection of accounts.

Once the strategic accounts are selected, there will be a time lag (that can last up to several years) between the selection of the account and the generation of value. This emphasises the future orientation of key account management and the importance of achieving coherence between the supplier and the customer expectations to avoid the 'supplier delusion' mentioned earlier.

The factors that influence the appointment of accounts may be diverse and vary from industry to industry. However, a key criterion for selecting a key account should consider the potential for profitable growth in the future. Another important element is organisational fitness; in other words, the degree of compatibility between the supplier and the customer. At the end of the day, both organisations will have to work together to co-create value and fulfil their respective objectives.

Given the protracted timeframes to realise effective key account management, the account portfolio needs to be reviewed regularly. Customers that are no longer aligned or whose future potential has been extinguished may need to be de-selected as key accounts. This is likely to trigger a contested process, particularly from account managers and teams dedicated to 'former' strategic accounts.

Organisations need to resource and plan both the process of selection as well as de-selection and have to be aware of some of the pitfalls and errors in strategic account selection such as:

- Lists of strategic accounts that are too long and unmanageable, resulting in potential failure to deliver the agreed value proposition.
- Not enough differentiation between accounts to give guidance on strategic resource allocation and dedicated structures.
- Insufficiently defined processes and confusing criteria that do not help to assess potential new key accounts.
- Overemphasis on current results rather than on the longer-term outcomes, sending the wrong message to the account about the genuine interest in the relationship.
- Internal pressure to include unsuitable accounts – often current customers that may be large but have limited prospects for future growth.

Phased approach in managing key account management programmes

The conception and planning of strategic account initiatives has generated much interest and literature over the years. Much of what we know about key account management is located within the foundation domain. Less is known about the implementation of key account management (Sengupta et al., 2000; Zupancic, 2008) and the evolution from sales to key account management approaches.

To address this gap, Davies and Ryals (2009) undertook an exploratory study to understand how companies transition to key account management. This study revealed four key phases in the implementation of key account management:

1. *Introduction*. This phase is characterised by a company's formal announcement of KAM initiatives and by the justification of the reasons for such programmes. The identification of strategic accounts and the appointment of KAMs is typically a key action at this stage. At this stage senior management commitment and the efforts of individuals are paramount for the success of the programme. There is rarely a significant re-structuring of the supplier's processes and functioning in this phase.
2. *Embedding*. This stage focuses on redefining the scope of the programme, in specifying the roles KAMs will play and how these connect with the rest of the organisation. Training and management development efforts are typically aimed at gradually creating a cultural change within the organisation. Teams often fulfil the management of the strategic account, so emphasis is placed on achieving inter-functional coordination and alignment. Formal procedures and processes are

defined, often including the creation of individual account plans and systems to monitor the activities of KAMs and the outcomes from the strategic accounts. This stage is seen to be crucial since a number of organisations have already committed significant resources, but may not yet have gained benefits from the programme. Thus, reassurance and renewed efforts from the leadership team may be needed.

3. *Optimising.* This phase is characterised by structural changes in the organisation to streamline processes dedicated to the strategic accounts, eventually making them scalable. Subtle changes transforming the culture of the supplier into a customer-oriented one typically emerge at this stage. This customer-centricity is translated into internal processes, policies and IT systems. More senior people become engaged in account management, either as sponsors or more directly involved in supporting strategic account operations. Value propositions and service levels for the key accounts become differentiated and often exclusive to dedicated accounts. Joint business planning, opportunity identification and problem resolution characterise the work with key customers.
4. *Continuous improvement.* Key account programmes rarely have a starting and end point. Quite the contrary – these are initiatives that require continual rejuvenation and support and understanding from across the organisation. Therefore, best-practice companies engage in continuous improvement of the programme, refining it to make it best value for the business. At this stage, companies revisit the business case for key account management, critically assessing investments made and future investments required. In addition, the portfolio of key customers is revisited, resulting in even higher customer selectivity – more defined selection criteria and clearer separation between strategic accounts and non-strategic customers. Further organisational change at this stage is rare and the customer-oriented culture is typically well established and recognised throughout the organisation.

The full implementation of strategic account programmes requires the organisation and the KAMs to critically assess each of the phases and parameters of the strategic accounts programmes. These questions for the 'organisation' and for the 'KAM' are meant to stimulate relevant discussions and to help effective implementation of the programme.

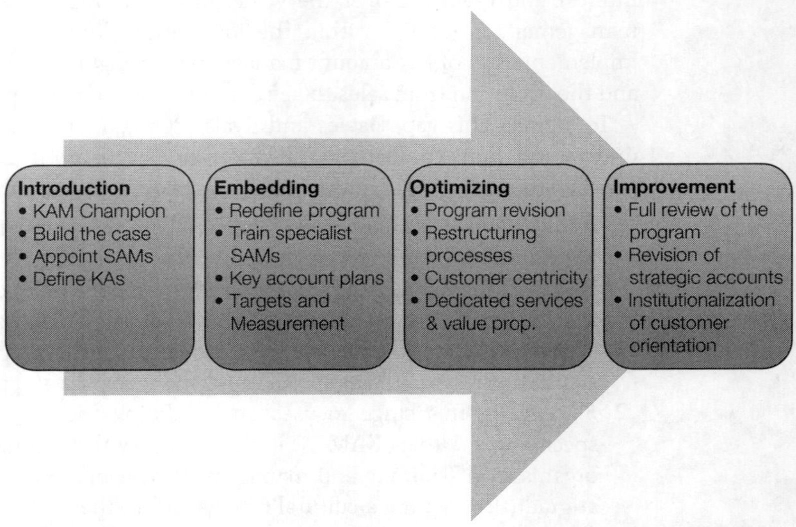

Figure 8.8 – Key phases in the implementation of key account management programmes

Development of actionable account plans

We have defined key account management as an integrated process for the profitable management of customer relationships (McDonald & Woodburn, 2007; Ryals, 2008). The integration process is a complex, multifaceted one. It requires enhanced awareness of the strategic customer's intent, the gathering and transfer of specific customer knowledge and ultimately functional alignment to realise joint business opportunities. The role of the strategic account plan is precisely to serve as the platform for integrating these elements of effective strategic customer management.

Account plans need to be seen as live documents that are regularly updated to capture opportunities and risks of the business with the strategic account. If the plans are based on insights supplied by the customer, and the relationship enjoys a high level of trust, the plans should be shared with the customer and used as a compass to direct and guide the allocation of resources and capabilities and the efforts for the value creation endeavour.

Strategic account plans may be lengthy documents or succinct sets of tools depending on the complexity of the account and on the thoroughness of the planning process. Typically, key account plans will contain the following sections (Ryals & McDonald, 2008; Storbacka, 2012):

- Description of strategic account: political, economic, social, technological, environmental context.
- Current offerings and value propositions: product and services sold to the customer and sales records.
- Customer business: customer's value-creating process, opportunities and threats, future business potential and opportunities.
- Customer management team: resource allocation and responsibilities between account manager and team.
- Customer profitability and financial information.
- Analysis of the relationship: including contact matrixes describing the contact points between firm team members and customer representatives.
- Action planning: goals and objectives, action plans with timelines and allocation of resources.

Figure 8.9 shows a framework for defining key parameters of a strategic account plan that the first author has used in management development programmes. The upper part prompts an analysis of the customer situation. The bottom part stimulates a systematic response to the insights identified in the first part. The framework is structured following a set of questions/challenges and established marketing tools and approaches to address these key challenges (Figure 8.9).

A key feature of powerful account plans is the degree to which the plan is actionable, hence the importance of translating strategic analysis into specific courses of actions. Overall, a solid strategic account plan is one that is linked to the overall business strategy.

Addressing the internal dimension and challenges of implementing KAM

When implementing KAM most organisations underestimate the importance of intra-organisational alignment, and put excessive focus on external, customer-facing processes at the expense of the necessary internal reorganisation and transformation.

Longitudinal case study research investigating the intra-organisational practices that facilitate the successful implementation of KAM programmes has revealed that

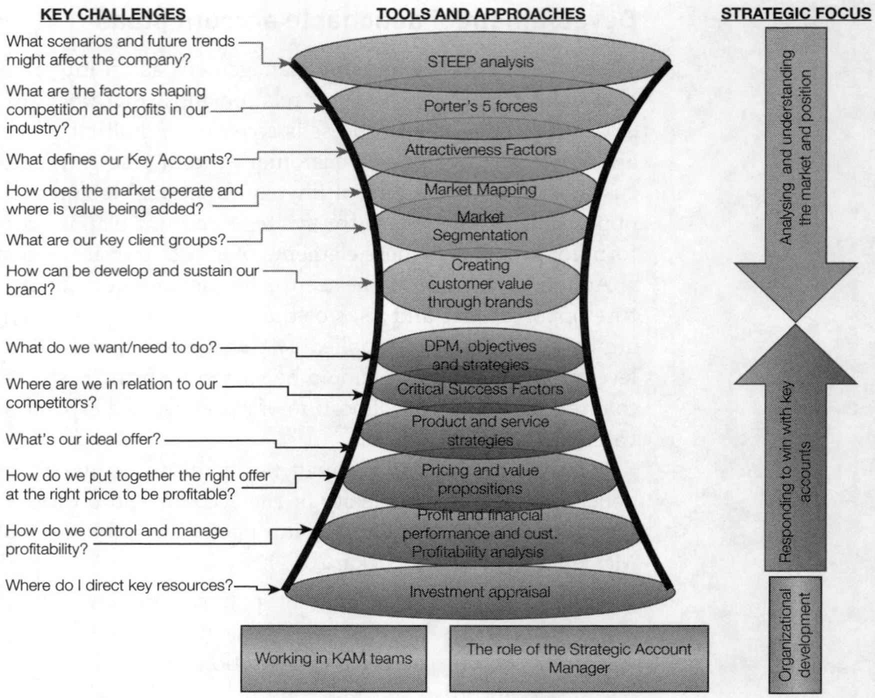

Figure 8.9 – A framework for strategic account plans

practices at two levels – 'strategic' and 'operational' – and the management of dilemmas associated with these practices underpin the ability to roll out KAM programmes successfully (Marcos-Cuevas, Natti, Palo & Ryals, 2014).

The *strategic practices* include:

1. Compelling business case for embarking on KAM, often as a result of a customer demand/need.
2. Well-informed understanding of KAM as a systematic approach to broaden and deepen relationships with customers, accompanied by training and management development initiatives for account managers and support teams.
3. Formal definition of structures and procedures but incorporating some flexibility and adaptation. These structures are customer-centric and sensitive to the way the key customer is organised.
4. Institutionalised KAM processes such as tracking and KAM evaluation schemes. Once they have embarked on KAM, companies follow up both inputs (activities and initiatives) as well as outputs (financial returns).
5. Establish support systems for KAM, both formal (e.g. committees) and informal (e.g. individual senior manager support).
6. Develop differentiated offerings and service levels exclusively for key accounts.
7. Management of trade-offs: balancing short- and long-term activities and results.

The *operational practices* supporting the implementation of KAM include:

1. Development of account planning tools such as key account plans including analysis, actions and planned investment; constant updating of plans.
2. Customer review routines that evolve over time including review protocols; value propositions; relational development matrices; insights from marketing research incorporated into key account plans, etc..

3 Measurement practices including key account items on board agendas; engagement of senior people in service delivery for key accounts, etc.
4 Incentive mechanisms that feature a balanced approach (input and output measures); incentives usually indirect or intrinsic.
5 Key account selection criteria that are clear and widely accepted across the organisation.

Overall, the effective implementation of KAM is characterised by context-specificity, which requires a mindful understanding of the organisation's local circumstances. When implementing KAM a balance between short vs. long term and forcefulness vs. flexibility needs to be achieved. Effective implementation of KAM involves both objective measures of progress and subjective appreciation of business relationship development. A KAM implementation endeavour entails changes in practices, processes and structures, but also in executives' mindsets.

Although KAM programmes can help achieve 'quick wins' the major contribution of KAM lies in its potential to help organisations renew their business. This requires relentless managerial effort, sustained support in continually reviewing practices, and an extensive critical mass of individuals supporting the organisational transformation of the supplier.

Measurement of account management programmes

Key account management programmes are often expensive interventions and, as such, need to be measured against goals and expectations. A key temptation senior executives need to avoid is an overemphasis on financial outcomes. Though we have argued that profitable relations are at the core of key account management, key measures of account management effectiveness go beyond financial measures (Workman, Homburg & Jensen, 2003; Davies & Ryals, 2014) and should take into account a wider range of aspects such as:

- Increased information sharing and transparency.
- Reduction of conflict.
- Customer commitment and satisfaction.
- Number and extent of relationships.
- Customer loyalty and retention.
- Revenue growth.

Jones, Richards, Halstead and Fu (2009) propose a framework to evaluate key account performance that includes relational outcomes as well as financial performance outcomes. They argue that a model of key account performance should consider the impact of strategic decisions made in the key account programme, and thus, it must capture their impact on both the quality of the relationship and the level of financial performance. The framework contemplates three types of customer equity: value equity, brand equity, and relationship equity, that together with trust and commitment affect the performance of the key account. Value equity refers to an objective and rational view of a firm's product or service offering and typically has been found to centre on price, quality and convenience. Brand equity denotes the customer's subjective appraisal of the brand. This evaluation is often intangible and represents the value involved in a product or service beyond the physical product itself. Relationship equity includes the customer's willingness to remain in the relationship and the intangible benefits it generates such as knowledge and insight generation.

The purpose of measuring key account management performance is to ascertain the value created in the relationship and to gain insights into how the value has been created. The measurement of value creation in buyer–seller relationships needs to acknowledge that value co-creation occurs during three cyclical and interrelated phases through which customers and suppliers interact: (1) joint crafting of value propositions, (2) value actualisation and (3) value determination (Lambert & Enz, 2012). Thus, the measurement approach could consider outcomes as well as input processes. Representatives from the supplier–key account dyads can qualify (rather than quantitatively measure) the extent to which joint efforts are enabling innovation, creative problem solving and value co-creation.

Enz and Lambert (2012) argue that in that in addition to considering subjective measures, financial measurement of value co-creation is important in business-to-business contexts. An individual key account manager is rarely familiar with all of the initiatives that occur within a key account relationship since the key account programme could encompass activities ranging from product development to manufacturing process improvement, quality improvement and the provision of market information. Value created and captured can be measured financially by the discounted present value of all future economic profit that the customer relationship generates, and this can be used as a proxy for the shareholder value creation (Storbacka & Nenonen, 2009).

Overall, a holistic approach to measuring account performance should not trade off between objective and subjective, financial and relational outcomes. A well-designed measurement system will measure retrospectively and also prospective indicators.

Continuous revitalisation of the account management programme

Throughout this chapter the nature of key account management as a process has been emphasised. This final section aims to further stress the importance of continuously reviewing and revitalising key account programmes. These efforts require investments throughout the lifecycle of key account management (Storbacka, 2012) from (1) knowledge generation, disseminating and interpretation to (2) selling process agreeing on orders/contracts, (3) to the delivery of the agreed value proposition and (4) relationship strengthening and development (Figure 8.10).

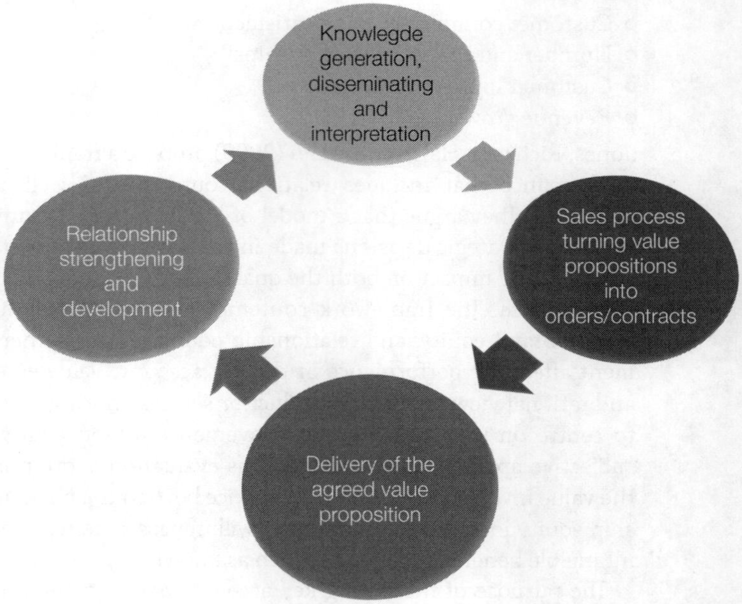

Figure 8.10 – Review and revitalisation of account management programmes

KAMs and senior executives need to devise comprehensive frameworks to enable the continuous development of account management programmes. These frameworks often include the following dimensions (Zupancic, 2008) (Figure 8.11):

- *Strategy*: covering the relational purpose for the selected key accounts and how the strategic account programme fits within the overall corporate strategy.
- *Product/service solution*: includes the bundles of products and services that will be offered to the strategic account in order to co-create the expected value, deliver against the account plan and build a profitable long-term relationship.
- *People*: include the definition of roles, competency profiles, reward systems and succession planning. A key aspect is the leadership approach adopted for the people involved in the supplier–key customer relationship.
- *Structures and processes:* a broad category that includes current and future ways of working with the account, performance targets and the processes that are necessary to serve the key account. The relationship structure or 'contact matrix' needs to be included either as part of structures or the definition of roles.
- *Knowledge capabilities:* include activities, systems and information to generate insights, measure process and monitor account activities. Organisational learning and knowledge sharing are also included in this category.

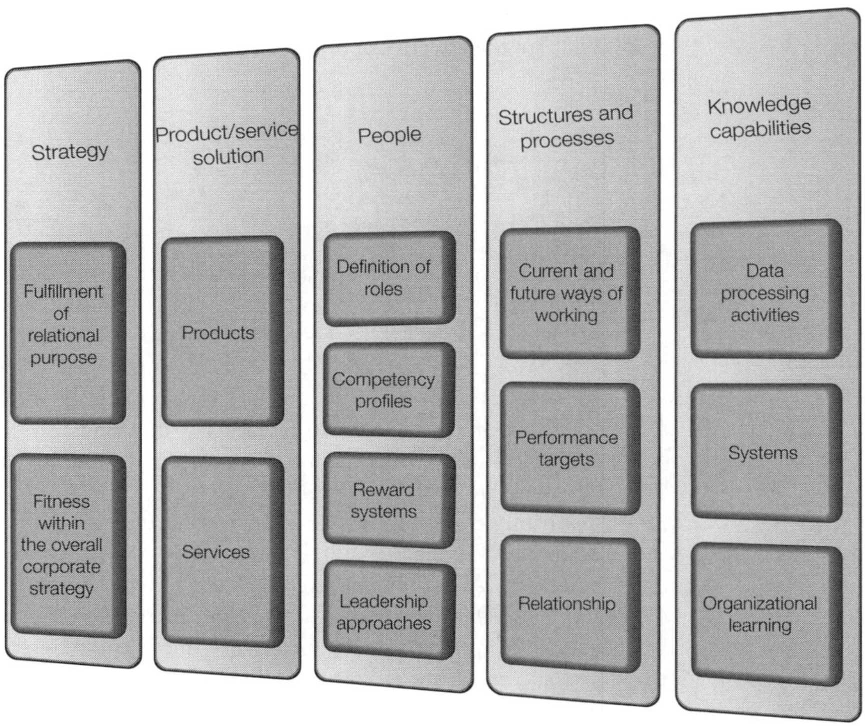

Figure 8.11 – Key dimensions for continuous development of account management programmes

SUMMARY

In this chapter, two major components of effective key account management programmes have been presented. First, the foundations or design parameters and second the key processes for implementing these programmes. Although these are presented separately, in reality they are often addressed in parallel. Key account management has been framed as a way of structuring around key customers and as an approach to develop long-term profitable relationships. This chapter provides a structured answer to these fundamental questions. The sections presented above form the route map to achieve an increased focus on key customers and to develop the capability to co-create sustainable value with them.

QUESTIONS

- What are the fundamental types of business relationships and what characterises each of them?
- How can I differentiate the relationship strategy with customers that are different?
- How important are customer insights in the strategic account programme?
- What are the key roles and functions of account managers?
- How can my organisation consistently select (or de-select) key accounts?
- What are the typical phases an organisation goes through when implementing a strategic account programme?
- What is the role of key account plans within the key account management programme?
- What are the effective approaches for measuring the effectiveness of KAM?

CASE STUDY

Case Company: Siemens Ag

Siemens AG is a global manufacturer and services company in electronics and electrical engineering, operating in the industry, energy and healthcare sectors. For over 160 years Siemens has stood for technological excellence, innovation, quality, reliability and internationality. The company is one of the world's largest providers of environmental technologies. More than one-third of its total revenue stems from green products and solutions. In 2010, revenue from continuing operations (excluding Osram and Siemens IT Solutions and Services) totalled €69 billion and net income from continuing operations €4.3 billion. Siemens has around 336,000 employees worldwide (Siemens, 2011).

Siemens AG was recognised by the Strategic Account Management Association (SAMA) for its successful customer management programme. Siemens CEO Peter Löscher claimed that 'proximity to our customers is decisive for our business success. I myself spend more than half my time with customers.' SAMA's president and CEO Bernhard Quancard explained, 'Siemens impressed us with its ongoing cultivation of customer relationships, its fostering of promising and talented sales employees and its practical implementation of customer proximity at the Managing Board level.'

Under the company's Executive Relationship Programme, the ten members of Siemens' Managing Board cultivate contacts with some 80 top customers. In order to better meet the needs of Siemens' international customers, Managing Board meetings have for several years regularly been held outside Germany and have also entailed customer participation. Most recently, the Managing Board convened in China, India, Brazil, Russia, the US and Mexico, among other countries.

Worldwide, more than 1,200 key account managers at Siemens serve over 2,000 customers, who generate 40 per cent of the company's revenue. To further expand its key account management system, Siemens is investing an amount in the triple-digit millions-of-euros range in the medium term. The investments will be used, among other things, to further expand the key account management system, provide training and continuing education for sales employees and develop improved software for managing customer processes.

Hajo Rapp, Senior Vice president, Account Management, and Market Development at Siemens when asked about the company's journey towards strategic account management, said:

> *[W]e started in the 1990s in the IT arena and in our manufacturing businesses. Key account management was growing in IT because there was a centralised person, the CIO, asking for somebody at the supplier side covering the same bandwidth of topics globally as him. At the same time in the manufacturing industry (e.g. automotive) the purchasers tried to aggregate their purchasing power in order to make sure that the delivery of parts they needed for production was secured. And now, two decades later we have grown several more key account management programmes for vertical markets, e.g. pharmaceuticals. In the future we expect more and more differentiation in sales. On the one hand customers need very cost-efficient sales channels (distribution) and on the other those that offer a customised treatment and close customer proximity will win.*

Siemens is recognised for high levels of customer-centricity. Pedro Miranda, a senior executive at Siemens One, reflecting on the challenges for the key account management function to overcome the difficulties of the current economic downturn, said 'basically what we want to do is to leverage customer development, that means engage account managers in a one-to-one with our customers, and bring the portfolio that makes sense for them, bring value to them'. In explaining the underpinning process for this, a fundamental principle is 'to really understand the needs and the growth needs of the customer, and leverage our portfolio of services and solutions for them to grow. If the customer is growing, we are growing behind them.'

Siemens account managers conduct detailed analysis of customer weaknesses and opportunities and provide Siemens with know-how to help the customer minimise the former and realise the latter.

A key milestone for Siemens, according to Pedro Miranda, is the achievement of 100 corporate account managers that look after about 150 global customers. Looking into the future, he declares: 'My vision for Siemens One is to be considered worldwide the benchmark for account management and customer development; this is what differentiates us from other companies.'

INTERVIEW – MARK DAVIES, SEGMENT PULSE

Mark is the Managing Partner and Founder of Segment Pulse Limited – an advisory firm that helps to develop commercial strategies for its clients, and a Visiting Fellow with Cranfield School of Management, where he coordinates Cranfield's Key Account Management Best Practice Research Club. This is a consortium that brings together leading academics with business leaders in blue chip organisations to research and disseminate leading-edge thinking in areas related to Key Account Management. Mark specialises in Sales Strategy Development, Innovation in Sales, and Key Account Management, having been Key Accounts Strategy Director for BP Castrol and having consulted internationally with global organisations.

Q: Overall, how do you define key account management?

MD: I like to think of a key account as a 'market segment of one' – if an organisation has decided that a customer within its portfolio is Key or Strategic, then it should do something that is unique and bespoke for that customer. In many ways, a key account requires the same approach and strategic thinking that is applied to the marketing of a sector, industry, or market. The difference for a key account is that the segment becomes one customer, and actually if you have, for example, 20 per cent (and more) of your business opportunity coming from that one customer, why wouldn't you do that!

Key account management (KAM) is the activity that organisations have to develop and embrace to develop these customer-specific strategies and to profitably implement them. KAM is an organisation-wide capability, and goes beyond the key account manager (although having the right key account manager is critical).

KAM is an essential activity to develop the commercial organic growth opportunity that resides in certain customers and it helps to mitigate the risk of losing established business. Organisations can also leverage their resources with key accounts if they consider the customer to be an important opportunity to gain traction in a new geography and/or industry that they see as strategically important.

Q: What are the key challenges you think organisations face in implementing key account management?

MD: Many organisations underestimate the complex nature of KAM and launch into training initiatives, often focused at *re-skilling* the existing sales force. For a successful KAM programme, however, there really needs to be a more strategic approach. This should be addressed and developed with senior leadership buy-in to establish exactly what the KAM initiative is trying to achieve, and the strategies the organisation will follow to deliver this future vision. KAM is an organisational capability, and requires consideration of the future design of the firm's structure, systems and processes, data and finance systems, culture and leadership, customer planning tools and of course its people. Jumping in and throwing KAM methodologies at salespeople is usually the wrong thing to do. A strategy should be set out that considers who are the key accounts, how will they be managed, who will do this, and describing what success look like. Failing to do this often leads to unsuccessful KAM programmes.

A further complexity is that KAM is different from one organisation to another. There really is no 'one size fits all'. Of course there are guidelines and methods that act as a *blueprint*, but every organisation has its own DNA, and this should be explored and understood during the development of the KAM strategy phase to ensure that an effective KAM programme is established and resourced correctly for that organisation.

Q: What are the key challenges you think key account managers face today?

MD: Perhaps the biggest challenge that I hear about from the clients that I work with in many sectors and many parts of the world is addressing the same issue: *how do I get the wider organisation to align, support and connect with my key account customer strategies and actions*? This is often phrased as a customer-centricity challenge, and in many ways it is not surprising that it is a problem.

Organisations become successful by providing core products and brands to target markets. The most cost-effective way to control activities and efficiencies of scale is to structure the business around product groups, and geographies. When a key account manager starts requesting time, energy, investment and focus for the customer, this can present problems and a tension/power struggle can arise.

The challenge of who owns the customer and who leads this agenda is a real issue for key account managers, and gets more complex as customers span geographies and business units. The secret to navigating through this is for the key account manager to accept that their own organisation is structured 'by silo', and these silos are very effective and productive at achieving business success. Great key account managers understand this, and have the leadership skills, gravitas and tenacity to coordinate and navigate their agenda internally and get their own organisations aligned behind the customer agenda. Easy to say, but really hard to achieve!

Q: To what extent can key accounts be both large in terms of volume and profitable? How do best-practice organisations manage this balance?

MD: It depends on many different circumstances. Quite often higher volumes will command lower costs per unit and that is to be expected, but the larger-volume business should always be tracked carefully to ensure profitable business is maintained. Measuring the profit by each key account customer is essential to track this, and this is often a key supporting action that is part of the KAM strategy.

Decisions can be taken to run a key account that produces less profitable business with higher volumes, especially if the volume relates to a manufacturing plant that requires a certain volume to be economically viable. Again, this needs to be considered carefully, because after all there is nothing strategic about losing money.

Best-practice organisations experience the reverse of what is suggested by this question; indeed, higher volumes can be obtained and higher costs per unit maintained. If KAM is conducted properly with the customer, they will see additional benefits and pay for this value added. I have seen many key accounts achieve this. The secret is always to really understand what is important to the customer and provide solutions that support the customer strategy and objectives.

The other aspect to consider is that the value proposition for the key account will probably stretch beyond the core product that the selling organisation provides, and an integrated offering comprising additional services will demonstrate significant benefits for the customer, again enabling a stronger position to have sustainable and higher levels of business at higher costs per unit.

Q: What are the key mechanisms to create value with key accounts?

MD: The first critical step is to establish the parameters to identify/segment the customer portfolio so that key account customers have been identified that have significant latent value residing in their operations, and that are also receptive to you as a key value supplier. Setting a strategic plan and implementing these customer-specific strategies and actions will enable value delivery. The four main steps to unlock value are:

1. Gather value insights – *know thy customer* and really understand the world they operate in and what the customer strategies are. Understand the markets and customers that they are selling to: this is a key to significant sources of value.
2. Establish your value opportunities against this 'market segment of one'. By doing step 1, there should be a much stronger understanding of what is important to the customer and where your own organisation can provide value to help them be successful.
3. Innovate and create a unique Value Proposition – by definition, you will do something unique and bespoke for a key account customer. This stage is the crystallisation of that and captures what the offer could be. Really, this is the most important element of KAM; after all, your customer pays for value delivered, not the fact that you have a great KAM programme!
4. Value delivery – The value proposition is a promise of what *could be.* Delivery needs to make sure that this promise is delivered, does what was intended, and value captured and measured. Establishing strong measures in the form of key performance indicators and benchmarking the customers' business to capture and record the value created is critical and helps to ensure future business.

A critical point to remember is that it is not just about value for the customer. Strong rewards in the form of profit for the supplier must be achieved. Value co-creation should be achieved, ensuring a supplier profit is maintained. Healthy profits on both sides will ensure a strong and sustainable relationship.

Q: How important is it to have a differentiated offering for key accounts?

MD: Having a unique/bespoke Value Proposition and offering is critical, but actually not as difficult as it may sound. Many organisations consider innovation to be the bastion of the product and R&D department, and of course this is where significant competitive advantage is derived. Key account managers can, and should, pull lots of other levers to develop an innovative and unique offering. For instance:

- Unique commercial offering – *can the service level and pricing structure be unique? Can there be outcome-based / gain share reward systems?*
- People – *can there be specific people employed just for the customer, could they operate within the customer operations?*
- Channel/route to market– *can the customer be served via third parties, and can they be equipped to provide additional services and technologies to enhance the customer experience?*

Q: Based on your experience, what are the sectors (and or companies) that have made significant progress in KAM?

MD: The consumer packaged goods industry (organisations making branded products that they sell via retail/mass merchandising channels – companies such as P&G, Unilever, Mars) has very strong KAM capability. Historically they are obsessed about the consumer, and they have a very consolidated group of key accounts (mass merchandisers such as Wal-Mart, Tesco, Carrefour) to reach their consumers. Mass merchandisers are extremely powerful, and require strong investment and effort to establish trading relationships. The consumer packaged goods industry is possibly one of the sectors that KAM evolved within.

Also, some of the bigger technology organisations are very strong at KAM. Multi-million dollar enterprises selling complex global solutions to complex global customers again require exceptional KAM capability. IBM, HP, Siemens, Oracle and Cisco are good examples. An interesting observation with these organisations is the emergence of outcome-based contract structure. Rewards and payments are delivered after delivery of results (as outlined in the value proposition).

This adds a whole new dynamic to the value selling processes and the supplier to customer relationship. It also means that there is additional pressure on delivering solutions and services, with products sometimes becoming less important. These so-called Product, Service & Solution (PSS) value propositions have complex business architecture and need close collaboration between supplier and buyer. It is safe to say that key account management will become even more important for businesses in the future!

REFERENCES

Abratt, R. & Kelly, P. M. (2002). Customer–supplier partnerships. Perceptions of a successful key account management program. *Industrial Marketing Management*, 31(5), 467–476.

Davies, I. A. & Ryals, L. J. (2009). A stage model for transitioning to KAM. *Journal of Marketing Management*, 25(9–10), 1027–1048.

Davies, I. A. & Ryals, L. J. (2014). The effectiveness of key account management practices. *Industrial Marketing Management*, 43(7), 1182–1194.

Davies, I. A., Ryals, L. J. & Holt, S. (2010). Relationship management: A sales role, or a state of mind?: An investigation of functions and attitudes across a business-to-business sales force. *Industrial Marketing Management*, 39(7), 1049–1062.

Enz, M. G. & Lambert, D. M. (2012). Using cross-functional, cross-firm teams to co-create value: The role of financial measures. *Industrial Marketing Management*, 41(3), 495–507.

Fiocca, R. (1982). Account portfolio analysis for strategy development. *Industrial Marketing Management*, 11(1), 53–63.

Guesalaga, R. (2014). Top management involvement with key accounts: The concept, its dimensions, and strategic outcomes. *Industrial Marketing Management*, 43(7), 1146–1156.

Guesalaga, R. & Johnston, W. (2010). What's next in key account management research? Building the bridge between the academic literature and the practitioners' priorities. *Industrial Marketing Management*, 39(7), 1063–1068.

Holt, S. (2003). *The Role of the Global Account Manager: A Boundary Role Theory Perspective*, PhD Thesis, Cranfield School of Management, Cranfield University, UK.

Homburg, C., Workman, J. P. & Jensen, O. (2002). A configurational perspective on key account management. *Journal of Marketing*, 66(2), 38–60.

Honeycutt, E. D. (2002). Sales management in the new millennium: An introduction. *Industrial Marketing Management*, 31(7), 555–558.

Janda, S. & Seshadri, S. (2001). The influences of purchasing strategies on performance. *Journal of Business & Industrial Marketing*, 16(4), 294–306.

Jones, E., Brown, S. P., Zoltners, A. A. & Weitz, B. A. (2005). The changing environment of selling & sales management. *Journal of Personal Selling & Sales Management*, 25(2), 105–111.

Jones, E., Richards, K. A., Halstead, D. & Fu, F. Q. (2009). Developing a strategic framework of key account performance. *Journal of Strategic Marketing*, 17(3–4), 221–235.

Kalwani, M. U. & Narayandas, N. (1995). Long-term manufacturer–supplier relationships: Do they pay off for supplier firms? *Journal of Marketing*, January, 59(1), 1–17.

Lambert, D. M. & Enz, M. G., 2012. Managing and measuring value co-creation in business-to-business relationships. *Journal of Marketing Management*, 28(13/14), 1588–1625.

Lemmens, R., Donaldson, B. & Marcos, J. (2014). *From Selling to Co-creating: New Trends, Practices and Tools to Upgrade Your Sales Force*. Amsterdam: BIS Publishers.

Lusch, R., Vargo, S. & Tanniru, M. (2010). Service, value networks and learning. *Journal of the Academy of Marketing Science*, 38(1), 19–31.

Marcos-Cuevas, J., Natti, S., Palo, T. & Ryals, L. (2014). Implementing key account management: Intraorganizational practices and dilemmas. *Industrial Marketing Management*, 43(7), 1216–1224.

McDonald, M., Millman, T. & Rogers, B. (1997), Key account management: Theory, practice and challenges. *Journal of Marketing Management*, 13(November), 737–757.

McDonald, M. & Woodburn, D. (2007). *Key Account Management: The Definitive Guide*. Oxford: Butterworth-Heinemann.

Moncrief, W. C. (1986). Ten key activities of industrial salespeople. *Industrial Marketing Management*, 15(4), 309–317.

Moncrief, W. C. & Marshall, G. W. (2005). The evolution of the seven steps of selling. *Industrial Marketing Management*, 34(1), 13–22.

Montgomery, D. B. & Yip, G. S. (2000). The challenge of global customer management. *Marketing Management*, 9(4), 22–29.

Pardo, C.' Henneberg, S. C., Mouzas, S. & Naude, P. (2006). Unpicking the meaning of value in key account management. *European Journal of Marketing*, 40(11/12), 1360–1374.

Piercy, N. & Lane, N. (2006). The underlying vulnerabilities in key account management strategies. *European Management Journal*, 24(2–3), 151–162.

Rackham, N. & DeVincentis, J. (1999). *Rethinking the Sales Force: Redefining Selling to Create & Capture Customer Value*. New York: McGraw-Hill.

Richards, K. (2006). Relationship effectiveness and key account performance: Assessing inter-firm fit between buying and selling organizations. Working Paper. University of Houston.

Ryals, L. (2008). *Managing Customers Profitably*. Chichester: Wiley.

Ryals, L. J. & Holt, S. (2007). Creating and capturing value in KAM relationships. *Journal of Strategic Marketing*, 15(5), 403–420.

Ryals, L. J. & McDonald, M. (2008). *Key Account Plans: The Practitioners' Guide to Profitable Planning*. Oxford: Butterworth-Heinemann.

Salojärvi, H., Sainio, L.-M. & Tarkiainen, A. (2010). Organizational factors enhancing customer knowledge utilization in the management of key account relationships. *Industrial Marketing Management*, 39(8), 1395–1402.

Sengupta, S., Krapfel, R. E. & Pusateri, M. E. (2000). An empirical investigation of key account salesperson effectiveness. *Journal of Personal Selling & Sales Management*, 20(4), 253–261.

Shapiro, B. & Wyman, J. (1981). New ways to reach your customers. *Harvard Business Review*, 59 (July/August), 103–110.

Sheth, J. N. & Sharma, A. (2008). The impact of the product to service shift in industrial markets & the evolution of the sales organization. *Industrial Marketing Management*, 37, 260–269.

Siemens (2011). Siemens receives award for best key account management. Retrieved 22 December 2012, from http://www.siemens.com.

Speakman, J. I. F. & Ryals, L. (2012). Key account management: The inside selling job. *Journal of Business & Industrial Marketing*, 27(5), 360–366.

Storbacka, K. (2012). Strategic account management programmes: Alignment of design elements and management practices. *Journal of Business & Industrial Marketing*, 27(4), 259–274.

Storbacka, K. & Nenonen, S. (2009), Customer relationships and the heterogeneity of firm performance. *Journal of Business & Industrial Marketing*, 24(5/6), 360–372.

Talluri, S. & Narasimhan, R. (2004). A methodology for strategic sales alignment. *European Journal of Operational Research*, 154(1), 236–250.

Treacy, M. & Wiersema, M. (1995). *The Discipline of the Market Leaders*. London: Harper Collins.

Tzempelikos, N. (2006). Key account management orientation and company performance – Does relationship quality matter? *AMA Annual Conference*. American Marketing Association, pp. 1–19.

Ulaga, W. & Eggert, A. (2006). Value-based differentiation in business relationships: Gaining & sustaining key supplier status. *Journal of Marketing*, 70(1), 119–136.

Vargo, S. L. & Lusch, R. F. (2008). From goods to service(s): Divergences & convergences of logic. *Industrial Marketing Management*, 37(3), 254–259.

Wang, X. L. & Brennan, R. (2014). A framework for key account management and revenue management integration. *Industrial Marketing Management*, 43(7), 1172–1181.

Workman, J. P., Homburg, C. & Jensen, O. (2003). Intraorganizational determinants of key account management effectiveness. *Journal of the Academy of Marketing Science*, 31(1), 3–21.

Zupancic, D. (2008). Towards an integrated framework of key account management. *Journal of Business & Industrial Marketing*, 23(5), 323–331.

9 TECHNOLOGY AND SALES

OVERVIEW

Information technology (IT) is the set of systems dedicated to the processing and communication of information, including computer and electronic databases, advanced telecommunications, the Internet and electronic commerce. These technologies have led to new and powerful ways of reaching customers and are changing the way in which firms interact and sales organisations reach their markets. In this chapter, customer relationship management (CRM), database marketing, sales force automation (SFA) and electronic commerce (e-commerce) will be discussed. The use of new technology in the sales process is clearly having a significant impact on how sales operations are implemented and managed, and will continue to do so. This chapter considers these developments, the problems and opportunities arising from them and the implications for sales management.

LEARNING OBJECTIVES

This chapter aims to enable the reader to:

- Understand CRM and the importance of information in the sales process.
- Develop an understanding of sales information systems and sales force automation.
- Assess the efficacy of database marketing, telemarketing and the Internet.
- Outline key developments in e-commerce and Internet sales.

DEFINITIONS

Customer relationship management (CRM) is the integration of technology and processes in the acquisition, retaining and growing of selected customers.

Sales force automation (SFA) is the computerised integration of front and back office activity to create an information-rich context that can enable the sales force to improve sales processes and optimise sales activities.

Sales information system (SIS) refers to the combination of technologies that facilitate the collection and processing of information to assist the sales and customer management process.

Electronic commerce (e-commerce) is the use of web-based tools and other forms of business solutions such as electronic request for quotation (eRFQ), electronic request for information (eRFI), catalogue procurement or e-auctions, to conduct streamlined transactions.

Social media refers to the creation, dissemination and consumption of information through online social interactions and platforms.

Sales funnel is a structured, phased framework to classify sales opportunities according to the stage they are in from prospect to close.

INTRODUCTION: SALES INFORMATION SYSTEMS

The rising cost of personal, face-to-face sales calls (see next 'Did you know?' vignette) has triggered a fundamental reappraisal of the way companies interact with their customers. This applies, in particular, to customers that despite constituting a large number, only account for a relatively small proportion of sales. It is no longer economic to service these accounts with intensive personal means of communication and sometimes less effective where the information customers need is readily available online or relies on the company's information systems. Hence, the use of marketing and SIS has complemented other forms of communication, principally the telephone. These forms of communication, some of which have been around for some time, need careful evaluation and appraisal before being used by different organisations in different ways. They include the major tools of direct marketing such as catalogues, direct mail, television, radio/magazine direct response, electronic shopping, kiosk shopping and telemarketing. The basis for these integrated communication systems is database marketing. Key uses of SIS include:

1 *Sales reporting and analysis.* They offer improved speed and accuracy on previously manually operated information. In other words, the new technology helps with collecting, classifying, storing and analysing data. Such data might include:

- Call reports.
- Sales against plan.
- Sales by product, customer or segment.
- Profit and cost calculations per customer.
- Other dimensions of sales performance.

Nowadays, a large amount of information can be electronically handled and computer technologies provide the capabilities to analyse data and derive valuable customer insights. Information systems can also be modified to redesign work. Collecting data is not an end in itself but an enabler to facilitate the achievement of optimal selling time and face-to-face customer interaction. A key guiding principle for SIS is that the systems should fit the task, not the other way. Salespeople should find the systems helpful in their role, which is often related to early involvement and participation in the design and implementation. The aim is to help salespeople and sales managers manage routine information more effectively, and ease the analysis and reporting of data. Sales managers can therefore measure variances between salespeople or against expected levels – enabling quicker and more appropriate responses.

2 *Sales planning.* Information systems are increasingly being used to help in three major areas: (1) identifying leads and classifying prospects, for example by geography, industry, market segment, turnover and potential; (2) building up customer profiles across a variety of criteria such as organisation, buying preferences or spending patterns and (3) helping with alternative call patterns and territory planning.

3 *Future options and projections.* Computerised information systems help the sales manager with 'what if?' types of question, with the evaluation of different options and with the prediction of future scenarios. This does not mean they provide the right answer every time, but they can assist in directing effort, improving productivity and making decisions which can subsequently be evaluated based on verifiable data. This enhances the ability to appropriately control and evaluate sales activities and results.

Did you know?

According to Mark Christie (*Sales Management*, March 5, 2015) if salespeople realised the real cost of making a sales call they might be more careful how they spend their time and who they spend it with. He calculated that a transactional sales call cost \$80–\$85; basic feature/benefit selling \$155–\$160; solution selling \$225–\$250 and value-based selling \$275–\$300.

Challenges in deploying sales information systems

When properly developed and implemented, an information system can provide timely and relevant information to decision-makers. Because of problems that are inherent in the decision-making and communication processes, a cost-efficient development of systems is not always possible. Common challenges when implementing SIS include the following:

1. *Information overload.* An efficiently designed information system should focus on the collection of information that facilitates decision-making. Research has shown that very little information solicited directly from the sales force is used in the SIS (Donaldson & Wright, 2002). Unfortunately, many sales managers do not always know what information is needed to make decisions. In some sales organisations valuable sales time is wasted collecting information that is not fully used. In order to minimise the information overload problem, it is first necessary to predefine the decisions to be made and then to identify the information that is needed to facilitate decision-making. Sales managers today need to be managers of information.
2. *Inaccurate input data.* Inaccurate input data not only impede decision-making but can destroy employee confidence in the information system. If this happens, salespeople may become disillusioned and dissatisfied with management and the software system being used.
3. *Functional language barriers.* People who develop systems are often technical people who may have limited knowledge of the sales manager's specific information requirements. Similarly, the sales manager may be unaware of what can be provided by an effective computer-based information system. The result is inadequate communication between the designer and the user. The sales manager tells the systems designer what is needed and the designer then converts that request into a prototype design. The translation of business needs into practical and compelling IT designs is far from straightforward. The request is often not interpreted correctly or the IT design driven by technical rather than selling process considerations. Even worse, sometimes, the designs of new systems are incompatible with other existing systems, potentially causing misunderstanding and confusion.
4. *Changing management requirements.* As firms grow and mature, the amount and type of information needed to manage the sales function effectively changes. Sales managers need more information on territory potential, customers' characteristics, sales force productivity, competitive activities and so on. They may also add new products, open new markets and change remuneration plans. These changes in information requirements lead to changes in data files and programs. Unless the system is flexible enough to accommodate these changes, extensive and expensive system modification may be necessary.
5. *Selling the system.* Systems frequently fail when psychological reactions and organisational factors are not considered during the design of the system. Firms

that do not train, educate and involve their employees in the development, uses and strengths of the system may find that it is underused by employees and does not deliver the expected benefits. To avoid such problems, firms should:

- Identify employee needs.
- Develop a system concept.
- Test acceptance of the concept among employees.
- Modify the concept to accommodate employee requests.
- Develop the system.
- Educate employees on the uses of the system.
- Promote the system to users.
- Redesign the system when needs change.

6 *Assessing costs and benefits.* Although costs of developing a system can be calculated and distributed to various operating divisions, benefits are not so easily identified and measured. Each manager must subjectively assess the impact of the system on the quality of decision-making:

- Are decisions made faster and more accurately?
- Are sales territories more productive?
- What effect has the system had on selling costs and gross margin?
- To what extent has staff turnover been reduced?
- How has the system improved employee morale?
- What effect has the system had on the compatibility of various operating divisions?

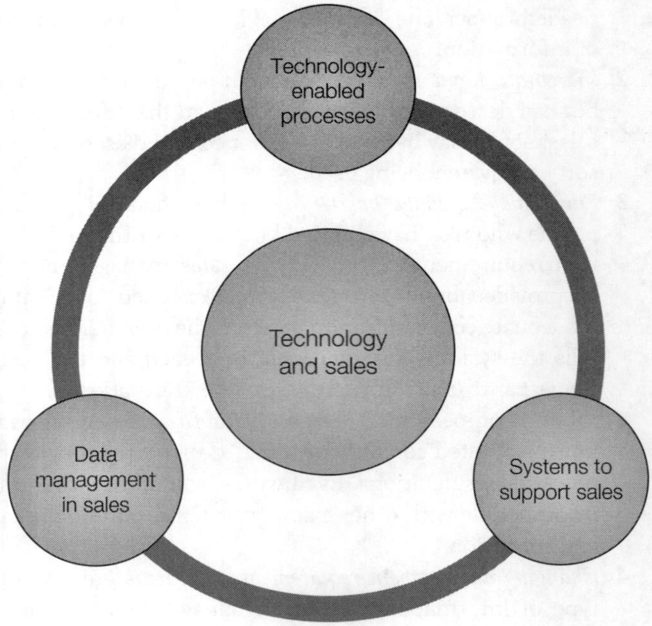

Figure 9.1 – Key areas in sales technology

SALES PROCESSES AND TECHNOLOGY

As discussed earlier, in particular in Chapter 1, the advancement of technologies has transformed the way sales operations are designed and implemented and the actual nature of sales work in many sectors. Four broad areas are fundamentally enabled by technology: customer relationship management (CRM), sales force automation (SFA), e-commerce and customer insights, and data management.

Customer relationship management (CRM)

Sales managers, like sales representatives, have been subject to a dramatic change in the environment where they work, both internally within their organisation and externally. Much of this change in recent years has been driven by the explosion of information technologies (IT), which continue to present challenges and opportunities for the sales function. Most academics and practitioners now agree that information systems should be focused on the customer, not just on the supplier's operations, hence the prominence of CRM. By CRM we mean the integration of technologies and business processes used to better understand the customers, satisfy their needs, and manage customer interactions in an integrated fashion. CRM involves acquisition, analysis and use of knowledge about customers in order to sell more goods or services and to do it more efficiently (Bose, 2002). While there are many varying definitions of CRM most analysts agree that CRM is a business strategy for using customer information to maximise the long-term value and profitability of its relationship with its customers.

CRM has been described as representing 'an enterprise approach to developing full knowledge about customer behaviour and preferences and to developing programmes and strategies that encourage customers to continually enhance their business relationship with the company' (Parvatiyar & Sheth, 2001, pp. 1–2). To achieve this, seamless integration of customer-facing personnel, front-office tools and data with the back office support functions is required. When this integration is achieved then it enables a unified view of the customer base that can be shared within the organisation. The result is potential better understanding of the customer, better service at lower cost and improved sales performance.

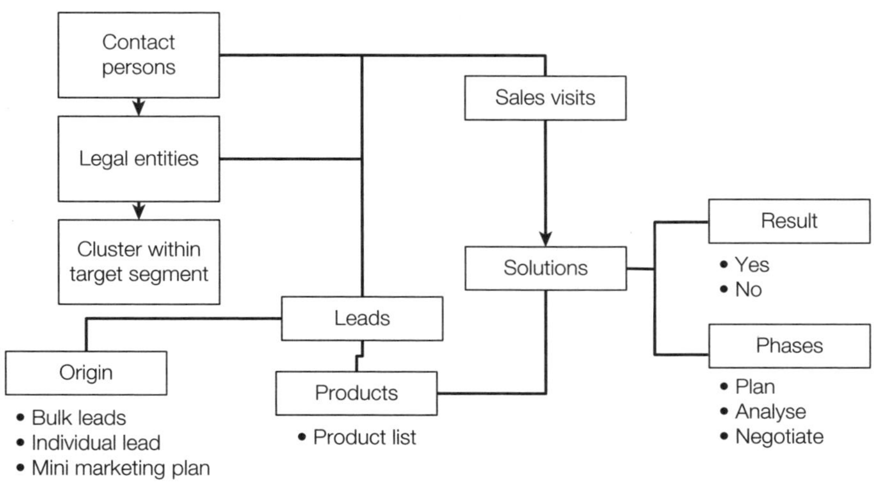

Figure 9.2 – Data available in SMS

As Figure 9.2 indicates, a major part of CRM is sales activity. In response, sales information systems (SIS) and sales force automation (SFA) are increasingly used as part of total CRM solutions. SIS broadly refer to data technologies that facilitate the collection and processing of information to assist the sales process. SFA is concerned with the integration of the front and back office to facilitate an information-empowered sales force that improves sales force productivity and enhances the customer relationship (Payne, 2000). Over the last decade interactive communication between the salesperson and the customer has been high on the sales management agenda of customer-orientated firms.

Traditionally, the role of salespeople has been perceived as crucial for the implementation (delivery) stage of the firm's operational marketing plans. However, the complexity of the relationship process necessitates a more advanced role for salespeople. Clearly, salespeople need to develop specific abilities to determine which accounts to target, who to focus on within that account and which combination of products and services to promote and sell. Sales forces also need to define how frequently they call or support a customer and how to divide their attention between servicing the customer, upselling and cross-selling. The internal organisation sometimes gets in the way of sales forces achieving maximum productivity. As Perrien and Ricard's (1995) study showed, internal management procedures can cause relationship breakdowns and reduce the quality of customer service. This outlines the importance of planning sales practices with a relationship orientation in mind and also of the need for integration and communication flow between the different functions as well as between the buyer and customer in the relationship.

Did you know?

Interesting CRM statistics in 2014:

1. CRM is expected to grow to a $36.5 billion market worldwide within the next three years!
2. 43 per cent of customers use fewer than half the features they have on their CRM.
3. 72 per cent of users would give up all the extra features just to get a CRM that's easier to use.
4. Only 47 per cent of all companies have CRM software.
5. 24 per cent of companies use software as a service (SaaS) to complement their on-site CRM solutions.
6. The average return on investment (ROI) for CRM is $5.60 for every dollar spent!
7. CRM increases sales by up to 29 per cent.
8. 25 per cent of Facebook and Twitter users expect a reply to their complaints via social media in less than one hour.
9. 66 per cent of social media users expect a response within a day.
10. 79 per cent of all marketing leads are never converted to sales.

Source: http://blog.capterra.com/top-crm-statistics-2014/ (accessed February 11, 2015)

We argue that CRM is about acquiring, retaining and growing profitable customers. This implies that the process must be not only closely linked with sales but should ideally be merged and integrated in a seamless enterprise process. Handen (2000) identifies four types of CRM programmes which highlight the need to mesh with sales force activity:

1. *Win back or save*. Selling to new customers is important but retaining existing profitable business even more so. To save a customer that you have failed to deliver to as promised, or one who is defecting because of some competitive weakness, is difficult and time-sensitive. Information, in the correct form as part of a customer database file, can identify declining sales, less frequent ordering and changing customer habits. On the positive side, the file can identify the most profitable and worthwhile customers. A customer once lost may be difficult to

recover. Winning back lost customers requires excellent sales and negotiating skills coupled with good data, the ability to analyse such data and to package this into a saleable customer proposition.

2 *Prospecting*. For most businesses repeat business is more important and more profitable than winning new business, but new customers are also the lifeblood of any enterprise. Leads from central databases, from individual salespeople and from various marketing plans and targets need to be input to the information system and used judiciously. Put simply, winning new business requires good leads. Focusing on leads which are unlikely to grow or which will be unprofitable is wasted effort; therefore it is not the number but the quality of leads that matters. A good CRM system can categorise leads, assist in evaluating credit ratings and assess the potential customer's future value to the business.

3 *Loyalty* is a much used and misused term in business, but as many utility companies know to their cost customer churn is a real business problem. Most telecom companies now categorise their business in terms of revenue assurance, given that customer churn can dramatically affect their future profitability. As a result, CRM is a profit centre rather than a cost overhead, and information that can identify and control subscriber churn is a critical source of competitive advantage. Such information may also create new opportunities such as affinity marketing, loyalty cards, customised billing and target-specific, cross-selling opportunities.

4 *Cross-sell/up-sell* opportunities are created by information that can identify customers' needs more specifically. As a result, complementary products and services can be offered which provide better solutions for the customer thus enhancing customer value. Customer profitability can improve by more than 10 per cent within three years if CRM strategies are correctly implemented and followed up consistently (Brown, 2000).

Sales force automation (SFA)

SFA systems have been defined, variously, as (1) centralised database systems that can be accessed remotely using special software – hence focusing on information-handling capacities (Parthasarathy & Sohi, 1997), or (2) as the converting of manual sales activities to electronic processes though the use of various combinations of hardware and software (Erffmeyer & Johnson, 2001). Perhaps the best compromise is to adopt a broad, practice-based, approach to SFA and SIS usage (Widmier, Jackson & McCabe, 2002). SFA often involves the automated collection of information to assist the sales and customer management process.

SFA enables easier communication across time and location, more rapidly and with greater accuracy and to the people that need to know within the network. Moreover, salespeople and sales managers require higher degrees of mobility. Thus, the collection and dissemination of information in real time is important within the sales function to enable salespeople to work smarter (Sujan, Weitz & Kumar, 1994).

Sales automation and sales information systems provide the salesperson with up-to-date relevant customer information such as orders, deliveries, invoices, customer contact details and other business-related issues. Salespeople can also work smarter by more efficient time management, call routing and targeting of customers and prospects. Indeed sales planning in terms of call preparation, customer information and sales presentation is enhanced if the account history is accurate, buyer profiles are complete and information about business opportunities is personalised in a number of sectors.

What do you think?

Salesforce.com, a leading provider of sales automation solutions, claims on one of its sites:

> Sales Cloud's sales force automation far surpasses that of traditional sales software of any other sales tool and, not surprisingly, has a customer satisfaction rate of 95 per cent. Cloud computing-driven sales management software has now pulled way ahead of traditional on-premises sales tools. This is because salesforce.com's Sales Cloud is so simple to use, is affordable and is globally accessible on demand! Server-based sales software can take forever to deploy. However, salesforce.com's cloud based sales force automation frees companies from huge and complex upfront investment.

Source: http://www.salesforce.com/uk/sales-cloud/overview/#more

The trend to be both flexible and responsive has accelerated in response to the increasing demand for customised products/services and rapid response to satisfy the requirements of custom-focused markets. Inevitably, there is conflict between the requirement for flexibility and the need for automation in systems and processes in order to reduce costs yet maintain quality service. Businesses are realising that to improve shareholder value whilst satisfying customer needs requires a re-conceptualisation of strategy, technology, people and systems. As a result, there has been an increasing investment in IT to create lower cost platforms to serve customers in multichannel environment. Part of this investment has been in sales automation systems that enable a more efficient and effective sales–customer interaction. Thus, leading firms have a multifaceted system of data mining, data warehousing, salespeople, call centre staff and others who interact with the customer. The current challenge is to manage sales data processing in an integrated fashion.

More recently, the strategic focus of information technology applications has moved from transaction efficiency to a relationship orientation that embraces customer-focused technology (Peppers & Rogers, 2004). The fundamental drive is to reduce transaction costs while maintaining or even enhancing service quality. A major benefit is to develop relationships with customers and new sales processes to enable the sales function to move from a focus on transaction to a new focus on 'enterprise' selling (Rackham & DeVincentis, 1998).

The adoption of SFA has not been as widespread, uniform or successful as early expectations predicted. Existing research has focused on individual-level factors – that is, at the level of the individual salesperson – explaining the degree of technology adoption and use amongst the sales force. Jones, Sundaram and Chin (2002) demonstrate the importance of salespeople's attitudes towards the new systems – including perceived usefulness and perceived compatibility with existing systems. Similarly, Venkatesh and Davies (2000) identified the importance of individual-level factors such as perceived ease of use and perceived usefulness – attitudes which themselves are shaped by general beliefs that the individual holds about computers – in the initial acceptance of SFA technology. Venkatesh and Davis (2000) extended this investigation by using three points of measurement – (1) pre-implementation, (2) immediate post-implementation and (3) three months post-implementation. These authors found that factors such as social influence (the pressure that meaningful others may have on a subject based on what they do/don't do) are important in explaining technology adoption. Other relevant factors such as job relevance, perceived quality of the output of the technology, and perceived ease of use explain the degree of adoption of SFA. Taken together, Venkatesh and Davis (2000) found that these factors accounted for about 50 per cent of the variance in usage intentions.

Widmier, Jackson and McCabe (2002) focused on the usage of adopted SFA and found that the major sales use was for sales calls and expense reports. However, fewer than one-half of the salespeople that they sampled used the technology for calendar reports. In addition, the majority of the applications of the SFA reporting technology were initiated by companies rather than by salespeople. This was because, Widmier et al. (2002) argued, the sales managers saw the SFA technology as a 'very useful tool in managing the sales force'.

Other studies such as Speier and Venkatesh (2002), who collected survey data from 454 salespeople across two firms that had implemented SFA tools in the United States, found that, immediately after training in the tools, salespeople had positive perceptions of the technology but, six months after implementation, the technology had been widely rejected by the salespeople and, at the same time, salesperson absenteeism and voluntary turnover had significantly increased. Interview data indicated that the SFA tools were a primary driver for those salespeople choosing to leave the two firms. It is argued that SFA technology may alienate successful salespeople in that the technology may change the salesperson's role if they generate internal conflict and power redistribution facilitated by managers quickly and easily assessing the number of, frequency of, and time allocated to sales calls. Increased monitoring often increases the power differential between manager and salesperson in favour of the manager, implying that SFA implementation need to be carefully thought through in terms of the 'knock-on' implications. Speier and Venkatesh (2002) thus develop the issue of the 'logic of opposition' raised by Robey and Boudreau (1999) in their analysis of the organisational consequences of information technology interventions.

Sviokla (1996) investigated the use of an expert system designed to support the insurance sales process at four insurance companies. Before the system was introduced sales agents 'often "owned" the clients and successfully took their business as they moved from one firm to another'. After the system was introduced, all the detailed client data were fed straight to the home office and so 'the company adopting the system could track its salespeople at a higher level of detail' (p. 32). Sviokla (1996) concludes that successful implementations were considerate of political ramifications of the adoption of technological innovation.

Sales funnel and opportunity management

In large sales forces or in contexts of high volume of operations, organisations often use the analogy of the 'sales funnel' to describe the sales processes from initial customer contact through to order confirmation and delivery (see Figure 9.3). The funnel represents the stage of sales opportunities, thus helping the company calculate conversion rates. Sales managers can then compare salespeople's ratios with the norm, in order to devise actions that may help develop the effectiveness of sales operations.

Technology companies provide a wide range of services and products to analyse the sales funnel activity. Typically these systems present sales transactions from a historic perspective, displaying information in such a way that marketing and sales campaigns can be evaluated, for instance calculating the number of leads generated that actually resulted in a sale.

Many technology companies and software vendors claim that sales funnel management and associated SFA can result in shortened sales cycles and higher levels of sales performance. SFA can help introduce the processes to encourage follow-through on deals, but SIS alone will rarely shorten cycles or improve sales outcomes. Customers

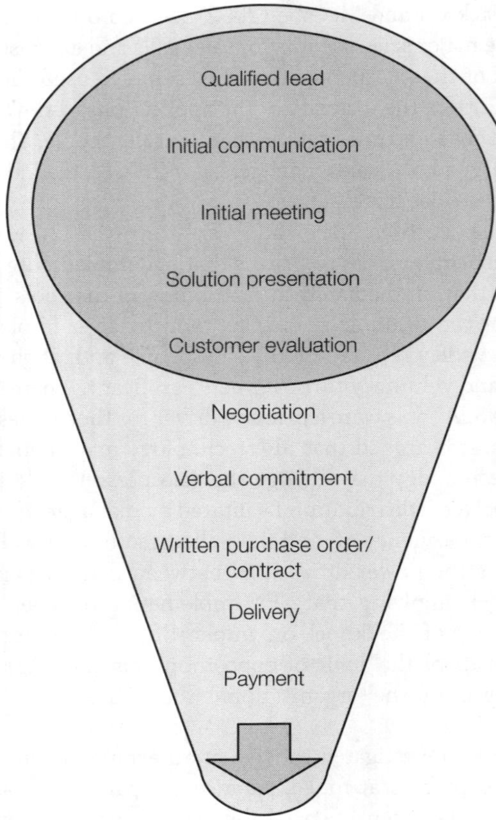

Figure 9.3 – The sales funnel

Source: Compiled by authors

are different and their purchase decisions are based on myriad factors, many of which cannot be captured and predicted by information systems. A key implication for salespeople is to understand in detail the customer's buying cycle. Then, sales organisations can 'map' these cycles and use technology to support the management of sales effectiveness-enhancing practices.

MINI CASE STUDY

Accelerating sales growth in SunGard.

SunGard is a global vendor of software and processing solutions for the financial services industries, government agencies and education institutions.

The executive team at SunGard recently faced the challenge of transforming the sales force to create sustainable growth. This aim was achieved by redefining Sungard's sales approach, giving rise to the so-called 'Selling the SunGard Way' and by investing in introducing tools and technologies to support sales operations and customer management processes. Initially, SunGard faced the challenge that only 30 per cent of total revenues stemmed from new business. Also, the executive team were concerned that Sungard's sales force focused on selling specific product to meet customer-expressed needs and did not engage in a deeper understanding of the customer and in exploring further opportunities. The company also recognised that the sales force was over-reliant on the brand's recognition and standing in the market place.

In addition to revisiting the sales approach SunGard engaged a few information systems partners to acquire sales-technology applications and integrated them using a Salesforce (see salesforce.com) platform. This platform, customised to support SunGard's specific sales processes, helped sales representatives understand when and how to move deals forward, having a positive impact on the accuracy and efficiency of the forecast. A new automated sales compensation platform was also implemented, allowing salespeople to quickly determine their incentives, and SunGard to move away from cumbersome, manual spreadsheets to calculate compensation.

The result of SunGard's renewed sales strategy has led to reduced turnover, increased sales and improved market receptivity. The company reports that it is on target for expected levels of growth with a promising pipeline (sales funnel). SunGard's case illustrates how re-focusing the sales strategy with the customer in mind, re-defining sales processes and supporting these with the appropriate technology can accelerate sales growth.

Source: SellingPower, 2014

Telesales and call centre management

Telesales (or telemarketing) is interactive communication with customers over the telephone which can provide the ability to target specific contacts quickly and at lower cost than can a person-to-person sales call. Telemarketing can also be used to prospect and qualify leads and for a range of service support activities other than merely order-taking. Customers who are small, make only a marginal contribution or are geographically remote can often be handled more effectively and more efficiently through telemarketing than in person. The telephone is obviously far quicker than a face-to-face meeting and has at least four key benefits:

1 Lower cost substitute for personal selling. On average, each telephone call is estimated to cost one-tenth as much as a personal call, mainly because of the absence of travel and waiting time, and this is clearly a more profitable approach for small accounts with limited potential. The telephone can be used productively with other forms of promotion and communication, such as television and radio direct response or mail order catalogues. Catalogue selling is far from a new channel but the speed and service that can be provided using today's technology coupled with the telephone interaction can greatly increase business done in this way.

2 To supplement personal selling calls. Salespeople themselves can increase their personal productivity by using the telephone wisely. Time and effort previously wasted by calling on accounts when not required can be replaced by a telephone call which, if the customer requires, can be followed up personally. It can generally be expected that most salespeople will increase their ratio of telephone to personal calls and, overall, fewer person-to-person calls will be required.

3 As an alternative to direct mail, especially if a 0800 freephone or reduced rate lines are used. Advertising and promotional campaigns can be targeted at encouraging customers to call for additional information and service or to place their order. In some cases, these sales leads will be followed up by personal selling. Most companies today provide a customer service telephone line that allows quick resolution

of concerns, and handling of queries, complaints or suggestions they may have relating to the products or services the company provides.

4 The use of the telephone can provide better customer support and service, particularly when integrating telephone activity with computer-based technology – to the extent that some companies such as Direct Line (www.directline.com) in the insurance sector or First Direct (www.firstdirect.com) in financial services have designed their business model entirely on telephone and Internet service. Where the customers are comfortable with this medium and with products which are fast moving and require no, or a limited, physical examination yet have a high value, telemarketing is very effective. The result is more effective communication at lower cost.

Telephone selling: Good practice

Like any management activity, telemarketing requires management of the process and not merely the activity itself. Six stages can be suggested:

1 *Define the objectives.* Since use of the telephone is now so widespread, so is its misuse. Most people receive many unsolicited telephone calls from companies they neither know nor care about and with whom they do not wish to do business. Despite some initial success, most companies are now wary of using the telephone for cold prospecting, although to sell new products or services to existing customers it is still a powerful and effective tool. Objectives can range from identifying leads and the qualification of prospects to order-taking and service activities. Clear objectives need to be set in terms of activity, response times, orders to calls and so on.

2 *Planning.* Alienating existing customers with overzealous selling by telephone is to be avoided but, equally, missing opportunities to cross-sell to existing customers means potentially losing the most lucrative sales prospects. Similarly, having several people, seemingly uncoordinated, contact the same customer on different issues is equally damaging to one's reputation and credibility. De-duplication and address and contact verification is essential. Using a variety of call strategies and different means of customer contact requires careful planning and coordination. This avoids multiple contacts at different times and ensures effective use of the telephone in a customer-friendly way. From a sales perspective, scoring and propensity modelling are some of the techniques now being used. This has important implications for marketing strategy since what can be observed is reverse market segmentation based on a bottom-up approach using an identification of individual customers in a more sophisticated way.

3 *Customer contact staff.* While certain aspects of selling by telephone are similar to those of personal selling, other aspects are quite different. As with personal selling, good communication skills, empathy and an ability to respond in the correct manner by asking questions will be helpful, but a different approach and different skills are also needed.

4 *Relationships with salespeople and other departments.* A key to an effective and efficient telemarketing operation is to obtain the early involvement and participation of other sales staff and functions in the organisation. In particular, competition between different departments or functions must be avoided, and there should preferably be some interchange of staff to appreciate what each department does, how and why.

5 *Sell the idea of telesales to the customers.* Most important in any telemarketing operation is to ensure that the customer is better served by the operation, that the system is designed to meet their needs and that there are benefits to the customer from operating in this way.

6 *Measurement and control*. Before introducing any telesales or telephone support operation, it should be critically tested and appraised to remove and avoid any pitfalls. Targets for performance should be set, effectiveness and efficiency measured and monitored, and adjustments made as necessary. Response times, the number of complaints answered by first operator, comparative sales and service levels are some of the areas that should be measured and monitored. Management of call centres or telemarketing operations has become a subset area of sales management. It requires an effective contact management plan, careful call list preparation and development and, very often, prepared scripts for staff to respond to customers in the correct manner. Furthermore, it is a management responsibility to ensure that what is promised is delivered so that customer expectations are met and, if possible, exceeded. Efficient call centre management, again using today's technology, should be able to provide management reports and statistics far in excess of any manual operation. The net result should be improved customer service, well motivated staff and a more efficient operation.

SELLING AND THE INTERNET

The Internet and associated technologies have changed, forever, the way we live, how we communicate and how we relate to others as individuals. Technology is transforming the way businesses are run across all functions. Perhaps the area where 'new' technologies are having the most radical impact is selling. The Internet has become the key tool for providing information, allowing efficient ways of searching for relevant information at an individual level. It has also made it easier to order and to process the exchange of goods, services and ideas. Customers now feel empowered to collect information and make more informed purchase decisions. From travel agencies and car dealerships to financial intermediaries – all are affected by this process and recognise that they are dealing with well versed and knowledgeable customers. Information itself is proving more robust and accurate. Information has become widely dispersed and accessible. It is argued, however, that at the organisational level businesses have been slower to adopt new technologies despite the potential value their use may bring about (Andzulis, Panagopoulos & Rapp, 2012).

Consumers readily use on a daily basis social media platforms such as Facebook, QZone (China), Flickr, LinkedIn, Myspace, Twitter, Google+, Slideshare, YouTube, etc. These ecosystems of resources present both unique opportunities and significant challenges to the players in the market place. The traditional purchase routes that existed pre-Internet were disrupted by the widespread expansion of the net. Then, customer choices when consuming products and services were transformed by the growth of connected devices and new apps making the act of purchasing easier and more immediate.

What do you think?

Just a vivid example of how the act of purchasing has become easier. We mentioned the launch of *From Selling to Co-creating* (Lemmens, Donaldson & Marcos, 2014) in one of our Sales Management classes. Minutes later, at a break, one of our students confirmed she had just bought it. It took her 90 seconds to purchase it using the Amazon app on her smartphone.

Consumers and customers preferences are changing and consumers are demanding higher levels of user-friendliness, more personalised communications and relevant information, provided when needed. Thus, companies need to be mindful about the amount and the nature of information they send to their customers and consumers.

The power of networks

Social media has boosted Internet-based platforms that enable individuals to share or trade with other people, removing the traditional barriers of other market channels. The success of eBay (www.ebay.com) as a platform to trade second-hand items was followed myriad websites from car sharing (www.liftshare.com) to courses (www.coursera.org), selling vintage and handmade items (www.etsy.com) or sharing spare rooms (www.airbnb.com), all matching offer and existing resources with latent demand. Networks facilitated by online platforms have revolutionised the service sector, creating unique opportunities for collaborative work from software development (www.github.com) to music making (www.kompoz.com).

The above are mostly examples of B2C, but companies are also exploiting the power of networks in B2B contexts. Firms as diverse as Caterpillar in the heavy machinery sector or ING in financial services create portals where customers are encouraged to interact and share their experiences. From these interactions, the firms can extract insights to further develop offerings and enhanced services.

Technologies are facilitating the development of not just services but also products. A new wave of micro-manufacturing techniques is allowing the creation of products in small batches, often customised for specific customers. An increasing 'desktop manufacturing revolution' (Anderson, 2012) is transforming the manufacturing sector. Tools and technologies that hitherto were only accessible to corporations with significant investment are now available to the wider population. Good ideas can find their way into assembly lines faster and easier. Then the web has made it easy to connect and bring creations fast into the market, with sites such as www.quirky.com, in ways unthinkable five decades ago. When it comes to financing, crowdfunding and social financing from companies like Kickstarter (www.kickstarter.com) means that entrepreneurs no longer depend on venture capitalists or investment banks to finance their ideas (GfK, 2014).

E-commerce

In an effort to drive down costs, improve efficiency and deliver competitive products buyers are increasingly using e-commerce systems. E-procurement is a specific form of e-commerce incorporating inter-company cooperation, supply chain management and instant data access between buyer and seller. Increasingly, these systems are using web-based tools and other forms of B2B solutions such as eRFQ, eRFI, catalogue procurement or e-auctions. These new forms of selling integrate information from several sources, but the ability of the sales professional to negotiate still prevails. For example, a study of electronic reverse auctions (eRA) in the automotive industry in Europe found that there are limitations to automated forms of exchange, and sales managers have very mixed attitudes to the use of eRA (Donaldson & Resch, 2006). It appears that to achieve more effective B2B exchange a compromise between relationship building and blind electronic auctions where lowest price wins is required.

However, eRAs are not free of disadvantages. Arguably, they can reduce the long-term competitiveness of both buyer and seller (Emiliani & Stec, 2002), if relationships are damaged. eRAs are widely perceived as a purchasing tool designed principally to reduce prices without giving adequate consideration to other factors like quality, relationship, experience or know-how (Tulder & Mol, 2002). They damage supplier relations and create distrust among incumbent suppliers (Emiliani, 2004). Some of the concerns over eRAs include the following:

- Gaining market data without having ambitions to award work to the bidders.
- Accepting bids from suppliers that are not qualified to do the work.
- Making side-deals, where work is awarded to bidders that didn't participate in the reverse auction.
- Not advising eRA participants of the outcome in a timely manner.
- Not awarding the work as quoted – for example, unbundling lots of partial lot awards.
- Not disclosing if buyer's internal operations are bidding on the work.

Some large industrial buyers, such as Toyota Motor Corporation, Honda Motor Corporation and Harley-Davidson, are reported to abstain from eRAs, arguing that they focus on price and not on total cost of acquisition and ownership, that buyers and sellers do not learn how to jointly solve problems and that eRAs may damage supplier relationships and teamwork (Emiliani, 2004).

These reservations are not specific to eRAs. Focus on price not on costs is independent from auction or traditional negotiation – it's a matter of purchasing professionalism. Purchasing managers who decide to use eRAs may be indulging in bad business behaviour regardless of whether they are negotiating online or not. Emiliani (2004) raises the interesting question with respect to the role of online auctions, that eRAs may just provide a short-term solution to much deeper problems within the buying firm, such as poor cost management and the inability to adopt modern supply chain management principles and lean production methods that 'are needed by both buyers and suppliers in order to truly eliminate waste and reduce total costs'.

Did you know?

Reverse e-auctions can be a good approach to drive down costs when they meet certain criteria, including:

- Spend characteristics: generic or commodity
- Product/service specifications: Industry standards
- Driver: mostly price and volume
- Supply market competiveness: very competitive
- Supply base: large number of potential suppliers
- Supplier relationship: transactional
- Switching costs and risks: low

Source: Procure Edge (2014). White paper. Reverse e-Auctions: A Recipe for Success

It can be argued that eRAs may shift existing markets between buyer and seller more to a kind of perfect market where knowledge is available very quickly and to many participants. During an auction, the buyer and supplier are informed almost immediately of changing conditions and prices. What took several days to negotiate before has become a matter of a few hours. eRAs have increased in popularity because they emphasise short-term price savings and can simplify and support negotiations (Jap, 2003). One benefit of eRAs, as well as e-commerce as a whole is speed. The use of the web enables a global sales management team to participate in real time in a bidding process. The quick collection of proposals speeds up the sourcing decision and enables more rapid award.

Suppliers want to maximise sales, particularly through long-term relationships that emphasise quality and delivery. These conditions can also breed discord and suspicion (Jap, 2003). Buyers can be greatly rewarded for saving money and lowering costs but also need to ensure consistency and reliability of supply. Online dynamic bidding systems require thorough preparation in advance, clarity about the walk away point and keeping emotions out of the process.

MINI CASE

The growth and expansion of Alibaba

Alibaba Group is a group of Internet-based e-commerce businesses that includes business-to-business online web portals, online retail and payment services, a shopping search engine and data-centric cloud computing services. It is privately owned and based in Hangzhou, the capital of Zhejiang on China's east coast. It is reported that in 2012, two of Alibaba's portals together handled 1.1 trillion yuan ($170 billion) in sales, more than competitors such as eBay and Amazon. The company operates primarily in China. Ma Yun founded Alibaba in 1999 in the living room of his house, and started operating as Alibaba.com, a business-to-business portal to connect Chinese manufacturers with overseas buyers. Today, the group employs 25,000 staff and trades 800 million products. Alibaba Group's sites account for over 60 per cent of the parcels delivered in China. Its CEO Lu Zhaoxi aspires to convert Alibaba into the second biggest Internet company, behind Google, and to triple its transactions by 2016 to surpass Wal-Mart as the biggest retailer in the world.

Sources: 'E-commerce in China: The Alibaba phenomenon'. The Economist. March 23, 2013. 'Una cueva de Alibaba en China – *Alibaba's cave in China*'. El Pais. April 12, 2014.

Selling and social media

In their paper 'A Review of Social Media and Implications for the Sales Process' Andzulis et al. (2012) argue that social media and its development has the potential to transform the way we as customers buy and thus the way suppliers sell, as well creating a new technological paradigm that sales researchers will need to consider. In their paper, four levels for the development of social media in sales are identified, which are labelled presence, influence, engagement, and value creation:

1. *Presence:* Establishing media presence to provide information (one way) from the company to the customer. The decision to have presence in social media is not linked to the sales and marketing strategy of the company in any fundamental way.
2. *Influence.* In this phase organisations make a conscious effort to direct customers to the company's social media platforms with a view to exchanging information, but not necessarily as part of a predefined sales or strategy. Forums and comments sections are opened.
3. *Engagement.* Social media is conceived as a core sales channel and a fundamental mechanism for customer engagement. It contributes to and largely shapes the sales strategy of the company.
4. *Value creation.* Social media is fully integrated with sales strategy; functionality such as real-time pricing and additional services are offered. As a result of the

way social media platforms are used, value is co-created via new insights and exchanges. Thus, meaningful learning emerges that businesses can use to provide a higher quality of service delivery and/or product development. The way the company uses social media enables the firm to enhance its overall value proposition. Insights can also be used to offer customised products and services to the customers.

These levels do not mean that all companies need to develop co-creating capabilities through social media. It means that depending on the nature and type of relationships with customers, social media can become a powerful leverage of sales and customer management strategies. All these levels have something in common: the customer has become the driver of the value creation and where sellers' efforts converge. The sharing of content and the creation of networks gravitate around the customer. The use of social media helps create new opportunities with customers, and enhances relationship management with positive effects on both relationship and outcome-based sales performance (Rodriguez, Peterson & Krishnan, 2012).

To achieve the benefits that social media usage may bring about, collaboration and alignment between sales and marketing is required. It is recognised (Andzulis et al., 2012) that some elements of the utilisation of social media naturally reside within the marketing unit, and some within sales. For instance brand awareness, advertising and market insights generation are traditional activities of marketing. Customer management and understanding is the remit of sales. The key then is to define the right set-up so integrative ownership structures allow the benefits of social media usage to be exploited by the function best placed to act on the results obtained.

The use of social media needs to be in sync with the sales processes and this can be achieved as follows (Andzulis et al., 2012):

1 *Prospecting* that includes opportunity identification and leads generation can be supported by becoming part of relevant interest groups on LinkedIn, establishing relevant alerts using keywords such as company names, line of business, product name etc., and extracting clues from company's product and service blogs.
2 *Research, planning and preparation* that includes insights gathering and anticipating potential professional/personal interests and risks can be enhanced by reviewing the customers' own presence in social media and what they are trying to achieve with their own customers/consumers, monitoring and analysing comments to understand attitudes toward purchasing and buying preferences and reviewing the LinkedIn and Facebook profiles of members of the decision-making unit.
3 *Approach and opening* including gaining interest, establishing credibility and rapport building can be facilitated by using LinkedIn surveys to generate industry discussion about relevant topics, posting insights with the results of these surveys, tweeting/re-tweeting links to the findings of the surveys, launching promotions inviting participation in new product testing on Facebook, sharing stories about your company's social responsibility initiatives and tweeting about conferences/results/innovation.
4 *Exploration of needs* including questioning, listening and understanding customer's motives can be enhanced by posting open questions to stimulate discussion forums, tweeting, emailing links to surveys that gather customer feedback and insights, analysing customer-generated content to understand their views of your product and services, as well as the customers' priorities and challenges.

5 *Presentation,* comprising the provision of product/service features and demonstrating advantages and benefits, is fostered by providing relevant information about your company's offerings in blogs, YouTube and Facebook, requesting customer reviews and posting them as 'case studies' on various media and sharing cases of positive impact on blogs, Facebook and YouTube channels.
6 *Handling objections* is eased by demonstrating and documenting how your company has helped other customers address their aims and objectives, and by using Chatter to communicate and personally address difficulties customers may have experienced.
7 *Closing* that involves generating commitment and negotiating is aided by tweeting and emailing/texting customers with special promotions benefits if they confirm a purchase and offering additional benefits that have high value for customers and low cost to the company.

We have outlined a number of ways in which social media can enhance the organisation's ability to be more relevant to its customers and to reach further. However, social media also brings a number of risks. Reputation risk in particular presents a threat to organisations when individuals using social media expose firms' vulnerabilities or malpractice, posing a challenge to firm's name (Aula, 2010).

Did you know?

On March 31, 2008, professional musician Dave Carroll and his band mates were travelling from Halifax, Canada, flying United Airlines to Omaha, connecting at Chicago O'Hare. The musician asked whether he could bring his guitar on board but was refused and asked to check the guitar in, so it could travel in the hold. He arrived at his destination, and to his surprise, his $3,500 acoustic guitar had been severely damaged. He spent eight months unsuccessfully trying to obtain compensation from the airline. United Airlines informed him that he was ineligible for compensation because he had failed to make the claim within its stipulated 'standard 24-hour timeframe'. He warned the company he would write a song about the incident and would post it in a social media platform if his request was not met.

On July 6, 2009, a video with a song titled 'United Breaks Guitars' was posted on YouTube. It amassed 150,000 views within one day, after which United contacted Carroll to find an amicable way forward. The video garnered over half a million hits by July 9, five million by mid-August 2009, ten million by February 2011, and 13.3 million by September 2013.

Four days after its launch, United stock went down 10 per cent, shedding $180 million in value. The musician attracted huge media attention, demonstrating 'the power of one voice in the age of social media' (Carroll, 2012).

CONCLUSION

Hardware functionalities, CRM application, the Internet and social media have completely transformed the way companies sell and the nature of interactions between sellers and customers. Online platforms are not becoming another way to interact with customers and develop relationships: many argue that nowadays they are the only way. A key challenge to consider is whether a firm is just aiming to be 'present' on the web by encouraging the public to like or recommend, or whether they will require a fundamental shift in what they do and how they do it. Just as organisations need to define the product strategy and its organisation, they also need a strategy for sales technology both internal and external.

QUESTIONS

- How can CRM systems help develop the sales process?
- What are the key benefits of sales force automation? And what may be the risks and shortcomings?
- How could you assess the efficacy of database marketing and telemarketing?
- In which ways have traditional sales techniques been changed by the Internet and other technologies?

CASE STUDY

Diversey: CRM in Action

Diversey Inc. is a leading global provider of cleaning and hygiene solutions to the institutional market place, serving customers in the lodging, food service, retail, health care, food & beverage sectors, as well as building service contractors worldwide. Diversey traces its roots back to 1886, but Diversey Corporation was founded in 1923 in Chicago. In 1996 it was acquired by Unilever to become DiverseyLever, and in 2002, Johnson Wax Professional acquired DiverseyLever and the combined companies became JohnsonDiversey until March 2010, when the name was simplified to Diversey.

The company has a large specialised sales force serving all sorts of private and public organisations. The sales organisation uses a range of sales reporting tools where they hold full details on all customers. Individual salespeople have access to specific customer information and contribute to update the system so the company can more accurately tailor its products and services to the needs of specific customers and customer types. The system is also used to monitor and measure sales force efficiency. Sales and customer management systems are integrated into wider Enterprise Resource Planning ERP platforms to provide an more integrated picture of sales and customer activities.

The success of FrontDesk, Diversey's CRM system, relies on the salesperson updating customer information in full every day, but less than 30 per cent of the sales force actually does so. This is despite full training and one-to-one training sessions with every member of the sales team. Changes have been made to work patterns and activities to ensure time and resources are available. Although some downsizing of the sales force has resulted in recent redundancies, changes were made to the pay structure with field salespeople receiving pay increases on the understanding that FrontDesk was rolled out and utilised. To date, no improvement in the usage of FrontDesk has materialised.

QUESTIONS

1. Why do you think there has been reluctance to use the FrontDesk system?
2. What else can the company/management do to increase usage of the system?
3. IT failures in Western Europe have been estimated at $40 billion (Dalcher & Genus, 2003). What proposals would you make to assess the financial worth of the system?

CASE STUDY

SAP A.G.: Transitioning to a cloud-based model

In a letter to SAP stakeholders in 2012, SAP's co-CEOs stated:

> The real-time world has now become reality. Cloud computing is changing the way software is consumed, evidenced by a shift in spending from hardware to software. Currently, there are more mobile devices in the world than people, giving billions of people computing power in their pockets. Fifteen billion of those devices are connected to the Internet, bringing people and businesses closer to each other across the globe. Technology has moved beyond supporting business. More than ever, technology is the business.

This statement marked an important development in SAP's strategy, with profound implications across the organisation and its ecosystem of customers, partners and suppliers. As part of this renewed strategy, SAP has further developed HANA, its cloud platform-based company's flagship in-memory data technology. HANA is becoming a full platform for building real-time apps in the cloud, including advanced analytical capabilities offering three main options: SAP HANA AppServices, SAP HANA DBServices, and SAP HANA Infrastructure Services.

Moreover, this fundamental change to cloud-based offering and unified platforms in the nature and the focus of its services has wide ranging repercussions for the sales and customer management strategies of the company. First, the sales and engagement process has changed, and the new SAP HANA marketplace has become, in the words of Vishal Sikka, one of SAP's board directors, 'a marketplace for the world we're coming into'. Bringing SAP HANA to the market, has already derived in changes in the way SAP structures its sales processes. Large companies, traditionally the target customers of SAP, may no longer be the largest contributors to the company's growth. The HANA cloud and market place is allowing thousands of startups to build products on HANA, creating a vibrant space for new developments.

A major transformation that new strategies are bringing about is the pricing models. The old model of generating income from design and on-premises installation is giving way to a consumption-based model that starts with a base price and increases as customers choose add-on options for more services as required. The launch of SAP Business Suite powered by SAP HANA in 2013 was recognised by the president of SAP Global Ecosystem and Channels as a move that 'will not only transform our customers' businesses, it is transforming our partnerships by unleashing unprecedented business opportunities. These opportunities include co-innovation and re-selling, high-value services, better differentiation, and more profitable and sustainable business.'

The 'radical' shift towards cloud computing brings a number of questions and issues that SAP will need to address. A key concern is whether well-established routes to market and organisational structures will be able to adapt fast enough. The transition from on-premises towards cloud-based computing triggers the worry of whether revenue secured through 'predictable' contracts will be maintained when licence schemes are introduced. Traditionally, pricing models rested on upfront, one-time licence fees negotiated by the sales teams. These teams typically were structured as direct sales organisations, at regional, national and international level. In addition, partners, distributors and value-added resellers form part of the go-to-market strategy.

Key contact people in SAP's customers are CIOs with whom SAP sales forces have, over decades, established and developed strong relationships. The introduction of cloud computing results in a reduction of the significance of the CIO in favour of the end user, who, though a subscription-based scheme, pays for what they use. It is likely that relationship development strategies aimed at persuading CIOs will become increasingly irrelevant with non-IT experts. Additionally, the value propositions for IT vs. HR or Marketing specialist change completely. Overall, a question for sales and customer management teams is the extent to which scalable and more versatile cloud technologies may co-exist with the hitherto sizeable on-premises business, minimising cannibalisation and still allowing cross-selling of traditional services.

The move towards a cloud-based business and the development of HANA has effectively meant transforming SAP from a conventional software provider into a cloud service vendor. SAP chief executives conceived cloud strategies relevant and applicable across the organisation. Thus, the new pricing schemes for cloud services suggested revamping the incentive structures that existed for sales teams primarily focused on on-premises offerings. The intention is to support the community of sales professionals to focus on the 'targets and measures that matter' and to engage in behaviours more in sync with the versatility and flexibility of new business models.

A key area of development to support SAP's growth is the selection and development of partners. SAP requires partnerships to be established with hardware & software vendors, systems integrators, and professional services firms. Currently, SAP establishes partnerships with firms throughout the spectrum of information technologies. SAP employs certified hardware partners for HANA on-premises installations that include hardware, the operating system and SAP software. Moving towards the full deployment of cloud environments, SAP has devised various options from full ownership of data centres and hardware to third party ownership where SAP provides services. SAP has made clear its commitment to roll out and develop its new platforms and to cooperate with partners for mutual success. As the president of SAP Global Ecosystem and Channels stated: 'SAP HANA will give partners the ability to transform our joint customers' business models ... Cloud is here to stay, and all our cloud solutions are now channel-ready under a unified partner program, making it very simple for partners to adopt and bring to customers.'

Sources: Annual Report 2012. Available at http://global.sap.com/corporate-en/investors/pdf/SAP-2012-Annual-Report.pdf. Accessed November 6, 2013.
http://www.zdnet.com/saps-new-cloud-strategy-includes-app-marketplace-new-pricing-scheme-7000027025/
Karim R. Lakhani, Marco Iansiti & Noah Fisher. *SAP 2014: Reaching for the Cloud*. HBS Case. No. 9-614-052
http://www.news-sap.com/why-sap-partners-have-a-competitive-advantage/

QUESTIONS:

1 How do you think SAP sales structures and routes to market will need to change to adapt to the new cloud-based business model?
2 How might customer expectations and demands change as a result of SAP's transition to a cloud-based model?
3 To what extent you think the skills and competences to sell on-premises are similar to selling on-cloud products and services?

INTERVIEW – ABBOUD GHANEM

Regional Sales Manager for Alterix, Inc., Abboud has developed a successful career in sales reaching senior client management positions at global technology companies such Oracle and Salesforce.com and co-founded 5W Consulting, a marketing technology business. Abboud discovered and practised the power of open questions (the 5Ws & How) to listen and to develop a full understanding of his clients' challenges and objectives, hence the name of the company he funded.

Q: In what ways is technology affecting professional selling?

Abboud: The ways in which technology affects selling are multifaceted. From an internal sales force perspective technology helps with the whole sales process: from prospecting to managing the sales cycle, technology helps sales professionals gather information, store it, share it, and collaborate around it. Availability of information is key to drive campaigns around one prospect (as an example through informed engagement). Therefore, technology creates efficiency, improves customer engagement (by being aware of past relationships) and ultimately helps drive more sales planning within accounts.

For example, in one of the organisations I worked for, technology helped me learn about previous engagements with the accounts when I joined, and provided a central point for all previous transactions and territory management information (historic sales/products data).

Reporting is also key when it comes to sales management. Technology offers a great opportunity for both sales executives and their managers to track campaigns, engagement, sales opportunities and forecasts, as well as being able to make sales decisions based on real-time data.

An increasingly adopted technology is sales collaboration tools – where the whole sales organisation collaborates in a Facebook-like environment. Sales executives can share presentations, plans, competitive information, meeting/call notes, all publicly which allows the wider team to comment, share, and add their work under one account record for example. The Chatter-type technology helps sales executives in getting approvals and order processing, and helps reduce email use. It's a single place or source of truth for your engagement with a customer.

Q: Tell me more; what in particular is technology enabling sales professionals to do they could not do say 20 years ago?

Abboud: One important element that technology plays an important role in is information. From a sales perspective technology helps with the gathering of information, analysis, sharing and helping a sales organisation to be more informed about existing and potential clients.

In addition, with the increased use of mobile technology as well as collaboration and cloud solutions, sales teams are more mobile than ever, efficient and can collaborate on the go – even with clients.

Q: What are the areas in which you think technology will not be able to replace sales forces?

Abboud: Unless technology can mirror human interaction and relationships, I don't see technology as a threat to a sales force but rather a positive enabler.

People buy from people and there has always been a great emphasis on story selling and therefore, organisations will always rely on sales professionals.

However, the success and efficiency of a sales organisations depends not only on talent but on adopting technology solutions to drive knowledge sharing, collaboration, time efficiency and allowing the sales force to be customer-focused.

In one of my sales roles, the organisation created a cloud solution allowing sales professionals to create a chat-type room to bring internal resources, customers and partner resources together to collaborate on projects.

I often heard customers frustrated with sales executives who don't do their research, or know about the industry or business. Technology certainly helps with knowledge gathering and sharing to better meet customer demands and collaborate on the go with mobile technologies.

Finally, let's not forget the phone which has immensely changed the way business is done. Take companies such as Salesforce.com where they've built their business with huge focus on telephone selling. Technology therefore allows sales management to make better decisions when it comes to resource allocation and territory management too.

Q: What is your view of the future? How will technology the future of personal and professional selling?

Abboud: We are seeing an unprecedented revolution in digital and social media. Whilst brands and organisations are taking this opportunity to engage with their customers and communities, sales professionals are taking on social media channels to build a reputation online and engage in thought leadership conversations on LinkedIn and Twitter. But where this is heading to is difficult to predict. Social is also becoming important within the organisation itself to encourage collaboration and engagement amongst employees – to share knowledge and best practices.

One can only think that innovation will change the way business is done – technology that enables the sales process and the interaction between sellers and buyers can only bring value in terms of increased competition, efficiency, collaboration, transparency. Having said that, professional sales executives who act as consultants, experts and advisors in the buyers' eyes aren't replaceable. Technology can only help them sell more, more effectively and efficiently.

REFERENCES

Anderson, C. (2012). *Markers: The New Industrial Revolution*. New York: Crown Publishing.

Andzulis, J. 'Mick', Panagopoulos, N. G. & Rapp, A. (2012). A review of social media and implications for the sales process. *Journal of Personal Selling & Sales Management*, 32(2), 305–316.

Aula, P. (2010). Social media, reputation risk and ambient publicity management. *Strategy & Leadership*, *38*(6), 43–49.

Bose, R. (2002). Customer relationship management: Key components for IT success. *Journal of Industrial Management and Data Systems*, 102(2), 89–97.

Brown, S. A. (2000). *Customer Relationship Management*. Ontario: Wiley.

Carroll, D. (2012). *United Breaks Guitars: The Power of One Voice in the Age of Social Media*. Carlsbad, CA: Hay House Inc.

Dalcher, D. & Genus, A. (2003) Introduction: avoiding IS/IT implementation failure. *Technology Analysis and Strategic Management*, 15(4), 403–407.

Donaldson, B. & Resch, G. (2006). Why it is too soon to kill off the salesperson: Some limitations with electronic reverse auctions. *Proceedings of the Academy of Marketing*. London: Middlesex University.

Donaldson, B. & Wright, G. (2002). Sales information systems: Are they being used for more than simple mail shots? *Journal of Database Marketing*, 9(3), 276–284.

Emiliani, M. L. (2004). Regulating B2B online reverse auctions through voluntary codes of conduct. *Industrial Marketing Management*, 34(5), 526–534.

Emiliani, M. L. & Stec, D. J. (2002). Realizing savings from online reverse auctions. *Supply Chain Management: An International Journal*, 7(1), 12–23.

Erffmeyer, R. C. & Johnson, D. A. (2001). An exploratory study of sales force automation practices: Expectations and realities. *Journal of Personal Selling & Sales Management*, 21(2), 167–175.

GfK (2014). Tech Trends 2014. Retrieved 13 July 2015, from http://www.gfk.com/Industries/technology/Pages/Tech-Trends-2014.aspx.

Handen, L. (2000). Putting CRM to Work, in S. A. Brown (ed.) *Customer Relationship Management*. Ontario: Wiley, pp. 9–18.

Jap, S. D. (2003). An exploratory study of the introduction of online reverse auctions. *Journal of Marketing*, 67(3), 96–107.

Jones, J., Sundaram, S. & Chin, W. (2002). Factors leading to sales force automation use: A longitudinal analysis. *Journal of Personal Selling & Sales Management*, 22(3), 145–156.

Lemmens, R., Donaldson, B. & Marcos, J. (2014). *From Selling to Co-creating*. Amsterdam: BIS Publishers.

Parthasarathy, M. & Sohi, R. (1997). Sales force automation and the adoption of technological innovations by salespeople: Theory and implications. *Journal of Business & Industrial Marketing*, 12(3/4), 196–208.

Parvatiyar, A. & Sheth, J. (2001). Customer relationship management: Emerging practice, process, and discipline. *Journal of Economic and Social Research*, 3(2), 1–34.

Payne, A. F. (2000). Improving sales force productivity, in Reeves, J. (ed.) *Customer Relationship Management*. London: Caspian Publishing Ltd, CBI Business Guide, pp. 58–62.

Peppers, D. & Rogers, M. (2004). *Managing Customer Relationships*. New Jersey: Wiley.

Perrien, J. & Ricard, L. (1995). The meaning of a marketing relationship: A pilot study. *Industrial Marketing Management*, 24(1), 37–43.

Rackham, N. & DeVincentis, J. (1998). *Rethinking the Sales Force: Redefining Selling to Create and Capture Customer Value*. New York: McGraw-Hill.

Robey, D. & Boudreau, M. C. (1999). Accounting for the contradictory organizational consequences of information technology: Theoretical directions and methodological implications. *Information Systems Research*, 10, 167–185.

Rodriguez, M., Peterson, R. M. & Krishnan, V. (2012). Social media's influence on business-to-business sales performance. *Journal of Personal Selling & Sales Management*, 32(2), 365–378.

SellingPower (2014). From strategy to execution: Accelerating sales growth. Retrieved 2 June 2014, from http://www.sellingpower.com/sales-transformation/?sp_src=SponsoredLink_092013.

Speier, C. & Venkatesh, V. (2002). The hidden minefields in the adoption of sales force automation technologies. *Journal of Marketing*, 66, 98–111.

Sujan, H., Weitz, B. A. & Kumar, N. (1994). Learning orientation, working smart, and effective selling. *Journal of Marketing*, 58(3), 39. doi: 10.2307/1252309.

Sviokla, J. J. (1996). Knowledge workers and radically new technologies. *Sloan Management Review*, 37, 25–40.

Tulder, R. V. & Mol, M. (2002). Reversed auctions or auctions reversed: First experiments by Philips. *European Management Journal*, 20(5), 447–456.

Venkatesh, N. & Davis, F. D. (2000). A theoretical extension of the technology acceptance model: Four longitudinal field studies. *Management Science*, 46(2), 186–204.

Widmier, S. M., Jackson, D. W. & McCabe, D. B. (2002). Infusing technology into personal selling. *Journal of Personal Selling & Sales Management*, 23(3), 189–198.

10 INTERNATIONAL SALES

OVERVIEW

Meeting the needs of any market or market segment can be daunting but as a firm moves into international markets it faces additional challenges. Marketing in another country means the business has to cope with many different issues, such as culture, legal systems, currencies and regulatory requirements. It will have to decide whether to use agents and distributors as its method of selling in foreign markets. Agents and distributors already have a sales organisation, understand the local culture and can be a more cost-effective means of market development than establishing a sales subsidiary. International marketing is littered with examples of firms that made expensive mistakes simply because they did not take the time to understand the market they were dealing with. In this chapter, we argue that taking time to assess the market and plan market entry and development will improve the chances of success.

LEARNING OBJECTIVES

This chapter aims to enable the reader to:

- Understand the complexities of selling in international markets.
- Discuss the different forms of selling and entry strategies used in international markets.
- Identify the main factors influencing the choice of selling mode.
- Present guidelines on how to manage agents and distributors in foreign markets.

DEFINITIONS

Culture is the sum of the knowledge, values, beliefs and attitudes that are shared by a particular group of people or society.
Born Global refers to companies that originate in small countries that almost by default have to sell internationally in order to grow because their domestic markets are small.
Global firm is a company that gains by operating in more than one country in areas of marketing, R&D or production, thus enhancing its reputation and reducing costs in a manner not available to domestic competitors.
Terms of trade refers to the specification of the duties and obligations of both exporter and importer when dealing in international trade.

THE INTERNATIONAL MARKETING ENVIRONMENT

The international marketing environment is undergoing profound and rapid change. In most industries today, competition is becoming fiercer as more firms enter international markets and access to markets becomes easier. This competition therefore has two dimensions: competition when selling internationally in foreign markets, and foreign firms selling in domestic markets.

According to the World Trade Organization (WTO, 2014), exports of merchandise in 2012 were US$5,803,285 million for the EU, US$2,048,714 million for the US and US$1,545,708 million for China. These figures illustrate the critical importance of international sales in the global economy.

To sell successfully in an international context, an understanding of the foreign marketing environment is vital, including the cultures, policies, legal and regulatory frameworks that apply. Cultural intelligence (CQ) has been developed in research in international business and refers to the ability of an individual to function and manage effectively in culturally diverse settings (Earley & Ang, 2003). In international sales it is argued that salespeople high in CQ are more likely to be effective when selling across cultures given their ability to better adapt to the cultural underpinnings of customers they sell to (Hansen, Singh, Weilbaker & Guesalaga, 2011).

The cultural environment

Culture underlies all our relationships in international marketing. It shapes the beliefs or standards of groups and helps individuals to decide what are appropriate behaviours and actions (Hofstede, 1981). One aspect of this is the existence of national or regional styles of doing business and conducting negotiations in regions such as the Middle East, Japan, North America and Britain. For instance some features that characterise doing business in Arab countries are (Usunier, 1996):

- Knowledge of the subgroup to which the negotiator belongs is essential; the relationships between the parties must be explored with great care, to find out who is who and what relationship each negotiator has with the different groups.
- The role of intermediaries, i.e. 'sponsors' in countries such as Saudi Arabia is very important. The majority of 'Middle Eastern' business people speak French or English and understand European cultures; whereas the reverse is not always the case. Intermediaries help in addressing cultural divides and differences.
- It must always be borne in mind that Middle Eastern civilisations were largely the founders of those in Europe. They have left many traces behind, and as far as art and culture are concerned, their influences were dominant for many centuries during the Middle Ages. The pride of the person with whom you are dealing must be – truly – respected.
- One must expect a great deal of emotion and demonstrativeness, interspersed with true pragmatism. Friendship is sought, relationships are personalised, and the idea of a cold 'business-like' encounter is difficult to envisage. Once a true friend has been made (which is far from straightforward), the sense of loyalty can be very strong.
- When loans and interest are discussed, it is best to be very cautious as interest or riba is forbidden by the Koran. There are acceptable forms of finance for business but the subject should be handled sensitively.

In contrast, the North American style of negotiations are often characterised by the following:

- A recognition that in conducting business negotiations the selection of negotiators and the preparation for talks is methodical.
- There is a tendency not to take sufficient account of the culture of other parties.
- Emphasis is placed on issues, facts and evidence in negotiation and the need to reach agreement by certain deadlines. Others groups, such as the French, have a

generally less timely sense of negotiations and like to debate more general principles of the sought agreements.
- Americans value frankness and sincerity, although being overly frank could be construed as arrogance in cultures which have a more restricted view of self-assertion.
- A recognition that contracts should be drawn up carefully and precisely in law and that these can be the basis of legal action if disputes arise in the future.

There are clearly major differences in the negotiating style of the Arab–Islamic and American cultures, which can lead to misunderstandings and failed negotiations. It is not the case that every member of the Arab–Islamic or American cultures exhibits all of the characteristics attributed to the cultures above, but as a group the negotiating styles are recognisable and are characteristics of the business groups. The key issue in discussing culture is to understand that culture plays an important part in international business and has tangible effects on selling and negotiation outcomes.

What do you think?

When doing business in international markets, it is important to take the time to find out about the culture and styles of negotiation before going into a market, so that the likelihood of mistakes and misunderstandings is reduced. Government export promotion agencies publish information on doing business in foreign markets, and talks with export promotion officials, chambers of commerce and businessmen who have knowledge of particular markets are a good starting point for understanding and working in a different culture.

Q: What other sources might be used to understand overseas markets?

Political, legal, economic and technological environments

Globalisation has become a key issue as a number of factors change the way in which companies, not only multinational corporations but also smaller firms, organise and carry out their business activities. Firms can now identify and sell to similar market segments around the world and have developed global marketing strategies to exploit these markets. Multinational corporations have gradually changed from conducting business on a country-by-country basis to conducting business on a regional or global basis. This is done to achieve cost savings through increased economies of scale and reducing the duplication of activities in markets. This is now possible because the information technology revolution enables firms to coordinate and control operations on a global basis. Communication within organisations and externally with customers and suppliers is now quicker and more informative with the advent of improved international telecommunications and the Internet.

The Internet offers new capabilities for selling in international markets, and firms are developing strategies to use the Internet to support their international marketing. The ease of communication between the exporter, customers and intermediaries will improve levels of customer service, speeding up the response to customer queries. There are new tools for selling, too. The provision of a website is feasible for any company and the Internet can be used to search for customer prospects.

From a political and economic standpoint, access to many markets is becoming easier with the increasing integration of markets. The European Union is dismantling barriers between member states and there has been a general reduction in barriers to trade, partly owing to the work of the World Trade Organization (WTO), formerly General Agreement on Tariffs and Trade (GATT). For example, under the auspices of the WTO, many countries have signed an agreement to eliminate almost all tariffs currently levied on information technology products, and other categories of products are being introduced into trade areas without being subject to tariffs.

Public bodies in international trade

Legal and regulatory systems also have a direct bearing on selling in international markets.

The World Trade Organization (WTO)

The WTO was born after a process of negotiations amongst various countries spanning 1986–1994 called the Uruguay Round and earlier negotiations under the General Agreement on Tariffs and Trade (GATT). The WTO is hosting new negotiations, under the 'Doha Development Agenda' launched in 2001. Overall, the mission of the WTO has been to articulate negotiations and help open markets for trade or to support maintaining trade barriers when appropriate – for example, to protect consumers or limit harm and damage. The WTO seeks to provide the legal frameworks to help producers of goods and services, exporters and importers conduct their business, and at the same time promote governments' social and environmental agendas. For international trade to flourish, it is necessary to have a framework that provides individuals, companies and governments with certainty that there will be transparent rules for trade and no sudden changes of policy.

At the core of WTO's mission are the WTO agreements, negotiated and signed by the majority of the world's trading nations. These documents provide the legal ground rules for international commerce. They are essentially contracts, binding governments to keep their trade policies within agreed limits. The system of agreements is designed to help trade flow as freely as possible and at the same time minimise undesirable side effects that may compromise economic development and well-being (WTO, 2014).

International Chamber of Commerce (ICC)

The ICC is a global business organisation whose role is to provide policy advocacy and other functions devoted to promoting international trade and investment. As the Secretary General states 'Indeed, much of our work is of a very practical nature, focused on making it easier for business to operate internationally. Our world-renowned commercial arbitration service is a form of impartial and dependable private justice that gives more security to commercial partners doing business across frontiers' (ICC, 2014).

Since its creation the ICC has developed a wide range of rules, guidelines and codes to facilitate international transactions and to help spread best practice among companies. One such set of rules is ICC's Incoterms® rules, first published in 1936, which are accepted as the global standard for the interpretation of the most common terms used in contracts for the international sale of goods. Incoterms specify the duties and obligations of the exporter and importer and defines costs and risks involved in the delivery of goods from the seller to the buyer. Incoterms do not constitute a contract or address the price payable, currency or credit terms. At the time of writing, the latest version came into effect in January 2011. The following are the key terms used in Incoterms (MIQ Logistics, 2013) (Table 10.1):

Table 10.1 – Description of Incoterms

CFR – Cost and freight	The Seller clears the goods for export and pays the costs of moving the goods to destination. The Buyer bears all risks of loss or damage.
CIF – Cost, insurance and freight	The Seller clears the goods for export and pays the costs of moving the goods to the port of destination. The Buyer bears all risks of loss or damage. The Seller, however, purchases the cargo insurance.

CIP – Carriage and insurance paid to	The Seller pays for moving the goods to destination. From the time the goods are transferred to the first carrier, the Buyer bears the risks of loss or damage. The Seller, however, purchases the cargo insurance.
CPT – Carriage paid to	The Seller pays for moving the goods to destination. From the time the goods are transferred to the first carrier, the Buyer bears the risks of loss or damage.
DAP – Delivered at place	The Seller delivers when the goods are placed at the Buyer's disposal on the arriving means of transport ready for unloading at the names place of destination. The Seller bears all risks involved in bringing the goods to the named place.
DAT – Delivered at terminal	The Seller delivers when the goods, once unloaded from the arriving means of transport, are placed at the Buyer's disposal at a named terminal at the named port or place of destination. 'Terminal' includes any place, whether covered or not, such as a quay, warehouse, container yard or road, rail or air cargo terminal. The Seller bears all risks involved in bringing the goods to and unloading them at the terminal at the named port or place of destination.
DDP – Delivered duty paid	The Seller delivers the goods -cleared for import – to the Buyer at destination. The Seller bears all costs and risks of moving the goods to destination, including the payment of Customs duties and taxes.
EXW – Ex works	The Seller's only responsibility is to make the goods available at the Seller's premises. The Buyer bears full costs and risks of moving the goods from there to destination.
FAS – Free alongside ship	The Seller delivers the goods to the origin port. From that point, the Buyer bears all costs and risks of loss or damage.
FCA – Free carrier	The Seller delivers the goods, cleared for export, to the carrier selected by the Buyer. The Seller loads the goods if the carrier pickup is at the Seller's premises. From that point, the Buyer bears the costs and risks of moving the goods to destination.
FOB – Free on board	The Seller delivers the goods on board the ship and clears the goods for export. From that point, the Buyer bears all costs and risks of loss or damage.

European Union: Agency law and regulations

European Union agency law in the form of the Commercial Agents Directive has widespread implications for firms selling in the European Union. The main points of the Commercial Agents Directive are as follows:

- The Directive applies only to agents who operate in connection with the sale of goods and only within European Union countries. Distributors who buy goods and then resell them on their own account are not covered.
- Where there is no agreement between parties, the agent will be entitled to remuneration that commercial agents 'are customarily allowed in the place where he carries on his activities'.
- Agents are entitled to commission on transactions completed, not only during the course of the agency contract but also afterwards if the transactions have been mainly attributable to their efforts.
- Agents must be supplied with a statement of commission due and the agent has the right to ask to see an extract from the principal's books.
- Where an agency contract is entered into for an indefinite period, each party is given a right to terminate it on notice. This provision may not be varied. The period of notice is one month during the first year of the contract, two months during the second year and three months thereafter.
- Agents are entitled to compensation for the damage they suffer when a contract is terminated.

- Compensation is not paid where the agent is in substantial breach of contract, if the agent terminates the contract, except where that termination is due to age or illness of the agent or due to facts attributable to the principal. There is no entitlement to compensation where the agent assigns the contract with the agreement of the principal to a third party (EC Agency Law – Exporter's Briefing 50:1).

When this legislation was introduced, many firms had to consider whether or not to change their sales and distribution network in the European Union because the new legislation gave much greater protection to agencies. As a result, some exporters replaced agencies with distributors, and firms that continued with their agencies had to make sure that their agency agreements complied with the legislation.

Exporters considering appointing agents in the European Union should consult a lawyer about the details of the Commercial Agents Directive. If the agency agreements are not carefully drafted and agreed, exporters may not realise the extent of their liability in the event of termination of an agency agreement. In some cases, companies may consider setting up a distributorship rather than an agency.

Countries also differ in the extent to which businesses and consumers will resort to legal action in the event of dispute or disagreement. One of the consequences of the propensity to sue in the United States is that firms are advised to insure against the crippling damages and legal costs that can be awarded. This is never truer than when a company is selling products that have a high consequential risk. For example, manufacturers of crash helmets have been sued by customers and relatives claiming that defects in the design and manufacture of helmets contributed to personal injury and death.

ORGANISING INTERNATIONAL SALES

There are many ways in which firms commercialise their goods in international markets. Some means of selling do not require the exporter to have a direct presence in the foreign market. Other selling modes require the exporter to play an active role in setting up the sales and distribution channels in the foreign market. When firms sell to international markets with little or no presence in the markets, this is referred to as indirect exporting, where the products are sold in foreign markets without any special activity for this purpose being undertaken within the company. The export operations, including all the documentation, physical movement of goods and selling of the goods, are carried on by others. In contrast, direct exporting occurs where the firm undertakes the export task itself, builds up contacts, undertakes market research, handles documentation and transportation and develops marketing plans for the markets, either in conjunction with agents and distributors or through its own direct salespeople or sales subsidiary (Young, Hamil, Wheeler & Davies, 1989).

As Figure 10.1 illustrates, direct exporting gives a firm more control of the market and more market information compared with indirect exporting, but more resources are committed. Export houses and buying houses are a low-risk method of selling but do not have the potential of agents, distributors and sales subsidiaries to develop sales in the foreign market.

Figure 10.1 – Market control and commitment of different forms of export

Indirect selling to international markets

Export houses

The functions performed by export houses vary but the most comprehensive role is where the export house buys from a firm and sells abroad on its own behalf. This has the following advantages for the firm (Young et al., 1989):

- It does not have to sell in the international market.
- It is paid in the currency of the home market.
- It is not responsible for any of the export operation or for collecting payment from the buyers in the foreign market.

There are, however, disadvantages:

- The lack of control over sales abroad, as export sales volume is entirely dependent on the performance of the export house.
- The image and reputation of the products is not within the control of the domestic firm.
- If the company sells on its own behalf at a later date, its efforts may be hindered by a product image and reputation not consistent with its marketing strategy at the time.

Confirming houses are normally used when a foreign buyer places an order with a manufacturer, and the manufacturer may want to protect himself from the possibility of non-payment by the foreign buyer. One way of doing this is for the exporter to agree terms with a confirming house, which will then guarantee payment to the manufacturer.

Local buying offices

Local buying offices are set up by organisations such as department store chains to buy goods from suppliers outside their home country. The buying office handles the export transaction with the exporter supplying the goods to the specification and price agreed. The manufacturer does not have any representation abroad and does not have any direct contact with the end user. The advantage for the exporter is that sales to the consumer or the end user are handled by the buying office and its parent company.

Piggyback exporting

As the term implies, this is an arrangement where a firm, the carrier, agrees to sell the products of another, the rider, through a sales network already built up by the carrier. The rider is often the smaller of the two parties. The agreement between the parties is usually that the carrier either sells the goods on a commission basis or acts as a distributor and buys the goods from the rider. Compared with export houses and buying offices, the rider may have more knowledge of the market depending on the relationship established with the carrier. Where this is the case, piggyback exporting has similarities with methods of direct exporting. For the rider, there are a number of advantages:

- The firm can use an existing sales network straight away, saving the time and costs of developing its own network.
- It is a comparatively low-risk method of selling because the investment in the international market is low.
- Being a low-risk, low-cost method of selling means that it is suitable for sales in markets where demand is small or unpredictable and would otherwise not be worthwhile. Agents, distributors and a firm's own sales force all require more time and money to develop than piggybacking.
- If the rider is not committed to exporting, piggybacking offers a way of developing international sales yet still leaves the rider free to concentrate on the domestic market.

The disadvantages are

- Finding a suitable carrier.
- That the rider's products may take second place to the carrier's product line, something which the rider may not find satisfactory.
- That the rider does not have direct access to the market and does not build up a knowledge of customers in the market.

Piggyback exporting, like export houses and other indirect means of selling in foreign markets, has the advantages of low risk and low cost for the new exporter, but knowledge of the market is restricted and sales growth is governed by the activities of the carrier.

Direct selling to international markets

Agents

Agents represent an exporter directly in the market. Effectively, they are the company abroad and if the relationship between the exporter and agents develops well, the exporter will have much greater knowledge of the market compared with other means of selling already discussed. In most situations, the exporter can actively manage the agency, developing market segments in a planned and progressive way. The exporter should be able to work closely with the agency to formulate marketing plans for the foreign market. To do this, the exporter has to:

- Be much more committed to exporting.
- Be prepared to invest the time and resources to find a good agent.
- Develop the relationship over a period of years.

Export agents have many roles in international markets. Some agencies undertake all the selling activities on behalf of the exporter while, at the other extreme, agencies are used simply as 'enquiry-finders' or 'lead generators' for their principals. Such agents are often small organisations. The agency's role is to pass on or generate enquires for the exporter, who will then visit the customer prospects, usually with the agent as well. This restrictive service is cost-effective and requires commission to be paid to the agent.

Distributors

Whereas agencies operate on a commission basis and do not take title to the goods, distributors buy the goods from the exporter and make their money from their mark-up; that is, the difference between the prices at which they buy and sell. Generally speaking, distributors are larger organisations than agencies and are able to offer a wider range of functions.

Company sales representatives

Using a company representative who travels to the foreign market has several advantages:

- They have specialised knowledge of the company's products.
- They are familiar with the company's marketing strategy and are able to give feedback on customers and markets directly.
- Being a company employee, the sales representative is much more easily controlled and evaluated.

The disadvantages of using a sales representative are as follows:

- Although international travel is nowadays much easier and arguably less expensive, there are limits to the time that a representative operating from the home market can spend abroad.
- If foreign languages are required, it may be difficult to recruit representatives who have the necessary language ability.
- They cannot be in the foreign market all the time, and consequently the use of an agent or distributor may be preferred by foreign buyers and be seen as a sign of greater commitment to the market.

Local sales subsidiary

This is generally interpreted by foreign customers as a sign of greater commitment to the market. The decision facing the exporter is how to staff the sales office. Should the exporter use salespeople from the home market or should local salespeople be recruited? Locally recruited representatives have the advantage that they know the local culture, can speak the local language, if required, and may have previous experience in the industry. On the other hand, they lack knowledge of the exporter.

One of the advantages of the sales office is flexibility. The number of people employed can be expanded or reduced as sales rise or fall. Nevertheless, starting a sales subsidiary takes a considerable amount of time and resources and would usually not be the first mode of selling considered by an exporter.

Furthermore, where an exporter sets up sales subsidiaries in several countries staffed by local sales representatives, the exporter will have to consider how best to manage sales forces of different nationalities and cultures. The management of a sales force in the domestic market is not likely to be an appropriate model for managing in other cultures.

Did you know?

A study of the management of sales forces in Japan and America (Graham, Ichikawa & Apasu, 1995) revealed that:

- Firms in Japan provided more training and organisational culture-building activities than in America.
- The preferred way of motivating a Japanese sales force was by fostering their commitment to the firm.
- Because Japanese sales representatives are more closely supervised, a sales manager would be responsible for fewer representatives than in the United States.
- In the United States, it is much easier to set up a sales force and financial rewards are a much more effective way of controlling the sales force.

A summary of the characteristics, advantages and disadvantages of selling modes is given in Table 10.2.

Table 10.2 – Characteristics, advantages and disadvantages of export modes

Export mode	Characteristics	Advantages	Disadvantages
Indirect Export houses	There are a number of types of export houses but the most commonly understood is the organisation that buys from a firm and sells abroad on its own account	May handle all aspects of the export operation	Little market control or information. Limited sales
Confirming houses	Act on behalf of foreign buyers who pay them on a commission basis. The confirming house guarantees payment to the exporter on shipment of the goods	As above, but also guarantees payment	As above
Buying houses	Acting on behalf of clients such as foreign department stores, buying houses purchase from domestic manufacturers	As above, but the domestic manufacturer is approached by the buying house and need have no involvement in exporting other than supplying the order	Finding a suitable partner. The domestic company's product may take second priority. Growth may be impeded by existing arrangements
Direct agents	There are several types of agent: some will sell only one company's products; other agents will sell products from a number of companies, some of which may be competing. An agent does not take title to the goods, is usually a national of the country concerned and is paid on a commission basis	More market control and information than with the channels mentioned above. Permanent presence in the market. Costs of agency are related to sales	May sell more than one company's products. Agency agreements can be difficult and expensive to terminate

Distributors	The distributor takes title to the goods and therefore earns revenue from the mark-up on the product rather than the commission	Like the agent, knows the local market. Able to provide after sales service. More control of the market channels	Costs of termination are high should exporter's market development plans require new arrangements with new distributors
Direct selling	Sales representatives operating from the home country may be used in foreign sales territories	Detailed knowledge of the company and its products. High level of market control and information	Suffers from a lack of market knowledge, increased travelling time and, depending on the country, language problems
Local sales offices	These may be staffed by representatives either from the home market or from the foreign market	Perceived as a commitment to the market. Easier for local companies to deal with the exporter. Flexible and can accommodate growth	Problem of choosing appropriate personnel for the sales force. Domestic reps may be reluctant to move overseas: Local reps have less company knowledge but more country/market know-how

MINI-CASE STUDY

AB Chemicals (name disguised) supplies fine chemicals in pre-pack and semi-bulk quantities for research and industry. As part of a larger group, AB Chemicals is well positioned to reap substantial economies of size. It can develop stable, long-term strategies required for product and market development and for broadening its product differentiation capabilities. This gives AB a strong starting position for winning new customers and improving its service to existing ones.

However, the market can be described as saturated and starting to decline. Many existing customers are moving their chemical production facilities to Asia because of less strict government regulations. Currently, 80 per cent of the market is in the hands of one monopoly player, 15 per cent is held by AB and the remainder divided over a number of smaller players.

The market is mature and the products are commodities. Price and delivery are the two main differentiators. There is very little opportunity to add value for the customer. Most users are experts or researchers, which offers limited opportunities for any add-on service support. Because it is a commodity product, ease of purchase is probably the single most important purchasing criterion. This can be translated into how easy it is to find the right reference to order the product and place the actual order. In many cases, the customer requires several products to conduct an experiment. These customers in pharmaceuticals, chemicals, healthcare and education will then try to order all these products from the same supplier if possible.

AB has been able to win market share thus far based on lower prices than the main competitor, a more user-friendly catalogue and 24-hour delivery. The field sales force visit the companies and users who received their catalogue. Because the main competitor no longer had a field sales force, this enabled AB to develop personal relationships between users and the company. Apparently, other things being equal, people still prefer to buy product from other people who they know personally.

Thus several channels to market were established – a field sales force; independent distributors for regions where no field sales force was available or where they were servicing a group of customer which were not well represented by the sales force; a call centre; an e-commerce web site. The channels were not chosen in terms of the costs involved to serve a customer but so that the maximum number of new orders could be obtained.

However, after early success, growth in market share has started to level off in several regions. This has led the company to ask itself the following questions:

1 Is expecting further growth in those markets realistic or have we achieved our fair share of the market?
2 How can the company bring its costs of sales in line with current sales revenue and growth?
3 If we reduce our sales force, how will our customers react?

As one manager explained it to us, we have to shift our sales approach from hard selling and calling on as many customers as possible to a smart selling approach where new opportunities will be looked for within specific accounts.

Called in as a consultant to AB, what solutions would you recommend and why?

MANAGING EXPORTER–INTERMEDIARY RELATIONSHIPS

Exporter–importer relationships are dynamic. Some relationships endure while others flourish, decline and die. This is partly because the exporter wants to develop markets and discards the first intermediary used, often indirect intermediaries, as the market develops. Agents particularly were traditionally used so that closer contact could be established and maintained with customers abroad.

The patterns of relationships built up during foreign market entry and development are complex. Table 10.3 shows the main forms of representation used by firms. On average, each exporter used four types of sales organisation for exporting, ranging from buyers based in the home market through to sales subsidiaries.

Not only are companies prepared to use several forms of selling in foreign markets but they will also use more than one means of selling in a market where necessary. Industrial manufacturers and providers of services often use more than one form of representation in the countries they export to (Turnbull, 1987).

Table 10.3 – Types of channel structure

Types of channel structure	% of firms using channel
Domestic-based buyers/buying agents	67
Domestic-based distributors	49
Domestic-based agents	63
Foreign-based agents	46
Foreign-based distributors	48
Firm's foreign sales offices/subsidiaries	61

If it is the case that exporters may work with several sales intermediaries, it is also true that agents and distributors frequently work for more than one exporter. Moore (1992) studied German agents and distributors working with UK exporters and found that four out of five agents/distributors worked with more than one exporter and there were instances of agents and distributors working with six or more exporters. Given the fact that the majority of intermediaries work for more than one exporter, the management of the exporter–intermediary relationship is especially important because if the exporter does not work effectively with the intermediary, the intermediary may put more effort into working with the other exporters it has links with.

Finally, it should be noted that sales subsidiaries set up by exporters also take on agents. In a study by Wheeler, Jones & Young (1996), the reason that sales subsidiaries gave for holding a number of agencies on behalf of other manufacturers was that this spread the costs of operating the subsidiary over a wider product range and careful selection of agencies could improve the attractiveness of the subsidiary's main product.

Evidence and experience show that more than half of export marketing ventures fail because the wrong distributor was selected. Usually the reasons for this were that the distributor company did not have the technical experience claimed, had exaggerated its influence with buyers, was poorly located, and wasn't prepared to commit itself to the exporter's products. Getting it right at the beginning is essential. This confirms the importance of agency/distributor relationships and underlines the fact that many firms do not manage these relationships well. This is supported by many studies in which firms cite establishing sales and distribution networks in foreign markets as a problem. How then do exporters manage these relationships effectively?

Selecting agents/distributors

The sources most frequently used to identify potential distributors are personal visits to search the territory, but government sources such as overseas Trade Boards or Chambers of Commerce are also used, as are colleagues, customer recommendations and trade fairs. Also, a number of firms find that their source for identifying overseas distributors is often an unsolicited contact by distributors.

Most exporters use similar criteria when selecting their agents/distributors. The criteria can be split into three categories:

1. Sales and market factors.
2. Product and service factors.
3. Risk and uncertainty factors.

The most frequently used criteria are market and customer knowledge and customer contacts, not carrying competitors' products, enthusiasm for the contract and willingness to succeed. These factors emphasise the basic reason for choosing foreign distributors, which is to obtain effective market representation. It is essential for the success of the exporter that the distributor has these characteristics. Exporters clearly prefer to have a distributor who concentrates on their own products rather than one who divides their time between competing products. It would seem, at least for some of the firms, that it is more important to have distributors who are enthusiastic and have good knowledge of the market than to have generally good track records and good financial standing. The majority of firms draw up a short list of potential distributors and interview them in their own country, which underlines the importance in the selection process of personal contact in market surroundings.

Motivation

An exporter needs to understand what will motivate their intermediaries abroad. With the caveat that different motivations may apply across different countries, exporters need to look carefully at each market. Perhaps most important element in this relationship is the need to maintain effective exporter–distributor communication. These include keeping the distributor up to date and maintaining regular personal contact.

Generally, the most important criteria in managing the exporter–agency relationship are:

- High/consistent product quality.
- Competitive prices.
- Suppliers' fairness and trustworthiness.
- An ability to keep his/her promises.

Clearly, fairness, trust and keeping promises are important issues in working with and motivating an agent/distributor.

Evaluation

Nearly all the firms evaluate their distributors, most on an annual basis. Criteria and standards vary but most exporters employ a wide range of criteria, with the achievement of sales outcomes the most frequently used evaluation measure. Sales volume, sales value and new business are commonly evaluated. In some situations, criteria include the quality of the distributor's market feedback, customer services and selling/marketing inputs. Comparison against past performance is an often-used approach.

The conclusion to be drawn about the management of exporter–agent/distributor relationships is that good personal contact and joint decision-making with the channel partner have a positive bearing on export performance. The rationale for this must be sought in the fact that increasing personal contact will lead the firm to a better understanding of customers and channel members' needs and behaviours. Improved target market selection, adaptation of marketing policy and better relations with channel members – including qualified joint decision-making – are the natural consequences which affect performance positively. The reason for better performance may be attributed to better decision quality and greater commitment from both parties. Good personal contact with the market and a close relationship with channel members further enhance the exporter's capability for careful planning and the control of sales in export markets.

There is a great deal of debate in the academic literature about exactly how firms increase their international activities, of which increasing the capacity to sell is one dimension. The competing explanations of internationalisation emphasise different aspects of firm behaviour and the environment. Internationalisation is not necessarily a formal rational process, although, as already identified, there is much support for the view that firms which assess international markets and plan their market entry and development improve their chances of success.

The discussion of the forms of organisation in this chapter has emphasised that, when firms are choosing sales intermediaries, there is a trade-off between the control of marketing activities and access to market information required versus the resources committed to that market. The decision to use a particular type of sales intermediary is partly based on the firm's assessment of these factors. Apart from this, the choice of sales intermediary is influenced by:

- The firm's own international marketing strategy.
- The structure of the exporter's industry, which may place constraints on the types of selling organisation used; for example, if competitors providing after-sales service is important, direct forms of export are more likely to be used.
- The operating environment of the firm abroad; for example, selling in Japan usually means working with an intermediary in the first instance (Turnbull, 1987).

PRICING

Compared with selling in the home market, selling in foreign markets entails a number of additional activities and costs that increase prices. This is sometimes referred to as price escalation and the effect on the final price of some of these factors is shown in Table 10.4. In the example, there are additional shipping costs and tariffs in the foreign market but otherwise both channels are similar. Nevertheless, the final price is 68 per cent higher in the foreign market. If more intermediaries are used, the price will increase even more.

Table 10.4 – Price escalation

	Domestic market £	Foreign market £
Manufacturer's price	10.00	10.00
Shipping costs		4.00
Landed cost		14.00
Tariff (20%)		2.80
Distributor's cost	10.00	16.80
Distributor's margin (33.33% on cost)	3.33	5.60
Retailer's cost	13.33	22.40
Retailer's margin (40% on cost)	5.33	8.96
Retail price	18.66	31.36
% Price escalation		+68%

Exporters, however, do have a choice of how they calculate the costs of manufacture of the goods exported. They may take a view that the fixed costs of manufacturing will not be spread evenly across all production, regardless of its destination, but attributed only to production for the home market. A decision could be made to attribute only the variable costs of production to the product destined for export markets. This means a lower price abroad.

Selling at low prices in a market may, however, lead to charges of dumping and governments may put an additional tariff on the goods to raise the price, but anti-dumping charges are fraught with problems because it is difficult to establish exactly what costs should be attributed to exported products. It is precisely this problem of determining costs that allows some governments to use anti-dumping charges as a barrier to trade. They unfairly protect local industry by imposing a levy when it is not warranted, in effect protecting inefficient home market manufacturers from genuinely competitive foreign incumbents.

An important aspect of pricing in international markets is how the price is quoted. One option is to quote a fully delivered price; that is, delivery duty paid, where the exporter quotes for delivery to the customer's premises and agrees to do all that is necessary, such as preparing the documentation, arranging insurance, shipping the goods, paying any tariffs and clearing customs. Another option is that the exporter might make the goods available at their own premises and quote an ex-works price which only includes the cost of manufacture. The customer bears all the costs and takes responsibility for transporting the consignment.

Another aspect of pricing is the cost and provision of credit. Exporters can arrange for their credit to be handled by other organisations, but many firms make their own arrangements for credit assessment and provision. It is important that credit references are taken out on customers initially and on a continuing basis. References can be taken out through credit-checking agencies based in the exporter's home country, such as Dun & Bradstreet or Infocheck, or it may be cheaper to go direct to foreign-based agencies which provide services across a number of countries. Examples of these are Sereco (based in Egypt, covering most of the Middle East), Harlow (based in the USA covering all of North America and Canada) and The Maypole (based in Bangladesh, which covers a very large area including the Far East and Africa).

In offering credit, the exporter has to balance the provisions of attractive, cheap, long-term credit to gain more orders against short-term and expensive credit which may lead to a loss of orders. To find the ideal balance, a firm should develop its own credit policy by deciding on such questions as:

- What percentage of total assets should be represented by debtors?
- What will be the range of credit terms on offer?
- How will the credit-worthiness of new customers be assessed?
- How will the company deal with slow payment and default?

Putting together tailor-made credit packages depends upon knowledge of the customer. The kinds of information sought should include the taking of credit references, credit terms desired and detailed information about the customer, possibly given through the use of a formal credit application. Clearly, the firm should have a clear idea of the cost of credit, which is determined by the quantity of credit sales; the average credit period; and the opportunity cost of capital.

A firm's credit policy should have a monitoring system to help to identify problems with customers and with the functioning of the policy within the firm's financial structure. For example, monitoring the ratio of credit sales to total sales enables the firm to see and assess changes in its risk exposure. The ratio of bad debts to total credit sales provides a view of how well the firm is managing the approval of credit applications and the collection of credit.

SUMMARY

Selling in international markets presents new challenges for the firm selling abroad for the first time. The various facets of the international marketing environment directly affect the selling activities of firms. Sales managers need to understand, for example, the role of culture in shaping diverse negotiating styles and the impact of legislation on the selection and management of agents and distributors.

Much of the research on successful exporting supports the view that planning pays. If the firm assesses a market it is interested in and plans how it is going to enter and develop that market; it will increase its chances of success.

The research on the management of agents and distributors underlines the unstable nature of some relationships and the necessity to select agents and distributors carefully. Export sales managers who consciously build close relationships with their agents and distributors will usually have more success in foreign markets.

Besides the above, there are many additional issues which the new exporter has to master. These include dealing with export documentation, selecting appropriate Incoterms and setting prices. Some firms may see these issues as a barrier to success but, given the commitment of management, there is no reason why a firm should not sell successfully in international markets.

QUESTIONS

1. In what ways can the overseas sales operations support the segmentation, targeting and positioning strategy of the firm?
2. Do you consider that relationship selling is more or less important in overseas markets than in the home country?
3. What are some of the difficulties with geographic distance that hinder effective international sales operations?
4. As trade barriers generally reduce, it becomes harder to control price across borders. What advice would you give to companies that sell at different prices in different geographical regions (for example, this is a common problem between western and eastern Europe).
5. Find at least three products where sales have grown substantially through online exchange. What does this imply for selling in international markets?

ONLINE SOURCES OF INFORMATION FOR INTERNATIONAL SALES

- For a director's briefing on research into export markets, go to **www.hie.cu.uk**
- Preparing to trade abroad go to **www.uktradeinvest.gov.uk**
- Help with exporting go to **www.export.org.uk**
- Trade associations use **www.taforum.org**
- Help through your chamber of commerce go to **www.chamberofcommerce.org.uk**
- Examples of purchase guides can also be found, such as Europages at **www.europages.com**
- Gaining access to trade-lead systems, such as **www.imex.com**
- Export credit, a UK government site may be useful **www.ecgd.gov.uk**

CASE STUDY: POINT INNOVATE

Point Innovate (http://www.pointinnovate.com) is a for-profit renewable energy business that designs, manufactures and distributes solar technology in developing markets in Africa and Central America such as Ghana, Nigeria, Honduras, etc. According to a report by the IEEE Smart Grid,[1] in the developing world 'the absence of a pervasive existing energy infrastructure – and the absence of a cumbersome regulatory apparatus – offer the possibility of introducing renewable technologies from scratch. This can be done with completely new methods and paradigms for meeting demand for electricity with highly distributed and heterogeneous sources of energy.' Point Innovative is developing such paradigms.

Point Innovate has three main parts of its business: retail, distribution and economic development.

- Point Innovate Retail sells personal solar technology (torches, lanterns, phone/tablet/laptop chargers), home system kits (from 90 watts to 3,000 watts), as well as providing scalable tailor-made energy solutions from 3,000 watts and above.
- Point Innovate sets up distribution networks throughout developing countries to facilitate the movement of product from its regional hubs.
- Point Innovate has developed a rural electrification programme that it offers to Governments, NGOs, NPOs and corporates as part of their energy and CSR programmes. These solar installations start at 3KVA and are scalable to meet the needs of the overall partner programme. The solar charging station acts as a community charging hub, where communities can purchase power. Families within the community are provided with home kits from which lighting and power points are installed.

The Opportunity

Over 90 per cent of people in Africa either live with no access to power or have severely interrupted access to power. Many believe that power is the primary hurdle that needs to be overcome in order to create economic development. Globally there is a growing movement, led by organisations such as the UN, to resolve this energy crisis and considerable financial resources have been mobilised to start to address this issue.

The ability of governments in developing countries to implement large-scale energy solutions is very limited given the huge costs, long time scales, and political stability required to complete these initiatives. Point Innovate, by comparison, is nimble with technology that is readily available and greatly need by individuals, as well as the distribution network to ensure that not only the product, but also services and support, can be delivered to the consumer.

The Challenge

The challenges facing Point Innovate as a start-up phase entity are many and diverse, and can be summarised as external and internal challenges.

External challenges

The level of economic development in each country or province can vary significantly for myriad reasons. The differences in disposable income can vary greatly from one region to another. This impacts not only price point in a region but also product distributed in a region and the manner in which a community is sensitised to the product, its use, as well as the benefits derived by the individual in those circumstances.

The global view of business in developing countries varies greatly depending on the world view of people with whom you are talking. If you are looking to procure product on terms, and the income stream supporting the payment of the product is coming from developing markets, it can create issues in negotiation of the terms of procurement, adding additional cost into the cost of goods sold (COGS), therefore decreasing your margins.

People in developing markets are suspicious and wary of organisations from developed markets entering their economies, taking their profit and leaving. To employ good sales staff and build sustainable sales and distribution channels, the market demands that you have a plan for longevity if it is to invest in relationships with your brand.

Finding strategic business partners who understand the nuances of business in developing economies is more challenging than it is in developed markets. You are often required to find local partners who can help you navigate the market landscape, identify credible distribution and sales networks, and help to identify the best channel to focus your sales efforts and staff.

Every developing country has differing in-country rules and regulations for business set-up, especially if you are a foreign-owned entity. Most countries require you to have a local equity partner in the business as well as onerous capital and labour requirements for entering the market. The resources required to navigate these issues can be significant and can even impact your operating model. Import/export duties and customs also vary greatly from country to country; if you are importing product into a country, it is imperative that you understand the cost involved in getting product in country because it has a significant impact on the COGS, which does impact your price point in the market.

Developing markets are renowned for their volatility. The success of Point Innovate in these markets rests on its ability to plan for and manage (hedge) the depreciation/appreciation of currencies, which is crucial to ensure that profits are protected as well as capital on hand. This allows assessing the ongoing viability of the sales environment, the impact on margins as well as the consumer price point.

Success in developing markets demands the construction of efficient manufacturer-to-market supply chain and logistics processes. This processes must ensure that you have consistent product servicing the market at all times, to give your business every opportunity to engage in a positive transaction with the end consumer.

Country-specific product selection must be developed to ensure that you are servicing the customer, as well as utilising your resources in the most efficient way. The only way to develop this strategy is to spend time with the end consumer to see and hear what they believe the compelling value proposition for your product is (or should be).

Internal challenges

Point Innovate had to acknowledge that it was trying to enter developing markets with a Western mindset when engaging in a sales transaction. The company quickly realised that in order to succeed at sales you had to adapt to the local mode of transaction, whether that be negotiation or payment terms.

Point Innovate has had to evolve away from the Western mindset for a product value proposition. The local market will always see your product in a unique way, and ultimately use your product in a way that you may not have considered. Capturing these insights is the key to conveying a value proposition in the future that customers will buy into.

Western businesses can often be inflexible in their approach for defining the payment terms of products and services: anything other than a 'cash in hand transaction' involves a level of risk. In developing markets you need to observe where consumers make cash transactions and when they don't, as well as understanding why they do and why they don't. Once consumer payment behaviour has been observed and understood, your business needs to assess whether it is willing to transact across multiple modes of payment to engage the market achieving maximum potential.

Appreciation and adaptability to diverse business and social cultural norms across developing countries is imperative. The willingness to engage on local terms, as a foreigner, goes a very long way. Similarly, when your staff are largely from the local community, the culture of your business is automatically different from any culture that you may have envisioned for your business. Subsequently, the motivational drivers for your staff are different, and may be outside of the norm of what you are used to. You need to understand these drivers and motivate staff accordingly. Well-motivated staff are brand ambassadors, engender a positive business culture and ultimately attract business from the communities within which they live and socialise, effectively lowering the threshold on some of your sales transactions.

Approach and key areas of work

Point Innovate's executive team has spent years developing their knowledge about business in developing countries and the accompanying challenges. As a new start-up, with a very large market opportunity globally, it was decided that the best way to tackle the challenges was to create a model or blueprint of how to successfully develop a sustainable distribution model in one country. Once this model was tested it could then be replicated, with the implementation of the necessary cultural adjustments, and with additional strategic distribution points in developing and emerging markets. Point Innovate's growth programme has three pillars: Knowledge of the consumer, Capacity building and Product development.

Knowledge of the consumer

Consumers in developing markets face many more challenges in their purchasing decisions than consumers in developed markets. Resources exist but are scarcer and disposable income not a widespread phenomenon, so prioritising purchases is almost an hour-by-hour process. Together with in-country staff and countless hours working with consumers, Point Innovate has identified three key areas that it must develop in order to know what the consumer wants and how to deliver to them:

a. Understand the customer's true needs. Often 'bright and shiny tech gadgets' are developed from the perspective of an outsider who has a particular product but has no knowledge of the local culture where the product will be sold. Point Innovate develops its product in the countries and environments where it will be used. Customer needs are understood by direct input and by developing and testing products with the end users. The world may think developing countries need 'multi mega watt' power plants but the end consumer just wants a single fridge, few lights and a TV to be powered.

b. Once the appropriate product is developed, Point Innovate, through direct interaction with its customers, seeks to understand the barriers of purchasing. Before a full-scale launch in a new market, solutions to customers' barriers to purchase are developed in order to address them during the sales process. Approaches to minimise the effects of barriers to purchasing in developing markets include: purchasing process and bartering, payment options, full-customer service and technical support.
c. Programmes, processes and routines are developed to aid staff in their jobs and interaction with customers. The systems that are developed are key to understanding consumer sentiment and providing a feedback mechanism that channels back to management in order to better understand product needs, R&D, consumer engagement, etc. With these programmes in place, productivity and sales increase and allow for a better understanding of consumers, and in turn, the development of the key drivers and performance indicators to help fine-tune the interactions with customers.

Capacity building

Building employees' capacity to run and manage business operations is required in order to create a sustainable business and to create a brand that is wanted by the target market. In developing markets, employees have the desire and the drive to be successful but the experience and knowledge required to be successful do not exist. Point Innovate must build the capacity of its employees in order to be successful and move its products into the many different channels. Real financial opportunity is provided. Hands-on training helps develop the capacity of employees to move product into the markets and ultimately create sustainable revenue streams. This requires a different mindset from Point Innovate: most business that enter developing markets look at employees as a mere tool to accomplish their financial goals and seldom provide opportunities for growth and wealth creation for their employees. Point Innovate is about creating wealth and opportunity for its employees. The motivation is that in the medium and long term this will result in larger market penetration and wider brand recognition.

Product development

Products must be designed and built to solve a problem and fill a customer need. Point Innovates product strategy focuses on the essential needs of developing communities and building products that are needed at all socio-economic levels in the market. To solve problems the product must be applicable to the poorest of the poor and the richest of the rich. The continuous development of new product and improvement of old product is essential to establish oneself in the market and stay ahead of the competition. Point Innovate currently develops renewable energy solutions that solve social core needs for all people living and working in developing countries. Point Innovate takes large-scale commercial solutions and brings them down to the consumer level at price points they can afford. It will continue to develop energy solutions but will also look at the other key areas of development such as water, sanitation, housing and food, where the appropriate market-based solutions don't exist or the current solutions are not feasible or affordable in order to solve the population's problems.

Questions for discussion:

- How important is it to adapt your sales processes to the local context when entering a foreign market?
- What are the relevant culture dimensions a Western company should considering when developing business in South America? and in Central Africa?
- What combination of agents, distributors and company sales representatives may be optimal to cover the Nigerian market?
- What would be the key factors to consider in sustaining strategic partnerships with distributors in emerging economies?

[1]http://smartgrid.ieee.org/december-2012/731-electrical-power-in-africa-challenges-and-opportunities

REFERENCES

Earley, P. C. & Ang, S. (2003). *Cultural Intelligence: An Analysis of Individual Interactions across Cultures*. Palo Alto, CA: Stanford University Press.

Graham, J. L., Ichikawa, S. & Apasu, Y. (1995). Managing your sales force in Japan and the U.S. In T. W. Meloan & J. L. Graham (eds.), *International and Global Marketing*. Chicago: Irwin.

Hansen, J. D., Singh, T., Weilbaker, D. C. & Guesalaga, R. (2011). Cultural Intelligence in cross-cultural selling: Propositions and directions for future research. *Journal of Personal Selling and Sales Management*, 31(3), 243–254.

Hofstede, G. (1981). *Cultural Consequences: International Differences in Work-Related Values*. Thousand Oaks, CA: Sage.

ICC (2014). International Chamber of Commerce. Retrieved 7 April 2014, from http://www.iccwbo.org.

MIQ Logistics (2013). Incoterms 2013. Retrieved from http://www2.miq.com/cms/INCOTERMS2013/.

Moore, R. A. (1992). A profile of UK manufacturers and West German agents and distributors. *European Journal of Marketing*, 26(1), 41.

Turnbull, P. W. (1987). A challenge to the stages theory of the internationalisation process. In P. J. Rosson & S. J. Reid (eds.), *Managing Export Entry and Expansion*. New York: Praeger.

Usunier, J. C. (1996). *Marketing across Cultures* (2nd edn). Hemel Hempstead, UK: Prentice Hall.

Wheeler, C., Jones, M. & Young, S. (1996). Market entry modes and channels of distribution in the UK machine tool industry. *European Journal of Marketing*, 30(4), 40–57.

WTO. (2014). World Trade Organization. Retrieved 4 April 2014, from http://www.wto.org.

Young S., Hamil, J., Wheeler, C. & Davies, J.R. (1989). *International Market Entry*, Hemel-Hempstead: Harvester Wheatsheaf.

PART III
PRACTICE

11 SALES FORCE RECRUITMENT AND SELECTION

OVERVIEW

A major determinant of sales performance is the quality of those recruited to the job. Training, leadership, remuneration and motivation are important but require quality talent to be developed. Careful attention and a professional approach are required to recruit and select the most appropriate candidates for sales jobs. The range of attributes required to satisfactorily perform the actions and processes mentioned in previous chapters makes it difficult to find the perfect recruit. Also, a good transactional seller or order-getter does not necessarily make a good technical sales specialist or key account manager and vice versa. The problems of status and role conflict in professional sales forces increase this difficulty, not only with securing the right candidates but also with keeping them. These key issues of recruitment and selection are the topics of this chapter.

LEARNING OBJECTIVES

This chapter aims to enable the reader to:

- Understand the importance of a planned approach to staffing the sales force.
- Help develop job specifications and descriptions for various sales positions.
- Critically evaluate different sources of new recruits.
- Identify the problems in selection and with selection techniques.
- Assess current techniques in recruitment and selection.

DEFINITIONS

Job description refers to the role and responsibilities that relate to a particular position in the organisation.

Job specification refers to how a particular job or position is described to potential applicants; it should be aligned with the job description, although the job description is normally used for internal purposes.

Psychometric testing is the use of validated techniques to assess an individual's attitudes and behaviour in different situations and circumstances.

THE RECRUITMENT PROCESS

Recruitment is important not least because of the costs associated with hiring new salespeople, the costs of employing the wrong people and the effect of mistakes on future business prosperity (Darmon, 1993). The effect on the individual's well-being should also be a major consideration when attracting and selecting. Salespeople are recruited to contribute to the development of a business. The starting point for recruitment is to assess the role of the sales force in the route to market strategy and then to determine their tasks and the appropriate size of the sales force to deliver their mission. An appraisal of manpower required, including estimates of those who might leave, be promoted or be dismissed, can help to complete the requirements for the sales force. The recruitment process considered in this chapter is outlined in Figure 11.1.

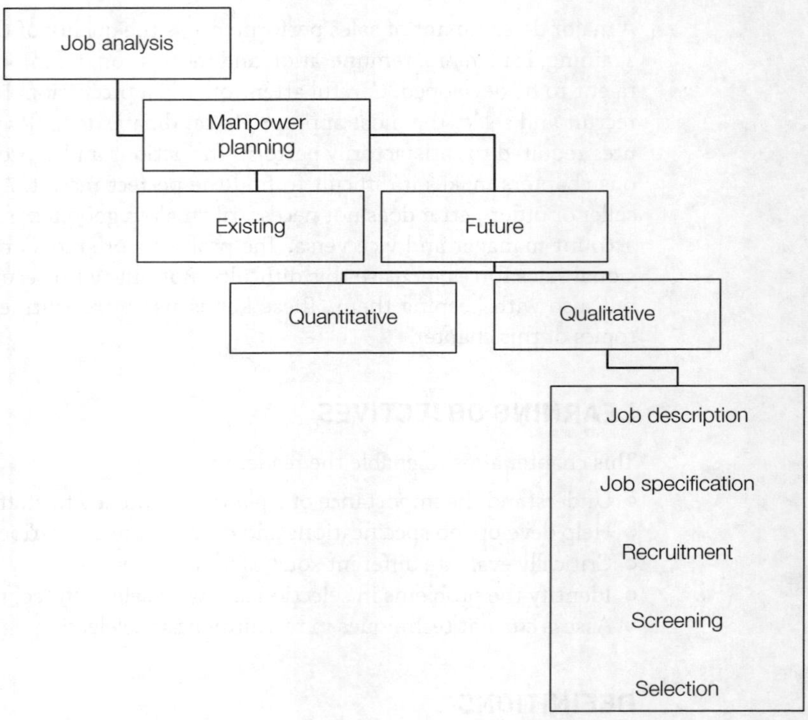

Figure 11.1 – The sales recruitment process

Sales managers often complain about a shortage of suitable applicants for some types of sales positions. It appears that people with the knowledge, skills and experience required, or perceived by sales managers to be required, are difficult to find. Formally addressing the recruitment process will help determine the required profile for the best candidates, thus avoiding unnecessary problems and costs. The time and expense in recruiting, including advertising, selection procedures and first and second interviews, are not insignificant. Added to this may be other costs, including induction training, the potential cost of lost sales, the costs of dismissal if the wrong applicant is selected and the cost of repeating the process. Recruitment costs can be a major issue for sales managers.

Another consideration, particularly in Western markets, is the anti-discrimination laws, ensuring equality regardless of the candidate gender, ethnicity, sexual orientation and age.

What do you think?

The following is a list of personal traits:

Appearance	Enthusiasm	Handshake	Numeracy	Courtesy	Flexibility
Friendliness	Non-smoker	Poise	Knowledge	Speech	Originality
Self-control	Persuasiveness	Handwriting	Mental alertness		
Ambition	Interest in the job	Curiosity	Healthy	Self-starter	

Evaluate each one distinguishing between essential, desirable, not relevant for a job in professional selling.

Select three types of sales jobs and discuss with others what you feel to be desirable characteristics or traits for these jobs.

Job analysis

Prior to drawing up the job description and independent of the job specification, the starting point in recruitment is job analysis. Job analysis specifies the tasks involved in a particular job and the factors which affect job performance. These factors might include:

- The type of selling job.
- The objectives of the job.
- The reporting relationship.
- The role and tasks necessary to perform effectively.
- The environment in which the job operates, including policies on sales, distribution and competitors.
- Company rules and regulations.

Sales managers should be rigorous in their job analysis and try to reflect in the job analysis corporate ethos, marketing strategy and the specific reporting relationships. Job analysis also requires assessment of what existing salespeople do. Surveys using questionnaires, observation and data returns can be used to confirm duties, tasks and time spent on the selling job. This information should be held as part of the sales automation system.

Manpower planning

The aim of manpower planning is to determine existing and future staffing levels. Manpower planning has both a quantitative dimension (how many?) and a qualitative requirement (what type?) as well as a geographical dimension (where?).

In Chapter 4 we presented approaches to calculating the size of the sales force. In addition to these models, and from a planning point of view, companies need to analyse the current sales force, its organisation and the profile of the salespeople in the context of the overall sales and business strategy. The starting point is to assess how adequate and effective the current sales force are in meeting sales objectives and the characteristics considered necessary to manage the portfolio of customers and to contribute to sales growth. Another factor to consider is the turnover of personnel. That is, people may be recruited to reinforce the existing sales structure while others will be recruited to replace those who are promoted, leave, retire or are dismissed.

A measure of turnover is the number of people who leave per annum, divided by the total number in the sales force.

Some of the factors that have been suggested to reduce salespeople's turnover are (Adidam, 2006):

- Appropriate setting of sales quotas that reinforce goal-oriented people when the targets are perceived to be fair and realistic.
- A positive relationship with the supervisor is associated with higher levels of retention.
- Opportunities for development that ensure salespeople remain marketable.
- Appropriate mechanisms to compensate individuals for the financial success their efforts help to generate.

Job description

Analysing and documenting the job/position is the cornerstone on which the job description for the salesperson is based. Therefore the job description should reflect the main duties, tasks and responsibilities of the job. Sales managers are responsible for recruiting new candidates so they should ensure that an adequate job description is produced and agreed. See Table 11.1 and Table 11.2, examples of job descriptions for a salesperson and a regional sales manager respectively. The key areas of a job description are typically job title, the main purpose of the job, key and secondary activities and performance measures. It is advisable to be as specific as possible in the job description about job functions and duties.

Table 11.1 – Example of job description – Salesperson

Job title	Sales Representative
Employment type	Full time
Description	The Sales Representative is a full-time outside business-to-business sales professional who is responsible for retaining and growing current accounts and for gaining new market share in a given territory.
Major responsibilities	• Articulate and position the company's products, services and solutions to key decision makers • Aggressively pursue competitive accounts; strive to differentiate the company from competitors • Manage entire sales cycle across customer accounts • Propose and close sales that achieve total revenue growth, profit and customer satisfaction plans • Sustain sales activities; appointments, demos, proposals, cold calls, and database updates • Keep abreast of changes in technology and understanding of basic user abilities
Basic requirements	• Proficiency using MS Office Suite (PowerPoint, Word, Excel & Outlook) • Excellent communication (oral, written and presentation skills) • Personal drive and internal motivation toward high achievement • Ability to work collaboratively and effectively in a team-oriented environment • Ability to influence, negotiate and gain commitment at all organizational levels • Demonstrated flexibility and adaptability; willingness to take risks and try new approaches
Desired qualifications	• BS/BA/AA degree in business or other related field • Previous sales experience preferred, but not required • Must have valid driver's license and minimum level of auto insurance coverage

Source: http://mrcopy.iapplicants.com

Table 11.2 – Example of Job description – Sales Manager

Job title	Regional Sales Manager, Food & Beverage – Foodservice
Reports to:	Director of Field Sales, Foodservice South Division
Key responsibilities	• Develop, coordinate and lead the region's execution of the company's Foodservice business (Food & Beverage) • Support and demonstrate the company's Vision, Culture and Principles • Help the team connect their responsibilities to delivering Our Purpose and Strategy • Enable the sales teams (direct and broker) to optimize region business opportunities • Promote clear communication and expectations • Recognize and adjust efforts to drive sales within a competitive industry and customer environment • Monitor and track progress vs. plan, adjust to business outages/needs • Sales Management • Lead and direct a Beverage sales team to achieve goals and objectives • Establish a strong top down relationship with the sales agencies representing food in the region • Deploy and execute solid, measureable initiatives in line with the company's Go-To-Market strategy • Develop and deploy joint annual business plans for strategic accounts • Train Broker Food sales teams on the company's branded product portfolio and applications • Review plan vs. quota, opportunities, red flags, gaps, etc. with Broker Account Executives on a weekly basis • Prioritize Resources to Implement and Deliver Region's Annual Plan • Target strategic customers and develop action/coverage plans • Initiate and develop annual customer action plans for region customers • Accelerate Volume and Profit Goals & Objectives • Implement strategic branded food & beverage category plans • Measure and track progress against budget goals and intervene when necessary • Execute and measure customer business plan's volume progress • Develop and maintain top to top business relationships with all key accounts • Maintain and optimize distribution of key the company's products • Work cross functionally (Sales Productivity, Marketing, Finance, Logistics, Product Development, HR,) to deliver the business results • Train and Coach Team Members • Effectively lead a team of two direct reports (Territory Sales Managers) • Act as a role model (coaches collaboration and teamwork) • Share successes / opportunities with team members • Accountable for Annual Budget • Actively review throughout the fiscal year • Effectively managing company assets • Customer Trade Funds and other support material/samples • Responsible for profitable qualified asset placements
Selection criteria	*Education* • Bachelor's degree is required *Experience* • At least five years of Foodservice Sales or Marketing experience (including knowledge of the industry, customers, products, and competition) is required • Sales Management experience is preferred • Must have proven experience selling nationally branded products and maintaining major customers (Top to Top) • Experience in strategic decision making, team building, and negotiations is a must • Proficiency in data analysis and capable of navigating and learning new technical systems is required

(Continued)

Table 11.2 – (*Continued*)

	Other • Understanding of Foodservice Supply Chain customer's needs and opportunities • Understanding of how to target, establish relationships, sell, and maintain Foodservice operators and distributors • Strong and effective communication skills • Must be willing to travel up to 60 per cent of work schedule • Must be willing to relocate in the future for growth opportunities within the Company • Must live in the Atlanta, Georgia area or be willing to relocate immediately to the area

Source: career4.successfactors.com

A job description can be defined as a written statement of the tasks to be performed and the relative importance of each. It should provide assistance and clarification on what functions and activities have to be performed and the priority of different tasks. A good job description is:

- *Written* to provide a formal statement of the expectations of the job.
- *Accepted* by salespeople, first-line managers and senior management. This is getting agreement on the priority tasks and evaluation criteria, and expected contribution of the job holder.
- *Specific* in terms of activities.
- *Comprehensive*, in that all key areas of the job, together with measures used to evaluate performance, should be included. Managers should not evaluate salespeople on dimensions not specified. If an adequate job analysis has been conducted, the measures listed in the job description should be appropriate and directly related to the specific tasks.
- *Reasonably short*, because if too short it may be too general to be of use. If too long, it becomes difficult to use and evaluate.

To facilitate writing a job description, a checklist of duties and responsibilities may help. Such a checklist may include: sales tasks, service tasks, management tasks, other tasks, authority, etc..

Profile specification

The purpose of the profile specification is to fit the most appropriate person to the required job description. The profile specification should list the desirable qualities and attributes that a person should have to perform to a high level in that job.

Not only is there a lack of consensus on these dimensions but also many of them are difficult to measure and assess. Inadequacies with new recruits in some areas can be overcome by suitable induction training, but a key problem for sales managers is whether to reduce the size of the pool of potential recruits by stipulating many qualifications, thus reducing training costs, or to reduce the entry qualifications and increase training costs. Remember also that there are legal restrictions on the extent to which employers can discriminate between applicants. Some guidelines to perform a quality profile specification include:

- Deciding on the most important aspects of the job.
- Identifying essential criteria.
- Identifying preferable criteria.
- Translating these into education, qualifications, experience and other attributes.

- Assessing validity and reliability (reliability is measuring accuracy, validity is whether the factor is a good indicator of future performance).

For example, certain tests may be reliable as measures of a person's personality, for example how extrovert someone is. This may or may not be a valid predictor of job performance. You need to consider the type of sales job. Job specifications offer some help but the evidence of the high turnover of salespeople and poor performance suggests that many companies are inefficient in recruitment and much greater attention must be paid by sales managers to sourcing, selecting and screening potential applicants.

Did you know?

When a salesperson leaves the business, the cost can be high. As much as six months in lost target and missed revenue is becoming increasingly typical, as the salesperson spends two months thinking about leaving without telling management (or, alternatively, being performance managed), a further two months leaving the business as they serve notice and wrap up pipeline, with an additional two months required for sourcing a replacement. This is before the new recruit is even trained and brought up to speed.

SOURCES OF SALES RECRUITS

A variety of potential sources can be used to recruit new salespeople. These sources can vary with respect to their adequacy and consistency in obtaining the best possible candidates for sales positions. However, an analysis of previous recruits can indicate more and less productive sources. This analysis can be extended to discriminate between high, average and low performers. One study (Avlonitis, Boyle & Kouremenos, 1986) suggested that sources of recruits can be linked to selling styles. For example, recruitment for direct to consumer selling jobs can be found through employment agencies. For trade selling, sources are primarily from advertisements and educational institutions, while for technical selling recruiters rely more on personal contacts. The use of different sources is, and should be, related to job- and company-specific criteria and, ideally, matching characteristics between buyer and seller. Effective recruiting is an organisational priority as many sales positions attain strategic importance for the supplying firm (Wiles & Spiro, 2004). The most important sources are as follows:

1. *Internet*. The most common way to source candidates for sales positions today is through the Internet. There are a number of ways in which the Internet can help match candidates and vacancies.
   - Through employment websites such www.Monster.com.
   - Posting a job vacancy on either the company's website or a third party's website.
   - Accessing relevant candidates through social media platforms such as LinkedIn (www.linkedin.com).
2. *Internal applicants*. People within the organisation may be ambitious to progress in their career. Selling may be seen as a more remunerative and satisfying job, especially by inside salespeople, designers, buyers or perhaps technical personnel. Careers in sales may be considered to be internal promotion and part of a management career. Such people are likely to be company-loyal and well versed in company policies, in particular in product knowledge. The uncertainty is likely to be with their selling skills.

3 *Recommended by existing employees, managers and salespeople*. Existing personnel offer a low-cost way of obtaining candidates through personal contact, friendship or third-party contacts. Such recruits are likely to have positive attitudes to the company and the job, but the recommendations are unlikely to be objective and representative. In some cases, the refusal to recruit could offend, putting unnecessary pressure on both manager and candidate. An even more delicate situation can arise when candidates are sourced through suppliers or major customers. Again, these situations must be handled carefully but in a positive manner.
4 *Unsolicited applications*. Intelligent, motivated individuals will attempt to find employment with companies they choose and take the initiative by writing to selected companies for a job. Unfortunately, in times of high unemployment, candidates tend to flood companies with such applications; at other times, far fewer are received. These applications should be assessed on their merits on the same basis as applicants from any other source.
5 *Employment agencies*. Professional recruitment agencies are an expensive source of recruits but so is the management time and effort if the entire process is handled internally. If using an agency, do the following:
   - Select a good one with a proven reputation and experience of your business and your sector.
   - Visit the agency personally, talk to the recruiters and examine their screening procedures.
   - If your company needs to recruit candidates regularly, aim to continue relationships with the agency rather than using them as a one-off. The agency's knowledge of your business may be a valuable asset.
6 *Educational institutions*. Colleges and universities are a rich source of high calibre applicants. In straight from undergraduate education, they lack business experience and perhaps have a low appreciation of what the selling job entails. Research conducted in the United States suggests that sales recruiters still have inaccurate perceptions of students' views on selling as a career. Generally they underestimate the importance of job satisfaction and career aspirations, which rate higher to students than salary alone (Wiles & Spiro, 2004). However, the gap in expertise of younger sales graduates is reducing in the US. Higher education institutions have responded to the need for qualified sales labour by increasing the number of sales-related courses offered in their curricula. For instance, sales education courses were offered by 44 universities in 2007 in the US and this number grew to 101 in 2011 (Cummins, Peltier, Erffmeyer & Whalen, 2013).

   A testimony of the importance for business of sales talent, and thus of sales education, is the creation in 2007 of the Sales Education Foundation (www.salesfoundation.org) with a vision of elevating the sales profession through university education. Also in 2002 the University Sales Center Alliance (http://www.universitysalescenteralliance.org) was established with the purpose of advancing the sales profession though teaching, research and further engagement with businesses.

7 *Professional bodies*. Associations and bodies such as the Sales Leadership Alliance (http://www.salesleadershipalliance.co.uk) and many other professional groups can be used to source applicants, often for senior sales positions.
8 *Advertisements*. Recruitment advertising, if well conducted, can be particularly effective in obtaining a large number of applicants. The size, message and

choice of media affect the response. Such advertising can also have a dual effect on company image and customers, but the appropriateness of advertising varies.

MINI-CASE STUDY – CHALLY GROUP

Chally Group is global leadership and sales potential and performance measurement firm. Chally Group Worldwide utilises industry leading research, predictive analytics and advisory services to ensure its clients have the vital information to minimise the risk associated with making decisions in selection, recruitment, development and succession planning.

Chally Group's advisors work with clients, helping them to match talent management strategies to their offering and sales strategy. Chally has well established links with sales academics and thought leaders to ensure the latest thinking and research informs the development of its services including:

- The creation of selection and developmental assessment profiles that are accurate in predicting future job performance.
- The evaluation of sales force performance against concrete benchmarks.
- The establishment of precise measurements of customer satisfaction with sales, service and leadership that accurately predict sales performance by individuals or teams.
- The definition of Talent Audit to review potential improvements in sales and management performance against forecast.

Source: www.chally.com

ASSESSING CANDIDATES

When the number and type of salespeople have been determined and the various sources have been selected to obtain the necessary applicants, it is then essential to define a rigorous process to evaluate these applicants in order to recruit those most suitable to the job and the firm. This is not an easy task for professional recruiters and may be extremely difficult for most sales managers. Consider some of the problems recruiting may have. First, the sales manager is in unfamiliar surroundings; that is, being objective, buying instead of selling. Second, the risk of selecting the wrong candidate is high, with consequences for the company and the individual. Third, there are a number of criteria to use in considering someone's suitability for a particular job. A systematic process will help to reduce error and bias but does not provide a guarantee. Recruitment is only one of the sales manager's tasks and the individual level of expertise is likely to be low. Sales managers are often under pressure to fill sales positions quickly. A degree of bias often means that sales managers attempt to recruit people who are similar to how a sales manager sees him- or herself.

Selecting applicants

In organisations, one possible cause of high turnover in sales personnel is that badly suited applicants are recruited in the first place. Turnover rates, that is, the number who leave per annum over the number in the sales force, which are above industry averages or seem to be increasing over previous periods indicate a problem and often hidden costs. Costs associated with turnover can include the fees of the recruitment agency, costs of advertising, training and development and unrealised business.

In addition to these costs, a salesperson leaving the company may well have a negative effect on sales in their territory and, if they join a competitor, business may be lost. The average lost sales multiplied by the number who leave will represent the total cost of lost business. Commensurate with cost is the time factor. From a decision to recruit or replace through sourcing, interviewing, screening, second or third interviews, checking references and the medical to placing and accepting an offer may take several months.

Despite the time and costs involved in this process, there is by no means universal agreement on the most effective selection tools. Cron, Marshall, Singh, Spiro and Sujan (2005) categorise selection procedures into five distinct domains: job skills/knowledge assessments, personality inventories, biodata, cognitive ability tests, and assessments for special sales purposes. Following we present well-established recruitment methods used in sales.

1 *Application forms* are very cost-efficient selection devices. They provide essential information on a person's personal history, educational qualifications and previous job experience. Forms are therefore a very useful first step in selection. The usefulness of such forms is as a first measure of suitability or otherwise. Forms are useful to identify areas of potential concern about the candidate such as:

   - Too many jobs in too short a time.
   - Inconsistent trajectory.
   - Employment gaps.

   These are particularly useful topics for clarification at the first interview.

2 *References*. A good candidate will often have previous commendations or letters of satisfaction from employers. References also have a use in verifying what is on the application form. It is often a useful technique to speak on the telephone to a referee to glean what is not written by asking pertinent questions.

3 *Interviews*. Interviews are rated highest in effectiveness but are also the highest cost selection tool. It is almost unthinkable to recruit a person for a sales position without some form of interview; indeed, it is used for virtually every job. More than one interview is recommended for sales jobs. The first may be a screening process whereas the second may help in finding the best candidate between equally qualified applicants.

   a) *First interviews* will tend to be more formal in structure to verify and clarify the application form details. Such an interview does not normally exceed one hour and must aim to assess the skills, experience and knowledge possessed by the applicant. One purpose is to save senior management time. First-line managers or personnel will conduct such interviews.

   b) *Second interviews* attempt to measure aptitude, personality and suitability factors that the candidate possesses relative to the requirements of the job. Interviews need to assess if this person can and will work with their customers, the sales team and the manager. Some sales managers may not be particularly effective in this role. Common failings include doing too much talking rather than listening, making frequent interruptions or overcorrecting. Inexperienced interviewers tend to be too incisive with the applicant or may alternatively be too nice. Asking the wrong or irrelevant questions and being self-opinionated are common mistakes in interviewing.

Interviewing is a skill which requires understanding and practice. Guidelines for those who *conduct interviews* include the following:

- Enlist professional help, an HR colleague or experienced interviewer.
- Be well prepared. Some list of prepared questions and rating charts can be used. It is also useful to rate key criteria separately using some form of (five- or ten-point) rating scale.
- Select a suitable interview environment. Avoid as much as possible all interruptions, calls and distractions.
- Establish a rapport such as a salesperson would with a prospective customer. Be at ease, be informal and start gently with easy questions. Maintain the candidate's self-esteem.
- Listen and observe. At least two-thirds of the time, the applicant should be talking.
- Use a pre-planned rating chart, to compare competencies and ratings of the candidates on these competencies.
- If possible, at least two interviewers should be used to compare findings and avoid bias. Variations of the interview situation can be suggested, including drinks, dinner and meet-the-partner sessions.

4 *Physical/medical*. This is quite important for salespeople. Physical and mental fitness will be required particularly in field sales jobs involving travelling, and possibly long working hours.

5 *Psychometric and other tests*. Such tests are extensively used, and when they are reliable, that is, when they measure a particular trait accurately they can provide very valuable insights that interviews can't reveal. Psychometric tests should have:

- Alignment with job analysis and a job specification.
- Reliability in results – if duplicated, would the results be similar?
- Validity – does it measure what it is intended to measure?
- Standardisation – is it uniform and fair?

6 *Intelligence and aptitude* tests may be relevant for certain sales positions These tests require extensive training and specialist skills to be conducted effectively. A structured approach to use the tests include:

- Determining what factors make for better performance. What evidence supports this? Does it apply to our industry?
- Questioning how these factors can be assessed. By interview, application form, reference, medical or test?
- If using psychological tests, the aim is to assess individual strengths and weaknesses relative to the job.
- Administering tests in order to complement rather than replace other methods.
- The test is only as good as its ability to identify those factors important in performance.

Did you know?

Our own research with European sales executives showed that, in seeking a new employer, 42 per cent of salespeople were looking for a company with interesting and challenging work, 24 per cent were looking for a good salary package and 13 per cent were looking for a good work–family balance.

THE ASSESSMENT CENTRE

Assessment centres are sets of techniques used by recruiters to test candidates for their suitability using a range of methods including tests, problem-solving exercises, group discussions and oral presentations. Originally used by the armed forces, they have proved worthwhile to assess managerial potential in a wide range of competences, and thus are increasingly being used to recruit salespeople. Large firms have both the resources and number of recruits to make this viable, although, increasingly, smaller firms are also recruiting in this way. An assessment centre will normally appraise six to eight candidates over one to three days using two or three trained specialists. It is therefore a high-cost selection approach, though it has a number of advantages such as:

- A wide variety of situations are created that will reveal the individual's abilities and reactions in different circumstances.
- A combination of selection techniques used with higher predictive validity than any one alone.
- The results cover a period of time rather than a one-off interview.
- The candidates have the opportunity to reveal particular strengths that do not appear through other mechanisms.
- The information can be quantified for subsequent use and validity.

SUMMARY

Recruiting and selecting suitable applicants is one of the most important and difficult jobs the sales manager can undertake. The process of job analysis, manpower planning, job description, job specification, recruitment, screening and selection should be systematic and thorough. Even professional recruiters cannot always claim reliability and validity in their selection criteria for salespeople. To reduce costs, improve selectivity and to be more effective, sales managers should follow a planned recruitment procedure, enlisting professional help as appropriate. A planned approach will increase the success rate in selection, and will help build positive reputation as employer. As the sales job becomes more complex and strategic the demand for more professionalised approach to recruitment and selection will become increasingly necessary.

QUESTIONS

1. Explain what steps might be taken to reduce the failure rate in selecting candidates for sales positions.
2. Discuss the benefits and drawbacks of recruiting graduates for selling jobs in fast-moving consumer goods companies.
3. Relatively new to recruiting salespeople, suggest how you would minimise your own personal bias and prejudices.
4. Put up an argument for or against the use of psychometric testing in recruiting salespeople.
5. Forecast in what ways the recruitment process might change over the next decade.

CASE STUDY: THE CARPHONE WAREHOUSE

The Carphone Warehouse (www.carphonewarehouse.com) has been in business since 1989 and has grown in size and now has over 1,400 stores in ten countries with the aim of achieving FTSE 100 status by 2007 and becoming a major consumer electronics retailer when it merged with Dixons in 2014. In Europe they have a network of 2,900 stores. The founder of the company, Charles Dunstone, originally worked for NEC and set up his business when he realised how difficult it was to buy a mobile phone. At that time, you could not go in to a shop and select but had to call a supplier who would send a salesperson to visit. The first retail outlet was set up in London and within weeks became highly successful.

Branches mostly sell from their premises, although personal visits to companies are also part of their customer portfolio and their B2B interests continue to expand. They do not favour cold calling or prospecting, relying on prospects to contact them through telephone, Internet or using their retail outlets. The company regard the personal selling of their products as requiring direct contact with the customer, in-depth product knowledge and personal adaptability and flexibility to respond to customers' needs in order to provide 'the right phone for the right person'. When recruiting, the company is looking for self-confident people who are able to make decisions and think for themselves. They must be able to show that they are capable of expressing technical knowledge in a language the customer will understand. Their policy is to promote retail and sales managers from within.

In the 'early days', the company recruited through word-of-mouth, basically recruiting friends of the original staff. As they expanded and moved away from London, this was no longer possible. They now recruit from a variety of sources, including recent graduates, although they prefer someone with a track record in sales and then to train them in mobile phone products. They are currently using advertisements, personal contacts, recruitment agencies and educational institutions but rely more and more today on their website as a source of recruits.

1. Called in as a sales recruitment consultant, what sources you would recommend the company should use to recruit new salespeople?
2. Go to www.careersatcarphone.com (select working at CPW) and critically evaluate their approach.
3. What advice would you give to the company about assessing potential applicants? Explain the selection procedure you would employ.

REFERENCES

Adidam, P. T. (2006). Causes and consequences of high turnover by sales professionals. *Journal of American Academy of Business*, 10(September), 137–142.

Avlonitis, C. J., Boyle, K. A. & Kouremenos, A. G. (1986). Matching salesmen to the selling job. *Industrial Marketing Management*, 15(1), 45–54.

Cron, W. L., Marshall, G. W., Singh, J., Spiro, R. L. & Sujan, H. (2005). Salesperson selection, training, and development: Trends, implications and research opportunities. *Journal of Personal Selling & Sales Management*, 25(2), 123–136.

Cummins, S., Peltier, J. W., Erffmeyer, R. & Whalen, J. (2013). A critical review of the literature for sales educators. *Journal of Marketing Education*, 35(1), 68–78.

Darmon, R. (1993). Sales force recruiting and training policies for minimising turnover costs. *Marketing for the New Europe: Dealing with Complexity. Proceedings of the 22nd EMAC Conference*, Barcelona, 27–44.

Stevens, C. D. & Macintosh, G. (2003). Personality and attractiveness of activities within sales jobs. *Journal of Personal Selling and Sales Management*, 23(1), 23–37.

Wiles, M. A. and Spiro, R. L. (2004). Attracting graduates to sales positions and the role of recruiter knowledge: A reexamination. *Journal of Personal Selling and Sales Management*, 24(1), 39–48.

12 SALES TRAINING AND DEVELOPMENT

OVERVIEW

This chapter is dedicated to one of the critical practices to enhance performance in sales management: training and coaching. The chapter covers the fundamental aspects of designing and evaluating sales training programmes and specifically focuses on sales coaching as a powerful approach to develop skills and competencies in salespeople. The chapter finishes with a reflection on the current and future trends in sales training and development.

LEARNING OBJECTIVES

This chapter aims to enable the reader to:

- Understand why and when sales training is effective.
- Define the principles of sales training programmes and how they might be delivered.
- Evaluate the impact of sales training.
- Describe how sales managers can coach salespeople and thus improve sales force job satisfaction and performance.

DEFINITIONS

Sales skills training refers to tuition to enhance 'how to' abilities with the purpose of becoming more effective at a particular task on a sales job.

Sales competence training is a development process that through increased awareness enables an individual to think and to behave differently to enhance sales performance.

Coaching is the means to enable people to achieve their objectives using feedback and reflection so the individual becomes more effective when using his/her knowledge, skills and abilities in work and personal contexts.

INTRODUCTION: SALES TRAINING

Sales training is a sizeable industry in mature markets. In the US, for instance, the American Society for Training and Development (ASTD, nowadays – Association for Talent Development – ATD) is estimated to be worth up to $15 billion per year (Salopek, 2009). Some companies spend on average up to $2,000 per year on training for a salesperson. Sales training should be specific for a particular job and organisation. Training design and delivery requires specialisation and focus on the specific circumstances of the individual and the organisation as well as observing the following principles:

- There is a clear purpose of what the training aims to do for the individual, how it can apply to their job and what benefits can be expected.
- There are opportunities to exercise and practise the new skills, to enable the individual to embody such skills.
- There is sufficient follow-up to ensure the learning process results in the application of new skills and competences.
- Encouragement of participation by the individual in the learning process.

Fundamental to the effectiveness of training is considering how learning occurs and the principles underlying adult learning. Stobart (2014), argues that ability is developed through applied learning and deliberate practice. In particular, Stobart's synthesis of existing research on the topic shows the importance of a few elements in developing expertise. First providing *opportunities and support* to develop skills, since people do not become experts accidentally. The place, context and time where someone is educated determine what we become experts in. For instance Tiger Woods used to play golf at the age of two with his father Earl. Bill Gates attended a school that had a computer lab funded by the mothers' club in 1968, unusual in schools at that time. In these two cases, the context facilitated their development into world-class professionals.

The second element in developing expertise is being *motivated to succeed.* Learning new skills will often involve sustained effort and overcoming difficulty, which is underpinned by intrinsic motivation. Csikszentmihaly (1990) claimed that:

> [T]he chief impediments to learning are not cognitive. It is not that students cannot learn; it is that they do not wish to. If educators invested a fraction of the energy they now spend on trying to transmit information in trying to stimulate students' enjoyment of learning, we could achieve much better results. (p. 118)

Third, undertaking extensive *deliberate practice* explains expert performance and a number of features believed to reflect innate talent are actually the result of intense practice at least over a period of ten years (Ericsson et al., 1993). Subsequent research found that other factors may also explain the level attained by expert performers and that at least one third of the variation in performance levels (for instance in chess players and musicians) is attributable to dedicated practice (Hambrick et al., 2014).

Expert performance is characterised by a fourth element, the creation of powerful *mental models* to handle and organise information. Experts can identify the principles that apply to a particular situation routinely, unlike novices who often see individual problems as new problems (Stobart, 2014).

The fifth element of developing expert performance is receiving continuous *feedback*. From elite athletes to musicians to salespeople, the quality, quantity and content of feedback will trigger reflection and will help develop specific skills, all resulting in enhanced performance.

Overall, the objective of sales training is to improve sales performance by adopting better work practices and behaviours. Not all training can achieve these desirable objectives directly, but they can potentially contribute in one or more of the following ways:

- Improving the salesperson's relationship with their customers by showing salespeople better ways to do business.

- Motivating the salesperson to develop their skills.
- Reducing staff turnover, which in turn reduces recruitment costs and the opportunity cost of lost sales.
- Making salespeople more flexible and innovative in meeting changing market conditions.
- Reducing supervision costs and requiring less management control.

PLANNING AND DELIVERING SALES TRAINING

Analysing training needs

Despite the importance and the pervasiveness of sales training, it has been claimed to be ineffective or less than useful (Salopek, 2009). Corporate sales education has in the past been 'prescriptive', 'linear' and content-centred rather than learner-centred. Cron, Marshall, Singh, Spiro and Sujan (2005) describe traditional sales training programmes as 'standardized (common to all salespeople), top-down (management decides), mandated (nonvoluntary), structured (formal and centralized), and offered in classroom' (p. 124). Thus in sync with the evolution of the sales function, there is increasing agreement of the need to further develop the approaches to sales training and education.

Factors associated with the lack of quality of sales training programmes include, among others, limited needs assessment, lack of training objectives, lack of alignment between training objectives and corporate goals, and inadequate sales training content (Ricks, Williams & Weeks, 2008).

Training needs' analysis typically cover three areas (Erffmeyer, Russ & Hair, 1991; Fan & Cheng, 2006) (Figure 12.1):

1. The analysis of the organisation's needs, ensuring that sales training programmes are designed to meet organisational needs and recognising the organisation's strategy and current structures, resources and organisational culture.
2. The analysis of the position, including the knowledge, skill and abilities required to perform the job.
3. The person or jobholder's needs, determining the extent to which the sales force possess the knowledge, skills and competences required by the job.

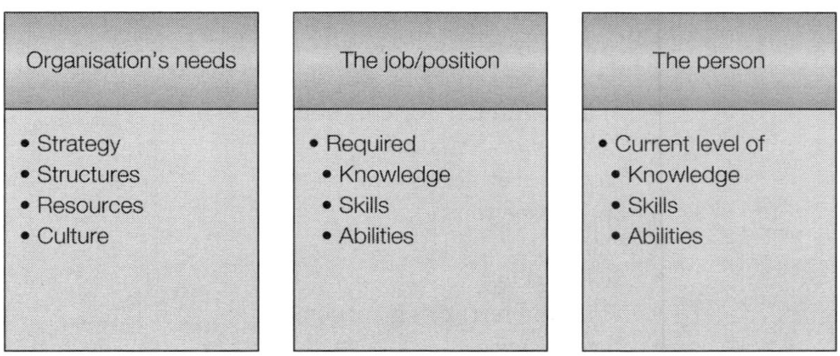

Figure 12.1 – Elements of training needs analysis

Training needs analysis must recognise that individuals will have different training needs. These differences may emerge when:

- New people are recruited.
- A salesperson takes on a new territory.

- New products are introduced.
- New business or new market segments are to be won.
- New company policies or procedures are introduced.
- Selling habits are poor or inappropriate.
- An individual is being considered for promotion thus taking new responsibilities.

Did you know?

Content of sales training programmes. The percentage of European firms providing sales training in specific areas was found to be as follows:

- Sales techniques (69 per cent of firms providing this).
- Market/customer knowledge (42 per cent).
- Computer knowledge (42 per cent).
- Product education (38 per cent).
- Company policy (35 per cent).
- Team work (30 per cent).

Source: Roman & Ruiz, 2003

Acknowledging types of sales training

We have argued that effective sales training has to be focused on the particular context of the salesperson. For example, some salespeople tend to favour existing calls with known customers and may have the need to develop skill in winning new business with new customers. Training can help them to do their job better. This might include the more efficient allocation of time, how to locate new potential customers, how to identify key decision-makers, how to arrange appointments, how to open a call, how to develop relationships, how to follow up and other aspects of what constitutes the complete selling job.

When addressing the type of training sales people require most organisations consider aspects of the job such as: task-related, personal, self-development (Cron et al., 2005):

- Task-related aspects: those that enable individuals to perform better on a particular job. Examples include:
  - Knowledge.
  - Product or service knowledge.
  - Market/Industry orientation.
  - Company orientation.
  - Legal and ethical issues.
  - Specialised topics.
  - Skills.
  - Selling skills.
  - Time and territory management.
  - Technology.
  - Relational skills.
- Personal aspects: Are focused on how individuals learn and mobilise skills, knowledge and abilities. These are often underpinned by learning theories that emphasise attitude change as a more enduring mechanism to achieve dynamic behavioural change (through practice). Examples include: practical intelligence, tacit knowledge, problem-solving skills, coping skills.

- Self-development: Focused on the personality and motivational underpinnings of personal development. Examples include: self-assessment, self-direction, self-monitoring, self-reinforcement, self-renewal.

What do you think?

Myths About Selling

Stanton, Buskirk and Spiro (1991) suggest that many managers and salespeople themselves are not receptive to training because of their attitude and philosophies about selling. These authors identified six myths which characterise this problem. What do you think?

Myth 1: Salespeople are born not made. Since there is great difficulty in identifying characteristics of successful salespeople, it is hard to explain why this myth is so popular. It is true that some people can never be trained to sell, and it is also true that others may be easier to train. Most people will become more effective through training. Successful companies invest heavily in training.

Myth 2: Salespeople must be good talkers. Evidence suggests that successful selling is about listening rather than talking. Probing and questioning which reveals the customer's real needs is more effective than talking.

Myth 3: Selling is a matter of knowing the right techniques or tricks. In some one-off, direct sales situations, and possibly some of the time in other situations, a canned approach may work if it is relevant. But selling based on insight and a combination of skills is far more effective.

Myth 4: A good salesperson can sell anything. Most successful salespeople started by failures with the wrong approach, wrong product or wrong customer. Success cannot be achieved where product, price, service and quality are inferior. Matching products to customers is the basis for success.

Myth 5: A good salesperson can sell ice to the Eskimos. A good salesperson wouldn't even try – the customer doesn't need it.

Myth 6: People do not want to buy and have to be conned. Most people enjoy buying and organisations have to buy for survival. Salespeople can help in this process.

Having identified that training is both necessary and desirable, decisions have to be taken on who will deliver the training, who should attend the training, where and using what methods. These points are covered in the following subsections.

Identifying sales trainers

The skills in teaching are quite different from those of actually doing a job. Good performers do not necessarily make good teachers. These two jobs are not comparable. Sales trainers can be inside specialists, external experts or experienced salespeople. In firms with large sales forces, training is more likely to be provided by company specialists who can assess individual needs and tailor programmes to suit both internal and on-the-job requirements. Where companies employ smaller sales forces outside experts are likely to be the optimal solution. Industrial goods companies typically rely on internal trainers/ experienced salespeople who have high levels of customer, company and product knowledge. Whoever undertakes the task, the skilled trainer/ developer/coach needs to be aware of adult learning theories to design and deliver meaningful programmes.

Considering sales training contexts

There are various contexts that sales trainers can use, and the most suitable ones depend on the nature and the intended outcomes of the sales training programme.

On-the-job training methods are effective ways of delivering sales training because sales people in most cases can carry on with their duties while receiving training. On-the-job training can take the form of:

- Teaming, bringing together people with different skills to help and support each other.

- Meetings, setting aside times when salespeople can get together on a particular topic or skill.
- Mentoring, providing formal and informal mechanisms for new salespeople to learn from more experienced ones.
- Peer-to-peer communications, creating opportunities for mutual knowledge sharing amongst salespeople.
- Sales coaching, establishing a structure to enhance specific competences.

Classroom-based training is effective when a number of people have similar needs and thus the content to be delivered is the same for every individual. This method is often used to train people in product knowledge, company polices, customer and market characteristics and certain selling skills. Classroom-based training has the additional advantage of enabling interaction amongst salespeople and building camaraderie. However, this type of training is often expensive, time-consuming and if too much material is imparted, less retention will occur.

Networked learning or online training is a growing method to deliver increasing numbers of topics and programmes. For most organisations, it will unlikely eliminate one-on-one training and classroom-based techniques, and rather than a substitute, most organisations think about these as complementary methods.

Experiential methods such as outdoor training are in growing demand. These approaches help develop effective training of competences such as teamwork, resilience and conflict management, all relevant to the world and work of sales. Intended learning outcomes must be well defined to avoid mistaking training for simply enjoyment activities.

Did you know?

US spending on corporate training grew by 15 per cent last year to over $70 billion. Worldwide, the industry is worth $130 billion.

This growth in training and development expenditure coincides with an explosive growth in technology-enabled resources including video, online communication, virtual learning, and massive open online courses (MOOCs) such as; Coursera, Udacity, Udemy, edX … As much as 18 per cent of all training is delivered through mobile devices today.

Source: *The Corporate Learning Factbook 2014*: Benchmarks, Trends, and Analysis of the US Training Market.

Specialist sales training can be delivered in a number of ways/locations:

1 Company specialist in an internal location. The advantage of this approach is that it enables company-specific and work-oriented training to be carried out. Sales trainers often involve field sales managers in the process to ensure that training is relevant to the realities of the job (Honeycutt, Howe & Ingram, 1993).

2 External location. Again, the experience and expertise of the trainer is important but specific customer, product and company knowledge may be lacking. Experienced salespeople tend to be skeptic of so-called outside experts. There may also be a lack of uniqueness and a possible lack of security with such programmes.

3 On-the-job, which, as described above, can be effective if knowledge and skills are put into practice, for which a process-oriented design of the training needs to be adopted (Lidstone, 1986) ensuring the trainer describes to salespeople what to do, shows them how to do it, gets salespeople to practise what they have been instructed to do, assesses what they do, corrects where necessary and instils a mindset of continuous practice. On-the-job training is often delivered by the sales

manager. Thus, sales managers need to develop an understanding of evaluation and follow up for on-the-job training to be effective.

On-the-job training occurs in real-life situations under actual market conditions. A possible shortcoming may be the lack of expertise in the trainer. Another weakness is that both good and bad habits can be learned. There is also a problem in being sales- rather than customer-focused, for example using sales technique as a solution to all sales tasks instead of building the ongoing relationship. In smaller companies, it is almost always the case that the trainer is the sales manager but such people tend to be weak on evaluation and follow-up, which are crucial to training effectiveness (Honeycutt, Ford & Tanner, 1994). No single approach is perfect and the method used in training should be considered and evaluated, as well as who is going to do it.

Selecting sales training methods

Sales training can be delivered using a number of different methods. The methods should be selected according to the skills to be developed. The most common methods in sales include:

1. *Workshops*. These can take a variety of forms and potentially offer the most frequent training opportunity at regional or national sales meetings or specially convened training sessions. The use of discussion topics, case studies or idea-generating sessions helps individuals to learn from peers and colleagues and to seek individual improvement.
2. *Seminars* are a traditional way of teaching large numbers at low cost. They are useful to convey factual type information but suffer from a poor retention of information by participants and sometimes the inability to adapt to some specific situations that appear in selling. A number of vehicles (visual aids) can be used including slides, flip charts, films and audio and video communications.
3. *Programmed and structured learning*. Developing on the previous approach, many sales trainers and companies are finding programmed learning to be a cost-effective training approach. This enables a substantial quantity of material to be given to new and existing salespeople at their own pace. The format uses a sales manual divided into relevant sections, for example, product knowledge and sales skills. General information can be supplemented with company- and product-specific data. Video and audio communication can be used together with assignments, exercises and possibly case examples to provide a comprehensive coverage of the subject. So-called high-tech training methods, including computer-assisted learning, computer-managed instruction, tele-training and interactive video, are likely to be increasingly used in the digital age.
4. *Role-playing*. A widely used technique in sales, whereby 'close-to-real' or artificial sales situations are constructed to educate salespeople in adopting effective behaviours in situations such as salesperson–customer interactions. Other options include recreating sales meetings to illustrate and highlight important points in selling and in sales management. Role-playing, using video recording and playback, is now widely used as a learning technique. The use of actors to increase realism is increasingly common as it provides unique insights into 'close-to-real' human interactions. Role-play in sales education typically involves:
   - Defining the sales situation; for example, to get a new product accepted by an existing customer.
   - Establishing the situation; for example, time of call, the individual you are addressing and relevant circumstances.

- Casting a buyer and a seller – roles will later be reversed.
- Briefing the participant (separately) on what their objectives should be – buyers can be told to raise specific obstacles or objections.
- Playing out the sales situation.
- Discussing and analysing the interaction getting individuals to reflect and to derive learning points to apply in real-life situations.

A good role-playing exercise is to create one or two salespeople acting as potential suppliers and three or four others acting in buying roles as might form the decision-making unit (DMU) to be found in organisational purchasing. This situation might be supplying a CRM system to a major bank, supplying process equipment to a major food manufacturer, environmental services to a major oil company or similar scenarios. By briefing the participants with alternative positions before or during the exercise participants can practise different approaches both strategically and in the sales/negotiation situation. Play-back of events provides strong learning and realisation of strengths and weaknesses in individual, team and organisational sales approaches.

5. *Observed sales calls*. Most managers and trainers use some form of behavioural observation of sales meetings, but very few are trained or skilled in the technique. The problem is often too much emphasis on specific strengths or weaknesses, mostly weaknesses. To be effective as a training method, it requires some skill in preparation, purpose, observation, analysis and coaching by the trainer. This participative approach, given its realism, is a powerful learning method that is discussed further below.

The reason for providing sales training is that the benefits to be derived from training often outweigh the costs. Sales training is not an end in itself. Managers must take cognisance of the fact that not all skills and attitudes can be learned and that individuals react to training in different ways. Some are more positive than others and training needs differ; for example, between new and experienced or between technical and non-technical personnel. Some salespeople will be more adaptable and receptive than others but training cannot help those who cannot or will not learn and adapt.

Sales training methods must be varied to be effective with individuals with different learning styles. Kolb (1984) proposed that combining perception and information processing one could identify four learning styles: diverging (concrete, reflective), assimilating (abstract, reflective), converging (abstract, active) and accommodating (concrete, active).

Sales training programmes should also focus on (and adapt to) the nature of the interaction between the supplier and the customer. In fact, the customer should be the focal point in the design of modern sales training. Understanding customer needs, problems and situations is fundamental to the selling job. Thus, training must be contextualised so it becomes instrumental in helping develop meaningful customer relations.

What do you think?

Job-related sales problems.

The following have been identified as some of the problems faced by salespeople:

- Failure to consummate a sale.
- Failure to achieve quotas.
- Failure to obtain new prospects.
- Inability to grant a prospect's request.
- Failure to achieve promotion.
- Failure to circumvent closed-door tactics.

Q: As a sales manager, what approaches would you suggest for these problems?

Evaluating sales training programmes

At the outset of this chapter, it was claimed that the purpose of training was to improve performance. This being so, it is necessary to evaluate the effectiveness of sales training. The costs of training are measurable and identifiable, but the outcomes of training are less measurable. Improvement can be measured on a variety of dimensions:

- *Outcome-related sales* – for example, value, volume, number of orders, average order size and new customers.
- *Sales activities* – such as number of calls, journey time and distance reports submitted.
- *Costs of sales* – including expenses, expense ratio and commission rates.

One approach to evaluate sales training is to collect relevant and measurable data on these parameters prior to training and immediately after. Results could show both the quantity and quality of sales performance. However, it should be acknowledged that factors other than the sales training may have considerable influence in sales outcomes. Pre- and post-training evaluation results need to be compared with a control group to ascertain the impact of training.

It has been suggested that sales training evaluation should encompass both the impact of training on trainees and the impact on the firm (Attia, Honeycutt & Leach, 2005). One of the most accepted frameworks for evaluating training programmes is Kirkpatrick's (1998) four levels of evaluation. The first is the participant's *reaction* to a training programme, which reflects how they feel about the training. The second level, *learning*, is the increase in knowledge and/or skills, and furthermore, the change in attitudes. The third level, *behaviour*, refers to the transfer of knowledge, skills, and/or attitudes from the classroom to the job. This evaluation is conducted between three and six months after the training programme has been delivered. The fourth level of evaluation, *results*, refers to the variety of outcomes that occurred due to the training.

Sales training programmes need to develop specific learning objectives so they can be assessed more objectively. There are benefits in involving experienced salespeople in the design and delivery process (Honeycutt et al., 1993). It is not just the sales training course that should be evaluated but also the training process, including the pre-briefing by the line manager outlining the initial training objectives; the event itself; the debriefing by the line manager; the subsequent encouragement and coaching and the opportunities for salespeople to implement change. This requires coordinated effort by the trainer, the manager and the salesperson to assess and to further improve sales practices (Figure 12.2).

Assessing selling skills and competencies

Training needs, often derive from significant gaps in selling skills, and the effectiveness of sales training is measured in terms of skill and competency development.

Furthermore, the evaluation of skills and competences feeds into the definition of sales roles, strengthening the design of the organisation and its performance. Selling skills and competences can be assessed through the following steps:

Step 1 Define the instrument

To assess the competence level of each salesperson you need an instrument. The simplest form is to list the skills/competencies and rate them on a scale of one (=inadequate) to five (=expert). Behaviourally anchored rating scales (BARS) can be used as a method to rate the level of competencies. This appraisal method aims to

Sales executive		5 = Expert 4 = Advanced 3 = Medium 2 = Basic 1 = Inadequate					✓ Ideal job skills profile 0 Personal skills profile	✓. . . . . 0 = Skills gap
		Skill level					Observations	
Skill sets		1	2	3	4	5		
Gaining and maintaining of accounts	Establish target customer portfolio		0	✓				
	Acquisition planning				0✓			
	Exploring & validating customer needs			0		✓		
	Product trials & demonstrations					0✓		
	Production and presentation of a proposal					0✓		
	Negotiating and closing the deal				0	✓		
	Implementation of the agreement			0	✓			
	Development of customer relationships					0✓		
	Maintenance of customer relationships					0✓		
	Mobilisation of internal organisation to deliver agreed service levels			0	✓			
	Servicing the customer				0✓			
	Optimising account profitability			0	✓			
	Identification of sales growth opportunities				0	✓		
	Identify and select co-suppliers	0	✓					
Co-supplier management	Management of co-suppliers			0	✓			
	Developing partnerships			0	✓			
General skills	Financial awareness				0	✓		
	Cost knowledge				0	✓		
	Self image projection				0✓			
	Internal & external communications					0✓		
	Collection and distribution of market information		0✓					
	Reporting written and verbal					0✓		
	Internal reporting / workflow updated			0	✓			
	Logistics and operations			0✓				
	Group presentations				0	✓		
	Customer records			0	✓			
	Selling skills				0	✓		

Figure 12.2 – Example of training needs analysis and appraisal form

combine both the ratings with descriptions of good, moderate and poor performance in a given skill/competence. So BARS differs from 'standard 1 to 5' rating scales in that it focuses on behaviours that are determined to be important for completing a job. By describing the detailed behaviour or knowledge for each competence level, you make the selection easier and more objective. BARS are intended to facilitate more accurate ratings of the person's skill/competence or performance (see Kingstrom & Bass, 1981).

Step 2 Define the method

There are several ways to analyse selling skills and competencies. An effective method in professional selling is to accompany the salesperson to real customer encounters to gain in-depth insights about the skills/competences of the sales person in the context where they are used. This engaged approach is consistent with established participatory and ethnographic approaches in sales and marketing research (Cayla & Arnould, 2013; Geiger & Turley, 2003).

Alternatively, skill/competency levels can be assessed via interviews. Since interview methods are prone to subjectivity and bias if only one interviewer is involved, 360-degree evaluation can be sought from a number of relevant stakeholders. The participants could include the individual's manager, customers, peers, and direct reports, among others (see Figure 12.3).

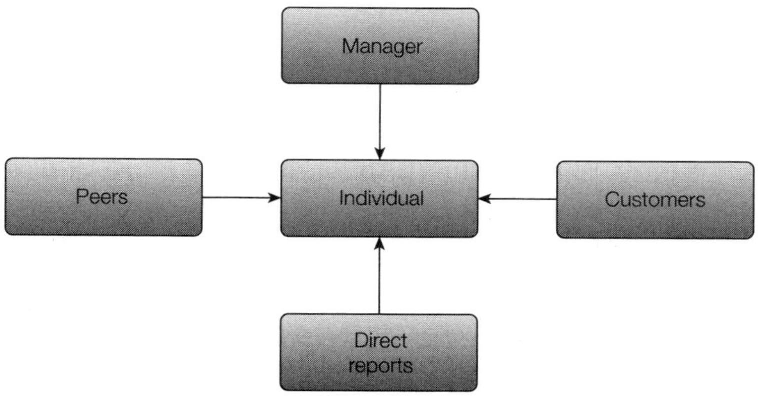

Figure 12.3 – Participants in 360-degree evaluation

The advantages of using such a method is to gather a more complete picture of the person's skill/competence level and also to reveal differences between one's own and other's evaluation of certain competences. This helps an individual to focus on specific skills and focus efforts on them. The outcomes of 360-degree evaluations often provide a meaningful starting points to discuss with the individual areas in need of further development. When performed for the whole of the sales team it allows the sales manager to identify areas to be developed through training (thus feeding into training needs analysis) and/or through coaching.

Step 3 Interpretation

The feedback of such a 360-degree analysis is often reported in the form of a radar diagram. The diagram shows the differences in perception between how the person sees him- or herself and how others see them (see Figure 12.4).

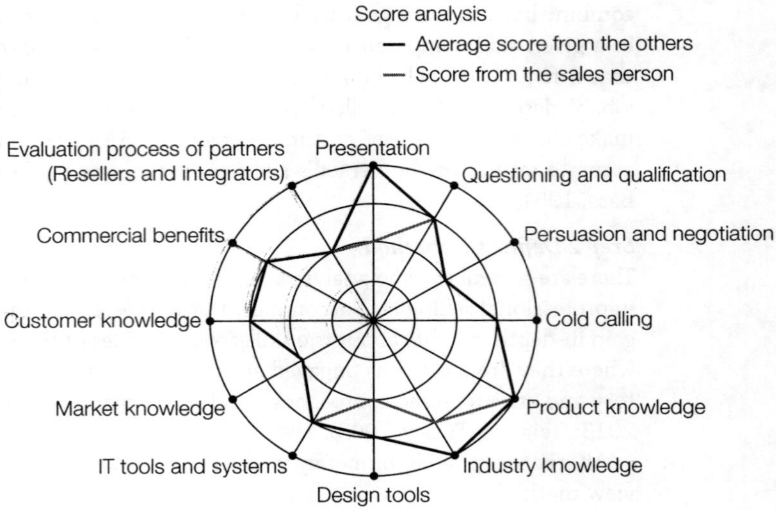

Figure 12.4 – Analysis of selling skills/competencies

SALES COACHING

Sales coaching is a powerful way to help an individual modify his/her behaviour and raise awareness to improve sales performance. Corcoran, Petersen, Baitch and Barrett (1995, p. 118) define sales coaching as a 'sequence of conversations and activities that provides ongoing feedback and encouragement to a salesperson or sales team member with the goal of improving that person's performance'. Rich (1998) argues that sales coaching is a multidimensional activity including three clusters of activities: (1) supervisory feedback, (2) role modelling and (3) development of a salesperson's trust in his or her manager. Guidance is also quoted by Ingram, Laforge, Avila, Schwepker, and Williams, (2001) as a major construct of sales coaching. When sales managers adopt a transformational leadership style and salespeople are highly coachable and competitive, sales performance increases significantly (Shannahan, Bush & Shannahan, 2013). Thus, effective coaching depends both on the sales manager effectively practising coaching and the salesperson being receptive to and impacted by the coaching efforts (Shannahan, Shannahan & Bush, 2013).

To understand sales coaching it is also important to understand the factors that affect sales managers' motivation to coach their people. These include extrinsic rewards due to managers' own performance, extrinsic rewards due to salespeople's performance and intrinsic rewards (Pousa & Sherbrooke, 2010). Coaching has demonstrated to impact salespeople's attitudes and behaviors. In particular, Onyemah's (2009) study demonstrates that coaching may impact (a) affective commitment; (b) intrinsic motivation; (c) role ambiguity; (d) satisfaction with job; (e) satisfaction with supervisor. However, the relationship between coaching and these variables is mediated by a number of contingencies. For instance, salesperson-organisation value fit reduces the likelihood that coaching will create more affective commitment to the organisation, improve satisfaction with job and supervisor and lower perceived role ambiguity. Quality of communication with the manager strengthens the positive relationship between coaching and intrinsic motivation. Interestingly, Onyemah (2009) demonstrates that a salesperson's organisational tenure has no impact on the effectiveness of coaching.

Overall, two types of sales coaching are practised in organisations: skills coaching and strategy coaching (Rackham & Ruff, 1991) which we now describe. (Note. We will use coach/sales manager interchangeably given that sales coaching is often provided by the sales manager.)

Skills coaching

Skills coaching aims to develop a very specific set of skills, mostly observable ones, through the use field observation, feedback and subsequent monitoring. Generally, sales managers can only coach a limited number of individuals, given that quality coaching is a time demanding activity. A number of suggestions for conducting effective skills coaching with salespeople are listed below.

1. *Careful planning* is paramount in sales coaching, and requires setting clear goals and expectations. Prior to engaging in 'live' skills coaching (i.e. with real customers and observing real sales meetings), managers need to agree on the customer that both the coach and the sales people will visit. For the coach, it is always useful to have an outline of the customer to enable the manager/coach to understand the intentions of the salesperson, and adequately interpret the reactions of both the salesperson and the customer.

   Coaches do not need to predefine what the behaviours of the salesperson should be, given that effective selling often requires a high degree of adaptiveness (Verbeke, Dietz & Verwaal, 2011) and that different customers may require different approaches in different circumstances. When the details of coaching sessions are jointly planned, this helps by putting the sales manager and salesperson 'on the same side'. This type of coaching is often an intense experience for the salesperson. Inevitably, many salespeople being 'coached' may interpret the coaching initiative as an 'evaluation', particularly if the coaching programme is defined and implemented by their own organisation. Thus, the sales manager/coach should acknowledge the perceived pressure that coaching may trigger and create a climate of receptivity and collegiality. The amount of time devoted to planning coaching will result in superior skill improvement (Rackham & Ruff, 1991).

2. *Conduct* the coaching session or day as planned. When doing so, it is important not to confuse 'selling' and coaching. Salespeople may have a tendency to let the coach/sales manager take over the sales meeting, particularly with challenging customers. If it is the kind of sales meeting the seller should be able to handle, it is better for the coach to stay quiet, and should the sales fail, reflect and learn the lessons from it. However, if the sales manager finds her/himself with something unexpected, or if it is a big sales opportunity, then pragmatism would suggest forgetting the coaching activity and to give 100 per cent of the attention to the customer and to the selling process. Typically, good coaching calls are those that happen early in the cycle, in safe selling situations with customers of moderate potential where the salesperson sells and the manager coaches. However, the types of calls that salespeople tend to set up are closing calls, in tough selling situations or high potential calls resulting in the manager doing the selling (Rackham, 2010).

What do you think?

Q: If a manager is skill coaching and sees that a call is going badly, what should the manager do?

3 *Debrief and review*

A key principle for effective coaching and the after sales call debrief is to focus on one skill at a time. If the sales manager aims to develop more than that, overload may occur and the coaching will be rendered ineffective. Good coaches listen carefully and establish a dialogue with the coachee. They avoid judgement or jumping too quickly into solutions and seek to understand the salesperson's perspective by asking in-depth questions about the salesperson's interpretations as well as the customer's problems. Good practice in coaching suggests fulfilling the plan specified earlier.

4 *Follow-up*

There is substantial skill loss with nonpractice and nonuse, in particular cognitive tasks both immediately after training and subsequently (Arthur, Bennet, Stanush & McNelly, 1998). Therefore, sales managers need to plan and agree with the salesperson the allocation of time and activities to perfect and develop those skills that were subject to coaching (Figure 12.5).

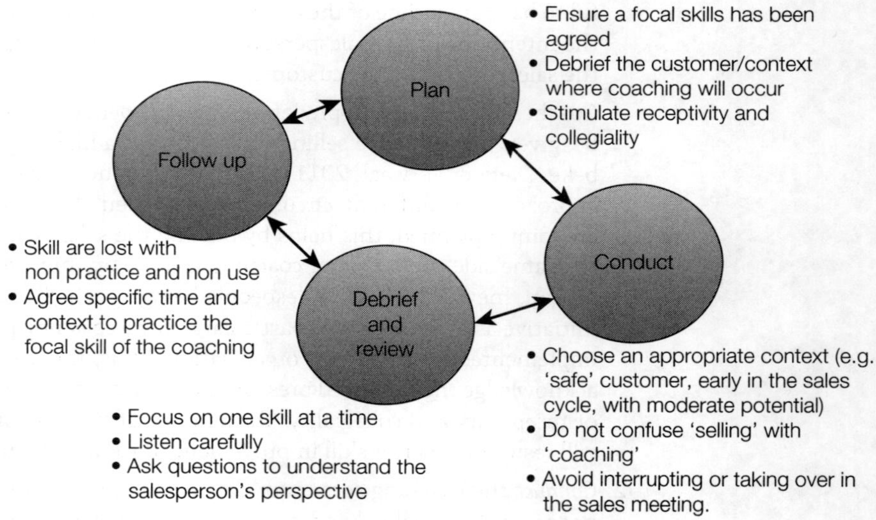

Figure 12.5 – Process for skills coaching

Doyle and Roth (1992) argue that the process of building relationships with customers is long and complex and requires more learning, making the 'once a month' coaching schedule insufficient. On this basis they argue that coaching by joining the salesperson on a single sales call cannot work because only the salesperson is able to place the call in the context of past conversations with all the unique personalities of that account. Therefore, coaching in relationship selling requires frequent interactions to jointly discuss and analyse account relationships, and potential and projected economic returns, with the aim of developing insight rather than evaluating a salesperson's behaviour in a particular sales call.

The complexity of the interactions between the seller and the customer suggests using additional material to help complete an in-depth diagnosis of the nature of interactions with particular customers. Such tools are diaries that may help structure relevant information about the customer, and feed into the coaching planning process.

These coaching discussions are led by the salesperson who analyses data for every call and describes the progress and problems encountered in the accounts. The sales manager should encourage insight by asking self-reflective questions. According to Doyle and Roth (1992) the result of the discussion and the self-reflecting questions should be new insight that the salesperson then commits to apply on future sales calls.

What do you think?

Some reflective questions that may help the sales representative and the sales manager to derive useful insights may include: 'Overall, how satisfied are you with this sales meeting'?' 'What is your view of the receptivity of the customer to your proposed solution?' 'Why do you think the customer did XYZ?', 'What could you have done to prevent that from happening?', 'What have you learnt as a result of this call?'

In Chapter 6 we argued that the role of a salesperson is more complex than ever before, requiring both action and reflection, analytical and management skills. Gosling and Mintzberg (2003) argue that management is about action on the ground and reflection in the abstract. Action without reflection is thoughtless, and reflection without action is just an illusion. These authors argue that events become experience only after they have been reflected upon, so that most people go through life undergoing happenings that are undigested into experience. On this basis, we can conclude that the role of the coach is no longer that of a teacher who tells the salesperson what and how to do his job. The role of the coach is to facilitate the interpretations of events that happened (e.g. during a customer interaction) so that the salesperson continuously enhances his or her knowledge about how to manage customer relationships in diverse contexts and settings.

Strategy coaching

Whilst skills coaching focuses specifically on a particular tactical aspect of 'how to' do a better job, strategic sales coaching is more about the 'what', such as the company's goals and strategies, key revenue drivers, optimisation initiatives and so on (Goh, 2014). Strategy coaching focuses on issues of planning, helping the salesperson think critically about a problem or challenge, and to devise creative ways of addressing that problem.

A *strategy coaching session* typically commences by clarifying the purpose and the structure of the session. This type of coaching is often aimed at enabling the sales manager and salesperson to jointly identify actions that when implemented will result in enhanced sales performance.

The manager often initiates a review of the current situation (market competition, company results) to establish the background upon which to frame the coaching dialogue. Then the coach aims to establish a collaborative and trustworthy exchange by recognising and acknowledging the key strengths of the coachee. By contrast a few problems or challenges can then be diagnosed following a clarification of needs either in the individual or in the context where the person operates. The last phases of strategy coaching typically involve the generation of alternatives and solutions and the definition of action plans and next steps (see Figure 12.6).

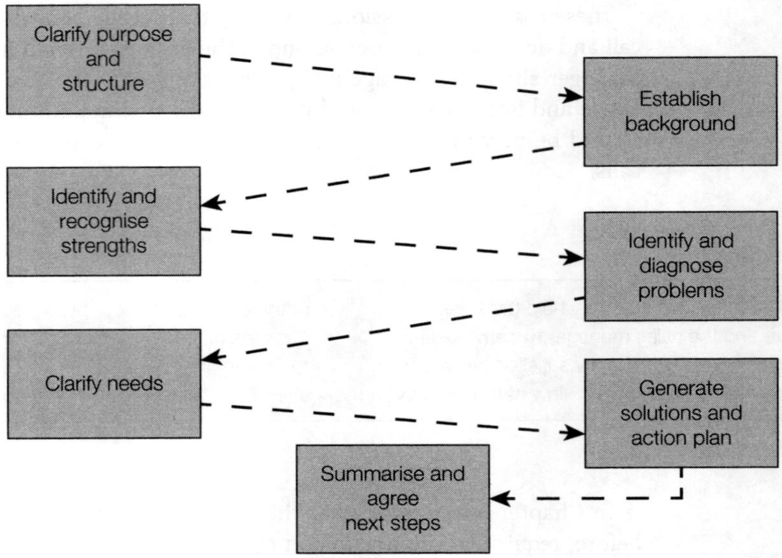

Figure 12.6 – Structuring a strategy coaching session

Coaching the right individuals

The last consideration of a well thought out coaching plan is the profile and characteristics of salespeople who would be priorities for coaching. As a general principle, volunteers are always good candidates for being coached because they will be motivated (Rackham, 2010). Very low performers, unless they are new, will be slow to change, so may not be a good priority. High performers may have unique features and competences and are already meeting the expectations of the manager. By coaching top people, the manager learns and also shows that coaching is not a remedial punishment. Mid-level performers are likely to respond more quickly to coaching.

Research conducted by the Sales Executive Council (Detterick & Spence, 2008) reveals that sales teams that report receiving high-quality coaching are likely to achieve up to 102 per cent to goal. This study suggests that performance improvements through coaching are likely to be marginal at either end of the performance spectrum (assuming a normal distribution of salesforce performance) and thus that medium performers should be coached to increase their results and high performers for retention.

Figure 12.7 shows a tool to help the sales manager prioritise coaching efforts. It first describes some elementary drivers of sales performance including competence, potential (to learn and develop) and motivation. It then features the payoff or return from the coaching investment. If a sales manager had four hypothetical salespeople, then the approach with each of them would be:

- Individuals B and C are the medium performers; thus, coaching would likely have a positive impact on performance.
- Individual D is someone with low levels of competence and motivation, therefore the return on time and effort invested is low. Rather than coaching, person D would require close monitoring and supervision.
- Individual A is a high performer with potential to achieve more, who would benefit only marginally from coaching on his/her current job, but would need and probably seek career advancement.

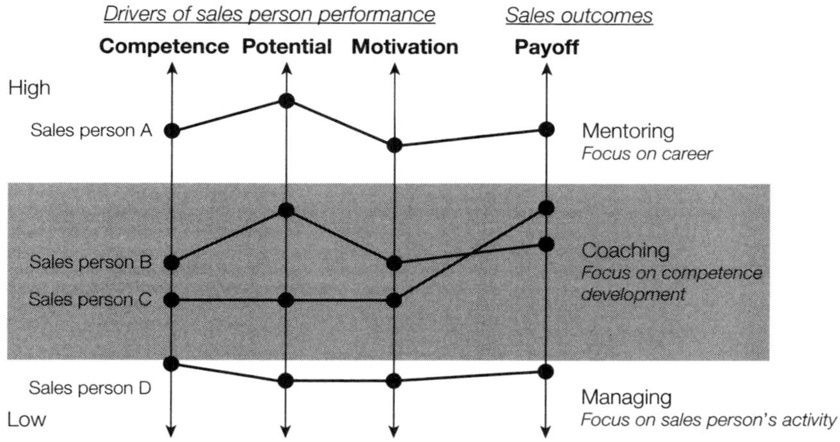

Figure 12.7 - Prioritising salespeople to be coached

THE FUTURE OF SALES TRAINING: TOWARDS SELF-DIRECTED LEARNING

In chapters 1 and 6 we argued that in an increasingly challenging environment sales forces will need to develop more complex competences and abilities to sustain performance. We also saw in Chapter 5 that sales leaders will require sophisticated approaches to enhance the contribution of the sales function to the long-term growth of the firm. A key question becomes, how can firms develop the future sales professional? Will established training and learning techniques in sales be sufficient to develop the emerging behavioural and cognitive variety required to succeed in the sales profession in the future?

The traditional functional boundaries of salespeople are opening up to a wider multi-functional profile where financial expertise and commercial acumen needs to be coupled with understanding of operational and supply issues. Relational competence goes beyond creating rapport towards developing a subtle understanding of human behaviour in context and the ability to interface and navigate organisational politics. Managerial competence in communicating and working with others will influence salespeople's ability to succeed internally and, as a consequence, externally with their clients. Finally we have argued in this chapter that enhanced skills and competences are required to match business growth with personal growth.

Traditional sales training approaches, whereby content is predefined and delivered via classroom interaction and technology-enabled platforms, is unlikely to equip sales forces with the range of competences mentioned above. A 'one size fits all' approach to design and deliver training, often group-based, is not likely to work. Decades of research in adult learning have shown that individuals have disparate learning styles (Mainemelis, Boyatzis & Kolb, 2002). Thus, sales training has to embrace different learning styles in its design, but also offer differentiated approaches to develop the required skills in those performing potentially repetitive sales activities for transactional customers, and for those who are required to contribute with higher levels of commitment and dedication to develop demanding, top end customers.

Despite being a sizeable industry, sales training has been claimed to be ineffective or less than useful (Salopek, 2009). A recent academic review of sales training

(Lassk, Ingram, Kraus & Di Mascio, 2012) and earlier contributions to the field (Cron et al., 2005) advocate for salespeople to have more input into their training programmes, engaging in both content development and in delivery mode. Self-directed learning approaches help address the challenge of individual idiosyncrasies by providing an individualised approach that is learner-centred. In addition, self-directed learning focuses on areas perceived as relevant by the individual and not just by the organisation.

Self-directed learning does not need to replace other forms of standardised and centrally managed sales learning and training, but it can complement such training. At the heart of this approach stands the sales manager, who can encourage different types of self-directed learning initiatives to help tailor the independent learning conducted by salespeople to their individual needs taking into account a number of personal and contextual circumstances (Artis & Harris, 2007). This approach has been found to enhance sales performance by helping salespeople develop their own competence – a meaningful and powerful intrinsic objective.

As noted in Chapter 6 sales models have experienced dramatic change in the last ten years. However, the pace of change is increasing and selling is undergoing a new transformation with very different challenges and opportunities. On one hand, customers are seeking suppliers who can add value to their business and are willing to build stronger, strategic relationships with those that can. At the same time, customers will demand more for less, plus the highest ethical standards. The willingness to adapt, the ability to develop long-term strategies, and the motivation to see the implementation through to completion will be keys to long-term sales success.

Did you know?

In 2010 in the United States there were 40 approved degree courses in sales. Three years later this number had risen to 160. In the United Kingdom there are at least seven undergraduate degree programmes in sales and five post-graduate programmes aimed at raising the professionalism of sales.

SUMMARY

How to get the best out of the people in the sales force is a management challenge for sales leaders. One way of boosting performance is through training to improve individual sales force productivity. Good training has a specific purpose, is planned and is aimed at the individual. Various people, locations and content can be used. To be effective, training requires behavioural aspects of buyer–seller interaction to be developed, individualised coaching and sustained practice.

QUESTIONS

1 How would you ensure that the customer is fully embedded in sales training programmes?
2 Salespeople are required to be aware of changing market conditions. Using your own examples, indicate which areas of training might be necessary because of changes in today's environment.
3 Sales training programmes vary from company to company because of differences in products, markets, company policies, organisational size and trainees'

experience and ability. Discuss the elements of sales training that would be common for most companies.

4 It is often postulated that top sales performers may not make the most effective sales managers. Explain why this may be the case.

CASE STUDY: EDMUNSON ELECTRICAL DISTRIBUTORS

Edmunson Electrical Distributors (www.edmundson-electrical.co.uk) is a leading distributor of electrical equipment and components with over 230 branches in the United Kingdom. The company is a wholesaler of electrical products acting as an intermediary between manufacturers and customers. Accounts are classified according to turnover and margins achieved. The 'bread and butter' of the business is the electrical contractor, who provides high turnover but low margins. The more significant the purchases, the higher are the rebates and discounts awarded to these customers. A second important group of customers are hotels, hospitals and other institutional customers who provide less volume but better margins. It is company policy to maximise the turnover of each customer so that Edmunson can, in turn, command a better price from the manufacturers. With such a wide range of product lines and items, the company cannot afford to stock every product so their own competence is measured not only in price but also by their service, especially delivery reliability.

The company uses a SPI (standard practice of initiation) to give similar accounting procedures for stocks, invoicing, ledger entry and so on. Branches in all other respects compete with each other in terms of orders, charges and revenues, which are the sole responsibility of the branch manager. Each branch is a separate profit centre and operates more like a franchise since the capital is given directly to the branch, although 19 per cent of annual profits go to the parent company. The branches compete with each other, but the sales representatives feel that the system is fair and motivating. The manager is usually supported in each branch by an accountant and at least one representative as well as buyers, telesales and store personnel and van drivers.

Branch A is one of the most successful in the group. There are several major accounts but relatively few electrical contractors and competition is not well represented in the area. Turnover is higher and costs are lower than in many other areas. The branch manager is well respected and highly successful, the youngest within the group, and last year steered his branch to a £3 million turnover with a profit share between the eight employees of £160,000. This success, combined with the hunger created by the profit share, has produced a highly motivated team. This team spirit is encouraged by the manager with open plan offices and an easy communication style. People are allocated to tasks according to their suitability – one salesperson actively seeking new accounts, another servicing existing accounts. All staff are aware of the 19 per cent profit levy so they aim to beat this on all business negotiated. However, because these figures are based on previous year's targets, in some months sales are held back if the increase was too great, in the knowledge this will raise next year's figure. Salespeople have been sent on training courses, but no qualitative targets are set for them.

Branch B is currently in financial trouble and operates in stark contrast to Branch A. In the past two years turnover fell by almost one-half, a stock deficit was recorded and, since 19 per cent of profit was to be paid, no profit sharing to staff was achieved. Competition is fierce in this area, with 30 other wholesalers operating, but no involvement of salespeople in setting targets is allowed. For example, a new recruit with two weeks' experience was given the task of opening 40 new accounts in 12 months. He failed and left the company. No sales forecast is set and people are encouraged to get business wherever they can. The result is that several people left and, after two years of disastrous results, the manager was asked to resign.

- From the information given, suggest what factors contributed to the diverse performances of the two branches.
- What training programme would you develop to help their sales operations?

REFERENCES

Arthur, W., Bennet, W., Stanush, P. & McNelly, T. (1998). Factors that influence skill decay and retention: A quantitative review and analysis. *Human Performance*, 11(1), 57–101.

Artis, A. & Harris, E. (2007). Self-directed learning and sales force performance: An integrated framework. *Journal of Personal Selling and Sales Management*, 27(1), 9–24.

Attia, A. M., Honeycutt, E. D. & Leach, M. P. (2005). A three-stage model for assessing and improving sales force training and development. *Journal of Personal Selling and Sales Management*, 25(3), 253–268.

Cayla, J. & Arnould, E. (2013). Ethnographic stories for market learning. *Journal of Marketing*, 77(July), 1–16.

Challagalla, G. N. & Shervani, T. A. (1996). Dimensions and types of supervisory control: Effects on salesperson performance and satisfaction. *Journal of Marketing*, 60(January), 89–105.

Corcoran, K. J., Petersen, L. K., Baitch, D. B. & Barrett, M. F. (1995). *High Performance Sales Organisations: Creating Competitive Advantage in the Global Marketplace*. New York: McGraw-Hill.

Cron, W. L., Marshall, G. W., Singh, J., Spiro, R. L. & Sujan, H. (2005). Salesperson selection, training, and development: Trends, implications and research opportunities. *Journal of Personal Selling & Sales Management*, 25(2), 123–136.

Csikszentmihalyi, M. (1990). Literacy and intrinsic motivation. *Daedalus*, 19(2), 115–140.

Detterick, M. & Spence, A. (2008). *Improve Rep Performance Through Coaching*. Sales Executive Council Report. Arlington, VA.

Doyle, S. X. & Roth, G. T. (1992). Selling and sales management in action: The use of insight coaching to improve relationship selling. *Journal of Personal Selling and Sales Management*, 12(1), 59–65.

Erffmeyer, R. C., Russ, K. R. & Hair, J. (1991). Needs assessment and evaluation in sales-training programs. *Journal of Personal Selling & Sales Management*, 11(1), 17.

Ericsson, K. A., Krampe, R. T., Tesch-romer, C., Ashworth, C., Carey, G., Grassia, J. & Schneider, V. (1993). The role of deliberate practice in the acquisition of expert performance. *Psychological Review*, 100(3), 363–406.

Geiger, S. & Turley, D. (2003). Grounded theory in sales research: An investigation of salespeople's client relationships. *Journal of Business & Industrial Marketing*, 18(6/7), 580–594.

Goh, G. (2014). What is strategic sales coaching? InsightSquared: The sales & marketing analytics blog. Retrieved 11 August 2014, from http://www.insightsquared.com/2014/05/what-is-strategic-sales-coaching/.

Gosling, J. & Mintzberg, H. (2003). The five managerial mind sets. *Harvard Business Review* (November), 54–63.

Hambrick, D. Z., Oswald, F. L., Altmann, E. M., Meinz, E. J., Gobet, F. & Campitelli, G. (2014). Deliberate practice: Is that all it takes to become an expert? *Intelligence*, 45, 34–45.

Honeycutt Jr, E. D., Ford, J. B. & Tanner, J. F. (1994). Who trains salespeople?: The role of sales trainers and sales managers. *Industrial Marketing Management*, 23(1), 65–70.

Honeycutt Jr, E. D., Howe, V. & Ingram, T. N. (1993). Shortcomings of sales training programs. *Industrial Marketing Management*, 22(2), 117–123

Ingram, T., Laforge, R.W., Avila, R. A., Schwepker, C. H. & Williams, M. R. (2001). *Sales Management: Analysis and Decision Making* (4th edn). Orlando, FL: Harcourt Inc.

Keusel, H. N. (1971). Six deadly diseases that can affect your sales force, in Kurtz, D. L. & Hubbard, C. W. (eds.) *The Sales Function and its Management: Selected Readings*. Morristown, NJ: General Learning Press, pp. 148–153.

Kingstrom, P. O. & Bass, A. R. (1981). A critical analysis of studies comparing behaviorally anchored rating scales (BATS) and other rating formats. *Personnel Psychology*, 34(2), 263–289.

Kirkpatrick, D. L. (1998). *Evaluating Training Programs: The Four Levels* (2nd edn). San Francisco, CA: Berrett Koehler.

Kolb, D. A. (1984). *Experiential Learning: Experience as the Source of Learning and Development.* Englewood Cliffs, NJ: Prentice Hall.

Lassk, F. G., Ingram, T. N., Kraus, F. & Di Mascio, R. (2012). The future of sales training: Challenges and related research questions. *Journal of Personal Selling & Sales Management*, 32(1), 141–154.

Lidstone, J. (1986). *Training Salesmen on the Job*. (2nd edn). Aldershot: Gower.

Mainemelis, C., Boyatzis, R. E. & Kolb, D. A. (2002). Learning styles and adaptive flexibility testing experiential learning theory. *Management Learning*, 33(1), 5–33.

Onyemah, V. (2009). The effects of coaching on salespeople's attitudes and behaviors: A contingency approach. *European Journal of Marketing*, 43(7/8), 938–960.

Pousa, C. & Sherbrooke, U. De. (2010). Sales managers' motivation to coach salespeople: An exploration using expectancy theory. *International Journal of Evidence Based Coaching and Mentoring*, 8(1), 34–51.

Rackham, N. (2010). Managing the sales force. Building global sales & marketing strategies. Bangalore, 19 February. Retrieved 11 August 2014, from www.kcapital-us.com/neil/presentations/complete3.

Rackham, N. & Ruff, R. (1991). *The Management of Major Sales*. Farnham, Surrey, UK: Gower.

Rich, G. (1998). The constructus of coaching: Supervisory feedback, role modelling and trust. *Journal of Personal Selling and Sales Management*, 18(Winter), 53–64.

Ricks, J. M., Williams, J. A. & Weeks, W. A. (2008). Sales trainer roles, competencies, skills, and behaviors: A case study. *Industrial Marketing Management*, 37(5), 593–609.

Roman, S. & Ruiz, S. (2003). A comparative analysis of sales training in Europe: Implications for international sales negotiations. *International Marketing Review*, 20(3), 304–327.

Salopek, J. J. (2009). The POWER of the pyramid. *T+D*, 63(5), 70–75.

Shannahan, K., Bush, A. & Shannahan, R. (2013). Are your salespeople coachable? How salesperson coachability, trait competitiveness, and transformational leadership enhance sales performance. *Journal of the Academy of Marketing Science*, 41(1), 40–54.

Shannahan, K., Shannahan, R. J. & Bush, A. (2013). Salesperson coachability: What it is and why it matters. *Journal of Business & Industrial Marketing*, 28(5), 411–420.

Stanton, W. J., Buskirk, R. H. & Spiro, R. L. (1991). *Management of a Sales Force* (8th edn). Homewood, IL: Irwin.

Stobart, G. (2014). *The Expert Learner: Challenging the Myth of Ability*. Maidenhead, UK: Open University Press – McGraw Hill Education.

Verbeke, W., Dietz, B. & Verwaal, E. (2011). Drivers of sales performance: A contemporary meta-analysis. Have salespeople become knowledge brokers? *Journal of the Academy of Marketing Science*, 39(3), 407–428.

13 SALES TARGET SETTING

OVERVIEW

Sales targets are extensively used by sales organisations. Performance goals define a 'desired', 'promised', 'minimum' or 'aspirational' level of performance – for example, to attain 10 per cent more profits, usually within a specified time limit. About 95 per cent of Fortune 500 companies use performance goals in their sales compensation schemes (Joseph & Kalwani, 1998). Zoltners, Sihna & Lorimer (2008) estimate that sales compensation in the US economy totals about $800 billion, almost three times the amount spent on advertising. Targets are mainly used for motivating specific behaviours, establishing expectations, evaluating and rewarding performance. At present, the use of performance targets seems to be ubiquitous; however, a high proportion of organisations have reported that they are dissatisfied with their targets, arguing that this management practice is often not generating the expected results (Marchetti & Brewer, 2000). Target setting is grounded in an area of organisational behaviour called 'goal-setting' theory (Locke & Latham, 1990). It is argued that people perform better when they are assigned specific and difficult targets than they do when they are assigned easy targets or 'do your best' type of targets. However targets are not free from issues and challenges when implemented. A key problem with the link between sales effort and sales response is that it is neither simple nor direct. We will explore these and other issues in this chapter and will present established practices to conduct sales forecast and budgeting.

LEARNING OBJECTIVES

This chapter aims to enable the reader to:

- Understand the importance of sales target setting.
- Describe the process of forecasting and some of the established techniques.
- Explain the connection between sales forecasts, sales budgets and sales targets.
- Consider the different ways of setting sales targets.
- Evaluate the options in sales targets both quantitative and qualitative.

DEFINITIONS

Sales target (or quota) can be defined as the level of performance an individual or a group is expected to achieve.

Sales forecast is an estimate of the level of company sales for a future time period.

Sales budget is the sum allocated to convert sales opportunities into sales over a definite time period.

SALES TARGETS

In sales, there are various types of targets including sales volume or value, costs of sales, selling activities and, in some cases, profit contribution. Most companies use sales volume or sales value for an individual salesperson as a basic sales target, within a temporal timeframe – annually, quarterly or monthly. Targets are often set by geographical area, product line, customer segment or a combination of these. Alternatively, targets can be set against operating costs or expenses and measured on net profit or some contribution rate of return. Another way in which targets can be set is against some activity measure such as call rates, new business or specific tasks set by management. Many companies use a combination of targets, the appropriateness depending on both their objectives, the ability of salespeople to achieve them and the potential to be achieved.

Purpose of sales targets

1 *To evaluate sales performance*. To be workable as a means of evaluation, targets set should be realistic and based on accurate information (e.g. forecast) for each territory if they are to be used as a measure of productivity for salespeople. Since many factors affect performance, such targets should incorporate sales, budget costs and activity measures. Indeed, in many service selling jobs, 'activities' may be more important to success than a purely quantitative sales objective. If sales alone are used to measure performance, other tasks, identified as crucial to the selling job, may be neglected. This is yet another reason for specifying in writing what needs to be done, and for having a job description and a fair evaluation procedure.
2 *As an incentive for salespeople*. Self-motivation and drive are characteristics sought after in salespeople. Targets are designed to stimulate a 'go for it' attitude. Salespeople, more than those in most categories of job, will have an in-built desire to achieve and beat target. Targets, to work as motivators, must be set neither too high nor too low or they may become counterproductive in subsequent trading periods.
3 *As a means to calculate remuneration* when it is linked to specific targets. A combination of methods of payment, such as salary and commission or salary and bonus, is common in remuneration structures. This is because incentive payments are often powerful motivators for salespeople to achieve results. The achievement of sales above the target level results in a bonus that is paid out to people. Careful evaluation of these schemes is required to balance good and bad trading periods and to minimise potential dysfunctional behaviours associated with excessive focus on meeting the sales target.
4 *To control activities*. Targets permit specific objectives to be set which direct selling activity, such as the type of account to be pursued or specific product targets. Again, these types of targets will be more effective if rewards and appraisals are built into the scheme.

Well-designed targets may achieve all of these purposes to a great extent, but it must be borne in mind that sales do not operate independently of marketing policies, product acceptance, competitive factors and the overall promotional spend. It follows that the onus is on management to set and control targets on a realistic and fair basis.

Methods to calculate sales targets

The most common methods used to determine sales targets are:

1 *Based on economic or leading indicators in the market*. Economic growth, disposable income, and other macro and micro economic indicators. These data provide a basis for setting specific targets and expected performance levels.

2 *Targets based on territory potential*. This indicator enables targets to be set on the basis of sales potential. Quality information and accurate forecasts are needed to set realistic and achievable targets. Lack of accuracy in reporting sales against target, expense levels against budget and customer-specific data can have a negative effect on salesperson motivation if they are used to determine sales target level. Territories often have differences, some of which are unique to that area – its geography, level of competition and customer prosperity. The result is that direct comparisons between one salesperson and another are difficult, even where territory potential, age and experience may be similar.
3 *Historical perspective*. This is usually computed as last year's sales plus a desired percentage increase. This is a very quick and convenient method but has little else to commend it. It would assume that there is no variation between areas, individuals or growth rates in products. Any previous inadequacies or errors would be perpetuated ad infinitum. Past sales are one factor in setting sales targets but not the only one. Some account must be taken of changing conditions resulting in varying growth rates between products and territories.
4 *Managerial judgement*. In the absence of any other information, this is the way in which targets are set. They have the disadvantage of resulting in targets which are perceived to be arbitrary, unfair and ill informed.
5 *Salespeople set their own target*. Since it is desirable to enhance the managerial responsibilities and accountability of salespeople, one way of achieving this would be to allow sales staff to set their own objectives. The appropriateness of this method depends on salespeople's expertise and motivation and it must be ensured that they are not over- or understating the target.

Part of the sales management task is to get salespeople to do the job in a cost-efficient manner, to optimise the return on investment for the sales budget. Otherwise, salespeople will seek their own objectives, which may be inefficient and wasteful. It is necessary to set achievable targets which encourage improved performance but take into account many other factors, particularly the ability and experience of salespeople themselves.

Types of sales target

Targets in sales may have different emphases:

- Customer-related targets where the emphasis is on the investment that is needed in developing good customer relationships in order to generate longer-term revenues. Examples include customer satisfaction, number of new customers, market share at customer, number of qualified prospects, number of lost customers, etc.
- Activity targets emphasise the long-term investment of salespeople in order to identify and develop business opportunities. Examples include: number of visits, number of proposals made, number of days worked, number of sales plans made.
- Behaviour targets recognise the need for salespeople to develop their competencies, and the importance of these competencies to support the generation of future revenues. Example: number of training days, number of joint visits with coach.

Overall targets can also be classified into qualitative and quantitative.

Quantitative sales targets

Sales volume or value Almost all firms that set targets will use some sales volume basis. This is simple to understand and easy to calculate. Each salesperson must generate sufficient volume to cover the operating costs – salary, expenses, supervision, administration and contribution to profit. There are potential problems in such a direct approach. For example, on what basis is the target set, orders received or sales invoiced? Is it based on a geographical area, number of customers, time period, multi-products or total sales? The danger may be that, in answering these questions, achievement of the target may be well below the optimum.

Most salespeople find the easiest option is existing sales in existing products with current customers. Orders from existing accounts – service-selling – may be at the expense of potential new business. While some business may be lost and new accounts won, the amount of effort in one time period may not show until future time periods given the length of some sales cycles. Volume targets may discourage a balanced selling effort since they stress sales volume rather than profitable sales and to the detriment of non-selling activities.

Product targets These are similar to sales volume targets except that the salesperson is expected to achieve sales according to a specified product mix, thus partially overcoming one of the disadvantages of the sales volume target – that is, achieving a balanced mix of sales across product portfolios. In many industrial markets, information on customers and competitors may change, as could the added value of different product groups. The main criticism of product targets is that they are seldom market-oriented but are rather production-oriented. Salespeople are asked to sell more of what the supplier has in stock or in production, regardless of whether the customer needs them. This may be in conflict with the principles of consultative/solution selling.

Expenses to sales ratio In improving profitable sales performance, the combination of revenue increase and reduction of costs to sell need to be addressed. Yet, these objectives may be incongruent or conflicting. Expense to sales ratios attempt to motivate salespeople to be mindful of the sales-associated costs in order to improve profitability. Also, it is intended to allow for higher expense only if higher sales are achieved.

Gross margin on orders In line with the ratio above, this type of target assesses performance on profitability, usually by achieving a balance between product groups and customers. It requires sales people to have adequate information available about product gross margin so as to calculate customer profitability. In industrial markets, evidence suggests that rigid, 'one price fits all' schemes may be ineffective and that the positive effect of price delegation to the sales force on firm performance is strengthened when market-related uncertainty is high and when salespeople possess better customer-related information than their managers (Frenzen, Hansen, Krafft, Mantrala & Schmidt, 2010).

Market share One important measure of competitiveness is market share. For many products, especially consumer goods, market estimates by region or sales area are available from organisations such as Nielsen (www.nielsen.com). Then it is possible to set targets on the achievement of a desired market share level. Definition of what constitutes the market will be important. For example, market may be by volume, value or number of outlets, the share of each being quite different. Most companies operate multi-product lines in diverse markets, making the definition more spurious. Market share is not an indicator under the control of sales forces; thus, if it is used, the limitations must be acknowledged.

Sales versus potential When designing sales territories, the business potential is one of the most important discriminating factors in performance. If sources of market and customer information are reliable, it would be desirable to measure sales performance against potential. The practical difficulties lie primarily in the accuracy of measurement potential.

Average order size The aim is to improve average order size (that is, total sales divided by the number of orders) with a view to reducing small orders or unprofitable accounts. One problem is that particular situations may result in a relatively low figure as a consequence of intermediaries' own sales and stocking policy. This measure is effective in the context of direct selling where the sales representative has control over the selling process and can influence the size of the order the customer places.

Return on investment As described in the sales budget section, return on investment (ROI) can be used at the individual level by computing total net sales minus all related expenses such as sales expenses (merchandising, samples), salesperson (salary, car, mobile) and a portion of overhead costs.

The above list is by no means exhaustive of the quantitative targets which can be used. The level of sophistication in their use will vary depending on the type of industry and context, company structure and other economic or regional factors. Purely quantitative targets have potential weaknesses in addressing all the key facets of a business-to-business selling job. Therefore, a combination of quantitative and qualitative targets is advisable.

Qualitative sales targets

Sales activities *Number of sales calls made* is a basic indicator of activity that many organisations operating in business-to-business sales capture and monitor. Management can establish an average call rate for the sales force, and can compare this with averages within and outside the company. This indicator may help to identify problems in sales representatives' efficacy when below average, and to identify unproductive sales visits in those significantly over. Areas and customers vary considerably, as do specific call objectives and the type of selling; therefore, the statement 'calls do not equal sales' needs to be acknowledged.

Call frequency ratio is also captured and monitored in geographically dispersed sales forces. Salespeople's own input in defining this metric and associated targets is helpful to enable them to become more selective in customer field visits, thus improving journey planning. Sales calls can then be divided (and analysed) in terms of order-to-call ratio, calls to specific types of customers (e.g. new vs. established), etc.. These targets need to take into account territory differences, customer quality and competitive influences in an area.

Other qualitative targets could be related to tasks such as:

- Service to existing accounts.
- Joint sales calls with distributors' own sales force to sell on to end users.
- Provision of technical advice.
- Collection of market and competitive information.

The limitations of certain aspects of quantitative targets, together with a desire by management to focus sales staff on other non-selling tasks, suggest that qualitative sales targets can be used as part of the overall target-setting framework. Best-practice companies are typically flexible in their choice and the use of targets in choosing both quantitative and well as qualitative targets, both at individual and sales team level (Brown, Evans, Mantrala & Challagalla, 2005).

Issues in sales target setting

The use of sales targets may have several shortcomings. Latham (2004) suggests that for goals to be effective in motivating and driving performance, they need to meet a set of conditions. The individual responsible for achieving the goal has to have control over the actions needed to attain it, as well as the required ability and knowledge. The person has to be committed to attaining the goal, and the individual needs to receive feedback on his or her progress towards the achievement of the goal, so appropriate improvement actions can be taken. Furthermore, Latham (2004) argues that the use of goals may fail to achieve its desired outcomes if performance goals are set for complex tasks (where strategies and behavioural routines have yet to become automated) or tasks are interrelated, requiring a balance between individual and group goals. In addition, when targets are set for any single dimension of performance (e.g. quantity at the expense of quality) or for two or more potentially conflicting dimensions, goals may have detrimental effects. Despite these potential drawbacks of targets, goal-setting theory shows that goals are an effective tool for motivating people and improving performance.

The same year Locke and Latham's (1990) seminal work on goal setting came out, Deming (1990) – considered the 'father' of the Total Quality Movement– published a book reporting the detrimental effect of the use of goals in organisations. Deming argued that performance goals negatively affect continuous improvement; they diminish the level of trust in management; and compromise firm performance in the long run.

An additional unintended consequence of goals is unethical behaviour. Perceived external pressures to meet performance goals may induce cheating (Van Yperen, Hamstra & van der Klauw, 2011) and stating over-performance (Schweitzer et al., 2004). Other 'side effects' of using goals may be distorted risk preferences, corrosion of corporate culture, inhibited learning, and reduced intrinsic motivation (Ordóñez, Schweitzer, Galinsky & Bazerman, 2009).

Recent studies in sales management have challenged received wisdom about the (positive) effect of quotas in fostering sales performance. Misra and Nair (2011) describe a case where a new sales compensation plan without quotas resulted in a 9 per cent improvement in overall revenues. Once a quota-based incentive system is implemented, Larkin (2010) argues that a risk exists that employees will 'game' to fulfil the quotas, offering additional discounts of up to 6–8 per cent of the revenue generated. The consequences of not achieving quotas also need to be considered, particularly in relation to the future performance of individual salespeople (Schwepker & Good, 2004). Failing to meet sales targets may also be associated with perceptions of personal non-accomplishment contributing to staff burnout (Hollet-Haudebert, Mulki & Fournier, 2011). In sales, there is evidence that when reward schemes are based on high quotas, this stimulates excessive high-risk behaviours (Gaba & Kaira, 1999). Similarly, short-term sales goals may induce problematic behaviours when there is high motivation to attain them (Murphy, 2004).

Franco-Santos and Bourne (2009) conducted research in the underlying causes of the potential negative impact of performance targets on salespeople's behaviour. They identified ten common issues that undermine the effectiveness of sales targets:

1. *Targets were based on past performance* – so people have an incentive not to (over) perform as otherwise next year's target would be disproportionally higher, so harder to meet. This is often called the ratchet effect.
2. *Targets were allocated inappropriately across the sales force,* generating the threshold effect; that is, acting as a disincentive for people to continue working after the target was achieved.
3. *Targets were perceived to be either too high or too low* – too high de-motivates, leading to non-achievement – too low means paying bonus for poor performance. This is often the result of a forecast too high or too low.
4. *Some targets were based on the wrong performance measures* – This is often referred to as 'hitting the target and missing the point'.

5 *Targets were entirely based on financial indicators* – even when factors such as customer relationships were absolutely critical.
6 *The data analysis process on which targets were based was poor and lacked rigour.*
7 *Targets were not periodically reviewed*, so corrective actions could not be discussed and adopted in time.
8 *Targets were 'given' to the salespeople* – so not creating ownership.
9 *The interrelation between targets was not considered*, causing inconsistency and role conflict.
10 *Agreed action plans were the exception and not the norm* so not increasing the commitment towards achieving the targets.

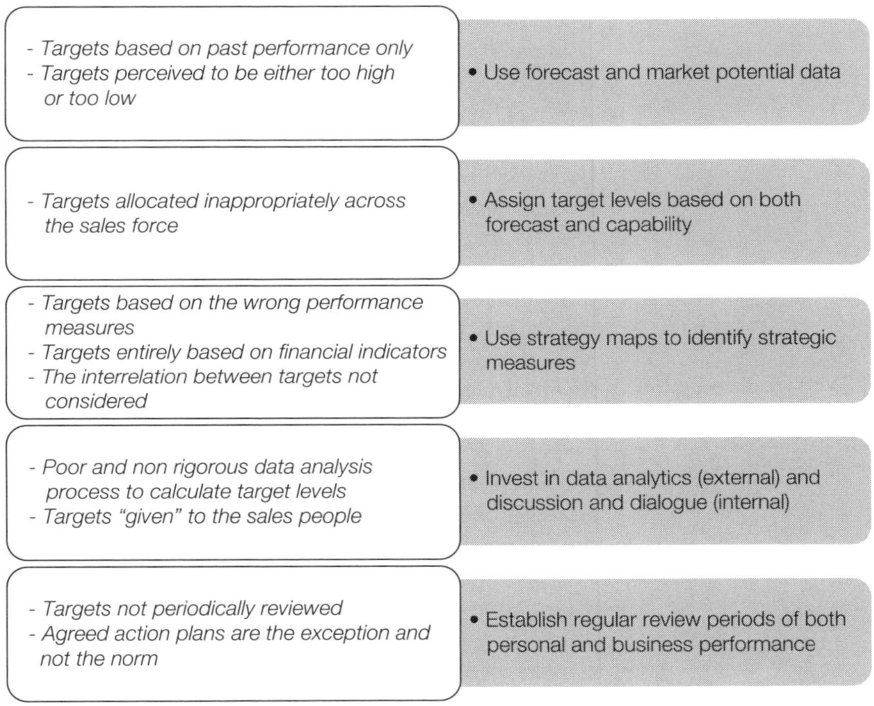

Figure 13.1 – Addressing issues in sales target setting

Source: Franco-Santos et al. (2009)

Sales targets also have profound consequences beyond sales performance into the overall organisational effectiveness and implications on organisational trust and customer-oriented selling culture (Schwepker & Good, 2012).

Overall, effective target setting requires the selection of the most appropriate quantitative and qualitative objectives relevant to the job and tasks. The best targets are not only the ones that direct the sales force to place effort in appropriate tasks, but also are aligned with the overall business objectives. The characteristics of effective targets include:

- Clear and concise.
- Measurable and attainable.
- Fit organisational goals.
- Cover short-, medium- and long-term objectives.
- Combine both qualitative and quantitative elements.
- Contribute to job satisfaction and improved performance.
- Do not encourage the salesperson to engage in dysfunctional behaviours.

A comprehensive framework for setting sales targets

To address the issues specified above, a ten-step framework is proposed (Franco-Santos & Bourne, 2009; Franco-Santos, Marcos & Bourne, 2010). Most organisations already have these practices in place, at least to a certain extent. However, there are other elements such as the understanding of variation in analysing capability or the discussion and agreement of meaningful action plans that seem not be widely adopted target-setting processes in business. This framework comprises key practices that are required for ensuring that the performance measures used in the target-setting process and the final targets agreed are effective (Figure 13.2):

1 *Review of stakeholders' expectations:* The first practice that should be undertaken when developing performance targets is a review of the organisation's stakeholder expectations. Questions such as 'who are the organisation's stakeholders?' and 'what do they expect from this organisation?' are critical at this stage (Neely, Adam & Kennerley, 2002). This practice will determine the areas that the organisation needs to address in order to be perceived as successful. Here the organisation's level of market- and customer-centricity will influence the areas of focus to be considered.

2 *Selection and clarification of strategic objectives to be pursued:* Once the stakeholders' expectations have been identified, the next step is to articulate these expectations into strategic objectives. Strategic objectives are clear statements of what the organisation aims to achieve. They must be few in number and they should address 'needs' and 'wants' of those key stakeholders (e.g. customers, employees, financial markets, etc.). This practice will help determine the types of measures the organisation may adopt.

3 *Definition of the organisation's success map,* also known as 'strategy map' (Kaplan & Norton, 2004) to show the cause-and-effect relationships among the different strategic objectives (Neely et al., 2002). The strategy map facilitates visualising the connections across functions that result in value creation for stakeholders. For a guide on how to use strategy maps see Armitage and Scholey (2007).

4 *Prioritisation of objectives.* Some strategic objectives will have more relevance than others at particular points in time. Therefore, it is crucial that the organisation clarifies its objectives and priorities.

5 *Identification of measures.* Strategic objectives need to be operationalised; this means defining how each strategic objective is going to be measured. The measures that provide information of strategic importance for decision-making and resource allocation are often referred to as key performance indicators (KPIs).

6 *Collection of activity and performance data.* Once strategic objectives have been translated into clear KPIs, organisations define the data collection methods for the different KPIs and the tools and technology platforms to handle and manage the data, as well as the frequency of collection and the individuals responsible for collecting the data.

7 *Data analysis:* At least two important aspects of data analysis must be conducted for each KPI. These are forecasting and capability analysis:

   a) *Forecasting:* in forecasting practices, careful consideration must be given to the methods used and to the intervening factors selected. As a rule of thumb, the more uncertainty there is in a specific market the more factors will be required in the forecasting (e.g. competitors' data, economic environment, internal capabilities). Also, in uncertain contexts historical information (i.e. past performance) may not be a useful or accurate predictor of future performance.

b) *Capability analysis:* After data have been collected for a particular KPI a rigorous analysis of this data must be conducted. The objectives of this analysis are (1) to understand how capable the organisation is at delivering the forecast figures, and (2) to identify the actions that must be taken in order to enable the organisation to deliver the forecast figures. A helpful tool at this stage is the use of control chart analysis. Control charts are tools used in statistical process control to determine if a process is in a state of statistical control. For instance, if a strategic objective is suggesting sales growth of 7 per cent for the next financial year and monthly historical data of the last three years suggests that 7 per cent is outside the capability (i.e. outside the control chart) of the existing process, the target may be unachievable with the existing organisational resources and processes. If 7 per cent sales growth must be attained for budgeting purposes (or to meet shareholders' expectations), then the way the organisation operates must be changed: increasing the sales force size, introducing a new training/coaching programme, or expanding the product/service portfolio.

8 *Setting targets:* Once a forecast has been conducted and a proper capability analysis has been developed, then specific targets for the organisation's sales KPIs can be defined.

9 *Action plan design:* After performance targets have been agreed, organisations need to spend the time deciding on the actions and initiatives that will help achieve the targets set.

10 *Action plan discussion and agreement:* Each target must be discussed and communicated together with the action plan designed to reach it. The action plan must be agreed with the team or individual who is going to be accountable for reaching the target. Action plans should not be 'given', they should always be discussed and agreed.

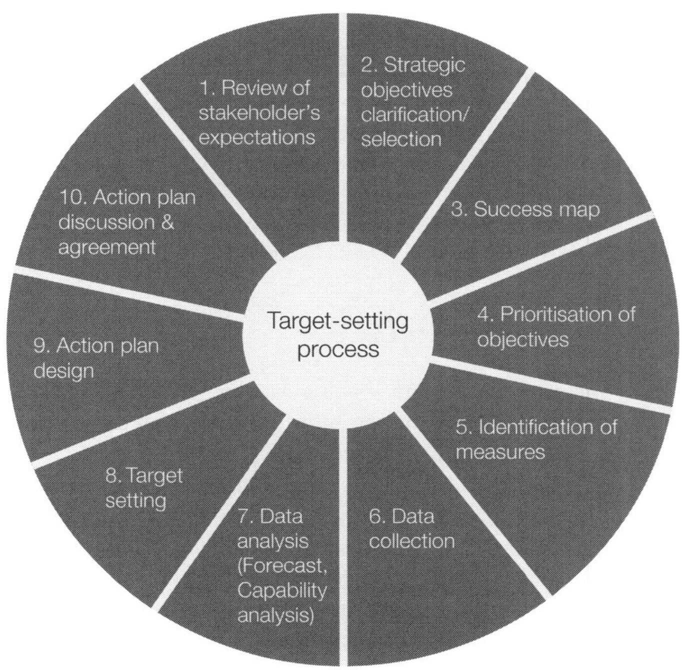

Figure 13.2 – A comprehensive framework for sales target setting

Source: Franco-Santos et al. (2010)

This section has addressed how to minimise the shortcomings of sales targets. Appropriate targets create a fruitful context for high performance in sales. This, combined with the right levels of training and development, will ensure sustained high performance. We have stated the importance of forecasts. The next subsection discusses sales forecasting in more detail.

Did you know?

According to Michael Dunne, a consultant with Gartner, an enterprise that lacks comprehensive insights is likely to miss the equivalent of 5–10 per cent of annual sales because of lost opportunities that could have been captured through improved management of sales territories, quotas and compensation plans. Instead sales managers typically employ a mixture of available data and intuition gained through previous experience to guide their decisions.

SALES FORECASTING

The aim of forecasting activity is to come up with an accurate sales figure, but it is more appropriate to view forecasting as a process, similar to the sales target setting process. It is important to be clear on the terminology as there is often confusion about the difference between forecasts, budgets and targets (Figure 13.3).

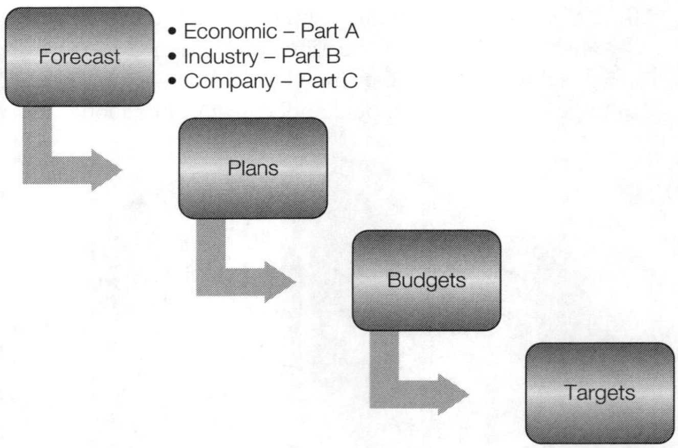

Figure 13.3 – The forecasting process

The sales forecast itself will normally be in three parts. Part A is a general forecast of economic and business conditions. This is an estimate of the total level of demand based on the number of consumers, their desires and their purchasing ability. Part B is an industry sales forecast including the anticipated effects of competitors' past, present and future activity. This represents the immediate market potential. Part C is the company sales forecast based on the company's share of the market but taking into account current business, marketing and sales planning activity. Beware of possible confusion over this circular process. Company plans are based on market and industry conditions and on aspects of strategic goals and environmental appraisals. Part C, the company sales forecast, must be based on the marketing effort planned and not the other way round. Sometimes if the company is large with monopoly power in the market, its plans will affect not only company sales but the industry and market forecast as well. The company sales forecast provides the input for budgets which are financial expressions of these plans. These budgets are used by individual functions and departments to monitor and control their activities, for example, capital budget, sales budget and so on.

With sales forecasting, the first step is to set objectives related to the purpose of the forecast and the time period. The relevant time period must relate to the nature of the business since the ability to react is clearly limited for a new power station or steel plant compared to a retailer. Forecasts normally relate to a given trading period but may be classified as:

- *Short-run forecasts* of up to one trading period which are used to decide operating budget levels, stock levels, production schedules and cash flow.
- *Medium-term forecasts*, normally covering one to three years ahead, although in some cases a five-year period; these forecasts help to decide on the number and type of machines, the raw material, manpower and other asset-building decisions.
- *Long-run forecasts* of up to ten years for decisions of a more strategic nature, such as the need for new plant, premises and technological developments; forecasts for the very long run or technological forecasting will not be covered in this section.

Sales forecasts are of critical importance in modern sales organisations, yet it is surprising to see the degree of sophistication in financial appraisal techniques that rely primarily on inaccurate sales forecast with low degree of exactness, sophistication or objectivity. The sales forecast is likely to be used by operations, logistics, supply-chain partners both up- and downstream, human resources, finance and marketing as part of their planning activities. Accuracy is important to all users, as each department uses the forecast as the starting point for its own operations and budgets. It should be apparent that accuracy is relative to the purpose the forecast is being used for and in some cases, such as cash flow, accuracy is crucial. In all uses, a trade-off between cost and accuracy has to be made. The management will require more explicit, quantifiable benefits of the accuracy versus costs of forecasting. The aim is to attempt to minimise the total cost, which is a summation of the cost of forecasting and the costs of inaccuracy.

Sales forecasting methods can be classified into three groupings: first, forecasts based on the use of market research and customer knowledge; second, using a consensus approach by the sales force or top management, and third, using statistical methods. These three approaches are not mutually exclusive and all three methods, and various techniques within each method, can be used together. There are some basic rules which need to be considered before choosing the most appropriate sales forecasting technique.

Rules of sales forecasting

Rule 1: *Distinguish between hard and soft data*. Hard data are facts which can be objectively assessed, such as past sales or verifiable information. Soft data are subjectively assessed, such as measures of opinion or attitude. When using soft data, questions need to be asked about how the data were collected, who collected the information, for what reason and by what method.

Rule 2: *Use as few variables as possible* and distinguish between dependent and independent variables. The dependent variable, normally sales, is related to changes in many independent variables such as sales activity, price, advertising and so on. If too many variables are included, the forecast model becomes complex and expensive but not necessarily cost-effective in terms of accuracy. Past sales, trend and seasonal and cyclical factors are usually sufficient to explain most variations.

Rule 3: Use general economic and industry indicators that have proved most reliable, such as housing starts or brick production in construction indices and disposable income for consumer markets.

Rule 4: Identify appropriate time relationships, particularly lag effects.

Rule 5: Do not use variables which cannot themselves be forecasted, such as the persuasiveness of salespeople.

Objective forecasts are those which use hard rather than soft data and incorporate quantitative and mathematical technique rather than guesswork. Subjective techniques are guesses about the future based on knowledge and experience. The advantage of objective or explicit techniques is that the assumptions and relationships on which forecasting is based can subsequently be evaluated for relevance and accuracy. This does not, however, mean that accuracy is more assured. As we know, all forecasts are wrong but they differ in the extent of their wrongness.

There are problems which beset any forecast and which must be at least anticipated if not always measured. Such problems include:

- The multivariate nature of marketing problems – many factors impinge on the sales response function and, while models can reach high levels of complexity, every eventuality in a dynamic situation cannot be incorporated.
- Related to the first problem is the difficulty in detecting and isolating the interaction effects between different elements in the marketing mix.
- Competitors' actions, which are difficult to predict yet crucial to the outcome.
- Short-run fluctuations, such as increased stocking prior to a price increase, which affect sales stability and possibly long-run trends.
- Some variables such as selling effort and advertising, which have a significant effect yet are very difficult to measure; this leads to quantifying subjectivity and often spurious accuracy.
- New products, which are always likely to be a special case.

A *model-building*, more explicit approach to forecasting should be preferred to the use of hunch, guesswork or consensus methods. Models may at some point lose realism by becoming over-sophisticated and unrealistic in their assumptions and common sense is required in the application of any technique.

Methods of forecasting

Using market research and customer knowledge

To implement the marketing concept, the most appropriate approach is to understand and assess the needs of both current and potential customers. As a method of forecasting this is not always possible, seldom easy and not always accurate. It can be done by senior executives and salespeople in industrial goods where there are only a few large customers with readily identifiable needs. Generally, customers themselves do not know their own requirements and, in the case of consumer goods, there is a lack of hard data on a large numbers of customers. 'Will you buy product X?' could provide answers of 'yes', 'no', 'don't know', 'maybe' and 'maybe not', which is quite different from what consumers actually do.

More sophisticated market research techniques and questioning can minimise the error and improve accuracy, but it is costly for individual products and a weak means of continuous forecasting for purposes such as stock levels, production scheduling or cash flow. The main difficulties are over-optimism by customers and a lack of commitment. Important, too, is the representativeness of the sample and the quality of respondent, since many markets are characterised by a few large buyers such the retail sector in some countries. The uncertainty of competitive actions and reactions compounds the problem. The use of these assessment methods of forecasting should be restricted to cases where there are only a few users who are likely to know their future requirements, where competition is known and where inertia between buyer and seller is strong. This means that consistency and predictability will exist. The use of continuous survey material, retail audits and omnibus surveys can contribute to build better forecasting methods, especially where distribution channels are long and complex. If suppliers become separated and remote from buyers or end users, such information is vital. Even in these circumstances, surveys are best used in conjunction with other forecasting methods.

Since salespeople are an expensive resource, the amount of time they should spend on information gathering is a hotly debated issue among practising sales managers. This issue also relates to the sophistication and use of sales automation systems discussed earlier.

Using a consensus approach

This is normally conducted by a panel of executives, experts or by the sales force. The advantages of sales force consensus methods are primarily that each person within the organisation who is closest to their customers provides the input. Other advantages could be that it provides a necessary discipline for the salesperson to identify opportunities and understand market trends. As noted earlier, the modern salesperson has had to be more strategic so that they know, understand and help their customers' own marketing and sales plans. Also, participation and involvement in future planning is important for salespeople's morale and motivation.

Some of the disadvantages also need to be considered:

- Forecasting can be time consuming when there are many customers and product groups.
- Accuracy on individual customers and products is likely to be variable.
- Value forecasts are subject to inflationary distortion and future price changes that salespeople will have limited understanding of and even less control over.
- It is difficult to set individual sales targets, which may conflict with the salesperson's own forecast.
- Salespeople want to beat their forecast rather than achieve accuracy.
- Salespeople are generally optimistic – too optimistic over the longer term – and the future always shows unjustified increases, making long-run predictions overstated.
- The use of salespeople as providers of market information has to be considered carefully and the information they provide treated as objectively as possible. If salespeople have a few large customers on single or limited products and have regular contact with informed buyers, their input will be invaluable.

The other consensus methods, such as the jury of executive opinion, vary from the board agreeing that next year's forecast will be this year's sales plus a per cent figure, to using a range of experts such as investment analysts or using internal personnel, such as the sales manager's estimate. The main advantage of expert or executive opinion is that people making such a forecast are also the people who have it within their power to achieve it.

Using objective techniques

The objective techniques fall into two categories: time series and causal methods. Time series refers to a family of techniques where time is used as a proxy to replace all other independent variables and thus permits the application of straightforward arithmetic to what is a complex problem. The evidence for this approach can be summed up as a combination of cost and pragmatism. Sales do not depend on time, and the longer the time lapse, the less appropriate the method becomes, but the inertia between buyers and sellers referred to earlier does permit the use of this notion in sales forecasting. Dramatic changes do not normally occur overnight and ceteris paribas (other things being equal) assumptions can be used.

With causal methods, an attempt is made to predict the dependent variable (sales) from one or more identified independent variables (price, promotional effort, economic and industry trends, etc.), the value of which is known or can be predicted with reasonable accuracy. If the independent variable cannot be estimated, there is no point guessing it or using this method since this is tantamount to guessing the forecast. Certain indicators, for example economic growth, industrial production and housing starts, are well predicted and hence good indicators which can be used for the particular product or market in question. The sales manager should not worry about their quantitative skills with these techniques as modern computer software provides the calculation. However, it is important to understand the basic concept and appropriateness of each technique. Remember:

- That forecasting is a process.
- To identify the uses of the sales forecast and the time periods covered; new products will create special forecasting problems.
- To clarify the purpose of the forecast, follow the basic rules and be clear on problems and assumptions; particular attention must be paid to matching the sales forecasting technique to the decision task.
- To set up and use a forecast procedure.
- To use a combination of techniques and approaches to verify the result.

What do you think?

According to www.Anaplan.com, in order to accurately set sales targets, organisations should consider adopting a variation of zero-based forecasting, where each period is treated independently, free from strong historic biases. While this method can be initially more difficult to implement, its results outperform other methods and the process becomes much easier in subsequent years.

SALES BUDGETING

The sales forecast is the base prediction of future sales, given certain assumptions which form the basis for the company's operations in the next trading period, usually one year ahead. From this, budgets can be set within different departments and operating areas of the business. For example:

Forecast sales revenue for the period	20 million
Material Costs	6 million
Operational costs/ gross margin	4 million
Contribution (50%)	10 million
Selling, administration and distribution (SAD)	5 million
Profit (25%)	5 million

In formulating budgets, account has to be taken of strategic and marketing objectives such as the planned increase in market share, the means to achieve this and the degree of realism in these plans. A 10 per cent increase in sales does not materialise from being written or stated. It comes from successful implementation of the sales plan. At this stage of planning the inputs from marketing research can be added to existing policies on product, price, promotion and distribution in the marketing operations plan. An essential ingredient is the financial expression of these plans in the form of a series of budgets which turn intentions into assignments at a cost, capital budgets, expense budgets, cash flow appraisals and schedules, of which the sales budget is a part.

The sales budget therefore is the sum allocated to convert sales effort into sales over a definite time period. Since resources are scarce, growth in profits is achieved by greater efficiency in returns over expenditure. The management decides where to allocate each pound of expense to best effect – a new machine, a market survey, an advertising campaign or an extra salesperson? The sales manager is primarily concerned with the sales budget. Decisions have to be made to achieve a certain sales revenue with certain investment on people and incurring in certain costs of expenses. For instance, should the sales manager offer greater incentives to existing staff, offer better car and expenses or recruit extra salespeople?

The sales manager's problem is deciding on the required amount of money and the best means of allocation. Improvement comes from increasing sales, reducing costs or changing the product mix to produce a more profitable result. If the manager tries to economise on the budget (reducing costs), the risk increases of sales volume not being achieved. Conversely, if sales volume is achieved or increased but at a higher cost, the overspending may reduce profitability. This is a basic dilemma for management, or, as the Americans might say, 'You put your budget money where you get the most bang for your buck'.

Sales budgets set out in financial terms the desired level of financial achievement. A budget is a financial or quantitative statement prepared and approved prior to a defined period of time for the sales policy to achieve a given objective. The sales budget has three benefits:

1. *Planning*. The cost of different options can be assessed, revealing whether the selected approach is satisfactory.
2. *Coordination*. It helps management to link the different cost centres to coordinate responsibilities and objectives within marketing as well as between sales and production.
3. *Control*. Since budgets serve as a quantitative expression of measuring performance, they indicate if things are going off course and provide a warning to take remedial action.

There are several methods for setting sales budgets, each with many variations:

- *Percentage of sales*. The most convenient for administrative reasons, but this method – for example, sales costs at 10 per cent of revenue – has little to commend it apart from simplicity and clarity.
- *Executive judgement*, which is often vague in justification but does have the advantage of top management involvement, also implying commitment.
- *Unit build-up method*, which attempts to allocate on the basis of specific objectives for a salesperson or area. Funds can be increased or reduced between weak and strong areas to improve effectiveness. The advantage should be greater flexibility since cost centres will otherwise tend to repeat the previous period's allocation, regardless of need. Experience may encourage managers to request more than is needed and to spend all they can get. A variation of this method is the so-called zero-base budget which expects each manager to identify the tasks, costs and benefits of each area of responsibility and assign a priority to its execution. This clearly requires time and effort to complete but avoids the year-on-year ritual of spending without real objectives or justification.

- *Rate of return on investment*. The sales force can be viewed as both investment and expense. For most sales forces, variations at the margin are not easily achieved. The case can be put forward for treating sales revenue and expense as an investment decision on which the rate of return can be calculated. By increasing sales, reducing costs or influencing the deployment of assets the rate of return can be improved.

SUMMARY

In this chapter we have presented the process of setting sales targets as a key practice in managing an effective sales organisation. Often linked to sales measures and incentives (see following chapters), sales targets are powerful mechanisms to help strategy execution, performance and motivation. However, sales targets can also have detrimental effects when they are not defined in accordance with solid calculations and aligned to the company's strategy. Thus, we have introduced sales forecasts as a fundamental practice with direct implications on sales management, and indirect effects on other functions such as production, operations and supply chain.

QUESTIONS

- Why are sales targets import in achieving sales effectiveness?
- What are the potential dysfunctional effects of sales targets?
- Describe established forecasting processes in sales force management.
- In what ways are sales forecasts connected to sales budgets and sales targets?

REFERENCES

Armitage, H. & Scholey, C. (2007). Using Strategy Maps to Drive Performance. *CMA Canada*. Retrieved 28 July 2015, from http://www.cimaglobal.com/documents/importeddocuments/tech_mag_strategy_mapping_march07.pdf.

Brown, S. P., Evans, K. R., Mantrala, M. K. & Challagalla, G. (2005). Adapting motivation, control, and compensation research to a new environment. *Journal of Personal Selling & Sales Management*, 25(2), 155–167.

Deming, W. E. (1990). *Out of the Crisis.* Cambridge: Massachusetts Institute of Technology Center for Advanced Engineering Study.

Franco-Santos, M. & Bourne, M. (2009). The impact of performance targets on behaviour: A close look at sales force contexts. *CIMA Research Executive Summaries Series*. Retrieved from http://www.cimaglobal.com/Documents/ImportedDocuments/cid_ressum_impact_performance_targets_behaviour_sales_force_oct_2009.pdf. (28 July 2015)

Franco-Santos, M., Marcos, J. & Bourne, M. (2010). The art and science of target setting. *IESE Insight*, Issue 7, 34–41.

Frenzen, H., Hansen, A.-K., Krafft, M., Mantrala, M. K. & Schmidt, S. (2010). Delegation of pricing authority to the sales force: An agency-theoretic perspective of its determinants and impact on performance. *International Journal of Research in Marketing*, 27(1), 58–68.

Gaba, A. & Kaira, A. (1999). Risk behavior in response to quotas and contests. *Marketing Science*, 18(3), 417–435.

Hollet-Haudebert, S., Mulki, J. P. & Fournier, C. (2011). Neglected burnout dimensions: Effect of depersonalization and personal non accomplishment on organizational commitment of salespeople. *Journal of Personal Selling & Sales Management*, 31(4), 411–428.

Joseph, K. & Kalwani, M. (1998). The role of bonus pay in sales force compensation plans. *Industrial Marketing Management*, 27, 147–159.

Kaplan, R. S. & Norton, D. (2004). *Strategy Maps: Converting Intangible Assets into Tangible Outcomes*. Boston, MA: Harvard Business School Press.

Larkin, I. (2010). *The Cost of High-powered Incentive Systems: Gaming Behavior in Enterprise Software Sales*. Working Paper, Harvard Business School.

Latham, G. P. (2004). The motivational benefits of goal setting. *Academy of Management Executive*, 18(4), 126–129.

Locke, E. A. & Latham, G. (1990). *A Theory of Goal Setting and Task Performance.* Englewood Cliffs, NJ: Prentice Hall.

Marchetti, M. and Brewer, G. (2000). The art of setting sales quotas. *Sales & Marketing Management*, 152(4), 101.

Misra, S. & Nair, H. (2011). A structural model of sales-force compensation dynamics: Estimation and field implementation. *Quantitative Marketing & Economics*, 9(3), 211–257.

Murphy, W. M. (2004). In pursuit of short-term goals: Anticipating the unintended consequences of using special incentives to motivate the sales force. *Journal of Business Research*, 57(11), 1265–1275.

Neely, A. D., Adams, C. & Kennerley, M. P. (2002). *The Performance Prism: The Scorecard for Measuring and Managing Business Success*. London: Pearson Education.

Ordóñez, L. D., Schweitzer, M. E., Galinsky, A. D. & Bazerman, M. B. (2009). Goals gone wild: The systematic side effects of overprescribing goal setting. *Academy of Management Perspectives*, 23(1), 6–16.

Schweitzer, M. E., Ordóñez, L. D. & Douma, B. (2004). Goal setting as a motivator of unethical behavior. *Academy of Management Journal*, 47(3), 422–432.

Schwepker C. H. & Good, D. J. (2004). Understanding sales quotas: An exploratory investigation of consequences of failure. *Journal of Business & Industrial Marketing*, 19(1), 39–48.

Schwepker, C. H. & Good, D. J. (2012). Sales quotas: Unintended consequences on trust in organization, customer-oriented selling, and sales performance. *The Journal of Marketing Theory and Practice*, 20(4), 437–452. doi: 10.2753/MTP1069-6679200406.

Van Yperen, N. W., Hamstra, M. R. W. & van der Klauw, M. (2011). To win, or not to lose, at any cost: The impact of achievement goals on cheating. *British Journal of Management*, 22, S5–S15.

Zoltners, A., Sihna, P. & Lorimer, S. (2008). Sales force effectiveness: A framework for researchers and practitioners. *Journal of Personal Selling and Sales Management*, 28(2), 115–131.

14 SALES COMPENSATION AND REWARDS

OVERVIEW

In previous chapters we have seen how motivation underpins salesperson performance. Compensation and reward practices have the potential to enhance sales person motivation and performance. We looked at motivation and leadership in Chapter 5, and argued that different individuals are motivated by different factors, thus suggesting that different leadership approaches need to be considered. In this chapter we acknowledge the significance of extrinsic motivation in sales professionals, and thus the importance of compensation and rewards. Both monetary and non-financial rewards will influence people's attitudes towards work. Most people weigh up potential monetary gains against the cost in time/effort/difficulty of the job and the opportunity of doing what they like and enjoy. Individuals' needs vary, but money is an important factor in most cases. Likewise, for the company, there is a balancing act between higher levels of pay and keeping costs down. In this chapter, we present the principles behind good compensation plans and the elements that can be considered for rewarding salespeople.

LEARNING OBJECTIVES

This chapter aims to enable the reader to:

- Understand the role of financial incentives in sales management.
- Assess the appropriate levels and methods of payment for financial compensation.
- Evaluate the design of compensation schemes in the context of sales management and sales performance.

DEFINITIONS

Compensation: although there are no widely agreed definitions of the terms used in this chapter, 'compensation' is often used to refer to the financial remuneration given in a job.

Rewards also refers to the financial provisions made to employees, thus used interchangeably with 'compensation'.

Incentive is a variable payment received for achieving a particular result. Variable pay schemes in business include performance-related pay and profit-sharing schemes.

Benefits are non-financial elements such as health care, company car, house and school allowances, etc..

INTRODUCTION: MOTIVATING AND REWARDING SALESPEOPLE

For more than two decades, research interest has focused on the link between sales force compensation and intrinsic motivation. This link is particularly relevant in contexts of long-term relationship development and relationship selling (Pullins, 2001). The quest to understand the components of motivation and its impact on performance in sales has generated interest for decades (Basu, Lal, Srinivasan & Staelin, 1985; Brown, Evans, Mantrala & Challagalla, 2005) and it is still a question featured in both academic and practitioner-oriented publications (Steenburgh & Ahearne, 2012).

In the motivation theories outlined in Chapter 5 we explain how motivation is affected by rewards and the desirability of higher rewards. We argue that compensation and rewards are powerful mechanisms to increase extrinsic motivation and thus complement other approaches to enhance intrinsic motivation such as:

- *Individual recognition and status enhancement*. Acknowledgement of a job well done, a more prestigious title, and other ways of recognising effort act as a stimulus.
- *Positive communication*. People are more motivated when they have positive views about the job, the company or their performance. These views can be influenced by management's communications and messages. Enhanced organisational communications can be achieved with suggestion boxes, employee surveys, exit interviews (for leavers) and other techniques to improve two-way exchanges.
- *Supporting their self-concept and esteem*. Especially in newer recruits, this helps to salespeople handle rejection in customer encounters and internal conflict.
- *Group involvement*. Since salespeople operate on their own, fostering team spirit, camaraderie and group involvement are part of the management task.
- *Accessibility and understanding*. As with any employee, individuality is important. At any one time, salespeople may face personal problems that personal connection and intimacy can help alleviate.
- *Engagement*. Sales managers who interact with their salespeople on an individual and on a team basis to further their organisation's objectives are likely to be more productive in their sales effort and performance.

COMPONENTS OF REWARDS IN SALES

When designing a sales force compensation scheme there are a few factors that inform the pay mix (Zoltners, Shina & Lorimer, 2006):

- Sales process and roles.
- The extent to which results are measurable.
- The situation and organisational culture of the company and its philosophy.
- Industry norms and practices.

A number of instruments exist in sales compensation. Generally speaking, two groups are often used: financial and non-financial. These are briefly explained below (Johnston & Marshall, 2013).

Financial rewards

Salary

A salary is a fixed sum of money that is paid at a regular interval and is a function of age, experience, competence, and the management's judgement about the quality of the individual. Basic salary enables companies to compensate effort on non-selling activities or activities that may not result in immediate sales results. These activities include market research, problem analysis, customer service, etc. Salary also enables the firm to moderate for accurate allocation of sales territories with disparate levels of workload and/or potential.

Salary can be 'a floor which many salespeople desire and a ceiling which many dislike' (Tosdal, 1953b). Salary levels should be set at a level sufficient to attract, retain and stimulate the type of salesperson desired. The salary rates for similar jobs at competing firms also needs to be taken into account. Pay has to be attractive enough to appeal to sales recruits and retain good salespeople yet not out of line with other employees. Underpaying may increase staff turnover, adding to recruitment costs and possibly lost sales.

Advantages of basic salary are:

- A basic level of pay is assured, providing security for the salesperson.
- A known cost – easy to administer for the company.
- It encourages loyalty and commitment of the salesperson.
- It enables transfer of individuals from one area to another.
- Control can be exercised on activities.

Disadvantages associated with salary-only pay schemes include:

- No direct incentive to greater effort.
- Costs being fixed regardless of sales levels.
- That it will result in below-par performers being overpaid and high performers underpaid.

In order to minimise the limitations of compensation schemes based solely on salary, other mechanisms are widely used. We present them below.

Commission

A commission is payment for achieving a certain level of performance whereby sales people are paid for the short-term results they produce. Usually commissions are paid based on sales volume or sales profit generated by the salesperson. Commissions have a direct link with job performance, which strongly motivates salespeople to improve their performance in order to increase their earnings. On the other hand commissions have the disadvantage of directing the sales force towards short-term sales revenues which may be at the expense of long-term profit and even customer satisfaction. Commissions are often combined with a salary in an effort to share the performance risk between the organisation and its sales force.

Commission is often used in direct to consumer selling (e.g. Tupperware, Avon cosmetics) where salespeople work on a part-time basis. The individual may choose to work as hard and long, or as little, as they like and they receive the commission according to volumes of sales. For smaller companies with no resources, commission-only payment protects cash flow by relating sales costs directly to sales made. With commission schemes, the sales manager has to decide the basis of the commission (volume, value or profit), the starting point (minimum order level), the time it is to be paid (e.g. when customer places order or settles the account) and the rate (usually a percentage of sales).

The advantages of commission-only schemes are:

- Payment is related to results for both individual and company.
- It is easy to calculate once the scheme has become established.
- There is no ceiling.
- Costs relate to sales.
- No other evaluation method is required.
- Individuals can be virtually self-employed.

Problems might include:

- A lack of loyalty, commitment and time from salespeople.
- A lack of service, customer-building and non-selling activities.
- A large turnover of people (recruitment and training costs may rise).
- Other sales activities being ignored.
- Cost control coming at the expense of area coverage, quality of presentation and company image.

Bonus

A bonus is a payment for achieving or surpassing a certain level of performance. A bonus is usually paid only after a salesperson has reached a certain level of performance such as reaching a particular quota or target. Individuals can achieve a bonus for reaching their individual target or a team-based goal. In this case, if the target is achieved each member typically receives the bonus despite different individual contributions. This method should be closely linked to clear and well agreed targets, as discussed in Chapter 13.

Most firms pay sales forces combining various reward instruments. This helps capture the diverse corporate and sales objectives and the variety of selling situations and sales tasks such as the buying process complexity or the number of influences in a purchase decision. Where there is a high-risk or large-value purchase, the time lag in the sales process may be prolonged. Short-term incentive mechanisms may not be adequate for this type of sale. Thus, payment plans have to combine different elements of salary and bonus to provide flexibility and control for sales managers but also to compensate sales professionals for focusing on the activities that add value in the medium and long term. Problems with combination schemes usually relate to the expense of administering them. As with some tax systems, if it's fair, it won't be simple; if it's simple, it won't be fair!

Sales contests

Sales contests are short-term initiatives to encourage additional effort. The winners of the contest could receive additional monetary payments or non-financial rewards. Sales contests are not considered part of the compensation package. They are an opportunity for the salespeople to gain additional rewards, whether financial or non-financial. Sales contests, in addition to other programmes such as incentives and recognition programmes can, when used appropriately, improve morale and team effort (Zoltners et al., 2006).

Other incentives

Other payments (e.g. lump sums) can be awarded for achieving or exceeding a particular performance target.

What do you think?

Rewarding will not affect performance but it will affect loyalty.

Non-financial rewards

Benefits

This category of rewards can include items such as health insurance, pension funds or a company car. It can also include shares or stock options in the firm.

Opportunity for promotion

For younger salespeople this is the number one reward which even tops financial rewards. Promotion does not necessarily mean promoting someone from sales to management. It can also be to a promotion along a set career path.

Sense of accomplishment and purpose

A sense of accomplishment is one type of reward that the organisation cannot provide for its salespeople. It comes from the sales people themselves. Organisations can, however, facilitate the process by making sure their salespeople understand the importance of their role and what they have achieved so far. Organisations can ensure through communication that salespeople feel a sense of purpose in their role.

Opportunity for personal growth and mastery

Personal growth rewards could comprise reimbursement of tuition fees for university, seminars, workshops and training. They can also be more personal by offering fitness memberships, financial advice or even eco-checks. The ability to develop themselves further is one of the main motivators for young people who seek to start employment and combine it with additional studies. One of the main examples is the increasing amount of people taking part-time MBA courses while they are working.

Recognition

Recognition can be provided both informally and formally. Informal forms of recognition consist of feedback and praise usually delivered by the sales manager to their salespeople during sales meetings or private conversations. Formal forms of recognition are part of clubs such as Xerox's President Club or GTE's Winner Circle. Formal recognition takes the form of public events where salespeople, in the presence of their peers and even family members, receive formal praise for their accomplishments. These usually include some form of symbolic award meant to sustain psychological value over time such as small statue or even a piece of jewellery.

Did you know?

Traditionally, salespeople were product-focused – 'the talking brochure' – but according to Huthwaite, 86 per cent of companies with high growth and profitability employ customer-focused targets that are quantifiable. In the same survey 71 per cent of businesses saw their main issue being the gap in the value claimed by salespeople and perceived by the customer, and how to close it.

LINKING COMPENSATION PLANS AND BUSINESS STRATEGY

Like any management activity, determining the remuneration package should be planned and coordinated. The first step in deciding reward is to carefully review the job specification and job description. This will indicate what the company must pay to get the people required. For example, graduates' technical expertise or sales experience requires a premium on standard wage rates. Similarly, salary levels will be on average less for companies that recruit young, inexperienced people than for those that hire experienced salespeople. The job review should indicate the importance of non-financial aspects in the job from the individual's point of view. These may include a desire for personal recognition in the company, a desire for status, a desire to excel and the need for job satisfaction. These needs cannot be met exclusively by financial incentives and rewards. Objectives motivate individuals to plan ahead and use time effectively. They encourage salespeople to do what management wants done in the way they want it done. The result is higher sales, lower costs and more profit.

Company objectives might include the following:

- Increasing volume. Sales increases, in real volume terms, have a positive effect as long-term cost curves fall, improving market share and profitability. Commissions on the sliding scale are more effective than bonuses in achieving such an objective.
- Increasing profits. Again, increased sales normally lead to increased profits but a different product and customer mix can have different effects. Too much volume on low contribution may be at the expense of profit. Profit-sharing schemes would be beneficial in raising profits in this case.
- Increasing sales of specific products, especially new products. In this case, special commissions or bonuses can work but the complexity of the plan may be such that it results in demotivation or excessively high administrative costs.
- Achieving a predetermined sales level. In this case, it is appropriate to pay on a regressive scale of commission.
- Increasing sales to particular classes of customers, for example large buyers, new types of outlets or specific market segments. Selected groups of customers such as government departments may not respond in a similar way and a selective commission is more appropriate.
- Achieving adequate across-the-range stocking policies. Here the emphasis is on obtaining and retaining distributor loyalty. Incentives are paid on all product lines or a product mix. A bonus would be appropriate.
- Adding new customers. Again, a bonus would be preferable or a contest can be set up.
- Increasing goodwill, sustaining long-term customer benefits and providing advice are more salary-related.
- Encouraging missionary selling. A fixed salary, contract or payment per call is more appropriate. Commissions on indirect sales through wholesalers can be added if sales areas are reasonably self-contained.
- Doing a good job – salary with annual merit awards.

Personal sales objectives emerge from a different perspective. Individuals are concerned with achieving adequate income as represented by:

- Ensuring a minimum salary.
- Achieving a regular income – frequent commission or bonus.
- Removing excessive fluctuations, especially downwards.

Salespeople, like other workers, are also motivated by non-financial incentives. It is important with remuneration to consider non-financial incentives. While money is important, it may not be the prime motivator, but other pecuniary rewards can stimulate extra effort. A sound remuneration plan comprises financial as well as non-financial incentives, and takes account of:

- What the job is and specific individual and company objectives.
- An assessment of the appropriate level of pay which is neither too high nor too low; the plan should determine minimum, average and maximum desirable levels of pay, considering new and existing staff, competitive pay levels and individual company needs.
- The method of payment, which could include a fixed element, an incentive element, a reimbursement of expenses element and any appropriate or desirable fringe benefits.
- A means of involving, consulting, communicating and testing the remuneration package prior to and during implementation.
- A follow-up to check that objectives are being met.

EFFECTIVE REWARDS SYSTEMS IN SALES

Principles for creating a sales reward plan

There will inevitably be a conflict of interest between the company and the individual when it comes to pay levels. The company would like, and need, to keep wage costs down whereas individuals naturally prefer as high an income as possible. Even in the most committed individual and in the most enlightened organisation, this underlying difference will exist.

Traditionally, in deciding the remuneration package, the following factors have been considered (Tosdal, 1953a):

- *Fairness*. To overcome the basic dilemma of paying too little or too much, the first issue to resolve is fairness, to both the employee and the company. Wage levels can be a morale builder in a job where other role demands create problems.
- *Income and security*. Companies that are tempted to pay on results, through commission only, overlook an individual's need for a predictable wage and the security of at least some earnings regardless of circumstances.
- *Incentives*. Above a minimum level of pay for security, there is an added incentive for individuals to work harder for more money. Sales performance does respond to sales effort, so offering a reward produces results.
- *Flexibility*. Salary levels should be relatively stable, avoiding high/low fluctuations. For this reason alone, combination methods are to be recommended but excesses in one period cannot be redressed by scarcity in another. For example, some firms operate retrospective commission payments above a target level. In a subsequent period, if target is not reached, the previous surplus is claimed back. This is to prevent salespeople from artificially pulling sales into a period to make a bonus at the expense of the next period's sales. This kind of approach, however, satisfies neither salespeople nor the company.
- *Economic*. Systems of pay, including expenses, should be economic in operating terms. Salespeople are a significant overhead cost and must justify their existence in cost/revenue terms. Complex payment schemes which are difficult, time consuming and costly to operate should be avoided.

The profound changes in the nature of selling and sales force management have resulted in changes in sales compensation plans. The following are considered good practice in effective sales compensation plans (Ingram, Laforge, Avila, Schwepker & Williams, 2012; Rouziès, 2011; The Chally Group, 2012):

Alignment with the overall business strategy

- Allows the company to secure profit margins and thus are designed in the context of the overall business planning process, providing an acceptable ratio of costs and value created.
- Encourage activities that are consistent with the firm's overall marketing and business strategies.
- Reward securing, building and maintaining long-term relationships with profitable customers.

Consideration of key features of design and operationalisation of compensation plans

- Include both fixed and variable elements that are easily managed by the company and well understood by the salesperson.

- Tied to measurable criteria that accurately match the critical sales success factors for the company.
- Establish fixed base lines that support the long-term security of both company and salespeople.
- Clearly differentiate payouts for top, average, and inadequate performers.
- Distinguish between performing tasks and achieving results.
- Reduce the variable component (often linked to targets) when environmental uncertainty is high.

Fostering of positive effects in the individuals

- Focus on motivating salespeople to meet both tactical and strategic company goals.
- Allow salespeople to plan how to best achieve these goals, thereby reducing stress.

Minimising dysfunctional effects

- Are sufficiently flexible to change as goals or the environment change, but they are not changed 'suddenly'.
- Reduce role conflict, ambiguity, and stress.
- Avoid direct competition between salespeople.

Levels in designing sales compensation plans

When designing a sales compensation scheme two key decisions need to be taken: the overall level of pay and the variance; that is, the difference between the highest and the lowest paid salesperson (Zoltners et al., 2006).

Pay level

The criteria for deciding how much to pay salespeople should be informed by three different drives: the sales role, market, company. Overall the lower the requirements for the sales role the lower the pay level expected. If the market is not contested and margins are healthy, companies can afford to offer lower levels of pay. The extent to which a sales job adds value to the company is the third consideration (Figure 14.1).

	Low pay level	**High pay level**
Sales role drivers	• Requires modest knowledge, skills and capabilities • Local responsibilities • Customer has multiple links to the company • Sales due to 'non-sales' factors	• Requires considerable knowledge, skills and capability • National/international responsibility • Customer has limited links to the company • Sales due to 'sales' factors
Market drivers	• Labour supply exceeds demand • The selling process is easy • The industry is low margin • Competition is low	• Labour demand exceeds supply • The selling process requires high levels of competence • The industry is profitable • High competition
Company drivers	• The sales job create moderate value to the firm • The firm attracts people through other non-monetary factors (culture, values, etc.)	• The sales job create considerable value to the firm • The firm attracts people by paying more than others in the industry

Figure 14.1 – Sales pay level

Source: Zoltners et al. (2006)

Pay variance

Organisations should consider low variance in pay when (Figure 14.2):

- Sales are influenced by non-sales factors.
- Team work is required.
- Top performers in the industry earn only slightly more than average performers.
- There are high similarities in salespeople's knowledge, skills and capabilities.
- Personal development is more valued than results.
- Salespeople care more about non-monetary factors.
- There are many levels of salespeople (individual pay is based on promotion).

Figure 14.2 – Pay variance

Source: Zoltners et al. (2006)

On the contrary, high pay variance or difference is justified when:

- Sales are highly influenced by salespeople's skills, effort and motivation.
- Salespeople work alone.
- Top performers in the industry earn multiples of what average performers earn.
- Low similarities in sales people's knowledge, skills and capabilities.
- Results are highly valued.
- Salespeople are highly motivated by money.
- There are few levels of salespeople (individual pay is based on performance).

Issues in rewarding salespeople

In line with the issues reported with the use of sales targets in Chapter 13, the use of compensation and rewards is not free from some issues and potential limitations that could result in dysfunctional effects in the company. Some of the problems in remuneration apply in greater degree to the *financial incentive* element of pay and reward. In particular:

- The incentive has to be sufficiently lucrative to be continuing and ongoing over time.
- The incentive must not be so insignificant that it ceases to function in a trade downturn or unfavourable economic conditions.
- Incentives must be easily understood and economical to operate.

Sales contests, commonly used in commercial sales forces, may have positive effects as described earlier. However, care has to be taken over how long the contest will run and how valuable participants will perceive the prize to be. Contests work as motivators because they provide recognition (status and enhanced self-esteem), excitement (risk and a change from routine) and reward. Contests often backfire because of poor management. Weak prizes, or too difficult targets, are common failures. Some of the common problems are:

- Failing to set clear objectives for the contest.
- Bad timing.

- The contest being too complicated.
- Quotas being too high.
- The wrong type of prize.
- A lack of promotion.
- No manager or customer involvement.
- Being too slow in assessment and reward.

Contests must be assessed on their individual merits in terms of the objectives set. They cannot overcome basic management deficiencies but, properly conducted, do provide incentives. They are short term rather than long term in duration. The effect must be evaluated in total business over the longer period and on sales force morale. Care has to be taken on the basis for a contest so that everyone has an equal and fair chance of success. If, early on, two-thirds of the sales force opt out, it may be self-defeating. Competition for reward and recognition can be a great motivator.

Companies may offer a range of fringe benefits to encourage greater commitment by their staff. The perceived worth of these may differ, especially between company and individual, but more evidence is required on their effect on job performance. The car and an expense account (telephone, meals and so on) are the most obvious. Other fringe benefits include share options, private health care, club membership and travel perks. The approach that sales managers take to handling expenses incurred by salespeople in the course of their job has an effect on the individual's earnings, their morale and their performance. From the company point of view, especially with a large sales force, the cost of expenses is significant. At the same time, it is unwise to look at expenses as a necessary evil when they are in fact a legitimate expense. The difficulty is to determine what is and is not legitimate. One approach is to classify expenses into:

- Essential, such as petrol, car and telephone.
- Reasonable, for example lunch allowances.
- Borderline, including personal gifts.
- Definite 'no's.

The responsibility for design and execution of the expense budget rests with the sales manager. The principles on which it is designed need to include the following:

- It should be fair in that expenses actually incurred are fully reimbursed but earnings are not through 'hidden' expenses. As well as being a weak method of remuneration, this is likely to incur the wrath of the tax inspector.
- The expense plan should also be flexible to take account of regional and customer variations. In particular, legitimate long-run customer-building expenses or costs of prospecting should be encouraged and reimbursed.
- Expenses should also be assessed and paid with minimum time and administration costs.
- Expense plan rules should be simple and unambiguous.

Other undesired consequences that excessive focus on incentives can bring about include (Zoltners, Sinha & Lorimer, 2012):

- For the salespeople: low organisational commitment, turnover and lack of teamwork.
- For salespeople's activities: propensity to engage in unethical behaviour, self-serving behaviour, lack of focus on non-selling activities.
- For customers: less customer orientation, selling products that are not needed or beneficial, lower levels of satisfaction.
- Business results: lost sales and profits and eventually lawsuits.

> **Did you know?**
> 98 per cent of UK businesses are establishing compensation packages after their financial year has begun, reducing their ability to plan ahead the best strategies to accomplish their established goals (www.anaplan.com)

PAY AND PERFORMANCE: A REVIEW AND CRITIQUE

Deciding and administering the methods and levels of pay are management tasks. Ambiguity, inconsistency and errors with pay create special problems for individuals. For example, bonus or commission related to performance creates problems if the target level set, and its parity with previous periods or other salespeople, does not seem equitable. Some of the problem areas may include the following:

- Most salespeople use value as a measure of performance comparing against a previous time period. As the basis for evaluation, however, real increases in sales can only relate to volume- or price/inflation-corrected values.
- Payment by results has to relate to invoiced sales rather than orders received. The problems with goods returned or orders cancelled can be a source of frustration to salespeople who feel they won the order only to be let down by quality, delivery or service problems.
- In certain types of selling, the problem of bad debts and poor credit risks may mean that business won is of poor value to the organisation. Salespeople incorrectly assume that this is not their problem.
- Salespeople paid on performance may benefit or be handicapped by dual contribution sales situations where sales are generated by more than one person. For example, distributors or intermediaries may operate in several sales areas. Since these purchase decisions may involve a number of personnel at different locations, the origins of who won the sale may be in dispute and uncertain. Another example would be where an order has been won yet sales are administered elsewhere. For example, suppose Wimpey decide to adopt a particular product, for example doors, for their house building programme in the north-east. The credit for this may be due to the salesperson for the door company in that area yet the product may be supplied through a builders' merchant group whose headquarters may be in a different area, for example, Yorkshire, a region serviced by a different salesperson. The actual number of units supplied by this merchant may be impossible to separate from the Wimpey contract.
- A related problem is the credit for house accounts. Many companies have subsidiaries which trade with each other. Sales in these situations may require extensive sales support but are not considered a basis for remuneration to individual salespeople.
- Key accounts are also a bone of contention with many salespeople. Although orders may be attributed to a central head office location, the size of these orders may owe much to the efforts of individual salespeople at branch level. Conversely, if no credit is attributed, certain necessary merchandising and service tasks, vital to support major accounts, may be neglected by individual salespeople.
- The problem of identifying sales performance as the result of sales effort may also be greater if the size of business is significant. Let us use the Wimpey example again. A medium-sized joinery firm winning such a contract from a large house builder would perhaps see this as the result of product quality, price, service and other customer-related benefits. To pay one person high commission as a result of this 'windfall gain' may be seen as inappropriate – although not by the salesperson who won the contract.

- In other sales situations, such as direct selling of, for example, cars, the value given to trade-ins may affect the real value of the sales, which in turn affects the commission paid.
- A related problem may be the treatment of instalment sales and credit agreements. For example, sales of many investment plans only become profitable for the company after year 1. Early payments only cover the salesperson's commission.
- The problem of telephone sales and posted orders has always been difficult to attribute to the individual. The developments in e-commerce will exacerbate this problem. Fairness and flexibility are needed in these situations but they are difficult to resolve.

SUMMARY

One of the most important factors in sales performance is the motivation of salespeople. Extrinsic motivation of sales professionals is fundamentally influenced by rewards and compensation. Pay is important to individuals and companies alike. Both the level and method of payment can affect salespeople's performance. This relationship is not an easy one to evaluate since people react differently to pay and incentives. As expected, monetary rewards and good management practices seem to be important. Emphasis should not be placed on job satisfaction at the expense of job performance. An integrated managerial approach to the motivational mix, taking cognisance of individual and situational factors, is recommended.

QUESTIONS

1 To what extent do you agree that, after a certain level, monetary rewards lose their power as motivators for salespeople?
2 Explain how and in what ways salespeople may differ in their motivations from workers in other occupations.
3 A toy manufacturer whose sales are highly seasonal is thinking of introducing a new remuneration package for the sales force. What elements of the remuneration packages should be considered?
4 What potential problems and advantages are there in using sales contests? Is this form of remuneration appropriate for all sales situations? What are the critical considerations in designing a successful sales contest?
5 A company is about to launch a new product range on the UK market. What are the probable effects of low sales force morale on this venture? Outline steps which could be taken to increase sales force commitment to the new range.

REFERENCES

Becherer, R. C., Morgan, F. W. & Richard, L. M. (1982). The job characteristics of industrial salespersons: Relationship to motivation and satisfaction. *Journal of Marketing*, 46 (Fall), 125–135.

Brown, S. P., Evans, K. R., Mantrala, M. K. & Challagalla, G. (2005). Adapting motivation, control, and compensation research to a new environment. *Journal of Personal Selling & Sales Management*, 25(2), 155–167.

Doyle, S. X. & Shapiro, B .P. (1980). What counts most in motivating your salesforce? *Harvard Business Review*, (May–June), 134–139.

Ingram, T. N. & Bellenger, D. N. (1982). Motivational segments in the sales force. *California Management Review*, 24(3), 81–88.

Ingram, T. N., Laforge, R. W., Avila, R. A., Schwepker, C. H. & Williams, M. R. (2012). *Sales Management: Analysis and Decision Making* (8th edn). London: M. E. Sharpe Inc.

Johnston, M. W. & Marshall, G. W. (2013). *Sales Force Management – Leadership, Innovation, Technology* (11th edn). New York: Routledge.

Maslow, A. H. (1970). *Motivation and Personality* (2nd edn). New York: Harper & Row.

Pullins, E. B. (2001). An exploratory investigation of the relationship of sales force compensation and intrinsic motivation. *Industrial Marketing Management*, 30(5), 403–413.

Rouziès, D. (2011). Sales force compensation, in Guenzi, P. & Geiger, S. (eds.) *Sales Management: A Multinational Perspective*. London: Palgrave Macmillan, pp. 413–432.

Steenburgh, T. & Ahearne, M. (2012). Motivating sales people: What really works. *Harvard Business Review*, 71–75.

The Chally Group (2012). *16 characteristics of effective compensation programs*. Retrieved 1 August 2014, from http://www.cpsa.com/knowledgecentre/SRCArticleRead.aspx?articleID=158.

Tosdal, H. R. (1953a). Administering salesmen's compensation. *Harvard Business Review*, (Mar–April), 70–83.

Tosdal, H. R. (1953b). How to design the salesman's compensation plan. *Harvard Business Review*, (September–October), 61–70.

Zoltners, A., Shina, P. & Lorimer, S. E. (2006). *The Complete Guide to Sales Force Incentive Compensation*. New York: AMACOM.

Zoltners, A., Sinha, P. & Lorimer, S. E. (2012). Breaking the sales force incentive addiction: A balanced approach to sales force effectiveness. *Journal of Personal Selling & Sales Management*, 32(2), 171–186. doi: 10.2753/PSS0885-3134320201.

15 SALES PERFORMANCE MEASUREMENT AND MONITORING

OVERVIEW

Throughout the previous two chapters, 'Sales target setting' and 'Sales compensation and rewards', we referred to the concept of 'sales performance' many times. In this chapter we focus on this concept defining its dimensions and the complex issue of its measurement. We also take a close look at the art of evaluating and monitoring the performance of the salesperson. Measuring and monitoring performance requires an evidence-based approach, to be able to evaluate the causes as well as the outcomes of it. Control that results in enhanced performance in sales forces implies setting standards, comparing results achieved with these standards and taking corrective action to balance these practices with the specific circumstances and situation of the salesperson. While sales performance is about results, sales performance management is about understanding the root causes or the behaviour and activities that led to these results and determining what needs to be changed. We therefore adopt a holistic approach to creating effective performance measurement systems. Thus, in this chapter we present recent research on performance measurement effectiveness bringing together the literatures of business performance management and personal sales performance.

LEARNING OBJECTIVES

This chapter aims to enable the reader to:

- Scope the concept of sales performance.
- Present the key antecedents of sales performance.
- Devise an integrated framework to measure sales performance at the organisation level.
- Present guidelines to evaluate salespeople's performance.

DEFINITIONS

Sales performance: assessment of how well the organisation's sales operations compare with competitors given market conditions.

Salesperson's performance: assessment of how well individuals or sales teams compare with others both in their own organisation and in other organisations in similar industries or sales situations.

Benchmarking is a management process whereby an organisation compares its performance with that of its competitors and with others in the same or related industries with the objective of establishing best practice. This enables the organisation to apply learning from the best performers to its own organisation.

SALESPERSON PERFORMANCE: CONCEPTUALISATION AND DIMENSIONS

Most sales leaders have two key objectives as part of their job: to enhance the performance of the individuals in their sales force, and to achieve sales effectiveness at the level of the organisation. At the individual salesperson level, evaluation is necessary to identify above- and below-average performers and to understand what lies beneath different levels of performance, particularly in individuals with similar levels of qualifications and experience. Differences in performance may also reveal vulnerabilities of practices such as territory deployment, recruitment, training and remuneration policies. Finally, evaluation is necessary to modify the sales tasks in line with customer and company needs so that sales plans are compared with the most appropriate criteria for improved sales performance.

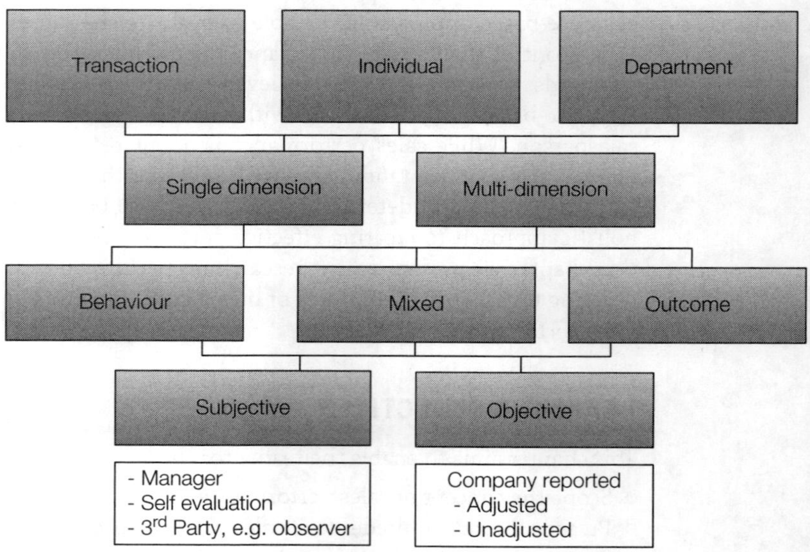

Figure 15.1 – Approaches to measuring sales performance

When assessing performance, a number of options need to be considered:

Level: whether individual or team/unit. Most research is focused on individual salespeople, but team-based selling has grown significantly over the last two to three decades (El-ansary, Zabriskie & Browning, 1993) and is increasingly used to bring about enhanced performance (Cravens, Grant, Ingram, LaForge & Young, 1992).

Single vs. multiple measures: there is consensus that the use of multiple metrics is more likely to capture the scope of salespeople's effectiveness (Johnston & Marshall, 2013).

Outcome vs. behaviour measures are well established in the literature. At present, most organisations use both types of measures in order to influence behaviour and performance (Zoltners, Sinha & Lorimer, 2006). Behaviour-based measures of performance are less quantifiable and tend to be oriented towards the longer term. Examples include: sales force product knowledge, relationship management and selling skills. Behaviour-based measures require high levels of managerial observation. Outcome-based measures have high measurability and are oriented towards the short term as their impact can be fully realised during the incentive period. Some examples of these measures are: sales revenues, profits, market share and sales growth from existing customers. Outcome-based measures are more appropriate for target-setting purposes and are often linked to incentive compensation.

Table 15.1 – Advantages and disadvantages of behaviour vs. outcome-based performance approach

'Sales performance' approach	Advantages	Disadvantages
Behaviour-based	• Allows management to dictate approach and focus • Removes factors outside a salesperson's control	• Requires significant monitoring of salesperson • Introduces subjectivity bias
Outcome-based	• Allows salespeople to develop situation-specific strategies for success • Ties compensation to firm financial performance	• Salesperson focus may not align to organisational priority • Difficult to identify and manage uncontrollable factors influencing outcomes

Subjective vs. objective. Each of these approaches has its merits and disadvantages, and as Rich, Bommer, MacKenzie, Podsakoff and Johnson (1999) suggest, 'salesperson performance are not interchangeable, and that the choice of the most appropriate measure may require a trade-off between accurately tapping the domain of the performance construct and minimizing measurement error' (p. 41).

Adjusted vs. unadjusted: In most sales contexts differences exist between territory potential, distribution of customers, etc., suggesting the need to adjust measures of performance to specific individuals and circumstances.

Determinants of sales performance

Early research into the determinants of sales performance (Walker, Churchill & Ford, 1977) showed that a salesperson's performance is a function of four factors: (1) personal, organisational and environmental variables, (2) role perception, (3) competence and (4) motivation (Figure 15.2). This conceptual framework suggested that when performance increases and the associated rewards (both internally and externally mediated) are achieved, the salesperson's satisfaction (intrinsic and extrinsic) will also increase, reinforcing the level of motivation. Below we outline the key characteristics of each of these four determinants.

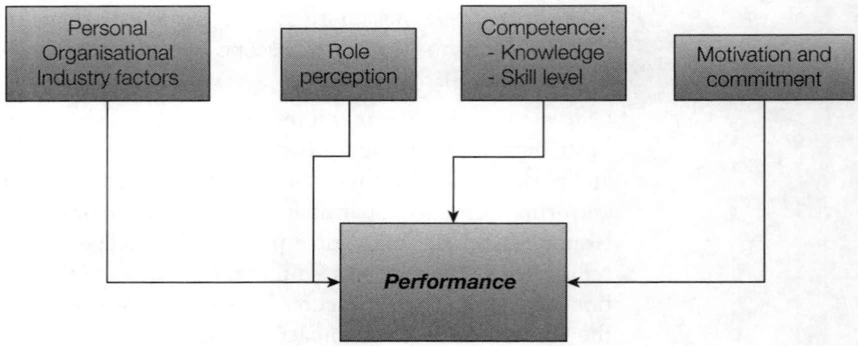

Figure 15.2 – Determinants of salesperson performance

Source: Adapted from Walker et al. (1977)

External and individual influencing variables

Organisational variables such as territory potential, organisational structure and industry conditions can influence sales performance directly. Territory potential is determined by concentration of customers, intensity of competition, amount of advertising expenditure and market share. In addition, closeness and the standards of supervision have an influence on an individual's role perception (see next subsection). The activities of sales managers have a great impact on the performance of their salespeople – particularly the emphasis that sales managers place on actively helping their salespeople to improve and develop their capabilities and motivating them to perform. Personal variables include job experience and training.

Role perception

Role perception refers to how the salesperson perceives the expectations the organisation has on him/her in terms of activities to execute or the behaviours to display. In particular three key dimensions were identified in Walker et al.'s (1977) framework:

- Role accuracy.
- Perceived role conflict.
- Perceived role ambiguity.

Sales professionals are believed to enjoy a high degree of independence, which may be associated with problems such as role clarity. The role of the salesperson is mainly defined and communicated to salespeople through expectations, demands and pressure expressed by all the people who have a stake in how they perform. How salespeople perceive these expectations determines their definition of their role. When the salesperson believes that the demands of several stakeholders are incompatible, role conflict emerges.

Competence

Refers to the personal and professional abilities of the salesperson to do his or her job. These competences may be cognitive (knowledge or what is known), functional (what the person knows to do) and behavioural (how the person tends to behave). Behaviours are influenced by factors such as personality, mental ability, values and experience.

Motivation

Refers to the extent to which a salesperson is willing to make an effort to achieve certain goals in their position. Motivating factors can be very different from one

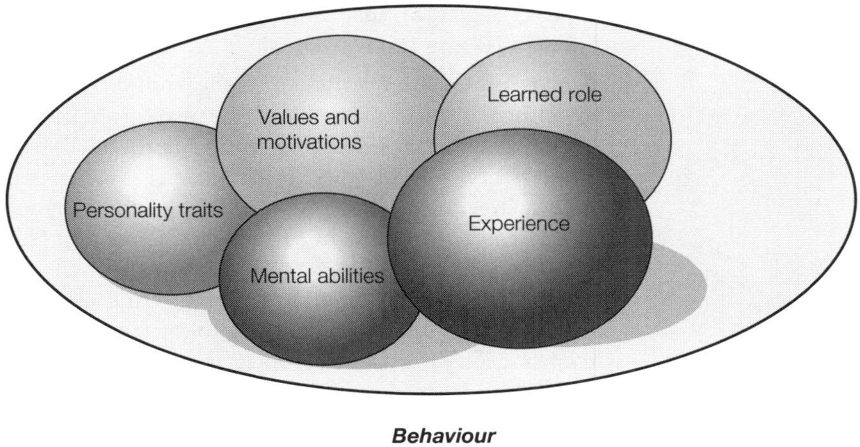

Figure 15.3 – Influencers of behaviour

salesperson to the next. Different sales professionals have different levels of ambition and drive. Motivation has traditionally been divided into extrinsic and intrinsic. Intrinsic motivation refers to the passion for the sales profession and the genuine sense of fulfilment for doing a good job. Extrinsic motivation refers to the level of importance the salesperson attributes to external rewards, such as money and incentives.

The work by Walker et al. (1977) was followed by myriad studies all aiming to establish the extent to which certain variables have an influence on sales performance. Verbeke, Dietz and Verwaal (2011) conducted a meta-analysis of 268 studies that included 292 samples in total 79,747 salespeople from 4,317 organisations. Initially, they identified the following categories as having a potential effect on salesperson performance:

- Role conflict.
- Role ambiguity.
- Role overload.
- Burnout.
- Dispositional traits.
- Personal concerns.
- Identity.
- Cognitive aptitude.
- Interpersonal.
- Degree of adaptiveness.
- Selling-related knowledge.
- Cognitive choice.
- Goal orientation.
- Motivated behaviours.
- Biographical.
- External environment.
- Internal environment.
- Supervisory leadership.

Employing advanced statistical analysis, their study revealed five sub-categories that were shown to have significant relationships with sales performance: selling-related knowledge, degree of adaptiveness, role ambiguity, cognitive aptitude and work engagement (Figure 15.4):

- *Selling-related knowledge*: Refers to the knowledge of products/services and customers necessary to present and 'co-create' solutions for customers. It includes how individuals make decisions in organisational settings and the ways in which products/services add value to customers. Overall, selling-related knowledge is about answering questions related to 'the know-why' of a product, how it might produce a solution (know-how) and who will adopt it ('know-who') (Verbeke, Dietz & Verwaal, 2011, p. 422).
- *Degree of adaptiveness*: refers to the ability to use tacit and explicit knowledge to change the sales approach according to the customer's situation, buying cycle and circumstances. Effective salespeople are able to 'select', from all the available repertoire of behaviours, those that best match the customer's preferences.
- *Role ambiguity*: the role of professional salespeople has increased in complexity over the years, resulting in less clear boundaries of work and influence. The clearer the expectations are for salespeople the better the focus and, thus, the results they will obtain.
- *Cognitive aptitude*: Higher levels of cognitive ability enables salespeople to select appropriate data to inform customers about the benefits of their products/services and to link these to areas of real interest to the customer. Furthermore, cognitive aptitude facilitates information processing, particularly from sales information systems. All this has the potential to enable sales professionals to achieve, over time, higher levels of performance.
- *Work engagement* facilitates the creation of networks, both internal and external. Individuals who are engaged and willing to work closely with others will most likely receive higher levels of support, thus resulting in higher levels of effectiveness with customers.

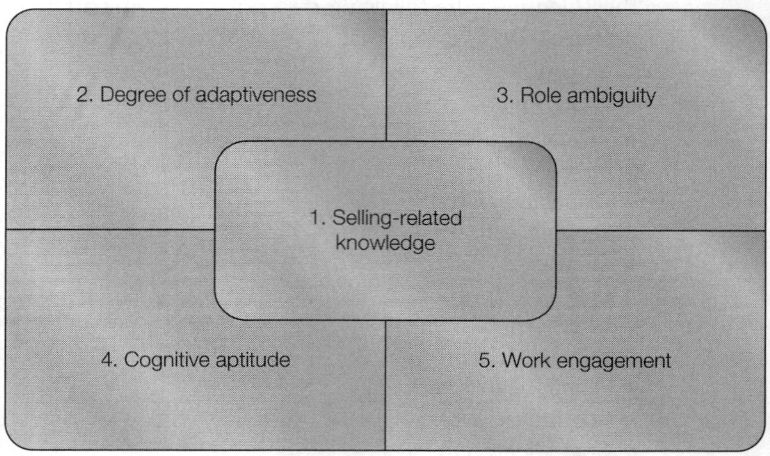

Figure 15.4 – Key drivers of sales performance

Source: Verbeke et al., 2011

Though the seminal paper by Verbeke et al. (2011) has consolidated a wealth of research into sales performance, the field is still a fertile domain to conduct further studies. Overall, their model and the factors described above only predict 32 per cent of the variance in sales performance. This suggests that more accurate measures of the phenomenon may be needed. This also reflects the possibility of a lack of agreement as to what constitutes sales performance. We now focus on presenting a framework of effective measurement systems in sales.

SALES PERFORMANCE MEASUREMENT EFFECTIVENESS

The types of sales performance measures used in businesses depend on the nature of firms' sales processes and their internal requirements. The selection of sales measures also depends on the maturity of the firms' data processing systems and sales automation solutions that enable the firm to capture, analyse and exploit its performance data. What only a few organisations realise is that the complexity of sales performance measures go beyond the difficulty of the gathering and the reporting of data. There are a number of factors that make measuring sales performance problematic (Marcos, Franco & Kerr, 2013):

The end–means paradox
The aim of measuring sales performance is to improve sales performance. This statement seems obvious and even redundant. However, many organisations design and roll out performance management systems and achieve precisely the opposite of enhanced performance. When salespeople are 'subject' to a set of strict measures they engage in behaviours to deliver against those measures. They perform activities without questioning the extent to which these activities add value to the customer and generate sustainable sales returns.

Linking measures with quotas
The potentially negative effect of having sales measures may be exacerbated when measures are linked to targets or sales quotas. If targets are perceived to be unachievable, evidence shows that this results in negative effects for both salespeople's trust in the organisation and their own sales performance (see Chapter 13).

The complex nature of measures
Organisational phenomena, including sales performance, are by their very nature complex, inter-connected and often subjective. Therefore, most attempts to measure 'performance realties' will be, by definition, limited. Sales managers need to be aware of certain characteristics of most sales measures such as:

- Imperfection: Some measures do not capture critical business development practices, thus resulting in the phenomenon known as 'hitting the measure but missing the point'. For instance, many organisations measure conversion rate, overlooking the 'quality' of those conversions. Equally, managers may focus on 'number of new customers', failing to scrutinise the quality and potential of such customers. The latter may be an 'imperfectly objective' but more meaningful measure than the former.
- Stickiness: once sales measures have been accepted they become uncontestable, thus promoting activities to increase a measure that may no longer be relevant, such as market share in highly volatile markets or sales by geography when dealing with global accounts.
- Conflicting roles: some measures that are useful as strategic information provision (i.e. for decision-making), are used for reward and compensation purposes. This induces distortion and manipulation of the metrics, like sales per customer segment.

- Inconsistency: over time, the validity of measures decreases. Measures will lose informativeness as individuals 'learn' what needs to be done to achieve the measure, so it no longer reflects the true performance of the sales and marketing organisation.

An approach to minimise the limitations of performance measures in sales is to develop holistic measurement schemes that address both the correctness as well as the appropriateness of measures used. Correctness is a function of measure validity and reliability. Effectiveness is seen as the measure's appropriateness relative to the context in which it is being used (Bourne, Kennerley & Franco-Santos, 2005).

Kerr and Marcos (2014) develop a conceptual framework which categorises the key contextual elements influencing sales performance measurement effectiveness. This framework shows that the properties of the measures (type and control orientation) are intertwined with situational variables in deriving effective measurement schemes. In addition, the purpose of the measure (e.g. compensation, promotion) and the characteristics of the phenomenon being measured also influence the effectiveness of a sales measurement scheme.

Even effective sales measurement systems are likely to produce organisational outcomes both desired and undesired. Therefore, to be considered as highly effective, sales performance measurement systems must go beyond ensuring measurement correctness and appropriateness to consider an optimal balance of both desired and undesired outcomes.

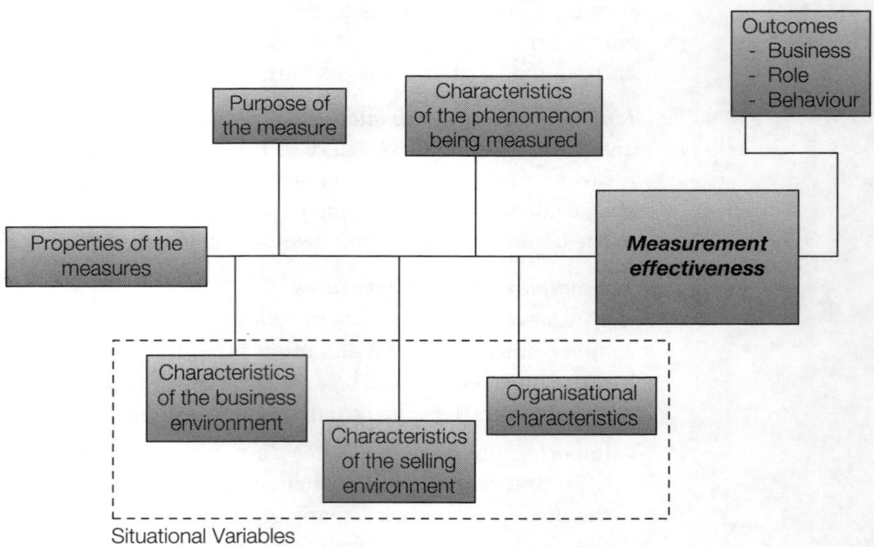

Figure 15.5 – A framework for effective sales performance measurement

EVALUATION OF SALESPEOPLE

A good sales force evaluation programme should be realistic and fair. It should be positive and contribute to motivation and improved job performance. It should be objective, involve salespeople and be economic in cost and time to administer. These aims inevitably conflict. Accountants, operational researchers, behaviourists, management scientists, economists and many other disciplines have tried to find better and more accurate measures of sales performance with varying degrees of success. It appears that evaluating salespeople is still something of an art struggling to be a science. Evaluation of salespeople is not easy. For example, eight calls per day may be better than six calls but what about the quality of each call? A higher sales value in one area may appear better than a lower value in another but what are the prevailing market and competitive conditions?

As with any management task, a planned approach is recommended for the evaluation task. This approach is typified by the following:

1 *Clarifying sales objectives*. These objectives normally mean sales volume levels but should relate to corporate and marketing strategy as well as sales objectives. The type of business, the type of customer, the sales, distribution and pricing policies and the level of service and support all need to be predetermined.
2 *Specifying sales tasks to achieve sales objectives*. Objectives must be translated into tasks. For example, gaining certain types of customers requires lead generation, prospecting, account development and a range of service and support tasks. Sales force productivity relies on other support from marketing, production, distribution, sales administration and service support functions. Task clarity enables a more objective evaluation which relates output measures to particular inputs.
3 *Writing, or rewriting, a job description with key and secondary tasks*. Evaluation is only possible according to preset written criteria. This removes much ambiguity about performance dimensions.
4 *Establishing suitable evaluation measures*. For various reasons, sales do not directly result from sales effort. Furthermore, improved sales productivity can be achieved by increased sales volume, reduced costs, a change in the mix of products and customers or a combination of these methods.
5 *Involving salespeople*. The most significant gains in sales force productivity will come from self-evaluation and self-improvement by salespeople themselves. Where management feels a need for greater control, a joint approach is recommended which at least involves salespeople in the process.
6 *Taking action*. As suggested earlier, the process is incomplete unless corrective action is implemented.

What do you think?

Sales managers underestimate the importance of behaviour.	**Q: Should sales managers spend as much time reviewing and analysing behaviours as they spend in analysing the business and financial outcomes?**

A six-stage, planned approach to evaluation implies a rather matter-of-fact situation. Before considering how information can be collected for evaluation purposes, it is worthwhile reconsidering the unique problems of the selling job:

- Salespeople have inadequate or incomplete information about their job, especially concerning the needs and preferences of customers and customer organisations.
- Salespeople mostly work alone and independently without direct supervision. Although considered by many to be an advantage, this independence creates other problems of role clarity.
- Salespeople operate in an inter-organisational boundary position which creates role conflicts.
- The sales job is demanding in terms of the degree of innovation and creativity required. There is no one right approach.

- The job requires adaptability and sensitivity by salespeople to the needs of customers yet is frequently met by different degrees of antagonism, hostility and aggression.
- Sales decisions may have to be made quickly, requiring decisiveness and mental alertness.
- Individual sales performance evaluation lacks direct observation of inputs – only outcomes are assessed.
- Evaluation is often inferred and subjective, and people are biased.
- Salespeople have little control over the conditions in which they operate.

Sources of information for evaluation

Conducting appropriate evaluation requires an adequate quantity and quality of information. Plans without evaluation are useless. Likewise, only by assessing variations against plan can the real reasons for performance be identified and corrected. Types of information are many and varied, from formal market research surveys, sales reports and management appraisal to internal records. These can all be used for sales force evaluation but each technique offers different benefits to the sales manager. It is good policy for information to be collected and assessed at the individual level where most use can be made of the data. With electronic capability now available through CRM and SFA the problem may well be too much data, some of which are not directly relevant to the particular person or situation. This may result in information overload. The temptation to exert excessive control needs to be resisted by new approaches in leadership and coaching to get the best from salespeople. Before considering the range and type of information that sales management can use, the main sources of information for evaluation of the sales force should be reviewed. These include the following:

- *Company records*. Sales orders, invoices and customer records form part of the marketing information system and can all be used to assess sales performance. The advantage of using internal records is that the source of the data is known and the data is available. Using company records should be quick, low cost and consistent. Records would normally be accurate and relevant. Disadvantages might be the absence of knowledge on relevant market conditions and the possibility of too much information being available for an individual's needs.
- *Sales reports*. Formal records can be time savers and helpful to management for evaluation. Salespeople are closest to the customers, their own records reflect a high level of involvement and information can be collected regularly. The disadvantages may be that reports show the truth, but not the whole truth; for example, call content may be disguised. Since peer evaluation of these reports is likely, salespeople may distort the content to gain favour, for example reporting favourably on new orders and new customers but omitting lost customers.
- *Managers' field visits*. This provides a useful comparison between different salespeople. If conducted well, it would entail joint involvement, which should also improve with practice, reinforcing the supervisor–subordinate relationship. The disadvantages with this method concern the people-to-people bias, the subjective views of managers, possible bias by salespeople in preselecting calls and the lack of quantification.
- *Customer contact*. Sales evaluation using customers provides first-hand, up-to-date information. It should be more independent and objective than other methods given that they capture an external judgements. It can also provide new insights

into customer needs. The problems may be the random nature of the response or the lack of representativeness; for example, small and big customers' views being given equal merit. The main disadvantage may be that this type of contact undermines the salesperson–customer relationship. It is, however, possible to use a combination of these methods in conjunction with other external hard data such as retail audit information to gain a more complete picture.

These sources have been at the disposal of sales managers for many years but using software to integrate information should give a more complete picture of performance. The danger is that data without a sound theoretical basis can tell what happened but not always why. Part of the problem is the lack of a theory which is comprehensive, accurate and testable. As a result, many sales managers still use traditional, obvious but inappropriate and inadequate measures of sales performance. Like other marketing problems, the dynamics of business plague accurate measurement. Not only are the goal posts moving, but the location of the pitch is also shifting. Another feature of the game is that any identified weaknesses are designed out as soon as practical. For example, if poor performers are observed to have lower call rates, this problem could be addressed rapidly by management dictum. Those with low call rates (and low performance) are immediately asked to increase call rates. Finally, the impact of other variables such as market conditions or competitive activity varies in importance, not only with the company but also between different sales areas and individual salespeople.

Weaknesses in traditional evaluation systems include the following:

- *An inadequate definition of the necessary inputs to achieve the desired outputs*. That is, the use of sales, call rates or other easily assessed measures is preferred to the more difficult quality dimensions of the job. The quality measures are often the most important. Anderson and Oliver (1987) call for more behaviour-based than output-based control. In a subsequent test of their propositions, they found support for the view that salespeople pursued organisation objectives more readily when control was behaviour-based whereas those using output-based control generated more self-interested behaviour in salespeople and less commitment.
- *Over-reliance on subjective factors*. Seemingly contrary to the first point, many managers seem to evaluate salespeople on selected personality traits or qualities. These characteristics are seldom proven measures of quality in sales performance. They are more probably factors that managers consider made themselves successful when they were selling.
- *Bias*. Managers themselves have particular personality traits, styles or techniques which affect their performance appraisal. These include the 'hire and fire' school, the overprotective 'mother-hen' syndrome and the 'wait and see' type. As well as being a management type, bias can also result from at least four causes. First is the halo effect, where performance on one or more characteristics is equated with performance on all dimensions of the job. For example, the salesperson who submits reports on time, has a high call rate, is punctual and has a good appearance may achieve higher performance scores than others who achieve higher sales in adverse market conditions. Second, there is the bias of central tendency. Managers may avoid assessing performance at the extreme ends (very poor and excellent) and play it safe, for example, with 'Please try harder' or 'Well done'. Since opportunity for observation is limited and the consequences of actions may be severe on pay or holding down the job, managers abdicate their responsibility for evaluation and play it safe. Third, an opposite form of bias is that to exercise,

or be seen to exercise managerial power, sales managers may be too lenient or too harsh. These decisions can have counterproductive effects on morale and motivation. Finally, bias arises for interpersonal reasons. Inevitably, managers may like some people more than others. DeCarlo and Leigh (1996) found that sales managers who like their salespeople as work partners (task attraction) and as friends (social attraction) were influenced in their performance appraisal. In particular, these managers were more likely to put weak performance down to external or other circumstances. Such bias is impossible to eliminate but should be acknowledged and guarded against.

These weaknesses relate to the management of the evaluation process rather than to the person being evaluated. It is incumbent upon sales managers to improve these evaluation procedures.

Conducting a performance evaluation

How organisations evaluate sales performance has been categorised into five classes of sales performance evaluation methods (Boles, Donthu & Lothia, 1995).

Class one evaluation methods (output only) rely on results as the criteria for evaluation and can include objective measures such as sales volume or subjective measures such as 'achieving sales objectives'. The main advantage of this evaluation method is that most measures can be directly related to the organisation's bottom-line results. The disadvantage is that it does not provide information regarding requirements in coaching, training or career improvement for salespeople.

Class two evaluation methods (input only) rely on input and output measures such as number of calls made and sales skills which are evaluated against performance goals. Porter, Lawler and Hackman (1975) argue that these measures may motivate activities rather than accomplishment. Rankings of the input and the output measures may be used but they are independent from each other.

Class three evaluation methods (individual evaluation) rely on both input and output measures combining both objective and subjective measures. These methods are described as supervisory methods incorporating both input and output into an overall assessment but with no explicit standards. Ratios can be developed and used for rank-order and may be particularly useful for assessing capabilities and further training needs.

Class four evaluation methods rely on the use of both input and output evaluation methods with explicit standards to compare salespeople with their peers. The comparison is performed either through supervisor evaluation or through statistical evaluation methods.

Class five is similar to class four with the exception that it relies only on statistical evaluation and compares the performance not against the average but the best performers in the sales team. Boles et al. (1995) argue that comparing salespeople's performance against that of the best performers is an important step towards achieving sales force excellence.

What do you think?

An IBM-sponsored study of the challenges faced by senior marketing officers revealed that data explosion, social media, growth of channels and changing consumer demographics are the top issues they face in today's competitive environment.

Q: How should these issues be considered when assessing sales performance and conducting sales practices benchmarks?

BENCHMARKING BEST PRACTICE

Understanding the cause and effect relationship between activities and their outcomes based on quantitative measures is part of a process known as benchmarking. In essence, benchmarking is the process of finding the best practice that leads to superior performance and implementing it. According to Zoltners, Sinha and Lorimer (2004) in order to improve sales operations a company needs to develop a set of best practices based on benchmarking methods that enables it to measure the cause and effect relationship between its sales activities and their outcomes.

Benchmarking has revitalised the old concept of performance comparison. It also involves a goal-setting process and in the achievement of these goals encourages empowerment of employees to effectively integrate the responsibilities, work processes and reward systems (Camp, 1989). Internal benchmarking is about comparing business units or processes within a single organisation, which overcomes the problem of finding an external organisation to measure against. However, only by external comparisons can an organisation hope to achieve 'best-in-class' performance.

Fong, Chong and Ho (1998) argue that benchmarking can be very expensive and top management must include instructing middle management and lower levels of management to use these techniques and provide adequate training to induce a planned transfer of knowledge. This is essential as findings must be adopted by both operational and management personnel. Employee commitment to the benchmarking project is essential as they are the people who will carry out the benchmarking practices. In order to gain support, the findings must be able to convince those requiring the data that it is from reliable sources and correctly analysed with clear and presentable findings (Fong et al., 1998). According to Biesada (1991) the toughest part of benchmarking is to get people out of their routine ways and to encourage them to think about the underlying process. Benchmarking will scare people if they think it is a device to get rid of them. Communication between management and employees is essential in order to avoid misinterpretation.

Chonko, Low, Roberts and Tanner (2000) argue that the sales manager must identify the relevant sales activities and for each of these activities define its goals, objectives, performance standards, what behaviours are needed to complete the activity and the relative importance of each behaviour. Developing benchmarks for selling activities may not be suitable for all types of selling environments. Rackham and De Vincentis (1998) argue that within a transactional sales environment selling costs are critical and non-selling time should be kept to a minimum. This selling environment is characterised by a simple sales process where one sales call is often sufficient to result in an order. Their advice is to assess activities that are easily measurable without going into too much detail. In a consultative selling environment, they argue, several process- and opportunity-related key performance indicators (KPI) should be measured. These selling environments are characterised by longer and more complex sales cycles, which include several individual sales calls to complete a sales process. Measuring the result of each sale call makes it possible to measure and track the individual sales process itself. Unlike transactional selling, consultative selling offers the ability to analyse and adapt the sales approach throughout the process. Figure 15.6 shows the stages in benchmarking the sales process.

This leads us to conclude that benchmarking systems, to be successful, need to be based on reliable data, correct analysis methods and clear presentation of the results. The employees need to be trained and management must obtain their commitment in order to implement and share best practices identified through the benchmarking process.

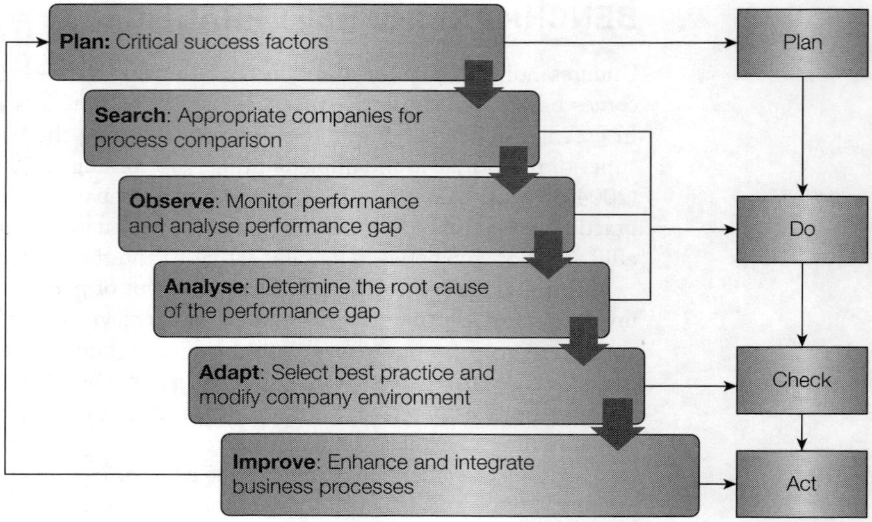

Figure 15.6 – Benchmarking sales processes

SUMMARY

Sales leaders and managers in organisations can use sales performance measures as key mechanisms to implement and communicate the business vision, inform decision-making, allocate resources and align sales behaviours with the overall sales strategy. Sales measurement and management systems are by their very nature complex and highly interactive. Data are rarely purely objective as we all use prior frames of reference and rely on assumptions to make sense of performance data to turn it into information. Moreover, sales and marketing managers often believe in the misguided motto 'what you measure is what you manage'. Customer experience is critical in many contexts, yet is difficult to measure as it is driven by subtle, intangible factors that may be observable but imperfectly measurable. Managing sales performance is a key foundation for creating winning sales teams that are focused on engaging valuable customers, with relevant offerings, through pertinent channels and approaches. Selling has evolved to become a highly situational profession where adaptability and customer-centredness differentiates moderate from high sales performance.

QUESTIONS

- How would you define sales performance? How does it differ from performance in other areas of the firm?
- Of the range of factors that may contribute to sales performance, which are the key ones?
- What are the fundamental aspects to consider when conducting effective salesperson performance evaluations?
- What are the steps of benchmarking sales practices?

INTERVIEW: MIGUEL CARRASCO HUERTA

Former Procurement Business Partner, Nestlé Latin America. Responsible for key relationships with suppliers, identifying best practice and knowledge sharing across supply chain, R&D and other departments for the breakfast cereal business units.

Q: In your role, what are the things you value most from your suppliers and their sales representatives?

Miguel: The most important thing for me is that vendors and their sales representatives get to have a deep knowledge of the company's buying process, the different steps that need to happen from the inclusion of a new vendor to the raising of a purchase order. I also value when the vendor makes available and brings their technical and organisational capabilities to add value to business – for instance, when engaging suppliers in the development of new products. Their knowledge of their own products may be instrumental in helping clients with research and development efforts. I also value that vendors deliver the specifications set and mutually agreed, not just a sole focus on 'selling'.

Q: How has the procurement function changed over the last few years?

Miguel: In South America, legislation and regulation is moving very fast. The requirements of the consumers are also moving very fast, and so our function has to contribute to responding to these trends.

Procurement has become more influential within the business. Years ago, it was seen as a secondary function. Now its involvement in core processes of the business is widely recognised.

Procurement must be involved early in the product development cycle, to find speedier and more effective product launches.

Q: I'd like to ask you about decision-making in procurement: to what extent can personal factors such as perceived trust, likeability and similarity influence rational decision-making in buyer–seller relationships?

Miguel: You do business face-to-face with other individuals most of the time. If you follow our predefined processes almost everything is under control and personal factors play a limited role. However, we are all human beings, thus trust, likeability and personal relationships are important, in particular for solving problems. When things go smoothly and as planned you do not need to talk to the vendor. However, when you have difficulties, then you have to talk to them, and that is where personal relationships can make a difference. They can provide valuable information, provide extra supplies to meet unexpected levels of production and help to source the materials needed. You may not need to have a great relationship with everyone all the time, but you need to trust the vendor. In my former role we aimed to develop long-term relationships with some vendors. In addition, the company tried to establish relationships with responsible suppliers, and thus developed a supplier code, specifying the expectations Nestlé has from its partners. These expectations are captured in its Supplier Code, which is publicly available (see http://www.nestle.com/aboutus/suppliers). When relationships with suppliers that observe this code are established, then Nestlé engages with these vendors in processes of mutual cooperation, information sharing, etc..

Q: We argue that sellers should adapt to the way in which the customer likes to buy. In general, to what extent you think suppliers are flexible in accommodating customer's buying methods and processes?

Miguel: Vendors must be flexible and adapt to clients' ways of working. Clients place a great value on that, as I indicated above. Then, clients are often willing to provide feedback on technical issues so they can work together more effectively. Since requirements are very high, and the companies often establishes standards that are even more stringent than the applicable legislation, sharing best practices with suppliers to help them fulfil the requirements is something that has to happen from the beginning of the relationship. That means for the supplier an investment in terms of time and willingness to adapt. In return, they expect higher volume of business. Sometimes, when they have more bargaining power, either because they are sole suppliers or because they are a local vendor, they tend to be a bit more inflexible. In that case, procurement has to stand up and refresh the terms and conditions to avoid an imbalance in the relationship.

Q: What is your view of the future of procurement? How will procurement influence professional selling in your industry?

Miguel: I think, given the trends and challenges in our market, that we have to work deeper with our suppliers. Supplier relationship management tools are likely to remain in use and even to become more critical. I expect that procurement, as a function, will become more professionalised, in particular in decision-making processes and other processes within the function. Supplier relationship management will be a key approach in the future, together with strategies to establish and to maintain relationships with certain vendors. We need to get more sophisticated and more forward looking.

The future will also see procurement enhancing their role as information brokers, sharing information and processes with strategic vendors within their own organisations.

Q: What advice would you give to a young professional sales representative in order to be effective in her/his relationships with corporate buyers?

Miguel: First, talk to the right people. In large companies the procurement processes need to be understood from the beginning.

Second, understand the processes of how to become a preferred vendor for the company and what is required. As mentioned, the expectations and requirements of our vendors are clear, explicit and publicly available. We may also have 'non-negotiable standards' – which we expect suppliers, vendors, contractors, employees, etc. to observe. These, as mentioned, form part of the code that we take for granted will govern the behaviours of partners.

And third, provide information about the product, know and offer what the procurement person values. Price is important, of course, but it is not only price that will define a sale. Focus on the value that your product can add to the business of the customer.

Q: Thank you Miguel, anything to add?

Miguel: Professional sellers need to know what they are selling beyond the price and the technical factsheet. They need to know how their products are produced,

where they come from – because that information is sometimes not so obvious. This will help persuade the customer that the seller has a good product and that it can add value. The seller in the end should be an expert on the product but also in the people who will have to deal with the product. Elevate the buyer's understanding and help her/him to understand why a particular product is better.
My last comment is that sometimes the buyer is not the sole decision-maker. Sellers have to have the support of a multi-disciplinary team and engage with individuals in different functions and again, to elevate the discussions about the product.

REFERENCES

Anderson, E. & Oliver, R. L. (1987). Perspectives on behavior-based versus outcome-based salesforce control systems. *Journal of Marketing*, 51 (October), 76–88.

Biesada, A. (1991). Benchmarking. *Financial World*, 17 (September), 28–47.

Boles, J. S., Donthu, N. & Lothia, R. (1995). Salesperson evaluation using relative performance efficiency: The application of data envelopment analysis. *Journal of Personal Selling & Sales Management*, XV(3), 31–49.

Bourne, M., Kennerley, M. & Franco-Santos, M. (2005). Managing through measures: A study of impact on performance. *Journal of Manufacturing Technology Management*, 16(4), 373–395.

Camp, R. C. (1989). *Benchmarking: The Search for Industry Best Practices that Lead to Superior Performance*. Milwaukee, WI: ASQC Quality Research.

Chonko, L. B., Low, T. W., Roberts, J. A. & Tanner, J. F. (2000). Sales performance: Timing and type of measurement make a difference. *Journal of Personal Selling and Sales Management*, 20 (Winter), 23–36.

Churchill, G. A., Ford, N. M., Hartley, S. W. & Walker, O. C. (1985). The determinants of salesperson performance: A meta-analysis. *Journal of Marketing Research*, XXII (May), 103–118.

Cravens, D. W., Grant, K., Ingram, T. N., LaForge, R. W. & Young, C. (1992). In search of excellent sales organizations. *European Journal of Marketing*, 26(1), 6–23.

DeCarlo, T. E. & Leigh, T. W. (1996). Impact of salesperson attraction on sales managers' attributions and feedback. *Journal of Marketing*, 60 (April), 47–66.

El-Ansary, A., Zabriskie, N. B. & Browning, J. M. (1993). Sales teamwork: A dominant strategy for improving salesforce effectiveness. *Journal of Business & Industrial Marketing*, 8(3), 65–67.

Fong, S. W., Chong, E. W. L. & Ho, D. C. K. (1998). Benchmarking: A general reading for management practitioners. *Management Decision*, 36(6), 407–418.

Heiman, S., Sanchez, D. & Tuleja, T. (1998). *The New Strategic Selling*. London: Warner Books.

Johnston, M. W. & Marshall, G. W. (2013). *Sales Force Management – Leadership, Innovation, Technology* (11th edn). New York: Routledge.

Kerr, P. & Marcos-Cuevas, J. (2014). Towards a framework of sales performance measurement effectiveness. In *Global Sales Science Institute Annual Conference*. London, 11–13 June. London.

Marcos, J., Franco, M. & Kerr, P. (2013). Measuring sales performance. *ADMAP* (March), 48–49.

Rackham, N. & De Vincentis, J. (1998). *Re-thinking the Sales Force: Re-defining Selling to Create and Capture Customer Value*. New York: McGraw-Hill.

Rich, G. A., Bommer, W. H., MacKenzie, S. B., Podsakoff, P. M. & Johnson, J. L. (1999). Apples and apples or apples and oranges? A meta-analysis of objective and subjective measures of salesperson performance. *Journal of Personal Selling & Sales Management*, 19(4), 41–52.

Verbeke, W., Dietz, B. & Verwaal, E. (2011). Drivers of sales performance: A contemporary meta-analysis. Have salespeople become knowledge brokers? *Journal of the Academy of Marketing Science*, 39(3), 407–428.

Walker, O. C., Churchill, G. A. & Ford, N. M. (1977). Motivation and performance in industrial selling: present knowledge and needed research. *Journal of Marketing Research*, 14, 156–168.

Zoltners, A. A., Sinha, P. & Lorimer, S. E. (2004). *Sales Force Design for Strategic Advantage.* Basingstoke: Palgrave Macmillan.

Zoltners, A. A., Sinha, P. & Lorimer, S. E. (2006). *How to Design and Implement Plans That Work: The Complete Guide to Sales Force Incentive Compensation*. New York: American Management Association.

CASE STUDY 1: SALES GROWTH AT UNILEVER FOOD SOLUTIONS

ALIGNING CUSTOMER & SALES FORCE MANAGEMENT

Global foodservice, a sector worth $832.4 billion with a compound annual growth rate (CAGR) of 4.8 per cent (MarketLine, 2012), is as extraordinary as the work of chefs: original, volatile, complex and unpredictable. Original, since 'globalisation' and 'localisation' can be combined in unique recipes. On the same dish, one can taste flavours from another continent perfectly blended with the best of local produce. It is highly volatile as a result of the high degree of fragmentation of food suppliers. It is complex since the market landscape is occupied by a plethora of diverse players: from small mobile kiosks to three-star Michelin restaurants through to global fast food chains. The offer and typologies of foodservice operators is endless. It is unpredictable, as random episodes have shown over recent years: food safety crises, dramatic price increases in raw materials and commodities, stringent regulation and potentially devastating consumer campaigns against certain brands or products.

Unilever Food Solutions (UFS) is a global provider of food products and ingredients aimed at creating solutions that help chefs and foodservice professionals in their jobs. Despite the complexities of the foodservice market and its decline in mature markets through the global economic recession, UFS has been growing faster than the market (Unilever, 2012a). This case presents UFS's success in a 'succulent' but 'hot' market, and describes its integrated approach to customer and sales force management that focuses on:

- Improving the routes to market.
- Delivering customer-focused and differentiated value propositions.
- Designing outstanding product–service innovations.
- Creating a winning sales force.

UNILEVER FOOD SOLUTIONS

The Unilever Food Solutions' 'journey' started at the end of 2000 when the merger with Bestfoods was approved, leading to the creation of the Foodservice Business

---

This case was written by Javier Marcos, published by The Case Centre. Reproduction authorised.

Group in January 2001, under the Unilever Bestfoods (UBF) brand. Back then, Patrick Cescau, the director for the Foods business (who later became chairman of Unilever) claimed that Bestfoods 'were much better focused on the customer'. The strategic priority after the merger was to create a unified organisation that was seen as a leader in foodservice and that achieved ambitious growth targets (Hay Group, 2006).

UFS currently operates in a market that offers huge potential: 35 per cent of the global 'food dollar' is spent out-of-home at about 12.7 million outlets worldwide (Unilever, 2012a). In this vibrant and dynamic environment, UFS's vision is to become the 'Best Solution Provider' for its customers. That means having a strong focus on understanding the customer, and designing solutions that specifically meet their needs, using specialist chefs and a well-trained sales force. UFS offers world-class expertise in food preparation and food technology to meet the highest standards of quality and effectiveness in foodservice (Unilever Food Solutions, 2012b).

UFS's product range is wide and covers a good number of applications in the kitchen including bouillons, stocks & seasonings, dairy cream alternatives, desserts, gravy & jus, mayonnaise, dressings & condiments, sauces, snacks, soups, spreads & cooking fats, and tea (Unilever Food Solutions, 2012b). Amongst others, UFS manufactures products under well-known consumer brands such as Knorr, Hellmann's, Lipton, Carte D'Or and Flora (Exhibit 2). However, the formats differ significantly from those found in retail shops. UFS packs in larger quantities and develops formulas and ingredients specifically designed for professional use.

UFS operates in 65 countries worldwide, directly employing 5,400 people including 2,600 salespeople and 150 chefs (Unilever Food Solutions, 2012b). Its customer base is broadly classified based on criteria of ownership (independent operators vs. chain accounts) and the context in which customers operate (social vs. commercial foodservice).

Independent operators are typically small or medium-sized establishments, often run as family businesses. ***Chain or key accounts*** are usually large organisations, often multinational, dedicated fully to the foodservice business (e.g. fast food chains) or where foodservice is a key part of their overall business portfolio (e.g. hotels).

Social establishments typically include schools, higher education institutions, hospitals, centres for the elderly, armed forces bases, etc. Large volumes of food are prepared at these premises, thus emphasis is placed on cost-effective menus. Social restaurateurs can be independent or international contract catering firms (e.g. Sodexho, Aramark).

Commercial foodservice, by contrast, is a vast group of for-profit outlets that includes restaurants (e.g. Tony Roma's, Fridays), cafeterias, hotels (e.g. Hilton), theme parks (e.g. Eurodisney), airports and stations, quick service restaurants (QSR) (e.g. Pizza Hut, McDonalds, KFC, Subway) and others.

UFS has established itself over the years as a premier provider and has achieved increasing recognition for quality, consistency and innovation. Some of the elements that underpin its sales and customer management strategy are presented below.

IMPROVING THE ROUTES TO MARKET

A key aspect in the business of fast-moving consumer goods manufacturers is the reach and coverage of their distribution network. Customers, no matter where they are located, whether a boutique hotel in the Rocky Mountains or a beach resort in Mallorca, will need to use products such as those offered by UFS in their food preparations. Achieving high levels of coverage requires close collaboration with food distributors, redistributors and cash and carry outlets.

Specialised foodservice distributors and wholesalers are independent or organised businesses with their own sales force, logistics infrastructure (warehouse, delivery fleets) and customer service staff (order taking, invoicing, etc.). The importance and size of distributors vary from country to country. In consolidated markets, such as the US, Sysco (a redistributor managing 125 distribution centres) and US Foodservice (with 100 warehouses) dominate the market (www.Foodservice.com, 2011). In the UK, distributors like P&H, 3663 or Brakes have leading positions in food distribution with double-digit market shares. In more fragmented and emerging markets, the foodservice distribution landscape comprises a large number of small distributors, sometimes with very modest turnover. These distributors often operate at a regional level, and are in close contact with food operators. Therefore, establishing business relationships with them becomes essential to achieving high levels of market reach and product penetration.

In addition to distributors, 'cash and carries' (C&C) play a key role in the foodservice market. C&Cs are large retailers specialising in products for grocery retailers and foodservice operators, with warehouse-type outlets that work on a self-service basis. Individual (i.e. non-professional) members are often allowed to buy in these centres subject to membership. Well-known C&Cs include Metro (often trading as Makro), Jetro (US) and Costco (US, UK).

Improving the routes to market is a huge endeavour in itself, and one that food manufacturers have to get right. Over the last few years, steadily increasing distribution costs have forced manufacturers and distributors to work together to gain supply chain efficiencies. Lack of collaboration in the distribution of food products often results in increased price for the operator who then reflects it in the final price to consumers. This may not be desirable as Tad Wampfler, senior vice president of supply chain management for Wendy's international, commented (Wells, 2008): 'we have to find ways to remove costs without taking money from the distributor or the manufacturer'. Wampfler added: 'If we can control costs, it's a win for the customer, distributors and manufacturers' (Wells, 2008).

In order to control costs and achieve efficiency gains, distributors often engage in network optimisation as well as rationalisation of their product portfolios. In the food industry where over 15,000 products are introduced annually (Cubitt, 2006), distributors and wholesalers need to conduct thorough analyses to decide which products to stock and which may be redundant. Achieving a balance between offering a wide range of choice to the operator, and deploying efficient logistics, is not easy. UFS supports its distributors with a range of services and initiatives to ensure a healthy sell in/sell out* ratio.

UFS has a dedicated field sales force focused on creating and following up business opportunities with customers. They can take orders for UFS products from customers that are then transferred to the distributor who delivers and invoices the operator. Overall, UFS' sales force work in coordination with the distributors' own sales representatives to achieve high standards of customer service and satisfaction. In foodservice, availability of products and supplies is a must, which means that having various touch points with the suppliers is a valuable service offered to the operator.

UFS helps its distributors by delivering specialist training to their sales forces, from product knowledge to selling techniques. These investments are aimed to equip the distributor sales force with arguments and insights to demonstrate the value of UFS products to the chef in a compelling way. A team of professional chefs from UFS deliver workshops and demonstrations of food preparation, showing how to make the most of UFS products. This culinary knowledge, when combined with operator insight, becomes a winning 'recipe' to enhance sales effectiveness.

Foodservice is a very competitive market where many operators are primarily driven by price. Therefore, to remain competitive, UFS offers special terms and conditions to channel partners. In addition, UFS designs a yearly promotional plan to help sustain demand. This promotional and activation plan is often linked to the season's culinary trends. To motivate sales efforts, UFS sponsors a comprehensive incentive scheme for the distributor sales force.

UFS employs joint business planning approaches to improve business relationships with channel partners. These plans specify sales growth expectations, key actions and initiatives, and a set of incentives for the distributor and its staff. UFS makes significant investments in its top tier distributors to support their growth to continuously improve its routes to market.

DELIVERING CUSTOMER-FOCUSED AND DIFFERENTIATED VALUE PROPOSITIONS

Working in a professional kitchen requires undertaking a detailed planning of the day, ensuring availability of ingredients and supplies. In order to optimise this planning, food positioning – 'old in front, new in back' – and expiration dates need to be carefully monitored. The peak hour in a kitchen often resembles the Underground: people in a rush and very little space. Placing all the necessary items at hand is advised to avoid having to look for them when the 'rush' starts. Coordination is essential, both with your fellow chefs and indeed with the waiters. Customers don't like to wait, and they want all the orders from the same table just at the same time, on time.

As mentioned above, UFS prides itself on being a customer-centric organisation; that is, rather than just a food product manufacturer, a 'solutions' provider, committed to adding value to the catering industry.

They realise this mission by sponsoring key industry events, helping customers with recipes and ideas for food preparation and presentation, food costing analyses, and working with their chosen channel partners to bring to their customers the best possible solution for their food-related processes (Exhibit 3).

UFS aims to offer its customers 'inspiration every day', helping them succeed in their own business with propositions such as (Unilever Food Solutions, 2012c):

- *'Your guests'*: Inspiring operators to understand more about their guests and their behaviour when eating out.
- *'Your menu'*: Encouraging food professionals to design nutritious and healthy meals, but at the same time profitable menus.
- *'Your kitchen'*: Providing operational insights to optimise kitchen processes, helping chefs to work smarter (rather than harder).

Drawing on a wealth of knowledge of food operations, consumers and markets (Unilever Food Solutions, 2011), UFS provides solutions that help foodservice business become more effective and competitive. UFS's chefs are a key element of the customer service strategy and their expertise is offered as part of a total value proposition. Overall, UFS sales and culinary teams are instrumental in offering advice on how to meet key challenges in foodservice such as quality, effectiveness, taste, originality and food safety.

Unilever Food Solutions has a long tradition of supplying value adding products and services to large and global operators and large customers. A wide range of initiatives (logistics, operational, focused on the end consumer) typically characterise the way UFS works with key customers. UFS marketing and sales teams work together with the customer's marketers and food operations staff to design ***concepts*** and new ideas. These concepts typically include a combination of branded products, merchandise and equipment. Altogether, these offer the end consumer an enhanced experience, and to the operator new opportunities to grow its revenues in food (Unilever Food Solutions, 2012a) and beverages (Unilever Food Solutions, 2012d).

Differentiated value propositions are designed for different types of customers, aiming to be consistent with the company's overall customer management strategy. In order to facilitate this, UFS classifies its customer base according to their turnover potential, not just based on current revenues. This potential is calculated using a composite algorithm that takes into account the customer's type of foodservice business and key aspects of its organisation. Based on this information UFS classifies customers from higher (A) to lower (D) potential. This classification aids in prioritising sales and service efforts. It also helps in devising and establishing more informative sales metrics. The differences between current vs. potential turnover help inform the development of distinctive sales growth strategies.

DESIGNING OUTSTANDING PRODUCT-SERVICE INNOVATIONS

UFS and Unilever pride themselves on their ability to listen to their customers and consumers. Award-winning marketing practices (Benjamin, 2012) and new products have often come from in-depth understanding of the consumer and meaningful customer insights (Von Krogh, Ichijo & Nonaka, 2000). Applying the latest technologies, the company aims to create products that provide consumers with a unique experience (Unilever, 2012b). Product innovation is at the heart of what the company does – in particular, product innovations that significantly increase consumers' well-being whilst reducing the company's environmental impact. For instance, in 2011 the company reported that 61 per cent of its products met salt levels equivalent to 5 g per day, and the total waste per tonne of production was reduced to 4.77 kg (from 6.48 kg in 2010) (Unilever, 2011).

A good example of UFS's concern in promoting healthier foods is Eatz4u (Unilever Food Solutions, 2012c), an initiative developed by UFS in the United Kingdom. The company recognised the challenge of achieving a balance in providing healthy and also cost effective meals to a growing number of diet-conscious pupils in schools. Eatz4u was created as an integrated range of products and services to help caterers in schools increase their uptake of meals. Nutritionists and chefs worked together to produce tasty, healthy recipes that also fitted within tight budgets and met the requirements of government regulations and guidelines.

Understanding consumer and customer needs is a key driver for product innovation at Unilever. UFS releases bi-annually the World Menu Report (Unilever Food Solutions, 2011). This document contains research into consumers' eating habits globally. It is recognised that eating habits have changed substantially in recent decades with increasing concern about the nutritional aspects of the food, but without compromising the enjoyment and pleasure of food tasting. In particular, the latest report indicated an overwhelming need for consumers to be provided with more information about the food they are eating when out of home. As a result, UFS is developing ways to raise awareness and increase transparency about what's in our food. As the report recognises:

> Chefs have the power to change the health of our world. And restaurants, shops, canteens, schools and cafeterias along with food service providers all need to be part of the solution. (Unilever Food Solutions, 2011, p. 11)

Innovation in business-to-business contexts does not just come from product innovation. It is widely acknowledged that sustainable competitive advantage can no longer be achieved just by improving existing products (Lusch, Vargo & O'Brien, 2007). As in other sectors, foodservice has seen the surge of service solutions, part of which is the co-creation of value and the adoption of a partnership approach with the customer (Occhiocupo, 2011). UFS has been pioneering innovative offerings and ways of working collaboratively that have become 'best practice' in foodservice.

CREATING A WINNING SALES FORCE

UFS's ability to effectively leverage routes to market, deliver compelling value propositions and innovate with the customer, largely depend on the calibre, structure and functioning of UFS's sales force.

Overall, the company puts a strong emphasis on training and developing the sales force, the marketing and the culinary teams to enhance their performance. A corporate framework of ***customer development*** skills and competencies provides the foundation for the design of training programmes for the sales and marketing communities. In addition, a Global Training Manager leads the design of UFS-specific learning solutions and programmes that regional and national trainers adapt and implement at a local level. Formal workshop-type courses are complemented with on-the-job training, providing individualised sales coaching. Overall, these initiatives contribute to create a strong culture of learning and performance within the company.

The structure of the sales force in UFS is designed to provide enhanced focus on its customer types and segments. At a global level, a group of Global Account Managers define and champion the relationship strategy with international companies such as Metro, Yum, MacDonalds, Sodehxo, etc.. At a national level, a Sales Director leads a sales force typically comprising the following roles:

- National Account Managers, who manage the relationship and business development initiatives with both national distributors and national chain operators.
- Regional Sales Managers, who are in charge at a regional level of monitoring the implementation of the company strategy, and developing the sales team.
- Field Sales Representatives are responsible for managing a portfolio of independent operators or customers. These customers are located within a given area (country, state or province). Tele-sales operators complement the customer-facing work of field sales.
- Trade Sales Representatives manage a portfolio of distributors across a region or a few large distributors. Their duties are to control the distributor's stocks, introduce new products, and, overall, to support the distributor's business.
- Chefs: act as technical experts, helping field and trade sales in their work. In so doing, they conduct product demonstrations and offer training to customers in the use of UFS products.

The functioning of the sales force; that is, sales processes, systems and resources, is reviewed on a regular basis. CRM systems' architecture as well as technical devices (e.g. laptops, tablets) are upgraded to facilitate sales force effectiveness. Back office support is available to facilitate rapid responses to customer demands or business opportunities. But first and foremost, world-class trade marketing and customer marketing resources help UFS' sales force to make a difference in their customers' food business.

THE WAY FORWARD: 'INGREDIENTS' FOR THE 'RECIPE' OF CONTINUED SALES GROWTH

The Unilever Food Solutions 'journey' that started about a decade ago after the integration with Bestfoods became a remarkable example of how to create what Anthony Burgmans, Unilever chairman at the time, called 'a formidable force in foodservice' (Hay Group, 2006). However, to maintain the levels of growth, customer-centredness and world-class salesmanship over the next decade, UFS may need to incorporate into its 'recipe' of success a number of new 'ingredients'. First, enhanced collaborative work with its distributors. Second, a critical evaluation of its selling approach. Third, an increased market-focused use of technology. Fourth, the reinforcement of the role of the sales force.

First, the nature of the relationship between manufacturers and distributors in foodservice is often fragile and needs to be managed carefully on an ongoing basis. Conflict emerges from diverging conceptions about pricing, exclusivity and 'ownership' of the end customer.

Pricing. In fragmented markets such as foodservice, it is not uncommon to find that a particular large (national) distributor or cash & carry buys certain products from the manufacturer cheaper than its competitors. This price advantage is often justified by volume of sales, and is then transferred to the operator/customer. In an environment where there is high visibility of prices in the market place, distributors often demand to have the conditions offered to the largest customers. Coherent management of the (necessary) differences in margins and terms & conditions across the customer base, is an issue foodservice suppliers need to address.

Exclusivity. Food manufacturers can sign either exclusive or non-exclusive distributor agreements. Non-exclusive arrangements allow the supplier the flexibility to appoint more than one distributor within a designated territory to sell its products. In turn, the non-exclusive agreement normally allows the distributor to buy and sell products of the supplier's competitors. UFS has a policy of 'partnership' where dedicated resources are invested in key wholesalers, rather than exclusivity. This creates stimulus in the distributor to 'win in the market'. It is believed that non-exclusive agreements often foster distributors' effort and focus on customer service, and help avoid complacency. UFS will have to continue working jointly with its partner distributors to minimise opportunistic behaviours such as stocking competitors' products or developing distributors' own brands (cheaper unbranded products that may have higher margins).

'Ownership' of the customer. Having both manufacturer and distributor's field sales forces selling to customers in foodservice markets has a number of advantages. The former can focus on opportunity identification and prospecting larger customers. The latter can complement these activities with regular order taking and customer service. UFS's sales forces can engage in a deeper-level understanding of the customer. They can propose combinations of UFS and distributors' products to create complete solutions for foodservice professionals. However, customer satisfaction requires alignment of these two sales forces and congruence in their respective selling approaches. Keeping the customer's best interests at the forefront as opposed to the interests of either the distributor or the manufacturers becomes critical.

A second 'ingredient' that UFS may need to consider in the future is the sustainability of its value-added selling approach. The emphasis in the current selling strategy is to sell to customers in a 'consultative' fashion: analysing their business and proposing ideas and products to enhance their menu, to streamline kitchen operations and to delight the end consumer. In order to do so, UFS invests heavily in a well-trained sales force, in chefs and in marketing tools. Thus, the operator receives a valuable service from UFS, but only pays for the products it buys from the company. In a tough market, with declining margins, many customers have shifted to cheaper, often unbranded products. If this trend increases and customers choose to switch to cheaper options in a wider range of products, the sales model may become unsustainable. UFS may end up delivering free valuable culinary ideas and solutions, and customers buying the products involved in those solutions from a cheaper source. UFS may need to review if and how the 'solution seller' approach can be maintained in the current market if conditions remain tough.

A third 'ingredient' for the recipe of continued success is to further embed and exploit available technologies in sales operations. In some countries the wholesalers and distributors have information systems that can be linked to UFS's legacy systems. Sell-out data of Unilever products is becoming increasingly available to UFS. Using data analytics brings opportunities to identify pockets for growth in untapped segments and customers. In addition, digital technologies are facilitating new ways of communicating with the customer, and creating platforms for co-creating innovation in foodservice. Leveraging the opportunities offered by technology will have to be high on UFS's business development agenda.

The fourth 'ingredient' for sustaining the sales performance 'recipe' is to reinforce the role of the sales force. UFS's ability to compete in a volatile market place rests on the calibre of its sales teams. Change happens fast in foodservice. For instance, traditional cash & carries are rapidly developing distribution platforms to deliver to the operator premises. This is posing a potential threat to traditional, local distributors. The sales force is in a unique position to sense these changes and to become internal champions and change agents to help UFS maintain its edge as a truly customer-focused organisation. The skills of the sales force will have to be developed so they can become 'business managers'. In this new role they will have to assign company resources to the best sales opportunities and will have to lead the delivery of increasingly complex and differentiated solutions.

If these challenges are addressed, very likely UFS will continue to make a difference in the work of chefs, helping them balance the 'odd combination of theatre, logistics, servility, and an ability to handle extreme pressure'. UFS will also continue to be a reference for customers in the foodservice market, and, for consumers, contributing to create more enjoyable, nutritious and healthy eating out experiences.

Bon appetit!

* Sell-in: refers to sales from the manufacturer to the distributor. Sell-out refers to sales from the distributor to the operator.

REFERENCES

Benjamin, K. (2012). *Unilever tops 2012 Marketing Society Awards nominations*. Retrieved 17 September 2012, from http://www.marketingmagazine.co.uk/news/1129581/.

Cubitt, B. (2006). *Food Distribution – The Supply Chain Optimization Challenge*. Retrieved 17 September 2012, from http://www.foodmanufacturing.com/articles/2006/03/food-distribution---supply-chain-optimization-challenge.

Foodservice.com (2011). *Top 50 U.S. Foodservice Distributors*. Retrieved 17 September 2012 from http://www.foodservice.com/foodshow/foodservice_distributors.cfm.

Hay Group (2006). *The Unilever Foodsolutions journey*. Retrieved 17 September 2012 from www.haygroup.com/research&opinions.

Lusch, R. F., Vargo, S. L. & O'Brien, M. (2007). Competing through service: Insights from service-dominant logic. *Journal of Retailing*, 83(1), 5–18.

MarketLine (2012). *Industry Profile: Global Profit Foodservice*. February 2012.

Occhiocupo, N. (2011). Innovation in foodservice: The case of a world leading Italian company. *The Marketing Review*, 11(2), 189–201.

Unilever (2011). *Annual Report and Accounts 2011*. Retrieved 17 September 2012 from http://www.unilever.com/images/Unilever_AR11_tcm13-282960.pdf.

Unilever (2012a). *Business to Business, Food Solutions*. Retrieved 17 September 2012 from http://www.unilever.co.uk/careers/carreerschoices/businesstobusiness/.

Unilever (2012b). *Product Innovations*. Retrieved 17 September 2012 from http://www.unilever.co.uk/innovation/productinnovations/.

Unilever Food Solutions (2011). *World Menu Report*. Retrieved 17 September 2012 from http://www.unileverFood Solutions.com/company/media-center/press-releases.

Unilever Food Solutions (2012a). *British Roast Dinner Week*. Retrieved 17 September 2012 from http://www.unileverFood Solutions.co.uk/promotions/roast_dinner/.

Unilever Food Solutions (2012b). Company website. Retrieved 17 September 2012 from www.unileverfoodsolutions.com.

Unilever Food Solutions (2012c). *Eatz4u*. Retrieved 17 September 2012 from http://www.eatz4u.co.uk.

Unilever Food Solutions (2012d). *Helping You Brew a Better Business*. Retrieved 17 September 2012 from http://www.ufs.teatips.co.u.

Unilever Food Solutions (2012e). *Our Services*. Retrieved 17 September 2012 from http://www.unileverfoodsolutions.co.uk/our-services.

Von Krogh, G., Ichijo, K. & Nonaka, I. (2000). *Enabling Knowledge Creation: How to Unlock the Mystery of Tacit Knowledge* (p. 60). Oxford: Oxford University Press.

Wells, I. (2008). Collaborative supply chain model can help control costs. *Nation Restaurant News*, February, 20–22.

CASE STUDY 2: LONGFELLOW OFFICE SUPPLIES

Longfellow Office Supplies (www.longfellowsltd.co.uk) was originally a sole-trader formed more than 40 years ago by Bill Sewell, Managing Director, who was succeeded by Christine Sewell at the head of the business. A strong customer base in the Lancashire area was created and maintained primarily through Bill's direction. The company name was chosen because Bill is a very tall man (long fellow) and an 'own-brand' product range of stationery items was created called Hiawatha (the legendary Indian, from the poem by H. W. Longfellow). Links between Bill himself, the name Longfellows (as it became known) and these products formed a very strong focus for customers both current and prospective.

Longfellow's product portfolio includes office furniture, office seating, equipment and stationery. The sales of office photocopiers have provided the majority of machine sales over the years and, having been sold on a 'cost per copy' maintenance basis, have provided the service department with a regular flow of work, albeit charged for by metered copy charges. The advent of cartridge-based copiers, removing much of the need for routine service as parts were incorporated into replaceable cartridges, has adversely affected the potential for profit of their service offerings.

As with many small and mid-sized businesses the company relies on strong personal relationships with customers. Longfellows still emphasises this aspect of professional selling. Longfellows has managed to retain a customer base which ranges from small businesses to large publicly listed corporations.

CURRENT SITUATION

The market for large-scale office copiers is continuing to decline, with more and more companies using laser printers to create multiple originals rather than using traditional photocopiers. Whilst Longfellows has made some small inroads into this market, there is little doubt that its traditional reliance on older copier technology is starting to have a severe impact on the revenue achieved through the 'cost per copy' metering arrangements. Although there has been an attempt to move into personal computers and related products, the skills required in terms of service backup for these items are substantially different from those available within the existing service engineer profile.

In terms of the general office products market, there is concern that consumer demand is slowing, and this is hitting the big suppliers. The increase in Small Office and Home Office (SOHO) markets means that a local presence, with shop facilities as an add-on to its main commercial distribution service, still has a reasonably bright future. Interestingly, one of the very large office products distributors, Corporate Express, recently handled its merger with other companies extremely well because of its strong customer relationship management (CRM) programme.

Longfellows invested in a computer system, although much data that would be considered as 'must have' for marketers (e.g. overall sales, costs, profits; sales and profit breakdowns by market segment, channel, brand, account and customer type; customer relationship monitors, etc.) is not yet readily available to management and has rarely been. The business has primarily been run based on an 'idea of what is happening' basis, which is now simply no longer viable. It is believed that appropriate procedures have to be put in place to ensure that all relevant functions of the legacy system are being used. The company is beginning to produce management accounts regularly which show, amongst other things, sales and profit breakdowns by product and account. This is a first step towards more meaningful planning.

Real benefits, however, will come from utilising the marketing database elements of the system and ensuring that the online updating features of this system enable a process of continuous analysis. The marketing tools available allow information to be input in respect of many attributes of a customer, and allow tailoring to track, for example, sales orders by individuals within a customer account. This data, combined with sensible promotional activity, targeted towards specific groups, will enable the company to develop strong relationship marketing capabilities. The IT system can store details right down to birthdays and anniversaries of the individual together with their likes and dislikes in terms of hobbies, although it is unlikely that Longfellows will use such data for marketing purposes in the foreseeable future.

It is argued that real value will begin to accrue when the historical data within the integrated database is interrogated to provide insight into possible sales opportunities. An example of this would be where the software is asked to report on all those customers who have bought printing machines within the last six months but who have not bought consumables for those machines. Such analysis is relatively easily carried out provided some sensible thought is given to the questions asked, and the results can be tailored to produce mail/email shot promotions for the items not bought.

INTERNET CAPABILITIES

More and more companies are sourcing products through the Internet these days and simply having a web presence is no longer enough. Electronic ordering is now commonplace and in some cases up to 90 per cent of purchase orders are done electronically. Longfellows has now invested in a website which has an electronic ordering catalogue facility, allowing customers to browse products or order from their paper catalogue by simply entering product code and quantity details. Currently, when transacting online, customers can choose instantly from a huge range of office supplies, benefit from discounts off first orders, recall saved orders, set up shopping lists, etc..

TRANSPARENT ORDERING ON TO SUPPLIERS

The existing integrated system within the company will support recent developments in the industry to allow fully transparent ordering from customers straight through to Longfellow's computer and then, if a product is not in stock, straight through to their preferred supplier's system. Such systems allow the customer to be sent an acknowledgement that the product is 'in stock' for next day delivery, even if it has to be ordered from Longfellow's preferred supplier. This type of facility, if developed properly, can enable vastly increased consumer participation in the ordering and supply process. The trend towards just-in-time purchasing by customers places ever-increasing demands on a company such as Longfellows and their existing capability to place orders with suppliers electronically for next day delivery to customers is a key source of advantage.

BRANDING

The marketing strategy for the Longfellow 'own-brand' Hiawatha is a contested issue. In order to compensate for the relatively weak buying power of a small organisation, the company is now a member of the North East Marketing Organisation (NEMO), which forms an alliance between competitors, similar to that formed between global players like Motorola, IBM, Philips, Siemens, BT and Toshiba. With buying power combined with other dealers around the world through Europa Office and BPGI, over £7.5 billion worth of purchasing is combined. This allows access to exceptionally priced branded and unbranded products together with private-label, mid-priced lines for general stationery sundries. The economics of sourcing Hiawatha branded product probably far outweigh the benefits gained by having this 'own brand'. The strength of the brand connection with the company name, however, is such that perhaps new means of linking the two together should be sought.

There is great advantage in retaining the association of such a brand, particularly when there is a 'story' behind it that can be told briefly and capture the imagination. Office products are dull lifeless things, and the big players such as Staples, Office International and the like have no such 'story' to link to their names.

QUESTIONS

1. How would you analyse Longfellow's current market position, and the key segments for its business?
2. Identify, within those segments, where the main growth opportunities lie.
3. What would be a suitable go-to-market strategy for one to three years?
4. How should Longfellows manage sales through the call centre, online and field sales to ensure minimum channel conflict?

CASE STUDY 3: SCORE GROUP PLC

Score Group plc (www.score-group.com) is an engineering solutions company providing engineering services across five continents within a range of sectors which include oil & gas, nuclear and marine. The Score Group of companies primarily provide services related to valves and industrial gas turbines in addition to training, specialist coatings and cell disruptors. Score Group plc continues to be guided by its founder Charles Ritchie from the group's headquarters in Scotland. In 2014 the Group employed over 1,700 people and is deeply committed to the training of its personnel with over 300 apprentices employed within the Group worldwide.

The company is well recognised for its business including engineering research, design, manufacture and repair offerings for oil companies in the North Sea. The company was founded in 1982 by Charles Ritchie. A qualified mechanical engineer, Charles is entrepreneurial, enterprising and assertive. His style is very much hands-on, and he has personally built up the business to the stage it is at now. As the company has grown, it has been able to compete for larger contracts where they are seen as competent and cost-effective, though on occasions still relatively small. Most of the managers in the organisation are also hands-on technical operators or highly skilled artisans with a limited knowledge and experience of sales and marketing. The basis on which Charles Ritchie has built the business has been mainly precision engineering with a focus on the service and maintenance of other people's equipment. The company consider themselves a quality supplier and are now operating in the big league of contractors to the oil industry, both in the North Sea and elsewhere in the world.

The UK oil and gas industry is in a mature stage of its development. This maturity is characterised by the decline of the larger, earlier discoveries in the North Sea, increasing smaller field development, but renewed exploration activity with an increasing emphasis on cost-reduction strategies by operators in both capital expenditure and operating costs. These development phases in the UK continental shelf oil industry, along with current revenues are summarized in Figures CS3.1 and CS3.2.

Despite price fluctuations, business activity is still high in this sector. This can be explained by a combination of the price of oil and high productivity, itself a result of two main variables, namely technology and efficiency. Advancements in technology, enabling the exploitation of smaller marginal satellite fields and innovative exploration techniques, indicate that the North Sea is only mature at certain geological levels. It is the increases in efficiency that are enhancing productivity rather than the price of oil itself which has fallen dramatically in 2014. These increases are also inspiring innovation and technology advances throughout the industry in an effort to reduce costs. Furthermore, these efficiencies are reflected in operators' recent claims that their cost-cutting initiatives have yielded savings of up to 25–30 per cent in both capital expenditure and operating costs. Such productivity enhancement transforms the economic viability of older fields that were previously threatened by closure as exploration and production became uneconomic.

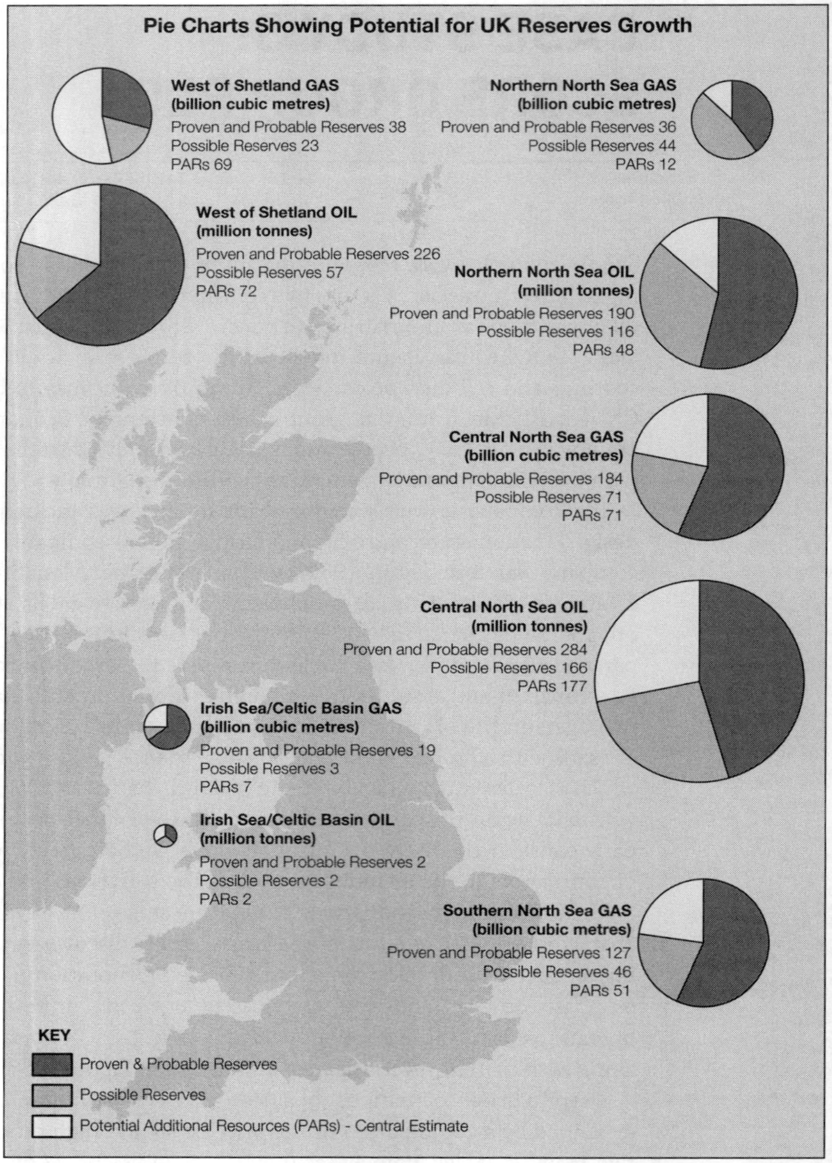

Figure CS3.1 – Pie charts showing potential for UK reserves growth

A pattern in North Sea exploration and production is emerging whereby, on the one hand, the established operators exercise cost-reduction initiatives to justify continued production from existing declining fields (Shell, BP, Exxon-Mobil), while, on the other hand, new operators are benefiting from technological advancements which enable them to develop and operate new smaller fields for the first time (Apache, Talisman, etc.).

Estimates of UK Oil Reserves and Ultimate Recovery at 31 December 2014[(1)(2)]					
			[figures in brackets for end 2013]		
Oil Reserves units - million tonnes	**Proven**	**Probable**	**Proven & Probable**	**Possible[(6)]**	**Maximum[(3)]**
Fields in production or under development[(4)]	374 [404]	255 [243]	630 [648]	312 [301]	942 [949]
Other significant discoveries where development plans are under discussion	0 [0]	86 [98]	86 [98]	32 [37]	118 [135]
Total Oil Reserves in million tonnes[(4)]	**374 [404]**	**342 [342]**	**716 [746]**	**344 [338]**	**1,060 [1,084]**
Cumulative Oil Production to end 2014[(5)]	**3,623 [3,583]**				
Estimated Ultimate Recovery in million tonnes	**3,997 [3,987]**	**342 [342]**	**4,339 [4,329]**	**344 [338]**	**4,683 [4,667]**

Figure CS3.2 – UK Oil Reserves and Estimated Ultimate Recovery 2015

Notes on Oil Table

(1) Includes onshore as well as offshore fields. All figures include condensate, gas liquids and liquefied products.
(2) All entries are rounded to the nearest one million tonnes.
(3) Maximum is the sum of proven, probable and possible reserves.
(4) The oil reserves include 104 (58) proven, 65 (59) probable and 42 (38) possible million tonnes in approved fields under development but not yet producing.
(5) Cumulative oil production includes 145 (101) million tonnes from decommissioned oil fields.
(6) Possibles include 82.2 million tonnes for EOR potential.

Note that there are also "Potential Additional Resources" (PARs) in fields and drilled prospects for which there are no current plans for development. These are listed in a separate section on the website.

	Forecast	Actual
Exploration Wells	25	14
Appraisal Wells	11	18
Production (Millions boe per day)	1.4–1.5	1.42
Expenditure (£billion)	25	26.5
- Capital expenditure	13	14.8
- Operating expenditure	9.6	9.6
- Exploration and Appraisal	1.4	1.1
- Decommissioning	1	1
Unit Operating Cost (£/boe)	18	18.5

Figure CS3.3 – Key Metrics Scorecard for 2014

Source: Oil and Gas UK

Either way, the industry is continuing to attract a substantial amount of risk capital which augurs well in terms of development expenditure (Figure CS3.3). Key metrics for the UK oil and Gas industry are shown in Figure CS3.3. However, this is a global industry which operates in various locations and countries each with its own rules governing explorations and extraction.

As a result of these market trends, operators seek to reduce their costs further by divesting certain operational responsibilities. This increasing focus on cost reduction for both new developments and the maintenance of existing offshore production facilities is leading to opportunities for contractors in the oil industry. For the contractor, the bid process begins at a prequalification stage and involves the application to operators for contracts which, according to European Union (EU) competition law, have to be advertised in the daily EU contracts publication for UK contracts. At this stage, operators will specify certain criteria to try to ensure that only the more suitable contractors apply. Such criteria will include:

- Experience in maintenance and modification.
- A proven track record and sound reputation within the industry.
- Satisfactory financial strength to perform the necessary work.
- Evidence of a complementary corporate culture with the operator.

These criteria will be specified in more detail in the tender document for those companies invited to tender. At this next stage, the companies will be given the opportunity to demonstrate their technical capability in relation to the job in question in more detail, they will be advised of possible contractual liabilities and the framework for remuneration will be discussed. With respect to remuneration, and despite the close working relationship between contractor and supplier, many contracts have contentious clauses in them involving risks that some contractors may not be prepared to take. In such cases, the contractor may account for such risks modifying the bid price or may qualify the risks to the operator, who would be expected to bear them. Depending on the nature of the contract, in terms of value and longevity, a post-qualification stage bid could cost the contractor as much as £100,000 to compile. Much of the expense will be in management time and the preparation of costings and promotional material for presentation to the client (operator). The general consensus among contractors in this context is that the minimum value of a contract needs to exceed £500,000 to make it worthwhile pursuing.

To recoup the considerable expense of unsuccessful bids and those won on the basis of a minimum cost tender, contractors sometimes attempt to increase their charges with each modification requested by the operator. This causes conflict, which is exacerbated by operators challenging contractors' estimates, both sides incurring further costs by employing additional personnel to assess claims and counter-claims. Contractors respond further by incorporating complex terms and conditions into their tender submissions along with extensive contingencies in cost estimates.

Research in the UK service and supply sector indicates that there are about ten companies that compete in the bidding for contracts put out for tender by the operators in the region. However, the picture is made more complex because of two particular factors. First, the range of services offered varies from contractor to contractor, each being recognised for particular areas of expertise. Second, some of the contractors are engaged in alliances or joint ventures with other contractors for certain projects where their own range of capabilities is not sufficient or adequately specialised. The ten or so contractors include large players such as Kvaerner, Haliburton and Hughes Christensen and others such as the Wood Group and Score. Turnover and profitability for each company will fluctuate from year to year depending on the number of projects and the stage of each project.

Naturally, the financial strength and resources of the organisation are important considerations for the operator when choosing a supplier of services. Score and its key competitors all possess the required depth of resources for the majority of the contracts for which they bid, by virtue of the fact that they are all members of multinational groups and have developed in recent years the status of preferred contractors by the operators to the detriment of smaller contractors.

The job of the salesperson or business development manager is to assess which projects are more suitable for their company to bid, to prepare a solution following discussions with the client and to coordinate and present the proposal to the client at the tender stage. Each solution will be customised to that project and to the client's requirements. For example, maintenance work in the southern North Sea will demand a totally different approach from fabrication work in the northern fields. For this reason, issues concerning price and product will be dictated by the market requirements of the project in question and finalised during the later stages of contract negotiations. The role of sales in this instance will be to provide the decision-makers with the relevant information based on sound analysis of the situation and particular requirements of the specific contract. As their work is mainly in the maintenance and refurbishment sector, Score's revenues and profits are more predictable since they come under the category of 'operating expenditure' (as opposed to capital expenditure).

However, the trend for partnering and forming alliances between large contractors and the large oil companies is creating problems for smaller players who are unable to offer a full service capability (Figure CS3.4).

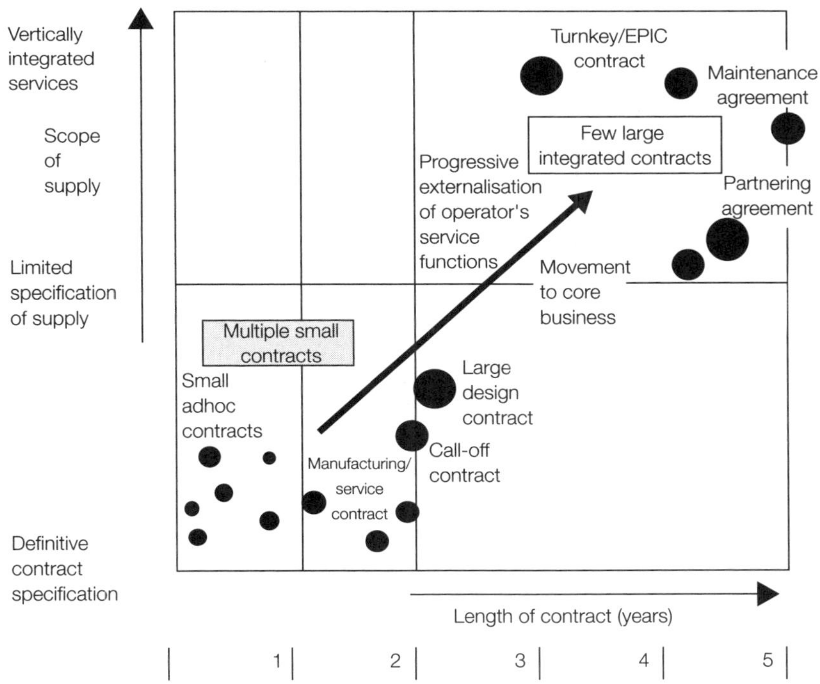

Figure CS3.4 – The changing nature of North Sea oil industry contracts (Drummond, 1993)

As with many of the contractors, the terms 'sales' and 'marketing' tend to be used interchangeably. Score puts little emphasis on formal marketing, publicity or PR activity. Their approach is for their commercial and technical staff to bid for and negotiate face to face the contracts which they feel are attractive and the company are capable of delivering. Presentations are made to clients and are primarily based on technical solutions.

All the contractors recognise the importance of personal relationships within the industry, which also serve as a network through which new opportunities are learned of and, where appropriate, exploited. The advent of EU competition rules, which demands that all new opportunities are documented, has created more bids for some of the contracts than was previously the case. Also, as the scale and variety of projects increases, so the number of personal relationships has also increased, requiring a more formal approach. The importance of personal relationships and contacts should not be underestimated, as the following quote from a manager of one of the contractors suggests:

> If you want to understand marketing in Aberdeen or North East Scotland the answer is simple. Befriend the chief buyers of the major companies, grease their palms, play golf with them and you will sell your product, unless it is really bad, of course. If you want to put icing on the cake then the answer is simple. Join the correct golf club or, better still, the Freemasons. After almost 25 years of oil and gas Aberdeen is still just a service and maintenance centre. It is nothing more than a source of partially skilled labour for the rigs and production platforms. It is a retail outlet like an industrial equivalent of Tesco. Anything that is really high-tech comes from outside Aberdeen but all this talk of quality being the only name in town is nonsense. The only quality that matters in the oil patch is the quality of the back-handers and who one knows.

Although this may be seen as an extreme view, those contractors who appeared to place a low priority on such visible marketing activity were those who placed an emphasis on sales, relying heavily on the personal relationships network, which manifests itself in corporate entertainment at sports and social functions. More than one contractor has suggested that the expense involved in the bid process, plus the costs incurred with corporate entertainment, are a severe strain on their budgets. The nature and history of the industry and the methods perceived necessary to win business are responsible for such attitudes. The benefits of a coordinated marketing strategy and a sound sales plan would suggest that there is considerable scope for a company such as Score to enhance their reputation and standing. Charles acknowledges that his marketing and sales operation needs to be on a more businesslike and professional footing but is uncertain how to proceed. At the same time, he realises that personal relationships in this industry are still vitally important.

Your tasks:

1. Draw up a strategic sales plan, with budgets, for Score Limited based on annual market potential of £500 million.
2. Outline an organisational structure incorporating marketing, sales and business development to support the growth of this company.
3. What development and training would you recommend for the existing sales/business development personnel at Score?
4. What criteria would you establish to qualify potential contracts and opportunities? In other words, how would you assess the attractiveness of new potential deals with customers?
5. If you were a small firm in this sector, what would you do in order to compete with the larger players?

CASE STUDY 4: BNP PARIBAS FORTIS

BNP Paribas Fortis https://www.bnpparibasfortis.com is a European bank, the market leader in Belgium and expanding its business banking network across Europe. The group operates in different markets across Europe and Asia. This expansion has been mainly through various acquisitions and mergers over the past ten years, which has resulted in different sales operations and practices in different markets. There are about 100 sales teams operating across Europe, each with an average of eight salespeople. In terms of their market growth, gross income and profit margins, they are a highly effective sales organisation.

Fortis operations cover three distinct markets. In the Benelux countries, they operate retail and business banking and insurance and their market coverage is intensive. Elsewhere in Europe, they concentrate on business banking, factoring and leasing, asset management and offshore banking. Finally, in the global arena, their focus is on selective businesses covering Bancassurance, offshore private banking, export and trade finance.

The company implemented a sales force automation (SFA) system and a sales reporting system across the network to enable each sales organisation to measure and track their salespeople's performance and activities. Until the introduction of this system, sales performance measures were gathered primarily through Excel sheets and used mainly by the salespeople and their sales managers. The evaluation method used corresponded with that of a class three 'supervisory' method as described by Boles, Donthu, and Lohtia (1995) (see Chapter 15). After the initial introduction of sales force automation systems, the organisation decided to enhance the SFA system to record sales process measures and to standardise the performance evaluation of its salespeople. This enhancement was followed by the introduction of a sales reporting system providing all sales managers with detailed performance measures of their salespeople and enabling them to benchmark the results of each salesperson with the rest of the team. The idea was that this system would enable sales managers to improve their sales performance evaluation methods evolving from class three to class four using statistical methods as a basis for their comparison. Figure CS4.1 gives an overview of this approach and Figure CS4.2 shows the range of reporting tools being used at different levels of management.

Results to date indicate that the system has not achieved all of its objectives. In particular evaluation and reporting are not being done to their full extent. Interviews with salespeople and sales managers revealed the following problems:

- The system of recording all the information required was excessively complex.
- Lack of training in use of the system.
- Existence of localised/customised sub-systems.

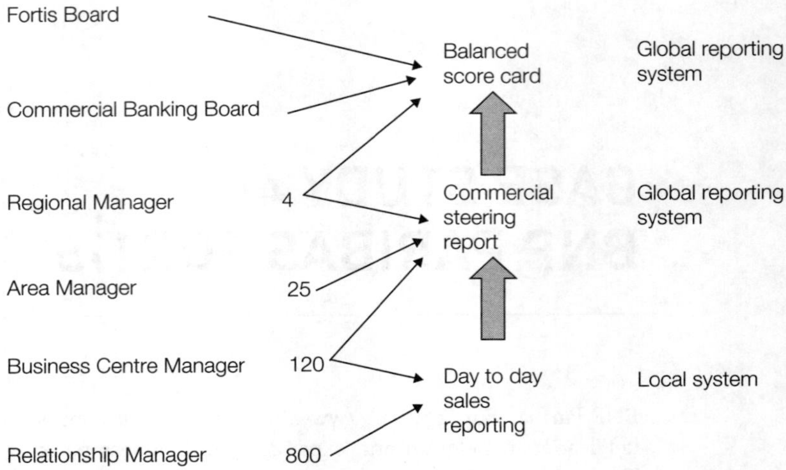

Figure CS4.1 – Fortis sales reporting systems in use

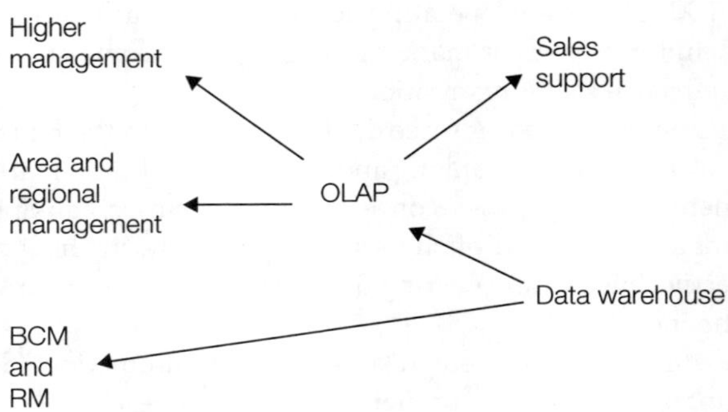

Figure CS4.2 – Sales reports must be available in SMS

- Inaccurate or selective recording of data.
- Smaller teams did not use the system.
- Sales managers only want to follow the progress of larger deals.

The interviews revealed that the sales managers do not know how to link financial objectives with activity objectives. However, the link between activities and financial result is assumed and objectives are given on both. The objective of introducing opportunity measures is a way for management to try and link activities, skills and results. These relationships are assumed but are not formally or statistically proven. The interviewees believe that given the quality of the data reported, a large volume of data will be required for statistical analysis. They also believe that the analysis should be by country because the market conditions are so different in each country. Others believe that the analysis will not be possible because the portfolios change too much and because the context in which each salesperson operates is too complex to measure.

At present, the information to be recorded includes calls made, conversion ratios, technical knowledge, customer portfolios, prospects and relationships. There is a yearly evaluation process linked to assessment and rewards, and the sales managers offer the salespeople steering and coaching on specific activities when required.

1 Given that the information is not being fully completed to conduct type four evaluation, could statistical relationships between sales effort and results be confidently established?
2 Assuming that relationships between sales effort and results could be measured, what would be the factors explaining their causal relationship?
3 How can salespeople and sales managers be encouraged to provide the data required?

REFERENCE

Boles, J. S., Donthu, N. & Lothia, R. (1995). Salesperson evaluation using relative performance efficiency: The application of data envelopment analysis. *Journal of Personal Selling & Sales Management*, 15(3), 31–49.

INDEX